S0-AVF-334

ONTARIO

Speed/Ontario Tourism

Editorial Director   Cynthia Clayton Ochterbeck

THE GREEN GUIDE ONTARIO

Editor   Gwen Cannon
Principal Writer   Margaret Lemay
Researcher   Ilona Kauremszky
Production Manager   Natasha G. George
Cartography   Mapmobility Corp., Peter Wrenn
Photo Editor   Yoshimi Kanazawa
Proofreader   Claiborne Linvill
Layout and Design   Nicole D. Jordan
Cover Design   Laurent Muller, Ute Weber

Contact Us: The Green Guide
                                Michelin Maps and Guides
                                One Parkway South
                                Greenville, SC 29615
                                USA
                                www.michelintravel.com
                                michelin.guides@us.michelin.com

                                Michelin Maps and Guides
                                Hannay House
                                39 Clarendon Road
                                Watford, Herts WD17 1JA
                                UK
                                ☎ (01923) 205 240
                                www.ViaMichelin.com
                                travelpubsales@uk.michelin.com

Special Sales: For information regarding bulk sales,
                                customized editions and premium sales,
                                please contact our Customer Service
                                Departments:
                                USA   1-800-432-6277
                                UK   (01923) 205 240
                                Canada 1-800-361-8236

Note to the Reader
While every effort is made to ensure that all information printed in this guide is
correct and up-to-date, Michelin Apa Publications Ltd. accepts no liability for
any direct, indirect or consequential losses howsoever caused so far as such
can be excluded by law.

One Team…
A Commitment to Quality

There's just one reason our team is dedicated to producing quality travel publications—you, our reader.

Throughout our guides we offer **practical information**, **touring tips** and **suggestions** for finding the best places for a break.

Michelin driving tours help you hit the highlights and quickly absorb the best of the region. Our descriptive **walking tours** make you your own guide, armed with directions, maps and expert information.

We scout out the attractions, classify them with **star ratings**, and describe in detail what you will find when you visit them.

Michelin maps featured throughout the guide offer vibrant, detailed and easy-to-follow outlines of everything from close-up museum plans to international maps.

Places to stay and eat are always a big part of travel, so we research **hotels and restaurants** that we think convey the essence of the destination and arrange them by geographic area and price. We walk you through the best shopping districts and point you towards the host of entertainment and recreation possibilities available.

We **test**, **retest**, **check and recheck** to make sure that our guidebooks are truly just that: a personalized guide to help you make the most of your visit. And if you still want a speaking guide, we list local tour guides who will lead you on all the boat, bus, guided, historical, culinary, and other tours you shouldn't miss.

In short, we remove the guesswork involved with travel. After all, we want you to enjoy exploring with Michelin as much as we do.

The Michelin Green Guide Team

PLANNING YOUR TRIP

INTRODUCTION TO ONTARIO

Ontario Tourism Marketing Partnership Corp.

Ontario Tourism

CONTENTS

DISCOVERING ONTARIO

MacDonald/Ontario Tourism

HOW TO USE THIS GUIDE

PLANNING YOUR TRIP

The blue-tabbed PLANNING YOUR TRIP section at the front of the guide gives you **ideas for your trip** and **practical information** to help you organize it. You'll find tours, ideas for recreation in the great outdoors, a calendar of events, information on shopping, sightseeing, children's activities and more.

INTRODUCTION

The orange-tabbed INTRODUCTION section explores **Nature** from the Great Lakes to Thunder Bay. The **History** section spans early settlement to the 21st century. The **Art and Culture** section covers art, literature, music, dance and cinema, while the **Province Today** delves into modern Ontario.

DISCOVERING

The green-tabbed DISCOVERING section showcases Ontario's Principal Sights, arranged geographically by region, and featuring the most interesting local **Sights**, **Walking Tours**, nearby **Excursions**, and detailed **Driving Tours**.

🛈Contact information,🖙admission fees, 🕔hours of operation and a host of other **visitor information** are given wherever possible. Admission fees shown are normally the single adult price.

STAR RATINGS★★★

Michelin has given star ratings for more than 100 years. If you're pressed for time, we recommend you visit the ★★★ or ★★ sights first:

★★★	Highly recommended
★★	Recommended
★	Interesting

Sidebars

Throughout the guide you will find peach-coloured text boxes (like this one) with lively anecdotes, detailed history and background information.

Address Books – Where to Stay, Eat and more…

WHERE TO STAY

We've made a selection of lodgings and arranged them within the cities by price category to fit all budgets (🔆 *see the Legend on the cover flap for an explanation of the price categories*). For the most part, we've selected accommodations based on their unique regional quality, their regional feel, as it were. So, unless the individual lodging embodies local ambience, it's rare that we include chain properties, which typically have their own imprint.
🔆 *See the back of the guide for an index to the accommodations featured throughout the guide.*

WHERE TO EAT

We thought you'd like to know the popular eating spots in Ontario. So, we selected restaurants that capture the regional experience—those that have a unique regional flavour (🔆 *see the Legend on the cover flap for an explanation of the price categories*). We're not rating the quality of the food per se; as we did with the lodgings, we selected restaurants for many towns and villages, categorized by price to appeal to all wallets.
🔆 *See the back of the guide for an index to the restaurants featured throughout the guide.*

MAPS

- 🔁 Regional **Driving Tours** maps.
- 🔁 Map of Ontario with the **Principal Sights** highlighted.
- 🔁 Maps for major **cities** and **villages**.
- 🔁 **Local tour** maps.

All maps in this guide are oriented north, unless otherwise indicated by a directional arrow. The term "Local Map" refers to a map within the chapter or Tourism Region. A complete list of the maps found in the guide appears at the back of this book, as well as a comprehensive index and list of restaurants and accommodations.
🔁 *See the Map Legend at the back of the guide for an explanation of map symbols.*

🔁 A Bit of Advice 🔁

Green advice boxes found in this guide contain practical tips and handy information relevant to the sight in the Discovering section.

ORIENT PANELS

Vital statistics are given for each principal sight in the DISCOVERING section:

- 🔲 **Information**: Tourist Office/Sight contact details.
- ▶ **Orient Yourself:** Geographic location of the sight with reference to its local core as well as surrounding boroughs, towns and roads.
- 🅿 **Parking:** Where to park.
- 🔁 **Don't Miss:** Unmissable things to do or see.
- 🕐 **Organizing Your Time:** Tips on organizing your stay; what to see first, how long to spend, crowd avoidance, market days and more.
- 𝙆𝙞𝙙𝙨 **Especially for Kids:** Sights of particular interest to children.
- 👌 **Also See:** Nearby PRINCIPAL SIGHTS featured elsewhere in the guide.

SYMBOLS

𝗦𝗽𝗮	**Spa Facilities**	🔁	**Tours**
𝙆𝙞𝙙𝙨	**Interesting for Children**	🅿	**On-site Parking**
👌	**Also See**	▶	**Directions**
🔲	**Tourist Information**	✕	**On-site eating Facilities**
🕐	**Hours of Operation**	🏊	**Swimming Pool**
🕐	**Periods of Closure**	⚠	**Camping Facilities**
⚬━	**Closed to the Public**	♨	**Beaches**
💳	**Entry Fees**	🍵	**Breakfast Included**
📵	**Credit Cards not Accepted**	🔁	**A Bit of Advice**
♿	**Wheelchair Accessible**	🔁	**Warning**

Contact – Addresses, phone numbers, opening hours and prices published in this guide are accurate at the time of press. We welcome corrections and suggestions that may assist us in preparing the next edition. Please send your comments to:

UK
Michelin Maps and Guides
Hannay House
39 Clarendon Road
Watford, Herts WD17 1JA
travelpubsales@uk.michelin.com
www.michelin.co.uk

USA
Michelin Maps and Guides
Editorial Department
P.O. Box 19001
Greenville, SC 29602-9001
michelin.guides@us.michelin.com
www.michelintravel.com

Rafting on the Ottawa River
Georgi/Ontario Tourism

MICHELIN DRIVING TOURS

Driving allows travellers to appreciate the vastness of this province, where distances between cities and towns can be great. The following two fast-paced tours, in duration 8 days and 18 days respectively, are intended as planning tools, not as fixed routes.

1 Northern Ontario

Trip of 1,495km/929mi from Ottawa to Thunder Bay. Time: 8 days. On this tour visitors can experience the wild, untouched beauty of the Canadian Shield country with its rocks, trees and lovely lakes. The drive around Lake Superior is particularly attractive.

DAYS/ITINERARY/SIGHTS

1–2 **Ottawa**★★★
3 **Ottawa – North Bay**
   (363km/226mi); North Bay★

4 **North Bay – Sault Ste Marie**
   (427km/265mi); Sudbury★★
5 **Sault Ste. Marie**★★
6 **Sault Ste Marie – Thunder Bay**
   (705km/438mi); Lake Superior
   Drive★★, North Shore Lake
   Superior★★ (described in other
   direction)
7 **Thunder Bay**★★
8 Thunder Bay – Kakabeka Falls★★

2 Southern Ontario

Round-trip of 1,737km/1,079mi from Niagara Falls. Time: 18 days. This tour combines the vibrant city of Toronto with the magnificent falls on the Niagara River, the highly cultivated southern Ontario, some Canadian Shield country and the nation's capital of Ottawa. In between are a host of interesting cities such as Kingston, Stratford, Goderich and Orillia.

WHEN AND WHERE TO GO

When to Go

CLIMATE

The climate varies widely in Ontario. Northern Ontario experiences long, bright but cold winters and sunny summers with hot days and cool nights. In the south the winters are less severe because of the moderating influence of the Great Lakes. The summers are longer than in the north but much more humid, again due to the Great Lakes. Daily weather reports by Environment Canada are available through television, radio and newspapers and at www.weatheroffice.gc.ca. Other useful websites are www.theweathernetwork.com and www.ontarioweather.com.

SEASONS

Ontario's main **tourist season** extends from Victoria Day (the last Monday on or before May 24) to Labour Day (the first Monday in September). Many attractions lengthen the season to the Thanksgiving weekend (second Monday in October). In mid-size to large cities, sights are usually open year-round.

From mid-March to mid-May, visitors can enjoy comfortable daytime temperatures but chilly nights in **spring;** the harvest of maple syrup is celebrated with sugaring-off parties. Most visitors go to Ontario during the **summer** season, extending from Victoria Day to Labour Day. May and June, particularly in forested and waterside areas, are high season for biting insects, so come prepared with repellents and protective clothing; arrival of hot weather kills most bugs. July and August are considered peak season and are ideal for outdoor activities such as sailing, kayaking, canoeing or hiking. Hot and often humid days with temperatures ranging from 22°-35°C/70°-95°F can be enjoyed in southern Ontario. May and September are pleasant months with warm days but cool evenings. However, many attractions have curtailed visiting hours, so phone ahead. The southern regions along the Canada/US border offer spectacular displays of **fall** colours from mid-September until early October.

For the sports enthusiast, the Ontario winter, generally from mid-November to mid-March, offers excellent opportunities to enjoy numerous **winter** activities such as downhill skiing, cross-country skiing and snowmobiling. Much of the province experiences heavy snowfall. Main highways are snowploughed, but vehicles should be winterized and snow tires are highly recommended. The provincial government provides road reports from late October to April at 1-800-268-4686 (416-235-4686 in the greater Toronto area) and online at www.mto.gov. on.ca/english/traveller/conditions

Note:
The extreme northern regions are most accessible during July and August since the temperature rises above 0°C/32°F for only a few months each year.

WHAT TO PACK

Warm clothing, including a hat, neck scarf and gloves, is necessary in early spring, late autumn and of course, winter, when heavy top coats, layers of clothing and warm waterproof boots are essential. Summer evenings can be cool in many places, so taking some warmer clothes is recommended. As there will be numerous times when walking is the ideal means of transport in both the cities and the countryside, comfortable footwear is essential, especially for sightseeing. If you are an outdoor enthusiast, pack your hiking boots as well, and be sure to have

insect repellent and long-sleeved shirts, slacks and a hat or bandana if you venture into the woods during insect season. In summer, bring a raincoat and umbrella, and be sure to include swim wear for enjoying the many lakes and rivers.

It's a good idea to take along an extra tote bag for shopping at outdoor markets, carrying a picnic and bringing your purchases home.

Themed Tours

Several **white-water rafting** excursions, led by experienced guides, are available on the Ottawa River *(May-Sept; round-trip 4-6 hours. From $105, including equipment and meals. Accommodations extra. Reservations required. Wilderness Tours, Box 89, Beachburg ON, K0J 1C0 ☎613-646-2291 or 888-723-8669. www.wildernesstours. com).* A fascinating all-day train trip, the **Polar Bear Express** takes the traveller across terrains of giant forests, bushland and muskeg through the Arctic watershed to Moosonee on Hudson Bay. Arriving at midday, visitors have ample time to tour Ontario's oldest English settlement, founded by the Hudson's Bay Company in 1673. *(Departs from Cochrane late Jun-Labour Day Mon-Fri 9am, returns to Cochrane 10pm. Reservations required. Round trip ☎$90 adult. ✗ &️ P. Ontario Northland, 200 Railway St., Cochrane ON, P1B 8L3. ☎705-472-5338 or 800-268-9281. www. polarbearexpress.ca).* Luxury steamboat cruising can be enjoyed aboard **MV Canadian Empress.** Cruises include shore visits to historic sites and to Ottawa, Montreal, Quebec City and other cities. Trips of 5-7 days available. *(Depart from either Kingston or Quebec City. Mid-May-late Oct. Reservations required. Contact St. Lawrence Cruise Lines, Inc., 253 Ontario St., Kingston, ON K7L 2Z4; ☎613-549-8091 or 800-267-7868. www.stlawrencecruiselines.com).* A scenic 2hr rail tour of the Algoma wilderness north of Sault Ste. Marie arrives at Agawa Canyon *(☾see East Shore Lake Superior)* on the **Algoma Central Railway**.

Algoma Central Railway in Agawa Canyon

Stradiotto/Ontario Tourism

KNOW BEFORE YOU GO

Useful Websites

Official Tourism Sites
www.canada.travel
(The official site of the Canadian Tourism Commission)
www.ontariotravel.net
(The site of the Ontario Tourism Marketing Partnership, a provincial government agency)
www.ontariooutdoor.com
(A website for northern Ontario)
www.soto.on.ca
(A website for southern Ontario)

Government Websites:
www.canada.gc.ca
(links to all federal government departments)
www.gov.on.ca
(links to Ontario provincial government departments)

Government Publishing:
http://publications.gc.ca
(federal government)
www.publications.service ontario.ca (Ontario provincial government)

Current information:
www.canoe.ca
www.canada.com
www.cbc.ca

Tourist Offices

Tourist offices operated by provincial, municipal and regional agencies distribute road maps and brochures and maintain websites that provide information on points of interest, seasonal events, accommodations and recreational activities. Local tourist offices (telephone numbers, addresses and websites listed under the symbol ⬛ under each entry heading in this guide) provide information about accommodations, shopping, entertainment, festivals and recreation.

International Visitors

In addition to tourism offices, visitors from outside Canada may obtain information from the nearest Canadian embassy or consulate in their country of residence. Embassies of other countries are located in Canada's capital, Ottawa. Most foreign countries maintain consulates in Canada's provincial capitals. For further information on all Canadian embassies and consulates abroad, contact the website of **Foreign Affairs and International Trade Canada:** www.international.gc.ca. For a complete list of Canadian embassies and consulates abroad go online to www.voyage.gc.ca

SELECTED CANADIAN CONSULATES AND EMBASSIES

US
1175 Peachtree St. NE, 100 Colony Square, Suite 1700, Atlanta, GA 30361-6205, ☎404-532-2000. www.atlanta.gc.ca
1251 Avenue of the Americas, Concourse Level, New York, NY 10020-1175, ☎212-596-1628. www.newyork.gc.ca
550 South Hope St., 9th floor, Los Angeles, CA 90071-2627, ☎213-346-2700. www.losangeles.gc.ca

Australia
Level 5, Quay West Bldg., 111 Harrington St., Sydney, NSW 2000, ☎9-364-3000. www.international.gc.ca/australia

Germany
Leipziger Platz 17, 10117 Berlin, ☎30-203120. www.berlin.gc.ca

United Kingdom
38 Grosvenor St., Macdonald House, London W1K 4AA, ☎020 7258 6506. www.london.gc.ca or www.canada.org.uk

ENTRY REQUIREMENTS

All travellers need a valid passport, Air NEXUS card or other valid travel document to visit Canada and return to the US by air. As of January 31, 2008, Canadian and US citizens must present a passport, or both a government-issued photo ID (such as a driver's licence) and a birth certificate, to cross the Canada/US border by land or sea. Parents taking children under 18 years of age into the US, or returning to the US after visiting Canada, must present a birth certificate for them. To bring children into Canada, single parents (divorced or simply unaccompained by their spouse) must present a notarized permission letter from the other parent; in addition, bringing a birth certificate for each child is strongly advised. As of June 2009, or earlier, only a passport or other appropriate secure document will be accepted for anyone, including US citizens, to enter the US. Check the websites www.canada.travel or www.travel.state.gov (US government site) for the most recent updates. All other visitors to Canada must have a valid **passport** and, in some cases, a visa *(see list of countries at www.cic. gc.ca/english/visit/visas.asp)*. No vaccinations are necessary. For entry into Canada via the US, all persons other than US citizens or legal residents are required to present a valid passport. Check with the Canadian embassy or consulate in your home country about entry regulations and proper travel documents. Most airlines, even smaller domestic carriers, require valid government-issued photo ID. Persons who have been convicted of a crime—or, in some cases, arrested—should be aware that they may be denied entry to Canada. If you have any doubt, check with Canadian border authorities before heading to Canada.

CUSTOMS REGULATIONS

Non-residents may import personal baggage temporarily without payment of duties. You must be at least 19 years old to bring **alcoholic beverages** into Ontario, limited to 1.14 litres (40 imperial ounces) of wine or spirits, or 24 bottles (355ml or 12 ounces) of beer or ale, duty-free. You may bring into Canada duty-free 200 cigarettes, 50 cigars and some other forms of **tobacco**. All **prescription drugs** should be clearly labelled and for personal use only; it is recommended that visitors carry a copy of the prescription. For more information, call **Border Information Service** ☎*800 461-9999 (within Canada) or* ☎*204-983-3500*; or visit **Canada Border Services Agency online:** *www.cbsa-asfc.gc.ca*. Canada has stringent legislation on firearms. A firearm cannot be brought into the country for personal protection while travelling. Only long guns may be imported by visitors 18 years or older for hunting or sporting purposes. Certain **firearms** are prohibited entry; restricted firearms, which include handguns, may only be imported with a permit by a person attending an approved shooting competition. For further information on entry of firearms, contact the **Canadian Centre for Firearms** *(284 Wellington St., Ottawa, ON K1A 1M6. ☎800-731-4000. www.cfc-cafc.gc.ca)*. Most animals, except domesticated dogs and cats, must be issued a Canadian import permit prior to entry into Canada. **Pets** must be accompanied by an official certificate of vaccination against rabies from the country of origin. Payment of an inspection fee may be necessary. For details, contact **Canadian Food Inspection Agency** *(59 Camelot Dr., Ottawa, ON K1A 0Y9; ☎613-225-2342; www.inspection.gc.ca)*.

CURRENCY EXCHANGE

⏷*See Money in Basic Information.*

HEALTH

Before travelling, visitors should check with their health care insurance to determine if doctor's visits, medication and hospitalization in Ontario are covered; otherwise supplementary insurance may be necessary. Manulife Financial offers reimbursement for expenses as a result of emergencies under their Visitors to Canada Plan. The plan must be purchased before arrival, or within five days of arrival, in Canada. For details contact **Manulife Financial** *(2 Queen St. East, Toronto, ON, M5W 4Z2. ☎800-268-3763. www.coverme.com)*. You may also be able to arrange travel insurance through your national automobile association, such as the American Automobile Association.

Accessibility

Full wheelchair access to sights described in this guide is indicated in admission information by the symbol ♿. Most public buildings and many attractions, restaurants and hotels provide wheelchair access. Disabled parking is provided and the law is strictly enforced. For details contact www.ontariotravel.net.
Many national and provincial parks have restrooms and other facilities for the disabled (such as wheelchair-accessible nature trails or tour buses). For details ☎888-773-8888 or *www.pc.gc.ca*. For Ontario provincial parks, access www.ontarioparks.com. Additional information is available from **Easter Seals Canada** *(Toronto; ☎416-932-8382; www.easterseals.ca)*. Passengers who need assistance should give 24-48hrs advance notice; also contact the following transportation providers to request literature for riders with disabilities:

Via Rail
☎888-842-7245
Special Needs Services:
☎800-268-9503 (TDD)
www.viarail.ca

Greyhound Canada
☎800-661-8747 (Canada)
☎800-397-7870 (TDD)
www.greyhound.ca

Reserve hand-controlled cars at rental companies well in advance.

GETTING THERE AND GETTING AROUND

By Plane

Lester B. Pearson International Airport in Toronto and Ottawa International Airport are served by major Canadian, US and international carriers, while some 39 smaller airports around the province are served by regional and charter companies; some of them are also served by US airlines.

Toronto (YYZ)
Lester B. Pearson International Airport 27km/17mi northwest of downtown ☎416-247-7678. www.gtaa.com

Ottawa (YOW)
Ottawa International Airport 18km/11mi south of downtown ☎613-248-2125
www.ottawa-airport.ca

Air Canada *(☎888-247-2262 Canada/US; www.aircanada.com)* flies to Toronto and Ottawa (as well as to other Canadian cities) from larger US and international cities, and provides domestic service across Canada. Air Canada Jazz *(☎888-247-2262 Canada/US; www.flyjazz.ca)* provides regional connections across the province and Canada. Westjet *(☎888-937-8538. www.westjet.com)* provides service to Hamilton, Kitchener-Waterloo, London, Ottawa, Thunder Bay and Toronto, as well as to other cities in Canada. Ontario regional airlines are Air Creebec *(www.aircreebec.ca)*, Bearskin Airlines*(www.bearskinairlines.com)*, Parry Sound Air Service *(www.inparrysound.com)* and Wasaya Airways *(www.wasaya.com)*.

Air service to remote areas is provided by many charter companies.

By Train

Amtrak offers daily rail service from New York City to Toronto; connections are offered from many major US cities. For schedules in the US ☎800-872-7245 or *www.amtrak.com*. **VIA Rail,** Canada's national passenger rail network, links many cities within the province. Amenities offered are dining cars, baggage handling (including bicycles), wheelchairs and preboarding aid with 24hr minimum notice. Unlimited train travel for 12 days within a 30-day period is available by **CANRAILPASS** *(Jun-mid-Oct, $837, 3-day extension $71/day; off-season $523)*. Special rates are offered for students with an ISIC card, youth and senior citizens.

For information, call ☎888-842-7245 *(US & Canada); www.viarail.ca*. The Travel Planner section of the Via Rail website lists overseas sales agents.

By Coach/Bus

Bus travel from the US is offered by **Greyhound** *(☎416-367-8747 or 800-661-8747,Canada or 800-231-2222, US; www.greyhound.ca)*. For information and schedules, visit *www.greyhound.ca* or call the local US bus terminal. It is advisable to book well in advance when travelling during peak season. The major intercity bus line is also **Greyhound.** Canada Travel Passes, which are sold internationally, offer unlimited travel from 7 days up to 60 days. Peak season rates range from $329 to $750 *(reduced rates available in off-season and for senior citizens)*. A 14-day **Rout-Pass** for travel from May to Oct ($263) is available for most of Quebec and Ontario *(☎416-393-7911; www.routpass.com)*.

By Car

Given Ontario's enormous size, it is impossible to cover the whole province during one visit. ⏱*See Driving Tours for suggested itineraries.* Ontario has an extensive system of well-maintained major roads. In the northern regions and off main arteries, however, many roads are gravel or even dirt. ⚠Extreme caution should be taken when travelling these roads, especially in bad weather.

DOCUMENTS

Foreign **driver's licences** are valid for 3 months in Ontario. Drivers must carry vehicle **registration** information and/or a rental contract at all times. Vehicle **insurance** is compulsory (minimum liability is $200,000). US visitors should obtain a Canadian Non-Resident Inter-Province Motor Vehicle Insurance Liability Card **(yellow card)**, available from US insurance companies. For more information contact the Insurance Bureau of Canada, *(777 Bay St., Suite 2400, Toronto, ON M5G 2C8; ☎416-362-2031; www.ibc.ca)*.

GASOLINE AND ROAD CONDITIONS

Gasoline is sold by the litre (1 gallon = 3.78 litres); prices many vary slightly from place to place, but are higher than in the US. All distances and speed limits are posted in kilometres (1 mile = 1.6 kilometres). During winter it is advisable to check road conditions before setting out. **Snow tires** from November to April and an **emergency kit** are imperative. The Ontario government provides road reports from late October to April: call 1-800-268-4686 (416-235-4686 in the greater Toronto area) or go online to www.mto.gov.on.ca/english/traveller/conditions.

ROAD REGULATIONS

Speed limits, unless otherwise posted, are 100km/h (60mph) on freeways, 90km/h (55mph) on the Trans-Canada routes, and 80km/h (50mph) on most highways and rural roads. Speed limits in cities and towns range from 40km/h to 60km/h (25-40mph). Service stations that are open 24 hours can be found in large cities and along major highways. The use of **seat belts** is mandatory for all drivers and passengers. Ontario prohibits **radar detection devices** in vehicles. Traffic in both directions must stop (except on divided roads) for a yellow school bus when signals are flashing. **Right turns on red** are allowed after coming to a complete stop, unless a sign indicates otherwise.

IN CASE OF ACCIDENT

If you are involved in an accident resulting in property damage and/or personal injury, you must notify the police and remain at the scene until dismissed by investigating officers. Highways are patrolled by the Ontario Provincial Police, as are other areas not served by municipal police; along highways, OPP stations are indicated by a small yellow sign with OPP in black letters. Hospitals are indicated by square blue signs carrying a big white H.

CANADIAN AUTOMOBILE ASSOCIATION (CAA)

This national member-based organization *(1145 Hunt Club Rd., Ottawa,* *ON K1V 0Y3. ☎613-247-0117. www. caa.ca)* offers services such as travel information, maps and tour books, accommodation reservations, insurance, technical and legal advice and emergency roadside assistance. These benefits are extended to members of other international affiliated clubs (proof of membership is required). The CAA maintains for its members a **24hr emergency road service ☎800-222-HELP.**

CAR RENTAL

Most major rental car agencies have offices at airports and in cities across Ontario. Minimum age for rental is usually 25. To avoid a large cash deposit, payment by credit card is recommended. More favourable rates can sometimes be obtained by making a reservation before arriving in Ontario, but be aware of drop-off charges.

- **Avis:** ☎800-331-1212. www.avis.com
- **Budget:** ☎800-268-8900. www.budget.com
- **Discount:** ☎800-263-2355. www.discountcar.com
- **Dollar Rent-a-Car:** ☎800-800-3665. ww2.dollar.com
- **Hertz:** ☎800-654-3131. www.hertz.ca
- **National/Tilden:** ☎800-227-7368. www.nationalcar.ca
- **Thrifty:** ☎800-847-4389. www.thrifty.com

Prince Edward County, Eastern Ontario

Gwen Cannon/Michelin

WHERE TO STAY AND EAT

Hotel and Restaurant listings fall within the Address Books in the Discovering Ontario section. For price categories, ♿see the Legend on the cover flap.

Where to Stay

♿For a selection of accommodations, see the green boxes titled Address Books within the major cities and areas described in the guide. Lodgings in this guide can also be found in the Index under the heading WHERE TO STAY.

Ontario offers accommodations suited to every taste and pocketbook. Luxury **hotels** generally are found in major cities, while **motels** normally are clustered on the outskirts of towns. **Bed-and-breakfast inns** (B&Bs) are found in residential areas of cities and towns, as well as in more secluded natural areas. Many properties offer special packages and weekend rates that may not be extended during peak summer months *(Jul–Aug)* and during winter holiday seasons. Most resort properties include outdoor recreational facilities such as golf courses, tennis courts, swimming pools and fitness centres. Activities—hiking, mountain biking and horseback riding—often can be arranged by contacting the hotel staff. Many cities and communities levy a **hotel occupancy tax** that is not reflected in hotel rates. Ontario provincial, regional and local tourist offices as well as chambers of commerce offer free publications and maintain websites listing accommodations by location. In less populated regions it may be difficult to find accommodations at the end of a long day's drive. Advance reservations are recommended, especially during the tourist season *(Victoria Day to Labour Day)*.

During the off-season, establishments outside urban centres may be closed; it is therefore advisable to telephone ahead. Guaranteeing reservations with a credit card is recommended.

HOTELS

Rates for hotels vary greatly depending on season and location. Expect to pay higher rates during holiday and peak seasons. For deluxe hotels, plan to pay at least $300-$500/night per standard room, based on double occupancy in peak season. Moderate hotels usually will charge $90-$200/night. When making a reservation, ask about packages including meals, passes to local attractions, etc. Typical amenities at hotels include televisions, alarm clocks, in-room phones, internet connections, smoking/non-smoking rooms, restaurants and swimming pools. Suites and in-room efficiency kitchens are available at some hotels. Always advise the reservations clerk of late arrival; unless confirmed with a credit card, rooms may not be held after 6pm.

MOTELS

Along major highways or close to urban areas, motels such as Comfort Inn, Quality Inn and Choice Hotels (☎800-221-2222; www.choicehotels. com), Travelodge (☎800-667-3529; www.travelodge.com) and Days Inn (☎800-325-2525; www.daysinnontario. com) offer accommodations at moderate prices ($50–$115), depending upon the location. Amenities include in-room television, alarm clock and telephone. Smoking and non-smoking rooms, restaurants and swimming pools are often available on-site. Some in-room efficiency kitchens may be available. Family-owned establishments and small, independent guest houses that offer basic comfort can be found all across Ontario.

BED AND BREAKFASTS AND COUNTRY INNS

Most B&Bs and country inns are privately owned; some are located in historic structures in residential sections of cities or small towns. In rural areas lodgings can be a rustic cabin or a farmhouse. At B&Bs the room rate includes complimentary breakfast ranging from continental fare to a gourmet repast; some offer afternoon tea and evening sherry or light snacks. Guests are invited to use the sitting room and garden spots. Country inns are larger establishments, usually with more than 15 rooms and with full-service dining facilities. Private baths are not always available, and often there is no phone in individual rooms. Smoking indoors may not be permitted. Reservations should be made well in advance, especially during peak seasons and holidays. Ask about minimum stay requirements, and cancellation and refund policies. Most establishments accept major credit cards, but some B&Bs may not. Rates vary seasonally ($75-$200) for a double room per night. Rates may be higher when amenities such as hot tubs, private entrances and scenic views are offered. *Also see Ontario's Finest Inns at www.ontariosfinestinns. com and Federation of Ontario B&B Accommodation at www.fobba.com.*

RESERVATIONS SERVICES

Numerous organizations offer reservation services for B&Bs and country inns. The **Federation of Ontario Bed & Breakfast Accommodation** provides names, as well as a printed guide, of member B&Bs by city, region or name *(FOBBA, 95 King St. West, Gananoque ON, K7G 2G2. www.fobba. com)* The **Professional Association of Innkeepers International** *(☎856-310-1102; www.paii.org)* and **Wakeman & Costine's North American Bed & Breakfast Directory** *(☎828-387-3697; www.bbdirectory. com)* include properties for Canada as a whole. The **Independent Innkeepers' Assn.** publishes an annual register that includes Canadian B&Bs and country inns; *☎269-789-0393 or 800-344-5244* or book online: *www. selectregistry.com*. For a complete listing, search the Internet using the keywords "bed breakfast Ontario" or ask your travel agent.

HOSTELS

Hostelling International Canada, affiliated with the International Youth Hostel Federation, offers budget accommodations in Barrie, Maynooth, Niagara Falls, Orillia, Ottawa, Toronto and Thunder Bay. A simple, no-frills alternative to hotels and inns, hostels are inexpensive dormitory-style accommodations (blankets and pillows are provided) with separate quarters for males and females. Many have private family/couples rooms that may be reserved in advance. Amenities include fully equipped self-service kitchens, dining areas, common rooms and laundry facilities. Rates average $15–$25 per night for members (higher for non-members). Hostels often organize special programs and activities for guests. Advance booking is advisable during peak travel times, but walk-ins are welcome. Membership is $35/year, but non-members are also admitted. When booking, ask for available discounts at area attractions, rental car companies and restaurants. For information and a free directory, contact **Hostelling International Canada** *(400-205 Catherine St., Ottawa, ON K2P 1C3; ☎613-237-7884 or 800-663-5777; www.hihostels.ca)*.

UNIVERSITIES AND COLLEGES

Most universities make their dormitory space available to travellers during summer vacation *(May–Aug)*. Rooms are sparse; linens are provided. Bathrooms are communal and there are no in-room telephones. Rates average $20–$35/day per person. Reservations are accepted. When booking, ask about on-campus parking and food service. For more information contact the local tourist office or the university directly.

FARM AND COUNTRY VACATIONS

The Ontario Farm and Country Accommodations Association *(www.countryhosts.com)* offers a list of some 50 members, located in five regions covering southern Ontario, who provide B&B style accommodations ranging from elegant old rural homes to working farms. Activities may include fishing, hiking and berry-picking. Breakfast is included. Other meals may be requested and may be taken with the host family. Rates begin at $80 for double occupancy, but often there are packages for longer stays. Inquire about deposit and refund policies and minimum stay requirements. Credit cards may not always be accepted.

For vacations in a country resort, contact **Resorts of Ontario** *(☎800-363-7227; www.resortsofontario.com)* which offers listings of resorts in seven regions of Ontario. Activities such as golf, winter sports, spa treatments, culinary lessons, hiking, or horseback riding may be included.

SPA RETREATS

Spa retreats are often found in restful rural settings, or in a city hotel, where day-long spa treatments offer a regenerating respite. To find a spa suited to your requirements, consult **Ontario's Finest Spas** *(☎800-340-4667. www.ontariosfinestspas.com)* which has 20 members, all in rural or semi-rural surroundings, or **Premier Spas of Ontario** *(☎800-990-7702; www.premierspasofontario)* which has 28 members, some rural, some located in hotels offering day spas, such as Toronto's Fairmont Royal York Hotel. Many spas offer special group rates, often in connection with meetings scheduled on or near the site. Prices for a country spa range from about $150 a night for double occupancy, to $500; many spas require at least a two- night stay. Day spa fees vary according to the treatments requested.

CAMPING AND RV PARKS

Ontario has excellent campgrounds that are operated privately or by the federal and provincial governments. Government sites are located in national and provincial parks. Fees are nominal. These campgrounds are well equipped and fill up quickly. Most park **campgrounds** *(open mid-May–Labour Day)* usually operate on a first-come, first-served basis. Dates are subject to change: visitors should check with park visitor centres for rates and maximum length of stay. Some parks offer reservation services; some offer winter camping. Campsites often include a level tent pad, picnic table, fire grill with firewood, and parking space near a potable water source. Most have toilet buildings and kitchen shelters. Some campgrounds are for tents only; others allow recreational vehicles; most do not have trailer hook-ups, although many have sewage disposal stations. Many accommodate persons with disabilities. Rustic campgrounds can be reached only on foot. Some parks offer hut-to-hut cross-country skiing with rustic overnight accommodations or winter tent sites.

NATIONAL AND PROVINCIAL PARKS

Campgrounds are relatively inexpensive but fill rapidly, especially during school holidays. Facilities range from simple tent sites to full RV hook-ups *(reserve 60 days in advance),* rustic cabins (☺*reserve one year in advance)* or even yurts. Fees vary according to season and available facilities (picnic tables, water/electric hook-ups, used-water disposal, recreational equipment, showers, restrooms): camping and RV sites $8–$21/day; cabins $20–$110/day. For all Canadian national park reservations, contact the park you are visiting or **Parks Canada** *(☎888-773-8888. www.pc.gc.ca).* For information on Ontario's 104 provincial parks, contact **Ontario Parks** *(☎800-668-2746. www.ontarioparks.ca)*

PRIVATE CAMPGROUNDS

Commercial campgrounds offer facilities ranging from simple tent sites to full RV hook-ups. They are slightly more expensive *($10–$60/day for tent sites, $20–$25/day for RVs)* but offer amenities such as hot showers, laundry facilities, convenience stores, children's playgrounds, pools, air-conditioned cabins and outdoor recreational facilities. Most accept daily, weekly or monthly occupancy. During the winter months *(Nov–Apr)*, campgrounds in northern regions may be closed. For private campgrounds contact the **Ontario Private Campground Association,** ☎*877-672-2226* or *www.campgrounds.org,* which lists some 500 private campgrounds in the province. Reservations are recommended, especially for longer stays and in popular resort areas.

FISHING CAMPS, FLY-IN LODGES AND WILDERNESS CAMPS

Ontario offers the experienced angler or the outdoor enthusiast a variety of fishing lodges and camps, some of which are so remote they can only be reached on foot or by private boat or float plane. Cabins, backcountry huts, main lodge and dormitory-style buildings are typical accommodations. Summer tent camping may also be offered. Outfitters offer packages that include transportation, accommodations, meals, supplies, equipment and expeditions led by experienced guides. Activities can include trail riding, ecotours, lake and stream fishing, hunting expeditions, boating and climbing. Some camps have saunas or hot tubs.

Wilderness camps offer all-inclusive hunting packages. Non-residents must be accompanied by licenced guides. Permits can be obtained through the outfitter, who can also assist with game registration *(*☺*required by law).* These packages are costly and the number of spaces is usually limited. It is advisable to make reservations well in advance. For information on fishing and hunting regulations and licence fees, as well as listings of outfitters, contact the **Northern Ontario Tourist Outfitters Association** *(386 Algonquin Ave, North Bay ON, P1B 4W3;* ☎*705-472-5552; www.noto.net),* which also offers a brochure, the Ontario Adventure Guide, describing trips and outfitting services and provides links to travel associations specializing in wilderness adventures.

Where to Eat

☙*For a selection of restaurants, see the green boxes titled* **Address Books** *within the major cities and other areas in the Discovering Ontario section of the guide. Restaurants in this guide can also be found in the Index under the heading* **WHERE TO EAT**.

Ontario's cuisines encompass traditional fare as well as novel creations. Originally, foods that were hunted and gathered (game, fish, goose, berries, and wild rice, for example) formed aboriginal and early Europeans' diets. Since then, traditional dishes favoured by early British and Loyalist settlers have been supplemented by those of a diverse ethnic population, resulting in a richly varied cuisine. The Niagara Peninsula of southern Ontario, which extends away from the rocky Canadian Shield that covers much of the rest of the province, benefits from good soil and a relatively mild climate that permit production of excellent fruit and vegetables, as well as a burgeoning wine industry. Development of tourism has created a demand for fine cuisine, and many restaurants and resorts use Ontario's natural bounty to create ambitious menus. In the spring, maple trees are tapped for their sap and sugaring-off parties are held; the Maple Syrup Museum of Ontario has all the information *(1441 King St. North, The Mill, St. Jacobs ON, N0B 2N0; www.stjacobs.com).* The tourism website **www.ontariotravel.net** lists places to go, as do regional and local websites.

WHAT TO SEE AND DO

Outdoor Fun

WATER SPORTS

Scenic routes to explore by boat are the Rideau Canal and lakes from Ottawa to Kingston, and the Trent-Severn canal system from Trenton to Georgian Bay via the Kawartha Lakes and Lake Simcoe. **Canoeing and kayaking** are among the most popular outdoor sports in Ontario, ranging from paddling across lakes and down rivers to whitewater kayaking. You can rent canoes and kayaks at many points.

Outfitters offer an array of excursions that include transportation, lodging and the service of experienced guides. The best-known regions for canoeing are **Algonquin Provincial Park** (*☎705-633-5572; www.algonquinpark. on.ca*), which has 1,500km/900mi of canoe routes, and **Quetico Provincial Park** (*☎807-597-2735; www. ontarioparks.com*) through which the Boundary Waters Fur Trade Canoe Route passes with 43 portages along 523km/325mi. Lifejackets are mandatory, and it's illegal to drink and boat. For trip planning and information, visit *www.paddlingcanada.com* and *www. canoekayakcanada.ca*. For leaving no trace travel, go to *http://lnt.org*.

FISHING

Ontario is an angler's paradise, especially in the north, where many fly-in lodges arrange expeditions. Non-residents must obtain a licence, available from a sporting goods store. For information on seasons, catch and possession limits, contact the Natural Heritage Information Centre (*300 Water St., Peterborough ON, K9J 8M5; ☎416-314-2000; www.mnr.gov. on.ca/mnr/fishing*). Some parks offer boat and canoe rentals.

HIKING

Ontario is crisscrossed with hiking trails, ranging from easy to strenuous; you can opt to hike only portions of longer trails. The famous **Bruce Trail** (The Bruce Trail Conservancy, *www. brucetrail.org*) follows the Niagara Escarpment for 692km/430mi across the southern part of the province. Along the shores of Lake Superior, hikers pass through wilderness on the Coastal Trail in **Pukaskwa National Park** (*☎807-229-0801; www.pc.gc. ca*). In national and provincial parks, hikers should ask park officials about trail conditions, weather forecasts and safety precautions. Overnight **hikers** in backcountry areas are required to register at the park office before setting out and to deregister upon completion of the trip. Trail distances are given from trailhead to destination, not round-trip, unless otherwise posted. Topographic maps and a compass are indispensable for backcountry hiking; Gem Trek Publishing (*☎250-380-0100 or 877-921-6277; www.gemtrek.com*) and Federal Maps, Inc. (*☎416-607-6250 or 888-545-8111; www.fedmaps.com*) are two sources for obtaining detailed topographic maps.

RIDING

Horseback riding opportunities range from hour-long trail rides to one week or longer expeditions. Also check the Royal Canadian Mounted Police Musical Ride for summer demonstrations or visit their stable in Ottawa, Ontario (*☎613-998-8199; www.rcmp-grc.gc.ca*). For equestrian events, contact Equine Canada (*☎866-282-8395; www. canadaequine.com*).

SKIING AND BOARDING

Thunder Bay, Blue Mountain (Collingwood) and the Gatineau Hills are popular alpine skiing and snowboarding areas. Although Ontario has no big mountains, there are local ski hills that offer programs and instruction; the province has produced several world-calibre competitive skiers.

For information, contact the **Ontario Snow Resorts Association** (☎705-443-5450; www.skiontario.on.ca).

WILDLIFE WATCHING

Ontario is renowned for its wildlife. **Point Pelee National Park** (☎519-322-2365; www.pc.gc.ca), which lies on migration routes, is a famed bird-watching site. For information about Canadian wildlife, visit the Canadian Wildlife Federation's website: www.hww.ca, and the Environment Canada Ontario Region website at www.on.ec.gc.ca/wildlife. Wildlife is best observed in the province's provincial and national parks, which include marine parks such as **Fathom Five National Marine Park** (☎416-519-596-2233; www.pc.gc.ca). When watching or photographing wildlife, a respectful distance is crucial. Stiff fines are given in parks for feeding and otherwise habituating wildlife: never feed, pet or disturb wild creatures of any kind. Large beasts such as bears and moose can be extremely dangerous.

Activities for Children Kids

In this guide, sights of particular interest to children are indicated with a Kids symbol. Many of these attractions offer discounted admission to visitors under 12 years of age as well as special children's programs designed for all ages. National and Ontario provincial parks usually offer discount fees for children. In addition, many hotels and resorts feature special family discount packages, and most restaurants offer children's menus.

Calendar of Events

Throughout the province, Ontarians hold annual fairs, festivals and celebrations, many of them seasonal, cultural, or ethnic. Here is a sampling:

SPRING

early Apr—**Maple Syrup Festival**; *Elmira; www.elmiramaple syrup.com*

Apr-Nov—**Shaw Festival**; *Niagara-on-the-Lake; www.shawfest.com* **Stratford Festival;** *Stratford; www.stratford-festival.on.ca*

May—**Canadian Tulip Festival**; *Ottawa; www.tulipfestival.ca*

SUMMER

Jun-Jul—**Summerfest**; *Windsor; www.summerfestwindsor.org*

mid-Jul—**Great Rendezvous**; *Thunder Bay; wwwfwhp.ca/events.html* **Muskoka Arts & Crafts' Summer Show**; *Bracebridge; www.muskokaartsandcrafts.com*

late Jul-early Aug—**Rockhound Gemboree**; *Bancroft*

early Aug—**Caribana** *Toronto; www.caribanatoronto.com* **Glengarry Highland Games**; *Maxville; www.glengarryhighland games.com*

mid-Aug—**Summerfolk Music and Crafts Festival;** *Owen Sound; www.summerfolk.org*

Aug—**Six Nations Native Pageant**; *Brantford; http://sixnations pageant.com*

FALL

early Sept—**International Film Festival**; *Toronto; www.tiffg.ca*

late Sept—**Niagara Wine Festival**; *St. Catharines; www.niagara winefestival.com*

mid-Oct—**Oktoberfest**; *Kitchener-Waterloo; www.oktoberfest.ca*

WINTER

mid-Nov–**Royal Agricultural Winter Fair;** *Toronto; www.royalfair.org*

Nov-Jan—**Winter Festival of Lights**; *Niagara Falls; www.WFOL.com*

Feb—**Winterlude**; *Ottawa; www.winterlude.ca*

Shopping

BUSINESS HOURS

Business hours in Ontario are, for the most part, Monday to Friday 9am–5pm. In general, retail stores are open Monday to Friday 9am–6pm (until 9pm Thursday and Friday), Saturday 9am–5pm.

In most cities, shops are usually open on Sunday afternoon; many small convenience stores in gas stations may be open much longer hours.

For banking hours, see Money in the Basic Information section.

GENERAL MERCHANDISE

Downtown areas provide opportunities for shopping at department stores, national chains, specialty stores, art galleries and antique shops. Founded in 1670, Hudson's Bay Company (known universally as "The Bay") has 35 stores across Ontario. The upscale Holt Renfrew (known as "Holt's") offers elegant clothing and toiletries in Toronto and Ottawa. Large **shopping malls** are generally located outside downtown areas, although Toronto's Eaton Centre and Hazelton Lanes, and Ottawa's 240 Sparks and Rideau Centre are squarely metropolitan. Bargain hunters will want to look for **outlet malls** that offer savings of up to 70% at brand-name factory stores. Canadian Tire, a national institution, is the ultimate hardware, housewares, athletic equipment (notably, hockey equipment) and car-parts emporium. For outerwear, companies such as Mountain Equipment Co-op (MEC), with stores in Toronto and Ottawa, equip customers head-to-toe for hiking, skiing, hunting and fishing. **Furriers** are plentiful, particularly in Ottawa and Toronto. For a list of shopping opportunities, consult the websites www.toronto.com and www.ottawakiosk.com. Also, the lovely towns in the Niagara Peninsula, Prince Edward County and other country refuges offer unique opportunities for finding antiques and crafts.

ARTS AND CRAFTS

Throughout Ontario, local artists and craftspeople produce and sell a wide variety of objects; local crafts fairs are common. The spectacular natural scenery of the province has inspired many painters; early in the 20C, Tom Thomson and the celebrated Group of Seven artists interpreted Ontario scenes, notably in Algonquin Park and Georgian Bay; their work is displayed at the McMichael Canadian Art Collection in Kleinburg (☎905-893-1121; www.mcmichael.com). Many local galleries feature contemporary Ontario artists whose work is often reasonably priced. The Thunder Bay Art Gallery (☎807-577-6427; www.theag.ca) features aboriginal and other local artists. Vacation areas such as the Muskoka Lakes region abound in small galleries and crafts shops; Muskoka has an annual crafts fair in Bracebridge each July (for a schedule of events, access www.muskokaartsandcrafts.com).

FARMERS' MARKETS

In Ontario, **Kitchener's** indoor market is held throughout the year, as is neighbouring **St. Jacob's,** a popular tourist attraction. St. Lawrence Market (open year-round) in **Toronto** sells fresh produce, seafood, baked goods, flowers, souvenirs and crafts. Nearby **Hamilton** boasts one of Ontario's largest indoor markets, open throughout the year. A festival atmosphere prevails at **Ottawa's** year-round ByWard Market, stretching over several blocks (indoors in winter). During harvest time, many farmers sell produce at roadside stands as well as at farmers' markets. Producers invite visitors to try the many varieties of apples, peaches, plums and other orchard bounty in the **Niagara Peninsula,** one of Canada's chief fruit-growing regions.

WINERIES

A wine-making industry thrives on the shores of Lake Ontario in the **Niagara Peninsula** and in and around **Prince**

Edward County, as well as on the north shore of Lake Erie and on Pelee Island. Most wineries welcome visitors, offering guided tours that include free wine tastings. During the fall harvest season, check with area visitor centres to find out about festivals and special events.

Sightseeing

HERITAGE SITES

Ontario Heritage Trust offers free admission to heritage properties in 55 communities throughout the province *(Apr-Oct)*. Sites range from small museums to historic houses and gardens. Call 800-668-2746 for a brochure, or access www.doorsopenontario.on.ca. Ontario Heritage Trust (www. heritagefdn.ca.on) owns 24 properties of special historical or architectural significance and more than 140 sites of natural beauty. Several are described under Sight headings in this guide. The Ontario Museum Association, based in Toronto, makes available a guide to museums located throughout the province: ☎*416-348-8672; www. museumsontario.com.*

There are 14 **National Historic Sites** and one **UNESCO World Heritage Site** in Ontario (the Rideau Canal in Ottawa). Designed for daytime visits, historic sites are open from Victoria Day to Labour Day, with reduced hours in the early spring and fall. Most charge a nominal admission fee and at many, interpretation centres and costumed guides provide insight into Canada's history and cultural heritage.

RIVER AND LAKE CRUISES

Cruising the Great Lakes, Georgian Bay or the St Lawrence River is a relaxing way to enjoy the province's natural beauty. Cruises are described under individual Sights: for details about specific cuises ⓒsee Georgian Bay, Goderich, Muskoka Lakes, Kingston and the Thousand Islands, North Bay, and Ottawa.

GARDENING

Perhaps it's Ontario's British heritage, but the care lavished on gardens, both public and private, strikes any visitor as an obsession. **Ontario Communities in Bloom** *(www.cibontario. ca)* lists participating communities on its website. For garden tours and flower shows, go to the website of the **Ontario Horticultural Association** (www.gardenontario.org) and click on "Events": most tours take place in late June and July, while flower and vegetable shows occur from June to September. The Ontario tourist board at www.ontariotravel.net lists remarkable public gardens, but for a look at photos of 19 lovingly maintained private gardens in Ontario, go to the **Canadian Garden Museum** at www. canadiangardenmuseum.ca. Members of **Rural Gardens of Grey and Bruce Counties** *(www.ruralgardens.ca)* open their 32 gardens on the Bruce Peninsula in Georgian Bay to visitors for a small donation. The illustrated book *Great Gardens to Visit* by Patricia Singer (Fitzhenry & Whiteside, 2003) describes 300 Ontario private gardens, with contact information.

NATIONAL PARKS AND RESERVES

General Information

Most points of interest are in the southern national parks, accessible by car. Hiking trails permit outdoor enthusiasts to enjoy the backcountry. Parks are open year-round; however, some roads may be closed during the winter. Daily entry or use fees range from $2.50 to $6 per adult. Discounts are offered at some parks to senior citizens (25%) and children (50%). Additional fees are charged for camping, fishing and guided programs. **Visitor centres** *(open Victoria Day–Labour Day daily; reduced hours the rest of the year)* are usually located at park entrances. Staff members are available to help visitors plan activities. Trail maps and literature on park facilities, hiking trails, nature programs, camping and in-park accommodations are available on-site free of charge. Interpretation programs, guided hikes, exhibits and self-guided trails introduce the visitor to each park's history, geology and habitats.

For a listing of in-park activities, see the description of specific parks within the Discovering Ontario section.

DISCOUNTS

For Students and Youths

Child rates usually apply to under 12 years of age, youth rates to ages 12–17 years. With a valid student card, any student 12 years and older can obtain an International Student Identity Card for discounts on rail travel and more (available at many ViaRail stations, or online from www.isic.org).

For Senior Citizens

To obtain discounts for visitors age 62 or older, proof of age may be required. National and provincial parks usually offer discounts. Canada has no national organization for older citizens, but visiting seniors should ask businesses if a discount is available.

Books

Roughing It in the Bush (1852, 1997). **Susanne Moodie.**
Sunshine Sketches of a Little Town (1912). **Stephen Leacock.**
Jalna (1927). **Mazo de la Roche.**
The Deptford Trilogy: Fifth Business (1970), The Manticore (1972); World of Wonders (1975). **Robertson Davies.**
The Wars (1978) **Timothy Findlay.**
Canada Made Me (1979) **Norman Levine.**
The Game (1983) **Ken Dryden.**
Black Robe (1985) **Brian Moore.**
In the Skin of a Lion (1987) **Michael Ondaatje.**
The View from Castle Rock (2006) **Alice Munro.**
The Blind Assassin (2000) **Margaret Atwood.**
Away (1993); The Underpainter (1997) **Jane Urquhart.**
The Meeting Point (1998) **Austin Clarke.**
Unless (2002) **Carole Shields.**

Crow Lake (2002) **Mary Lawson.**
The Group of Seven and Tom Thomson (2006) **David P.Silcox.**

Films

Below are notable Canadian films relevant to Ontario:

The Handmaid's Tale (1990).
Hollywood adaptation of Margaret Atwood's novel about a dystopian US run by religious fundamentalists; dissenters escape to Canada.

Black Robe (1991).
Film version of Brian Moore's novel about a young French Jesuit who, in 17C New France, encounters horrific violence on his way to the mission at Sainte-Marie-among-the-Hurons on Georgian Bay.

Last Night (1998).
Residents in a Canadian city come to terms with news that the world will come to an end at midnight.

Stardom (2000).
Young female hockey player evolves to celebrity status and scandal as a fashion model.

Possible Worlds (2000).
The permutations of George Barber's life in parallel universes.

Waydowntown (2002).
Four office workers bet a month's salary to see who can go the longest without leaving their apartment-office-shopping complex.

Men with Brooms (2002).
Antics of four curling buddies who reunite to realize their late coach's dream of winning a big trophy.

The Corporation (2003).
Documentary examines the impact of how a corporation, legally defined as a person, can operate without the moral responsibility expected of individuals.

Away from Her (2007).
Film interpretation of a short story by Alice Munro. A woman with Alzheimer's disease moves into a nursing home and to her husband's alarm, transfers her affections to another patient.

BASIC INFORMATION

Electricity

120 volts, 60 cycles. Most small American appliances can be used. European appliances require an electrical transformer, available at electric supply stores.

Emergencies

Ontario cities and many rural areas have **911** telephone service for emergency response. When 911 is dialled from any telephone in a served area, a central dispatch office sees the dialling location and can redirect the call to the appropriate emergency response agency—fire department, police or ambulance. Much of rural Ontario is not within range of cellular telephone service, and although coverage extends along most major highways, service can be unreliable in wilderness regions. *Also see Telephones.*
Public Safety Canada maintains extensive links to information and services on public safety: www.safecanada.ca.

Liquor Laws

The legal drinking age in Ontario is 19. Liquor is sold in government stores.

Mail/Post

Post offices across Canada are generally open Monday to Friday 8am–5:30pm; extended hours are available in some locations. Sample rates for first-class mail (letter or postcard; up to 30 grams): within Canada 52 cents; to the US 93 cents; international mail $1.55. Mail service for all but local deliveries is by air. Visitors can receive mail c/o "General Delivery" addressed to Main Post Office, City, Province and Postal Code. Mail will be held for 15 days and has to be picked up by the addressee. Some post offices have

fax services, and all post offices offer international courier service. In addition to post offices, postal facilities are located at selected Canadian retailers, offering convenient extended and weekend hours. For information regarding postal codes or locations of facilities call ☎866-607-6301 or access www.canadapost.ca.

Metric System

Canada has adopted the International System of Units popularly known as the metric system. Weather temperatures are given in Celsius (C°), milk and wine are sold by millilitres and litres, and grocery items are measured in grams. All distances and speed limits are posted in kilometres (to obtain the equivalent in miles, multiply by 0.6). Some examples of metric conversions are:
1 kilometre (km) = 0.62 miles
1 metre (m) = 3.28 feet
1 kilogram (kg) = 2.2 pounds
1 litre (L) = 33.8 fluid ounces =
  0.26 gallons
(1 US quart = 32 fluid ounces)

Money

Canadian currency is based on the decimal system (100 cents to the dollar). Bills are issued in $5, $10, $20, $50, $100, $500 and $1,000 denominations; coins are minted in 1 cent, 5 cents, 10 cents, 25 cents, $1 and $2. Exchange money at banks for the most favourable exchange rate.
You don't need to carry much cash while visiting Canada: ATM machines are widely available, and most merchants accept debit or credit cards. Self-serve gas stations, parking lots and even store check-outs are common. Do carry a few "loonies" or "toonies"—the $1 and $2 coins—for parking meters, tips and snacks. Most public telephones accept calling

cards at no charge, but local calls cost 25–50¢ (one or two quarters). Most ATMs dispense cash in increments of $20.

BANKS

Banking institutions are generally open Monday to Friday 9am–5pm. Some bank branches are open on Saturday morning, and some offer extended evening hours. Banks at large airports have foreign exchange counters and extended hours. Institutions generally charge a fee for cashing traveller's cheques. Most principal bank cards are honoured at affiliated Canadian banks.

⊚Use bank-branded ATM machines to avoid the higher fees charged by private operators.

CREDIT CARDS AND TRAVELLER'S CHEQUES

The following major credit cards are accepted in Canada: American Express, Carte Blanche, Discover, Diners Club, MasterCard/Eurocard and Visa. Most banks will cash traveller's cheques and process cash advances on major credit cards with proper personal identification. Be advised, however, that bank fees for cashing traveller's cheques are normally charged per cheque and are usually a substantial amount.

CURRENCY EXCHANGE

The most favourable exchange rate can usually be obtained at branch offices of a national bank. Some banks charge a small fee for this transaction. Private exchange companies generally charge higher fees. Airports and visitor centres in large cities may have exchange outlets as do some hotels. The Canadian dollar fluctuates with international exchange rates. Exchange facilities tend to be limited in rural and remote areas. If arriving in Canada late in the day or on a weekend, visitors may wish to exchange some funds prior to arrival (a few

banks are open on Saturday mornings in major cities, however).

⊚You can use ATMs to withdraw Canadian currency from your home account, but check with your bank first to see if it has reciprocal arrangements with a Canadian bank for a lower fee.

TAXES

Canada levies a 5% Goods and Services Tax (GST) on most goods and services. Ontario levies an additional Retail Sales Tax of 8% on some goods and services.

Public Holidays

The following holidays are observed in Ontario. Banks, government offices and schools are closed:

New Year's Day: January 1
Family Day: 3rd Monday in February
Good Friday: Friday before
   Easter Sunday
Easter Monday: Monday after
   Easter Sunday
Victoria Day: The Monday on or
   before May 24
Canada Day: July 1
Civic Holiday: 1st Monday in August
Labour Day: 1st Monday in
   September
Thanksgiving: 2nd Monday in
   October
Remembrance Day: 2nd
   Wednesday in November
Christmas Day: December 25
Boxing Day: December 26

Smoking

Ontario has one of the toughest anti-smoking laws in North America. As of 2006, smoking is banned in all public enclosed spaces, including restaurants, bars and private clubs. There are designated smoking rooms in hospitals and health institutions, but otherwise the only public place you can light up is outdoors. Smoking has been banned from aircraft, buses, trains and most offices for some time.

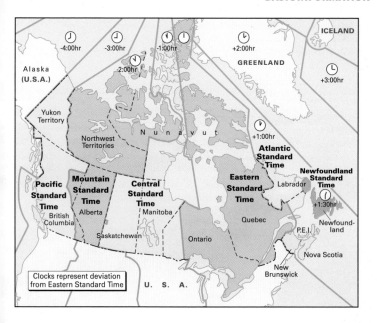

Clocks represent deviation from Eastern Standard Time

Telephones

To call long distance within Canada and to the US, dial 1+ area code + number. For overseas calls, refer to the country codes in most telephone directories, or dial "0" for operator assistance. All operators in Canada speak English and French. Collect calls and credit card calls can be made from public pay phones. For local directory assistance, check the white pages of the phone directory or dial 411; outside the local area code, dial 1+ area code + 555-1212. Telephone numbers that start with **800, 866, 877** or **888** are toll-free *(no charge)*.
A local call costs 25 to 50 cents. Be aware that many hotels place a surcharge on all calls.

EMERGENCY NUMBERS

911 service, operated through municipalities, is extensive in Ontario, and can be accessed from cell phones; if for some reason 911 doesn't work, dial "0" for the operator and ask for the police.

Time

Most of Ontario is on Eastern Standard Time. In the western third of the province (west of 90°, or to the west of Thunder Bay), Central Standard Time applies. Daylight Saving Time is observed from the 2nd Sunday in March to the 1st Sunday in November.

Tips

Tips or service charges are not normally added to a bill in Ontario. However, it is customary to tip for services received from food servers, porters, hotel maids and taxi drivers. In restaurants and for taxi drivers, it is customary to tip 10%-15% of the total amount of the bill (excluding taxes). In restaurants, one method of calculating the tip is to pay a bit more than the total of federal and provincial sales taxes, which comes to 13%. At hotels, porters should be tipped $1 per bag, and maids $1 per night.

Aerial view of Muskoka Lake
Ontario Tourism

NATURE

Ontario is Canada's second-largest province. Covering one million square kilometres (415,000sq mi), it stretches from Middle Island in Lake Erie (41°40' N latitude) to **Hudson Bay and James Bay** in the north. Quebec (the largest province) lies to the east, Manitoba to the west, and the US to the south. The southern border edges the **St. Lawrence River** and four of the five **Great Lakes,** which together form the largest body of fresh water in the world. Ontario takes its name from an Iroquoian word probably meaning "a large body of water."

Geologic Past

THE GREAT ICE AGES

Four times during the past million years, the North American climate has become progressively colder. Snowfall became increasingly heavy in the north and was gradually compressed into ice. This ice began to flow south, reaching as far as the Ohio and Missouri river valleys in the US before retreating. At peak coverage, 97 percent of Canada and all of Ontario were submerged under ice up to 3km/2mi deep at the centre and 1.6km/1mi deep at the edges. The last Ice Age receded more than 10,000 years ago.

A sheet of ice of such thickness exerts a great deal of pressure on the earth below. As the ice from each glacial advance retreated, hollows were scoured out of the land and filled with water, forming Ontario's characteristic rocky terrain indented with a quarter-million lakes; indeed, Ontario's lakes and rivers hold about one-third of the world's fresh water, besides providing sites of great natural beauty that have attracted artists and tourists for generations.

THE CANADIAN SHIELD

Canada has at its centre a massive upland known as the Canadian Shield, which encompasses nearly half of the country's area. It covers nearly two-thirds of Ontario, interrupted by lowlands stretching in a wide swath along the shores of Hudson Bay and James Bay

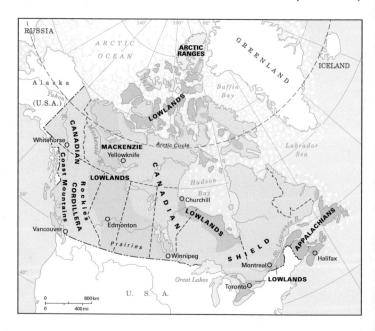

to the north, and in the province's southern tip, the fertile economic heartland framed by lakes Erie, Ontario and Huron. Much of the Shield is covered by glacial debris such as clay, gravel, sand, peat and thin soil, but some is exposed in all its rugged impressiveness.

The Canadian Shield is formed of ancient, hard rocks of the **Precambrian** era (more than 540 million years old) known for their great rigidity and strength. Yet, somewhat surprisingly, this harsh terrain has proven a vast treasure trove. It supports great forests that form the basis for the thriving forest products industry, as well as the fur trade, the original source of the province's wealth, and mineral riches including amethyst, cobalt, copper, gold, iron, nickel, platinum, silver and zinc. Historically, the Shield's many lakes and rivers provided the hydroelectric energy that launched Ontario's great manufacturing industries; about 20 percent of the electricity generated in Ontario today is hydroelectric.

GREAT LAKES/ ST. LAWRENCE LOWLANDS

Despite their comparatively small size, the southern Ontario lowlands, which extend south into one of the great industrial and agricultural belts of the continent, are home to about 80 per cent of the province's inhabitants. They were created in **Palaeozoic** times (251 million–542 million years ago) when great stretches of the region were flooded by the sea for long periods. During this flooding thousands of feet of sedimentary rock accumulated on top of the Canadian Shield, providing fertile soil that has made the region important for agriculture today. In addition, the proximity of the Great Lakes and the protective barrier of the Niagara Escarpment create a particularly favourable climate. The fertile soil and climate attracted settlers, while easy water transport to major US markets spurred trade and manufacturing. The result was that southern Ontario became Canada's richest and most industrialized area.

Geographical Features

VEGETATION

About 65 percent of Ontario is covered by forest, or some 70 million hectares (173 million acres). The largest region, the **boreal forest** of black pine and jack pine, interspersed with spruce, tamarack and other conifers, covers about 25 percent of Ontario, including most of the northwest and stretching east to the Quebec border. Between the boreal forest and the subarctic tundra in the far north lie the **boreal barrens,** a transition zone covering another 25 percent of the province, consisting of patches of black spruce and tamarack interspersed with bogs, muskeg and other wetlands; along riverbanks are found stands of white and black spruce, balsam fir, trembling aspen, balsam poplar and white birch. To the south, along the St. Lawrence River and across central Ontario lies the **Great Lakes-St. Lawrence forest** where yellow birch, sugar and red maples, basswood and red oak mingle with coniferous species such as eastern white pine, red pine, eastern hemlock and white cedar. In southern Ontario, the conifers of the north are completely left behind and a true **deciduous forest** exists. The remaining wetlands support cattails, water lilies, sedges and ferns,

Moose in Algonquin Provincal Park

G. Briand/Ontario Tourism

as well as successful alien species like purple loosestrife, which came from Europe some 200 years ago as seeds in cattle fodder.

WILDLIFE

Ontario's varied landscape hosts several species of animals typical of regional fauna. Vast forests provide habitat for **black bears, white-tailed deer, moose,** the largest of the deer family, and the **woodland caribou,** another member of the deer family. Trapped nearly to extinction, **beavers** once again thrive across the province, occupying the streams and ponds of forested regions. Once common to forest, prairies and tundra, **gray wolves** reside primarily in the northern wilderness. Other woodland denizens that campers and vacationers routinely encounter include Eastern cottontail rabbits, coyotes, Eastern chipmunks, groundhogs (marmots), muskrats, racoons, red foxes and squirrels.In the far north of Ontario, on the shores of Hudson Bay, are **polar bears** that feed on **ringed seals,** as well as **walruses**. **Beluga whales** can be sighted off Moosonee on James Bay.

Some 318 species of **birds** regularly appear in Ontario. Ontario's boreal forests provide breeding grounds for hundreds of species, while migrating birds—ducks, grebes, loons—depend on the forest for sustenance; some species—woodpeckers, finches, nuthatches, chickadees, owls, grouse and ravens—live in the boreal forest year-round.

Great places to view migratory birds include Point Pelee National Park (warblers) (www.pc.gc.ca), Rondeau, Long Point , Presqu'ile (waterfowl) or Grand Bend (tundra swans) provincial parks (www.ontarioparks.com), or the Jack Miner Sanctuary (www.jackminer.com) near Kingsville (Canada geese).

Fish abound in Ontario waters. In the warmer waters are bluegill, channel catfish, yellow perch, and largemouth and smallmouth bass. In cooler waters muskellunge, northern pike and walleye can be found. Lake trout, lake sturgeon, Chinook salmon, lake whitefish and brook trout prefer cold waters. Fishing opportunities are varied: fly-in resorts on pristine lakes and rivers offer thrilling struggles with game fish; fly-fishing in fast-moving streams and rivers is practiced all over the province; winter fishing through holes in the ice, inside heated huts, is popular on lakes. Consult *www. fishontario.com* or *www.gofishin ontario.com*.

In southern Ontario, Canada's most densely populated area, wildlife habitats are increasingly squeezed by development. Provincial parks, game preserves and protected areas—some 9.5 million hectares (23.5 million acres)—as well as national parks protect wilderness areas, while concerted efforts by government and many voluntary organizations enlist public support in preserving this important heritage.

CLIMATE

In southern Ontario, the climate is humid, with cold winters and warm summers. The coldest month is January, when temperatures around the Ottawa River in eastern Ontario average -13° C (9°F). From Niagara Falls to Windsor, where the Great Lakes warm the climate, the January average is about -4°C (25°F). In July, the warmest month, average temperatures range from 23°C (74°C) in southwestern Ontario, to 19°C (64°F) in eastern Ontario. As you leave the relatively benign Great Lakes area, temperatures become far more extreme. At Kapuskasing, along Highway 11 in the Cochrane area, the record low is -47°C (-53°F) and the record high is 38°C (101°F).

Ontario receives considerable precipitation throughout the year, due to cold polar air from the north meeting warm moist air from the south. Heavy snowfall is common along a belt reaching inland east of Lake Huron and Georgian Bay: at Owen Sound, annual snowfall can exceed 339cm (134 in). On the other hand, residents of Toronto may not wear snow boots all winter.

HISTORY

Immigration and exploration have shaped Canada's history, with archaeological evidence of people in the northwest of the country some 15,000 years ago. In Ontario there is evidence of human habitation dating back at least 10,000 years. The first French explorers entered Ontario via the St. Lawrence River and Lake Ontario: **Étienne Brulé** in 1610 and **Samuel de Champlain** in 1615. From the north, **Henry Hudson** claimed the Hudson Bay area for Britain in 1610.

Reports of abundant natural resources led to colonization and brought European conflicts to the New World, with the French and English forming alliances with various aboriginal peoples. The fur trade pushed exploration westward, and by the late 1800s, completion of a transcontinental railroad enabled the Dominion of Canada to extend to the Pacific Ocean.

Past to Present

NATIVE PEOPLES

By the time Europeans arrived in America, Northern Ontario was inhabited by Algonquin, Cree and Ojibwa who lived a nomadic existence fishing and hunting the abundant game. The south was the realm of Huron, Tobacco (Petun), Neutrals (Attiwandaron) and the Iroquois peoples, as well as some Algonquins. These people lived in fortified villages, around which fields of beans, corn and squash were cultivated. Every 10 years or so, when the land was exhausted, the village was moved to a new site. The men hunted and fished extensively, never staying away long from their palisaded villages.

Arrival of Europeans and subsequent development of the fur trade caused an upheaval in relations among the tribes and in their territorial positions. Composed of five tribes (Mohawk, Onondaga, Seneca, Cayuga, Oneida), the **League of the Iroquois** (joined by the Tuscarora in 1722) warred repeatedly with the early French settlers and defeated and dispersed the **Huron,** another Iroquoian group which had allied with the French; the Iroquois eventually allied with the British, and after the American Revolution those living in New York State moved to southern Ontario. On the other hand, the **Algonquin,** befriended by Champlain, became allies of the French. These alliances were to have important consequences during the struggle between the French and English to dominate Canada.

NEW FRANCE

Before their final defeat by the British on the **Plains of Abraham** outside Quebec City in 1759, the French not only established enduring settlements in the St. Lawrence Valley, but also explored half the continent. Known as **New France,** the empire they founded stretched, at its greatest extent, from Hudson Bay to New Orleans (Louisiana) and from Newfoundland nearly to the Rockies. What is now Ontario was crisscrossed during the 17C and 18C by French explorers in pursuit of furs. Fur traders **Pierre-Esprit Radisson** and his brother-in-law **Médard Chouart Des Groseilliers** succeeded in reaching Hudson Bay overland sometime around 1660. Unable to interest the French government in their proposal for a northern trading post to replace the dangerous St. Lawrence River route, the two men approached British investors. The Frenchmen's successful trip and wintering-over on James Bay in 1668-69 led to the founding of the **Hudson's Bay Company (HBC)** in 1670. The HBC gained control of all the lands draining into the great bay, establishing at **Moose Factory** on James Bay a settlement that is among Ontario's oldest.

Much French exploration was spurred not by commercial interests, but by the burning desire to save souls and by a penchant, quite inexplicable to modern minds, for martyrdom. In 1639 the Jesuits established a mission on the shores of Georgian Bay to convert the Huron to Christianity. In 1650 the settlement succumbed to attacks by the Iroquois, who martyred, after atrocious torture, five of the Jesuit fathers, including **Jean de Brébeuf** and **Gabriel Lalemant.**

TOWARD CONFEDERATION

In 1763, when the fall of New France was confirmed by the **Treaty of Paris,** the population of the future confederation of Canada was overwhelmingly French. A few settlements in Newfoundland and Halifax in Nova Scotia were the only English-speaking exceptions. This imbalance was not to endure. The aftermath of the American Revolution brought thousands of **Loyalists** to the remaining British colonies (Nova Scotia, Prince Edward Island and Lower Canada, later named Quebec) and led to the creation of two more colonies—New Brunswick and Upper Canada (later Ontario). The Loyalist influx into Upper Canada was reinforced by immigration from Britain. By 1812, the population stood at 90,000. The War of 1812 with the US resulted in serious skirmishes along the border, and in 1813 the Americans burned the Legislative Buildings in York (later Toronto); the British riposted by burning the US Capitol and the White House in Washington, DC. In 1814, the **Treaty of Ghent** ended the war and inaugurated—despite some tense moments in the early 19C—an era of trade and peaceful relations that endures to this day. Construction of the **Erie Canal** linking the Hudson River and the Great Lakes in the US, and of the **Welland Canal** (today, much modified, part of the St. Lawrence Seaway) around the Niagara Falls to link lakes Ontario and Erie, was a great impetus to trade. However, immigration and growing prosperity also brought restiveness. Before long, the colonial government was subjected to demands for representative government not dissimilar to those that had led to the American Revolution.

Upper Canada, governed by a legislative council dominated by a tight group known as the Family Compact, was shaken in 1837 by an uprising led by Scottish immigrant William Lyon Mackenzie, a newpaperman, president of the Legislative Assembly and first mayor of the City of Toronto (after the name had changed from York). At the same time, the Patriots' Rebellion erupted in Lower Canada (Quebec). Although neither uprising succeeded at the time, the unrest prompted a report by Lord Durham that led directly to the British Parliament's **Act of Union** in 1841, which united Upper and Lower Canada into the Province of Canada. The report proposed **responsible government,** a system of majority-party rule in the assembly (the British government did not formally implement this system until 1847), partly in the hope of reducing American influence.

Threats and incursions by Americans during the War of 1812, the Rebellions of 1837, the American Civil War and the Fenian Raids of 1866-70 convinced the British government that more settlers were needed if their colonies were to survive. The policy of offering free land to potential settlers played a significant role in the development of Ontario during the 19C and early 20C.

Fear of American takeover encouraged the small groups of British colonists to unite for common defence. Their actions helped to propel the British Parliament into ratifying the **British North America Act** of 1867, which provided for **Canadian Confederation.** The resulting new political entity, initially composed of four founding provinces—**Ontario, Quebec, New Brunswick and Nova Scotia**—adopted a parliamentary system of government and separation of federal and provincial powers. Even as confederation was negotiated, chief proponents John A. Macdonald and George-Étienne Cartier envisaged a dominion stretching from coast to coast. Between the eastern provinces and the small colony of British Columbia on the West Coast lay the immense, empty domain of the Hudson's Bay Company. Pressured by the British government, the company finally agreed to relinquish its lands to the new Confederation for a cash settlement and rights to its posts and some land.

THE TRANSCONTINENTAL RAILWAY

To encourage British Columbia to join Confederation in 1871, the province was promised a transcontinental rail link. After a few false starts, construction of the **Canadian Pacific Railway** finally got under way in 1881. It was an immense and difficult project, the western mountain ranges alone posing a formidable barrier. Serious problems beset the laying of track in the Canadian Shield country north of Lake Superior, through present-day Thunder Bay (then Fort William), where, at one moment, tonnes of granite had to be blasted out and at the next, track lines would sink into the muskeg. The CP track was nevertheless completed by 1885, a remarkable achievement. As track builders moved across the province, and as other railway builders constructed tracks, including the Timiskaming/Ontario Northland Railway, huge deposits of silver, copper and nickel came to light. By the early 1900s, northern Ontario was opening to development its great mineral wealth.

THE 20TH CENTURY

Canada's purchase of land controlled by the HBC opened the way for settlement of the West. By 1912 the remaining parts of the Northwest Territories south of the 60th parallel had been redistributed to Manitoba, Ontario and Quebec. At the same time, Canada's population was booming, particularly in Ontario, which took the lion's share of immigrants (one million to Canada in 1911-13).

The world wars, which Canada entered as part of the British Empire, had a major effect in forming the national consciousness. The poem, *In Flanders Fields*, written in 1915 by a young doctor from Guelph, Ontario, Lt-Col. John McCrae, serving in France, is almost certainly Canada's most-quoted literary work. Some 628,000 Canadians served in the first World War, and 66,573 were killed, a high toll for a small population; the taking of **Vimy Ridge** on April 12, 1917, is a celebrated moment in Canadian military history. More than one million Canadians served in World War II, and on June 6, 1944, Canadians stormed ashore at **Juno Beach** in Normandy and later liberated the Netherlands, events often evoked as key moments in the emerging national self-image.

Following the war, the area bordering on the Great Lakes in Ontario, from Windsor to Oshawa, including the "Golden Horseshoe" along western Lake Ontario from Oshawa to St. Catharines, became a major industrial centre. An influx of immigrants provided the skills and labour vital to economic growth. The population of Ontario increased 40 percent from 1945 to 1958, due to the baby boom and to immigration of 100,000 people per year; by 1963 one in five Ontarians was an immigrant.

At the beginning of the 20C, Ontario had a population of one million, of whom half worked in agriculture. By the end of the century, the population would reach nearly 12 million, with less than 2 percent living on farms, and less than 20 percent living outside cities. A major instigator of this dramatic change was Henry Ford, who in 1904 arranged to manufacture automobiles in Windsor, to supply the British Empire. In 1965, signing of the **US-Canada Autopact** permitted auto companies to manufacture efficiently on both sides of the border, and provided a huge boost, through many ancillary industries, to Ontario's entire economy. At the same time, the provincial government was building thousands of kilometres of highway; in 1968, the 800km/500mi Macdonald-Cartier Freeway, or Highway 401, opened across southern Ontario, soon becoming Canada's busiest highway.

The signing of the Canada-US Free Trade Agreement in 1989 between Canada and the US, superseded by the **North American Free Trade Agreement (NAFTA)** in 1994, has further strengthened Ontario's economy, now more than ever based on trade.

THE 21ST CENTURY

The city of Toronto has become the dominant financial centre of Canada, defacto headquarters of four of the five big banks (Canada, unlike the US, has a system based on big national banks), headquarters of the biggest stock exchange (again unlike the US, financial market regulation is a provincial, rather than national, responsibility), and the home of major corporate head offices. At the same time, the province dominates the country's intellectual life. Ontario-based media and publishing inform much of the country's opinion, and despite strong claims from Montreal and Vancouver, Toronto is the country's overwhelming cultural centre, much as New York City is for the US.

Meanwhile, Canada's capital city, Ottawa, lying in the extreme east of the province, has changed from a sleepy backwater to a vibrant cultural centre, with the National Arts Centre lit up almost nightly for lively productions. All around Ottawa are found high-tech companies, a sort of Silicon Valley North.

ONTARIO'S FIRST NATIONS

Census results released in early 2008 showed that 1,172,790 of Canada's population is of aboriginal stock, defined as First Nation, Métis or Inuit; of these, 242,495 live in Ontario, or 21 per cent of the total, the largest number of any province. In Ontario, 60 per cent of native people live off reserves; over 50 percent of aboriginals across Canada live in big cities. Although Indian affairs are governed at the Federal level by Indian and Northern Affairs Canada, Ontario has a Ministry of Aboriginal Affairs that works with the Union of Ontario Indi-

ans, which represents 42 First Nations groups across the province. The most contentious issues involve land claims resulting from disagreements over treaties and agreements. In a dramatic incident in 1995, a protest concerning a former army base adjacent to Ipperwash Provincial Park resulted in the shooting death of an aboriginal protester. After an inquiry, the government announced in December 2007 that the park would be returned to the Chippewas of Kettle Creek and Stony Point First Nation. Both parties, shaken by the incident, are working towards better relations.

Time Line

PRE-COLONIAL PERIOD

10,000 BC — Date of earliest evidence of human habitation in Ontario.

1497 — **John Cabot** explores east coast of Canada.

NEW FRANCE

1534 — **Jacques Cartier** claims Canada for France.

1610 — **Étienne Brulé** enters Ontario via the St. Lawrence River.

1615 — **Samuel de Champlain** reaches Ontario, also via the St. Lawrence.

Welland Canal Opens in 1829

Ontario Tourism

1668-69 — Financed by the British, **Pierre-Esprit Radisson** and **Médard Chouart Des Groseilliers** establish a trading post on Hudson Bay.

1722 — **Six Nations Iroquois Confederacy** is formed.

1756-63 — Seven Years' War (French and Indian War).

1759 — British defeat the French in Quebec City.

1763 — **Treaty of Paris** is signed. France cedes New France to Britain.

BRITISH REGIME

1783 — American colonies gain independence from Britain. Loyalists and Iroquois allies of British immigrate to Canada.

1791 — **Constitutional Act** creates Upper Canada (Ontario) and Lower Canada (Quebec).

1793 — Capital of Upper Canada moved from Newark (now Niagara-on-the-Lake) to York (now Toronto), less vulnerable to raids from the US.

1812 — Population of Upper Canada reaches 90,000, from 15,000 only 20 years earlier.

1812-14 — War of 1812. Americans burn Legislative Buildings in York (later Toronto); British retaliate by burning Washington, DC.

1825 — **Erie Canal** completed, linking Hudson River to Lake Ontario.

1829 — **Welland Canal** opens, linking lakes Erie and Ontario, bypassing Niagara Falls.

1826-32 — Lt. Col. John By heads project to build **Rideau Canal** and lays out plans for future city of Ottawa.

1837 — **William Lyon Mackenzie** leads rebellion against Family Compact's dominance of the legislative council.

1841 — **Act of Union** creates the United Province of Canada. Population of Upper Canada reaches 430,000.

1843 — Capital of Canada moved from Kingston, Ontario to Montreal.

1847 — **Responsible government** system is implemented in Canada.

1857 — Queen Victoria selects Ottawa as capital of the Province of Canada.

CANADIAN CONFEDERATION

1867 — **British North America Act** establishes Canadian Confederation.

1870 — Canadian Confederation buys Hudson's Bay Company land; Ontario gains some of this land in the north.

1885 — Canadian Pacific Railway is completed.

1900 — Ontario population reaches 2 million.

1903 — Discovery of world's richest silver vein in Cobalt, Ontario.

1904 — **Henry Ford** begins manufacturing automobiles in **Windsor.**

1906 — Hydroelectric dam built to harness Niagara Falls; launch of Ontario Hydro-Electric Commission, which evolved into Ontario Power Generation, one of world's largest power utilities.

1914-18 — World War I. Some 628,000 Canadians serve.

1921 — **William Lyon Mackenzie King,** grandson of the leader of the 1837 rebellion, becomes prime minister of Canada.

1922 — Toronto Symphony Orchestra founded.

1939-45 — World War II. Ontario industry prospers during and after the war, and receives large numbers of European immigrants.

1943 — Progressive Conservative Party gains power in Ontario Legislative Assembly; remains in power for 42 years.

CONTEMPORARY ONTARIO

1954 — Canada's first subway built in Toronto.

1959 — **St. Lawrence Seaway** opens, creating a channel for ocean-going ships from the Atlantic to the western Great Lakes ports.

1962 — Trans-Canada Highway is completed.

1963 — Ontario Arts Council formed to promote the arts and assist artists with government funding.

1965 — U.S.-Canada Autopact signed, a major boost to Ontario's auto industry, related manufacturing and the entire economy.

1968 — Macdonald-Cartier Freeway, better known as Highway 401, opens across southern Ontario.

1969 — National Arts Centre opens in Ottawa.

1976 — First Toronto International Film Festival is held.

1982 — Roy Thomson Hall, a venue for the Toronto Symphony Orchestra and designed by Canadian architect Arthur Erickson, opens.

1985 — The Ontario Liberal Party breaks the Progressive Conservative Party's 42-year hold on power; David Peterson becomes Premier.

1989 — **US-Canada Free Trade Agreement** opens greater trade opportunities for Ontario.

1990 — The New Democratic Party, under Bob Rae, gains control of Ontario Legislative Assembly. This is first victory for NDP, a socialist party, east of Manitoba.

1993 — Negotiation of North American Free Trade Agreement (NAFTA) among Canada, Mexico and the US.

1994 — Approved by Canada, Mexico and the US, NAFTA takes effect, giving Canada secure access to US and Mexican markets.

1995 — New Democrats lose popular support and power; Progressive Conservatives return to power under Mike Harris.

1995 — Protest by aboriginals over land rights at Ipperwash Provincial Park results in death of protester Dudley George; park closes.

1998 — Canada experiences its worst ice storm in the country's history. Some 1.5 million people in eastern Ontario are without power; 57 Ontario communities are declared disaster areas.

THE NEW MILLENNIUM

2001 — A nationwide **census** confirms a population of 29.5 million in Canada, and 11.4 million in Ontario, or 39 percent of the total.

2002 — Canadian troops join international peacekeeping mission in Afghanistan.

2003 — A massive electricity failure blacks out parts of US and all of Ontario except some of the Niagara Peninsula. Ontario Liberal Party regains power under Dalton McGuinty.

2007 — In September, the Canadian dollar closes slightly above parity with the US dollar for the first time in 31 years. Announcement of amalgamation of Toronto Stock Exchange with Montreal Exchange; in effect, the TSE acquires the ME. After an inquiry into the shooting of a native protester in 1995, the provincial government returns Ipperwash Provincial Park to the local First Nation.

2008 — Census of the Canadian aboriginal population reveals that 21 percent, or 242,495, live in Ontario, the greatest number for any Canadian province or territory.

ART AND CULTURE

The culture of Canada, including Ontario, is rooted in a blend of British, French, and aboriginal traditions, and influenced by successive waves of immigration. American media and entertainment dominate, but various federal and provincial government programs and laws support Canadian cultural initiatives. The federally funded Canadian Broadcasting Corporation (CBC) provides country-wide television and radio coverage; in Ontario, TV Ontario (TVO) is a provincially funded educational television station that provides news, documentaries, drama and arts programming. The Ontario Arts Council offers funding for Ontario-based artists and art organizations.

Art

NATIVE EXPRESSIONS

Over centuries, Canada's indigenous peoples have developed diverse modes of artistic expression that bear witness to their distinctive lifestyles and beliefs. Since the aboriginal peoples were generally nomadic, little remains of their prehistoric art. However, petroglyphs, or carvings and paintings on rock, found in various sites in Ontario and British Columbia are as much as 5,000 years old. Decorated with representations of animals and geometric designs, Iroquoian pottery dating from 900-1600 has been unearthed in Ontario and Quebec.

Traditional Art

Most Algonquian-speaking aboriginals (notably Abenaki, Algonquin, Cree, Mi'kmaq, Montagnais and Naskapi) are descended from nomadic peoples, who excelled in the art of beadwork (shell, bone, rock or seed) and embroideries (porcupine quills and moose or caribou hair). Caribou-hide vests and moccasins and various birchbark objects were often adorned with geometric incisions and drawings. Elaborate belts of wampum (beads made from shells) feature motifs illustrating significant events in native history. **Wampum** was exchanged at peace ceremonies and during the signing of treaties. The smaller, quasi-sedentary, Iroquoian-speaking groups included Hurons, Mohawks, Onondagas and Senecas. As agricultural societies, they formed semipermanent villages and constructed multifamily dwellings known as longhouses; out of their sedentary lifestyle evolved an artistic repertoire free from the constraints of nomadism. Among their most beautiful works are exquisite moosehair embroideries that gradually began incorporating floral motifs under European influence. Wooden masks known as **false faces** represented mythological figures associated with traditional healing practices.

Contemporary Works

Native art has undergone a profound transformation in recent years. Whereas artists traditionally relied on the use of natural materials such as hide and bark, today they are experimenting with canvas, acrylics, charcoal and other new media; consequently, innovative techniques have emerged, although

Ontario Tourism

Dancers at the Six Nations Native Pageant in Brantford

inspiration is still drawn from social and cultural traditions. The result is a fresh, contemporary vision of aboriginal art that keeps alive the memory of the past.

Woodland artists in eastern Canada have been influenced by the iconographic style of Ojibwa **Norval Morrisseau** (1931-2007) in the 1970s, in particular his renderings of mythological creatures. His contemporaries Odawa artist **Daphne Odjig** (b.1919), born on Manitoulin Island, and Cree artist **Carl Ray** (1943-78), born on the same Sandy Lake Reserve as Morrisseau, further evolved Morrisseau's style through personal interpretation. The elegant but spare representations of birds and animals by Benjamin Chee Chee (1944-77) of Temagami are widely imitated.

PAINTING AND SCULPTURE

17C-18C

The arrival of French and British colonists in the early 17C introduced European aesthetics and forms to the artistic landscape. Religion dominated life in what was then New France; thus, church decoration was the focus of early Canadian art. Paintings and statuary were first imported from France, but craftsmen were soon trained locally. After the British victory on the Plains of Abraham (1759), religious art declined and nonreligious painting gained prominence. Artists, primarily European-trained, began producing works that focused on such popular subjects as **landscapes** and, above all, **portraits,** commissioned by an emerging and wealthy bourgeoisie.

19C

Secular art blossomed in the early 19C with such works as **William Berczy's** (1744-1813) Neoclassical painting *The Woolsey Family* and his portrait of Mohawk chief Joseph Brant, which can be seen at the National Gallery of Canada in Ottawa. (Berczy, a German adventurer, also led a group of German settlers who founded the town of Markham, a Toronto suburb; a public school in Unionville is named for him.) The expanding middle class wanted portraits of themselves, their pastimes and their business ventures. Robert Clow Todd (1809-66) was commissioned by the Gilmour family to paint its shipyards (*Wolfe's Cove, Québec,* 1840), for example.

Throughout the 19C, the arrival of European artists had a decisive impact on Canadian painting. **Paul Kane** (1810-71), born in Ireland, came to Toronto (then called York) as a child. His detailed portraits of native peoples (*The Death of Omoxesisixany* c.1856) are of historical interest today; his work can be seen at the National Gallery. Dutch-born **Cornelius Kreighoff** (1815-72) captured colourful French Canadian rural life in unprecedented detail in *The Habitant Farm* (1856) and other paintings. His work is displayed at the National Gallery and the Art Gallery of Ontario.

In Ottawa, governor general the Marquess of Lorne created the **Royal Canadian Academy of Arts** in 1880, which eventually became the National Gallery of Canada. At this time, however, most artists were trained in Paris (then the art capital of the world), though the subject matter of both their paintings and sculpted works was largely Canadian.

Early 20C

At the onset of the 20C, the influence of the so-called Paris school was visible in Canadian art, particularly in the works of Quebec artist Wyatt Eaton (1849-1896) and Montreal art professor **William Brymner** (1855-1925), one of the first

Museum London, Purchased with the Assistance of the Richard & Jean Ivey Fund, London, Ontario, 1987

The Young Botanist (1890) by Paul Peel, Museum London

Ontario Tourism

National Gallery of Canada in Ottawa

Canadians to study abroad; his painting *A Wreath of Flowers* (1884), which hangs in the National Gallery of Canada, is an embodiment of French techniques. **Robert Harris** (1849-1919) left Prince Edward Island to train in Paris, but returned to execute perhaps the most prestigious commission in Canada, *The Fathers of Confederation* (1883); the painting was destroyed when Parliament in Ottawa burned in 1916. Hailing from London, Ontario, **Paul Peel** (1860-92) studied and lived abroad, though he exhibited in Canada. His works, several of which were controversial (*A Venetian Bather* and *After the Bath*), gained international attention. His paintings hang in the London, Ontario museum as well as in the National Gallery and the Art Gallery of Ontario in Toronto, which possesses the two paintings mentioned above.

Sculpture
In the 1930s the Art-Deco style influenced several Canadian sculptors, including Torontonian **Elizabeth Wyn Wood** (1903-66) *(Passing Rain)*. Among her monumental works are the 10-foot statue of King George VI in Niagara Falls, the war memorial in Welland and the monument to John Graves Simcoe in Niagara-on-the-Lake. Her work is also displayed in the National Gallery.
Following World War II, Canadian sculpture was invigorated by the availability of many new materials, which fostered experimentation in techniques and shapes. In the 1960s Toronto painter, musician, and filmmaker **Michael Snow**

and Les Levine established reputations based largely on their sculpted works: Snow's stainless steel forms (he sculpted *Flightstop,* the Canada geese that soar at the Eaton Centre in Toronto) and Levine's plastic modules. Romanian-born **Sorel Etrog** is recognized for his signature knotted-bronze works, which suggest the influence of cubism; his works appear around Toronto, notably at the Toronto Congress Centre. **Walter Redinger** turned to fibreglass for his constructions; his work is displayed in towns around the province, including his native Wallacetown, and at the University of Western Ontario in London and the Museum of Contemporary Canadian Art in Toronto. **Michael Hayden** created his kinetic works from neon tubing; they can be seen at York University in Toronto, the Ontario Arts Council and the Art Gallery of Ontario, among other places.

Budding Nationalism
World War I profoundly affected artists who regarded Canada as a proud young nation to be accepted on its own terms: why look to Europe, they felt. Trained in commercial design, **Tom Thomson** (1877-1917), an expert outdoorsman, painted Algonquin Park and other parts of Ontario in a bold new way. Thomson's vibrant colours and intense brushwork infused his paintings of the rugged terrain with a vitality that leaps from the canvas. *The West Wind* and *The Jack Pine* are among his best-known works. Like-minded artist-friends based in Toronto

formed the **Group of Seven** in 1920, the first truly Canadian school, which included Lawren Harris (1885-1970), J.E.H. MacDonald (1873-1932) and A.Y. Jackson (1892-1974). Harris' austere depictions of the Canadian landscape, in particular *North Shore, Lake Superior* (1926), inspired the country's new modernists. Works by Thomson and members of the Group of Seven are on view at the McMichael Canadian Art Collection in Kleinburg, Ontario *(www. mcmichael.com)*. Influenced by members of the Group of Seven, **Carl Schaefer** (1903-95) painting in the 1930s, imbued psychological and sociological symbolism into his renderings of the Canadian landscape (*Ontario Farmhouse,* 1934); his works hang in the National Gallery. Ontario-born **David Milne** (1882-1953), a war artist during World War II, emphasized form and brush technique over subject matter; his paintings exhibited a wide variety of subjects, from cityscapes and rural scenes to still life (*Water Lilies and the Sunday Paper,* 1929). His works hang in the National Gallery.

THE POST-WAR ERA

World War II marked a turning point in the evolution of Canadian art. French influences towards abstraction, considered shocking, first appeared in Quebec. Modernism later struck in even more radical form in Toronto, where American influence, notably abstract expressionism, was strong. In the 1950s and 60s, a group of Toronto painters formed **Artists Eleven** to promote modernism. They held their first exhibition in Toronto in 1954, to public scorn. They were, however, championed by American critics, notably Clement Greenberg, at a show in New York in 1956, and gradually found supporters at home, especially journalist **Robert Fulford**. The leader was **William Ronald** (1926-98), whose 1967 mural decorates the National Arts Centre; in the 1980s, he painted a series of abstract portraits of Canadian prime ministers. Other notable members were **Jack Bush** (1909-77), who was respected for his use of colour and whose work *Big A* hangs at the National Gallery; and **Harold Town** (1924-90), a versatile painter whose work has been displayed at the Windsor Art Gallery and the Art Gallery of Ontario. **Kazuo Nakamura** (1926-2002), another prominent member of the group, was a Japanese-Canadian interned with his family in British Columbia during the war. He settled in Ontario, where he attended art school and began producing works influenced by geometry; his work is at the National Gallery. Artistic ferment in Ontario was not limited to Toronto: a community of artists in London, formed in the 1960s, is still active, and Ontario artists have fanned out across Canada and into the US. The influence of Artists Eleven on succeeding generations is not necessarily one of style, because these artists were strong individualists, but of doors opened and of more enlightened public taste.

THE CONTEMPORARY SCENE

In recent years, Canadian art has evolved alongside major international currents; it has distanced itself from traditional painting while emphasizing more diversified forms and techniques, including "installation," a primarily sculptural idiom that also encompasses other art forms, such as painting and photography. Art becomes "performance," having little intrinsic worth, in the mixed-media installations of such artists as Toronto-based A.A. Bronson, Felix Partz and Jorge Zontal. As new technologies emerge (lasers, computers, holograms), Canadian artists continue to express themselves in different genres and contexts. Contemporary movements aside, the precise realism of the paintings by **Robert McLellan Bateman,** who depicts animals in their natural habitats, remains popular with an international as well as a domestic buying public.

Literature and Language

LITERATURE

In large measure, Canadian literature resonates with a rich sense of place.

Whether in the explorers' journals of the early 17C-18C, the diaries and novels of 19C immigrant settlers, or the poems and literary works of the 20C and 21C, writers grapple with what it means to be Canadian.

Early Works

As settlement in Ontario was considerably later than in Quebec (at the end of the 18C, there were only about 15,000 Europeans in Upper Canada), literary expression until the 20C was very thin. English settlers, such as **Susanna Moodie,** described the challenges of making a home in the Canadian wilderness (*Roughing It in the Bush,* 1852). British publishers made it very difficult for writers elsewhere in the Empire to collect royalties, and Canadian tax laws as regards royalties were oppressive; it was impossible to earn a living as a writer.

Duncan Campbell Scott (1862-1947) and **Archibald Lampman** (1861-99), now recognized as the seminal "Confederation Poets" after Canadian Confederation in 1867, laboured in Ottawa bureaucracies. Scott had a successful career in the Bureau of Indian Affairs, drawing information from his day job to inspire his night-time writing. Lampman worked as a low-paid clerk in the Post Office Department. The poets, close friends, were inspired by their explorations of the Ontario wilderness; as a child, Lampman had known Susanna Moodie and her sister, Catharine Parr Traill, who wrote *The Backwoods of Canada* (1836).

Emily Pauline Johnson (1861-1913), born on the Six Nations Reserve near Brantford, achieved success through aboriginal-inspired tales and poems that she marketed with genius. She toured extensively in the US, Canada and Britain, giving recitations. These early writers faced a public that expected Canadians to be preoccupied with nature, Indian spirituality and animals (often talking animals); the writers seem to have accepted this limitation. Yet the only remembered poem of this era, *In Flanders Fields* (1915) by Guelph native John McCrae (1872-1918), speaks to greater universal concerns from a battlefield far away.

In another vein entirely, **Stephen Leacock** (1869-1944), a professor of economics at Montreal's McGill University, wrote widely appreciated humourous accounts of life in Orillia, Ontario, the family home where he spent vacations.

Mazo de la Roche (1879-1961) penned the very popular *Jalna* series, chronicling how generations of a Southern Ontario family adapted to life there between the years 1927 and 1960.

Contemporary Currents

After the Second World War, Canadian national awareness encouraged greater expression of a distinctly Canadian sensibility. The Canada Council, formed in 1957, and the Ontario Arts Council, formed in 1963, not only provided funding, but heralded a more favourable environment for writers and artists. What followed was a flowering of the arts across Canada, as well as in Ontario. Although **Robertson Davies** (1913-95) *(The Deptford Trilogy, The Rebel Angels, What's Bred in the Bone)* got his start before generous government funding, he rode the wave. A few of the many Ontario writers appreciated around the world are **Margaret Atwood** *(Alias Grace, The Robber Bride),* **Timothy Findley** *(The Wars),* **Michael Ondaatje** *(The English Patient, Anil's Ghost)* and **Alice Munro** *(Lives of Girls and Women, Runaway).* Atwood's book *Survival: a Thematic Guide to Canadian Literature* elevated the internationally acclaimed author to guru status, to the point where her questioning of Canadianness became a yardstick of Canadian culture. In the year 2000, Atwood won Britain's most coveted literary prize, The Booker, for her work *The Blind Assassin.*

Best-selling author **Farley Mowat** *(Never Cry Wolf, Sea of Slaughter),* born in Belleville, remains Canada's champion of the environment with his compelling recountings of humanity's destructive impact.

LANGUAGE

English is the official language of Ontario, but French is widely used in the eastern portion of the province and French language rights have been extended to the legal and educational systems. Ontario, like Canada, is a land of immigrants, and this fact is reflected in daily life, particularly in large cities. In Toronto, one of the world's most multi-cultural cities, some 70 languages are spoken. According to the 2001 census, the languages most often spoken at home in Ontario are English (8 million speakers), French (490,000 speakers), Chinese (405,000 speakers), Italian (296,000 speakers) and German (157,000 speakers). Other significant languages in Canada are Polish, Spanish, Punjabi, Ukrainian and Portuguese.

> "Canada could have enjoyed:
> English government, French culture,
> and American know-how.
> Instead it ended up with:
> English know-how, French govern-
> ment, and American culture."
>
> John Robert Colombo,
> *Oh Canada,* 1965

Music and Dance

CANADA'S MUSIC

The first European immigrants to Ontario brought their own musical traditions: British ballads; Irish, Scottish and French fiddle music; or German instrument ensembles. Initially, the desire was to enliven an often desperately hard life, but gradually a more educated leisure class wanted increasingly sophisticated European music such as orchestral music and opera.

The 1840s brought international touring performers such as singer Jenny Lind. Local and regional musical societies—the precursors of today's philharmonic orchestras—sprang up. By the 1870s, the Toronto Philharmonic Society was organizing concerts. The Toronto Mendelssohn Choir in 1902 began inviting orchestras from the US to perform, and in 1906, the Toronto Symphony Orchestra (TSO), was formed. The years between the world wars saw Canada's first musician to achieve national stature (and the only Canadian musician ever knighted):

noted conductor Sir **Ernest Macmillan** (1893-1973), closely identified with the TSO. He founded one of Canada's first string quartets, and his composition *Two Sketches for Strings* became a Canadian classic. Internationally renowned pianist **Glenn Gould** (1932-82) retired from concert tours in 1964, concentrating on studio recordings; he is noted in particular for his recordings of Bach's *Goldberg Variations.* Notable Ontario pianists performing today are **Angela Hewitt** and **Anton Kuerti.**

In Ottawa, the National Arts Centre Orchestra was formed in 1969 and has developed a premier reputation under a series of inspired conductors, notably **Mario Bernardi** and Pinchas Zukerman. Several outstanding Toronto-based Canadian voices—soprano **Isabel Bayrakdarian,** tenors **Richard Margison,** and **Michael Schade,** baritone **Gino Quilico** among them—are heard on the **opera** stages of Milan, New York, Paris and London, as well as in home-town concert halls. Composer **R. Murray Schafer's** *Ra* premiered in 1983 and at 11 hours in length, remains Canada's most experimental theatrical-music experience. In Toronto, the Four Seasons Centre for the Performing Arts, (opened in 2006) houses the Canadian Opera Company as well as the National Ballet of Canada, while Ottawa's NAC is home to Opera Lyra Ottawa.

Jazz, rock, folk and other contemporary music forms are vibrant, and there is a lively club scene in larger cities. Some figures such as **Shania Twain,** the darling of Timmins, Ontario, and the late jazz pianist **Oscar Peterson** (1925-2007) who lived in Mississauga, where a school is named after him, have attained iconic status.

DANCE

Early European explorers, such as John Cabot, chronicled the traditional dances of the aboriginal people. It was not until the early 20C, when Anna Pavlova toured the country several times, that **ballet** truly arrived in Canada. British dancer Celia Franca established the National Ballet of Canada in 1951 in Toronto. Ballet stars who raised the

Filming in Toronto

profile of the National Ballet company included Karen Kain, Frank Augustyn and Rex Harrington. Today's stars include Sonia Rodriguez, Greta Hodgkinson, and Chan Hon Goh. Choreographers Brian Macdonald and James Kudelka have gained wide recognition.

Modern dance in Canada owes its existence to European and American dancers and choreographers who established schools and troupes in the country. The **Toronto Dance Theatre** (1968) was established by Patricia Beatty, Peter Randazzo and David Earle, who trained in the techniques of American dance pioneer Martha Graham in the early 1970s.

Cinema

Although most films shown in Canada are imported from the US, Canadians factor significantly in a surprising number of major films—as actors, directors and animators. Toronto, a frequent location for filming US and international films, enjoys thriving production.

The Toronto International Film Festival debuted in 1976, when the Ontario Censor Board still operated; the sophisticated films shown helped finish it off. Reflecting the growing importance of animation in cinema, the Ottawa International Animation Festival has become North America's largest and most important showcase for the genre

and the second largest in the world since its founding in 1976.

Canada produces about 40 feature films per year with budgets of $3.5 million or more. Almost 40 percent of financing for English-language features and some 80 percent of funding for French-language features is provided by government.

Once reviled in the Canadian Parliament as a public menace, director **David Cronenberg** has unnerved film-goers with his gripping treatment of dark subjects—from his first commercial breakthrough *Scanners* (1981) to *The Fly* (1986), then *Crash* (1996), *A History of Violence* (2005) and *Eastern Promises* (2007). The films of Toronto-based director **Atom Egoyan** are more works of art than traditional movies; with *The Sweet Hereafter* (1997), he became a player in American commercial cinema. In 2002 his film *Ararat* premiered at the Cannes Film Festival, as did *Adoration* in 2008. *The Statement* (2004) is the most recent in a string of award-winning films by **Norman Jewison** that include his Oscar-winning *The Russians Are Coming, The Russians Are Coming* (1966), *Fiddler On The Roof* (1971) and *Moonstruck* (1987). Best known as the director of *Titanic* (1997), **James Cameron,** a native of Kapuskasing and Chippewa, also wrote and directed The *Terminator* (1984) and directed a series of successful science-fiction action films like *Aliens* (1986) and *Terminator 2: Judgment Day* (1991).

ONTARIO TODAY

Ontario is Canada's richest and most populous province. Home to 12,160,282 people, or more than one-third of the national population, Ontario is also Canada's industrial, economic, political and cultural heartland. Since the mid 1990s, sound financial management and rising natural resource prices have buoyed the country's economy. The Ontario economy, based on manufacturing and, increasingly, on the service industry, remains—by a significant margin—the largest contributor to the Canadian economy (nearly 39 percent of GDP).

The Economy

Statistics Canada provides electronic publications for readers seeking detailed information (fees may apply): www.statcan.ca. Another source is the Canadian government's website http://canada.gc.ca, which provides links to all government publications.

Ontario's economy was initially built on its wealth of natural resources—fur, forests, and minerals. From Upper Canada's earliest days, the Great Lakes, along with the many rivers, offered transportation routes to the rest of Canada as well as to the industrial heartland of the US. The completion of the **St Lawrence Seaway** in 1959 has had a powerful effect on the Ontario economy, providing access to the Atlantic trade routes and to the farthest ports on lakes Michigan and Superior. This network of lakes, rivers, locks and canals extends 3,790km/2,350 mi from the Atlantic to the western end of the Great Lakes.

DIVERSIFICATION

Mining and forestry still dominate the economy of northern Ontario, while the south has a diversified economy based on manufacturing; the fastest growing sectors are business services, finance, tourism and culture. Although agriculture is less important to the economy, southern Ontario has some of the best land and growing conditions in the country, possessing over half of Canada's Class 1 (highest quality) agriculture land, accounting for almost one-quarter of Canada's farm revenue.

Ontario's diversified economy is the engine of the Canadian economy, with about 40 percent of the country's total employment; it contributes 58 percent of Canada's total manufacturing exports. It is North America's second-largest motor vehicle assembler, after Michigan, and exports more vehicles to the US than do Japan or Mexico. In fact, more than 90 percent of Ontario's exports go to the US.

MANUFACTURING

Motor-vehicles and parts manufacturing is a major industry in Ontario, accounting for 38 percent of exports, but also important are the production of telecommunications systems, electronics and electrical machinery, primary and fabricated metals, rubber, chemical goods and food products, as well as printing and publishing. Most of these industries are concentrated in the Greater Toronto Area and along the Highway 401 corridor from Windsor to Kingston. Other significant industrial regions include Sarnia (petrochemicals), Niagara (auto parts), Sault-Ste. Marie (steel and paper) and Ottawa-Carleton (telecommunications, high technology).

MINING

No other province is as rich in minerals as Ontario. The **Sudbury Igneous Complex** contains one of the world's largest deposits of nickel and copper. Platinum, cobalt, silver, gold, selenium, sulphur compounds and tellurium are also extracted. Mines in Hemlo, Timmins and Red Lake produce a billion dollars of gold annually. Timmins is also the site of a large copper/zinc deposit, and the Lac des Iles mine produces platinum and palladium. Amethyst is mined near

The salt mine at Goderich's waterfront

Thunder Bay. Exploration continues for diamonds in the James Bay lowlands. Southern Ontario produces non-metallic minerals: salt is mined at Goderich and Windsor, limestone at Guelph and Hamilton, gypsum in Caledona and Hagersville, and talc at Madoc. Southern Ontario also exploits small oil and gas deposits, consumed entirely within the province: the first commercial oil well in North America was drilled in 1858 near Sarnia.

FOREST, FISHING, FURS AND HYDROELECTRICITY

The province is still largely covered with forest, despite harvesting in the last century. Today, pulp, paper and sawn lumber are the main products, and Ontario ranks third after British Columbia and Quebec in the value of total production. The forest industry is a major economic sector, employing some 90,000 people, with sales of over $15 billion a year and exports exceeding $9 billion. Ontario leads the rest of Canada in the value of fish taken from inland waters, thanks to the province's 250,000 lakes, and borders on four of the Great Lakes. Fur production is still carried out both by trapping and by fur farms. The harnessing of the Niagara River, the St. Lawrence and other waters was essential for early industrial development. Today Ontario ranks third after Quebec and British Columbia in hydroelectric power. Still,

the province's huge requirements for energy mean that nearly half is provided by five nuclear plants with a capacity of 14,000 megawatts, while fossil-fuelled plants provide another 12,000 megawatts. The 60 hydroelectric plants have a capacity of 7,000 megawatts.

AGRICULTURE

The southern part of the province boasts some of the richest soil in Canada as well as the province's longest frost free season. Dairy farming is the predominant activity in the southeast corner. Soybean and field corn are the staple crops of the southwest. The section of the Niagara Peninsula on the shores of Lake Ontario sheltered by the Niagara Escarpment is Ontario's most important fruit-growing region. A wine-making industry thrives on the Niagara Peninsula, on Pelee Island and in Prince Edward County.

THE NEW ECONOMY

Although the provincial economy is still dominated by the manufacturing sector, the services sector accounts for 70 percent of the overall economy, and more Ontarians work in the service sector than on assembly lines. Ontario accounts for about half of Canada's $120 billion trade in services.

On a per capita basis, Canada is next only to the US in the number of personal computers, with 669 per 1,000 inhabitants in 2005. Long considered one of the best-wired countries, Canada boasts comprehensive and inexpensive **telecommunications services**—no doubt a contributing factor to the nation's top ranking in worldwide Internet use per capita. Canada's long-distance telephone services were deregulated in 1992. Deregulation of the local telephone market in 1998 resulted in alternative carriers and resellers entering the market with new competitive services, although downturns in the worldwide telecommunications industry in 2001 led to consolidation and layoffs within Canada. Several Ontario-based companies are world leaders in the telecommunications equipment market. Biotechnology and information and communications technologies in Ontario are centred primarily in Toronto, Ottawa and Kitchener-Waterloo.

Toronto is a leader in new media and in film and television production. Cultural attractions, a strong element of the new economy, are powerful in Toronto and to a lesser extent, Ottawa. Tourism in Ontario is the country's largest such industry; the province attracts some 48 percent of visitors to Canada and generates about 37 percent of the nation's income from this source.

ECONOMIC PROSPECTS

Ontario's 2006 Gross Domestic Product of $557.8 billion represented 38.6 percent of the Canadian total, dem-

onstrating the province's dominant economic role. Ontario's economy has grown strongly in recent years. In November 2007, year-to-year inflation was 2.3 percent and job growth was robust, pushing unemployment to 6 per cent, the lowest rate in six years. A poll of manufacturers by Statistics Canada indicated general optimism about production prospects, but the looming downturn in US markets, destination of 86.5 percent of Ontario exports, means that optimism is guarded. For one thing, recent parity of US and Canadian dollars means that Canadian exports are more expensive than they were, while imports are relatively cheaper. However, Canada has not experienced the same turmoil in the housing markets as the US, although some of its financial institutions have been affected through purchase of asset-backed securities. In addition, in recent years both the federal and provincial governments have reduced debt and are in strong fiscal positions.

Government

Ontario is one of ten provinces and three territories composing Canada, a **federal state.** The central government in **Ottawa,** the federal capital, assumes responsibility for such matters as defence, foreign affairs, transportation, trade, commerce, money and banking, and criminal law.

Vineyard of Chateau-des-Charmes, Niagara-on-the-Lake

Richard Pierre/Ontario Tourism

Legislative Building in Queen's Park, Toronto

The system of government at both federal and provincial levels is parliamentary. Ontario's **Legislative Assembly** (known as "The House") sits in a grand old 1893 red sandstone building in the midst of **Queen's Park** in Toronto; the government is often simply referred to as "Queen's Park." During parliamentary sessions, which are televised and which the public can attend, the party in power sits on one side, facing the opposition parties. The parties represented lately at Queen's Park are the Liberal Party (currently in power), the Progressive Conservatives and the New Democrats. The representatives, elected from ridings around the province, are called MPPs, or Members of the Provincial Parliament. The premier is the leader of the party that had the most MPPs. The most interesting part of proceedings is the Question Period, lasting about an hour, when MPPs, usually from the opposition, ask pointed questions of the government. The premier or ministers respond, and the debate can become quite lively.

The **federal Parliament,** composed of a House of Commons whose members are elected from federal ridings across the country and an appointed Senate, sits in Ottawa, the capital of Canada. The Canadian head of state is the **British monarch.** Her authority is exercised by the **governor general,** who was at one time appointed by the monarch but today is chosen by the elected representatives of the Canadian people. Each province has its own **lieutenant governor,** selected by the federal government with the consent of the provincial government. Actual power lies in the hands of the Canadian **prime minister,** who is the leader of the majority party in Parliament. The prime minister rules through a cabinet drawn from elected representatives (and sometimes from members of the Senate), and must submit his or her government for re-election after a maximum of five years, or if he or she is defeated in the House of Commons.

Visitors to Ontario will notice the **Ontario Provincial Police,** which provide policing on highways and in some communities. The famous Royal Canadian Mounted Police, Canada's national police force, are found in airports and federal installations.

Population

As of July 2007, Ontario had a population of 12,803,861 people, or 38.8 percent of the Canadian total. Of the total population, 72.9 percent was Canadian born, while 27.1 was foreign born. Some 9 percent of the population had arrived since 1991. As a general rule, half of all immigrants to Canada choose to settle in Ontario. The labour force of Ontario was composed of 6.9 million people. Some 80 percent of the population lives along the southern border. Life expectancy for men was 78.3 years, for women 82.7 years.

Toronto Skyline
iStockphoto.com/Vertex IS

TORONTO AREA
AND LAKE ONTARIO

Situated on the southeast leg of the province and set on the broad north shore of Lake Ontario, Toronto is Canada's largest metropolis and one of the most populated cities in North America. This capital city of Ontario is the sprawling 600sq km/232sq mi hub of the Golden Horseshoe, the 60km/100mi arc stretching from Oshawa to Hamilton, where at least a quarter of the country's manufacturing is based. The area has benefited from the most favourable geographic position of any in Canada: it is set on some of the country's most fertile soil, with a climate moderated by the lake. It enjoys easy access via the lake, the St. Lawrence Seaway and canals, as well as road and rail, to the great cities of the US industrial heartland. The vast mineral resources of northern Ontario spurred industrial development. Free trade with the US since 1993 has further strengthened the economy.

The easternmost of the Great Lakes, **Lake Ontario** is the 14th largest lake on earth. It is the smallest of the Great Lakes in terms of surface area, measuring 311km/193mi long and 85km/53mi wide, with a shoreline of 1,146km/712mi. Its average depth of 86m/283ft is second only to Lake Superior, however, and prevents the lake from freezing. Major rivers that flow into Lake Ontario include Toronto's Don and Humber rivers.

The earliest European explorers in the area were Samuel de Champlain and his protegé, Étienne Brûlé, around 1615. Champlain called the lake Lac St-Louis, after the king of France, but the name was later changed to reflect a word in Iroquois thought to mean "large body of water." By the early 1680s, the Iroquois village called "Toronto" already appeared on French maps.

In the ferocious imperial contest that followed, the French and British built forts here (☞ see **Fort Rouillé** below), but British victory in the **Seven Years' War** ended French interests in the area. After the Revolutionary War, many people loyal to the British Crown fled the US and settled along the lake. Over time, immigrants poured in from Britain; since World War II, Toronto has become one of the world's most multicultural cities.

Yonge-Dundas Square, Toronto

Tourism Toronto

Address Book

🔖 *For price categories, see the Legend on the cover flap. For an additional selection of Toronto lodgings and restaurants, see* **Michelin Must Sees Toronto**.

WHERE TO STAY

$ The Residence College Hotel – *90 Gerrard St. W., Toronto. ☎416-351-1010. www.hostels.com.420 rooms (30 are double).* 🛏. A former nurses' residence, this high rise adjacent to Toronto Hospital offers very modest rooms with single beds, desk, telephone and climate control. Two washrooms per floor. Communal TV lounge, equipped kitchen and laundry facilities on each of 15 floors. The best features are the location and the fitness centre with its swimming pool.

$$ Cawthra Square – *10 Cawthra Sq., Toronto. ☎416-966-3074 or 800-259-5474. www.cawthrasquare.com. 32 rooms.* A few blocks from Church Street Village (Toronto's gay community), these inviting B&Bs offer lodgings in three restored period houses: an Edwardian at Cawthra Square, and Victorians at 512 and 514 Jarvis Street. A two-minute walk apart, the properties offer rooms at several levels of comfort; most have private baths and terraces. Rates include tea each afternoon, and guests have 24hr access to beverages and snacks.

$$ Hotel Victoria – *56 Yonge St., Toronto. ☎416-363-1666 or 800-363-8228. www.hotelvictoria-toronto.com. 56 rooms.* ♿🅿. Situated only a few blocks from theatres, shopping and restaurants, this small boutique hotel is dwarfed by Yonge Street skyscrapers. Small standard rooms, nicely decorated in dark woods and warm peach and grey tones, include standard amenities and high-speed internet access as well as access to a health club.

$$ Strathcona Hotel – *60 York St., Toronto. ☎416-363-3321 or 800-268-8304. www.thestrathconahotel.com. 194 rooms.* ✕🅿. Situated across the street from Union Station, smack in the middle of the Financial District, the Strathcona has a pleasant lobby facing busy York Street. Rooms are on the small side, but are cheery and comfortable, with modern amenities; corporate rooms are equipped with data ports and dual-line phones. Guests here have access to a nearby fitness club and spa.

$$$ Metropolitan – *108 Chestnut St., Toronto. ☎416-977-5000 or 800-668-6600. www.metropolitan.com. 422 rooms.* ♿🅿✕. Sleek, clean lines and Asian influences permeate this fine downtown hotel. Guest rooms have blond wood, glass, and neutral colour schemes as well as down duvets, Italian linens, in-room safes, Internet access and windows that open. The award-winning **Lai Wah Heen ($$$)** restaurant, whose name means "luxurious meeting place," serves some of the best Cantonese cuisine in the city.

$$$$ The Fairmont Royal York – *100 Front St., Toronto. ☎416-368-2511 or 800-866-5577. www.fairmont.ca. 1,365 rooms.* ♿🅿✕🛏Spa. Its noble facade a familiar part of the city skyline, Toronto's landmark hostelry is palatial. From its imposing chandeliered lobby to its grand ballrooms, the hotel exudes an aura of majesty. Kings, prime ministers, three generations of Britain's Royal Family, not to mention countless celebrities, have stayed here. Elegant guest rooms offer all the amenities and data ports.

$$$$ Le Royal Meridien King Edward – *37 King St. E., Toronto. ☎416-863-9700 or 800-543-4300. www.starwoodhotels.com. 298 rooms.* ♿🅿✕. The "King Eddie," as it's locally known, dates to 1903 and the reign of King Edward VII. Marble pillars, a vaulted ceiling, fine period pieces and lavish floral arrangements decorate the public areas. Edwardian guest-room decor is fit for a king, with mahogany furnishings and marble baths, but with modern amenities including data ports. Crowned by a baroque plasterwork ceiling, the airy, palm-studded **Café Victoria ($$$)** is a lovely spot for a meal.

$$$$$ Sutton Place – *955 Bay St., Toronto.* ☎*416-924-9221 or 866-378-8866. www.suttonplace.com. 294 rooms.* ♿🅿🔲. This stylish hotel in tony Yorkville is a favourite with visiting celebrities. Old World charm and discretion combine here with modern-day comforts. Marble floors, lush carpets, antique furnishings and big bouquets of fresh flowers adorn the lobby. Spacious well-lit guest quarters contain traditional furnishings in dark or blond wood and feature full amenities for business travellers.

$$$$$ Windsor Arms – *18 St. Thomas St., Toronto.* ☎*416-971-9666 or 877-999-2767. www.windsorarmshotel.com. 26 rooms.* 🍴❌🅿🔲🧖. Near Bloor Street and neighbouring Yorkville, this high-end boutique hotel occupies a 1927 Gothic Revival structure. Inside, luxury meets high-tech in 26 suites (and 2 deluxe rooms) outfitted with fireplaces, limestone baths and Frette linens as well as computer ports. The celebrated Tea Room becomes a champagne and caviar bar in the evening, and Club 22 features dancing, cocktails and a cigar lounge. In the **Courtyard Café ($$$$)** impeccable service complements fine continental cuisine.

WHERE TO EAT

$ The Gardens' Cafe – *In RBG Centre at the Royal Botanical Gardens, Hamilton.* ☎*905-527-1158, ext 540. www.rbg.ca. Open for lunch only 11am–3pm daily.* **Light fare.** This pleasant restaurant on the grounds of the Royal Botanical Gardens overlooks Spicer Court with its seasonal plantings. Sandwiches, soups and salads and seasonally changing entrées are offered.

$ Shopsy's Deli – *33 Yonge St., Toronto.* ♿☎*416-365-3333. www.shopsys.ca.* **American.** A Toronto institution since 1921, this breakfast-lunch-dinner spot is famous for its all-beef hot dogs and corned beef sandwiches enjoyed in indoor booths, on the spacious patio or as a takeout order. There's a good range of sandwich platters, burgers and salads as well. Walls are lined with celebrity photos and caricatures.

$ Spring Rolls – *85 Front St. E., Toronto. Also restaurants at 40 Dundas St.W., 45 Eglinton Ave. E., & 694 Yonge St.* ☎*416-365-3649. www.springrolls.ca.* **Asian.** Sleek Asian decor and tasty, affordable Vietnamese, Chinese and Thai dishes attract students, a local office crowd and tourists. Entrée specials change daily and include soup and salad. Pad Thai, Thai red curry and stir-fries with Szechwan or black bean sauce top the list of the most popular dishes. And don't forget the spring rolls!

$$ The Red Tomato – *321 King St. W., Toronto.* ☎*416-971-6626. www.theredtomato.ca. Dinner only.* **International.** One of many popular, bustling restaurants in the King Street entertainment district, this cozy lower-level eatery (its higher-priced sister, **Fred's Not Here,** resides upstairs) offers salads, gourmet pizza, pasta and grill-your-own tandoori dishes.

$$ Rodney's Oyster House – *469 King St. W., Toronto.* ☎*416-363-8105. www.rodneysoysterhouse.com.* **Seafood.** The house specialty is fresh Malpeque oysters presented on the half shell with a wide choice of condiments, including homemade pepper sauces. A meal at Rodney's is a night of boisterous, good old Maritime fun.

$$ Le Papillon – *16 Church St., Toronto.* ♿☎*416-363-3773. www.lepapillon.ca. Closed Mon.* **French.** This is one of the few crêperies in Toronto, serving up French and Québécois fare on a quiet street close to Sony Centre. Stucco walls and checkered tablecloths are resolutely French. In addition to a wide selection of crêpes—15 varieties, not including dessert—*plats principaux* include *tourtière* (a Québécois meat pie baked with seasoned pork, beef and veal) and *steak au poivre.* Le Papillon's onion soup, smothered with Emmenthal cheese and chunks of bread, is a meal in itself.

$$ Myth – *417 Danforth Ave., Toronto.* ☎*416-461-8383. www.myth.to.* **Greek.** One of a conclave of restaurants in Greektown, Myth is an open, high-ceilinged eatery with video screens and pool tables. A Mediterranean-style menu is available inside or on the sidewalk patio. Entrées include the inevitable souvlaki with Greek salad, but also a creative moussaka with goat cheese and vegetables; extensive menu of appetizers.

$$ Nice-Bistro – *117 Brock St. N. (Exit 410 off Hwy.401, then north), Whitby.* ☎*905-668-8839. www.nicebistro.com. Closed Sun & Mon.* **French.** Hailing from Nice, France, Chef Bernard and his Quebec-born wife, Manon, opened this charming restaurant in 1998. Dark wood and colourful Provençal-style tablecloths set the scene for classic French fare. Check the chalkboard's handwritten "menu du jour" to see what's in season: maybe bouillabaisse with mussels, scallops, shrimp and fish in a tomato-Pernod sauce, served with spicy cheese bread, or *grenadins de veau*—veal tenderloin with mushrooms in a Cognac cream sauce.

$$ Shrimp Cocktail – *843 King St. W. (at Thornton), Oshawa.* ☎*905-725-7500. www.shrimpcocktailcafe.com. No lunch Sun.* **Contemporary.** Located just over a block west of the Oshawa Centre shopping mall, this restaurant draws repeat customers for stylishly presented plates of seafood, lamb, chicken, beef and pasta. Chef Michael McKay keeps them coming back for creative concoctions such as red snapper filet in a lobster-infused king crabmeat cream or sugar cane, ginger, miso and cinnamon-poached chicken with tiger shrimp in a red Thai-curry cream. Choose a semicircular banquette near the bar, with its cooling aquariums, or a table in the industrial-chic dining space.

$$ Spencers at the Waterfront – *1340 Lakeshore Rd., Burlington.* ☎*905-633-7494. www.spencersatthewaterfront. com.* **Contemporary.** Splendid views of the lakefront from any table in this restaurant within the Discovery Landing enliven lunch or dinner. The restaurant maintains its own farm and offers local lamb, chicken, rabbit and pork dishes, fine Ontario wines and fresh garden produce. An example is the braised lamb shank with curried vegetables. Ample seafood is also on offer, such as seared scallops with Niagara bacon, along with crispy salads. On weekend evenings, musicians entertain diners.

$$$ Ancaster Old Mill Inn – *548 Old Dundas Rd., Ancaster. Exit Mohawk Rd. from Hwy. 403 West.* ☎*905-648-1827. www.ancasteroldmill.com.* **Contemporary.** In Ancaster, just west of Hamilton, an 18C stone mill has been converted into an upscale restaurant with seven dining rooms, the most popular overlooking a waterfall through floor-to-ceiling windows. Two prix-fixe menus are prepared daily. An example: smoked trout and Bosc pear salad, venison on parsnip purée with seasonal vegetables and vanilla and plum soufflé for dessert, with a selected wine for each course.

$$$ Sassafraz – *100 Cumberland St., Toronto.* ☎*416-964-2222. www.cafe sassafraz.com.* **French.** This trendy eatery on one of Yorkville's prime corners offers a bistro lunch of steak-frites, salade Niçoise and other dishes, available on the sidewalk patio. Inside, the sunny yellow garden room blooms year-round with herb trees under a 40ft atrium. Dine on creative cuisine such as bison carpaccio, or roasted lamb with eggplant croquant. Jazz on occasion.

$$$ Southern Accent – *595 Markham St., Toronto. Dinner only.* ☎*416-536-3211. www.southernaccent.com.* **Cajun/Creole.** Housed in a former Victorian residence, this funky Mirvish Village restaurant attracts a mixed crowd to its outdoor patio and small, mood-lit rooms on different levels. Start your meal with a Creole martini, made with Cajun pepper vodka. Favourites include Creole jambalaya and blackened chicken livers. Everything is à la carte, including sides and yummy corn bread.

$$$$ Canoe – *66 Wellington St. W., Toronto.* ♿☎*416-364-0054. www. oliverbonacini.com.* **Canadian.** Overlooking the harbour and the Toronto Islands from its perch on the 54th floor of the Toronto Dominion Bank Tower, this perennial hot spot combines haute Canadian cuisine with excellent service. Signature dishes include venison loin, roast suckling pig and Maritime lobster salad. Minimalist decor mixes country pine and polished concrete.

$$$$ Splendido – *88 Harbord St., Toronto.* ♿☎*416-929-7788. www. splendido.ca.* **Canadian.** This Annex neighbourhood restaurant offers fresh Canadian ingredients with Mediterranean accents such as baked halibut filet with Tuscan bean ragout, or smoked pork belly with cauliflower tortellini. For dessert, try the chocolate truffle cake.

Toronto ★★★

METROPOLITAN AREA POPULATION 5,113,149

MAPS P 65, P 69 AND P 78

A vibrant, multicultural city with a liveable downtown core, Toronto offers a vigourous cultural scene, professional sports teams, great shopping and many recreational activities. The provincial capital enjoys a buoyant economy driven by finance, telecommunications, biotechnology, aerospace, film and television production and media. Major Canadian corporations have their head offices here. Recent major projects—the new Four Seasons Centre for the Performing Arts and renovations of the Art Gallery of Ontario and the Royal Ontario Museum—have confirmed the city's role as the epicentre of Canadian culture. Toronto possesses a fine harbour, punctuated with a chain of offshore islands that provide the city with an expanse of parkland. No wonder fortunate Toronto is known as the Queen City.

Information: Toronto Visitors Centre, 207 Queens Quay W. ☎416-203-2600 or 800-499-2514. www.torontotourism.com

▶ **Orient Yourself:** City centre stretches northward from the waterfront opposite the Toronto Islands. Its two main south-north arteries are University Avenue and Yonge Street. Historic Fort York stands not far from the water, at the southwest corner; **Old Town of York** lies on the opposite side of the city's core. **Downtown,** site of many of Toronto's skyscrapers, encompasses the Financial District and City Hall Area. Major **shopping hubs** include Eaton Centre and The Bay department store, both east of City Hall and the upscale Bloor-Yorkville district just north. South and westward, West Queen West *(Bathurst to Shaw Sts.)* holds boutiques of up-and-coming designers as well as vintage clothing shops. College Street caters largely to students. North of City Hall, the University of Toronto and Ontario Parliament flank **Queen's Park.** North of the park, Bloor Street anchors the city's major **museums:** the Royal Ontario Museum, Gardiner Museum and Bata Shoe Museum (the Art Gallery of Ontario, another heavyweight, occupies a growing complex west of City Hall).

Parking: Street metered parking is available but hard to find; timed parking (signed) and permit-only parking is strictly enforced. It is prudent to park in lots. Museum parking, when available, must be paid for, often in cash only.

Don't Miss: CN Tower and the Royal Ontario Museum. For innovative opera or ballet, visit the new Four Seasons Centre for the Performing Arts. And, since this is Canada, why not see the Hockey Hall of Fame?

Organizing Your Time: Public transportation (Toronto Transit Commission, or "TTC" as locals call it) with its network of subway trains, buses and streetcars (trams) is efficient, safe and inexpensive. When driving, avoid the crowded north-south artery, Yonge St.; try Avenue Road, Bathurst or Don Valley Parkway.

Especially for Kids: The Ontario Science Centre, the amusement parks at Toronto Islands, Ontario Place, and the Toronto Zoo.

Also See: SOUTHERN ONTARIO

A Bit of History

"Toronto Passage" – Prior to 1600, the **Huron** and **Petun** peoples abandoned their north shore lands to the warlike **Iroquois Confederacy,** which dominated the fur trade. The Iroquois in turn ceded to French traders control of the "Toronto Passage" of trails and canoe routes between Lakes Huron and Ontario.

The French Regime – As early as 1615 the site of Toronto was visited by **Étienne Brûlé,** one of Champlain's men. Years later French traders met native and English traders on the Humber River in what is now Toronto, a Huron word for "meeting place." The French began construction in 1720 of forts around Lake Ontario; remains of **Fort Rouillé** have been found in Toronto's Exhibition Grounds. The Seven Years' War (1756-63) brought an end to French presence in the area.

York – In 1787, **Sir Guy Carleton,** the governor of British North America, arranged to buy land from the **Mississaugas,** who had occupied the Toronto area after the Iroquois. Loyalists fleeing the US had also settled along the lake; their demands for English law led to the formation of Upper Canada (now Ontario) in 1791. Colonel **John Graves Simcoe,** lieutenant-governor of the new territory, chose the site for a temporary capital, because of its fine harbour and distance from the American border. It was called **York,** after the Duke, a son of George III. In 1813 an American fleet set fire to the legislative assembly and other buildings. In retaliation, the British set Washington, DC, on fire, including the Capitol and the White House, in 1814.

The Family Compact – After 1814, immigrants flooding in from Britain began to challenge the power of what was called "the Family Compact," a small group of wealthy men who dominated the government of York and Upper Canada. An outspoken Scot named **William Lyon Mackenzie** (1795-1861) attacked the group in his newspaper, *The Colonial Advocate*. He was elected to the legislative assembly (although not allowed to take his seat) and in 1835 was elected the first mayor of the City of Toronto (the name was changed as the Duke of York continued to lose in battle). In 1836, Gov. **Sir Francis Bond Head** dissolved the legislature.

The Rebellion of 1837 – Mackenzie turned to armed rebellion in 1837. When Toronto's garrison was away in Lower Canada, he gathered supporters and marched toward the city. British reinforcements arrived under Col. Allan MacNab, the revolt collapsed and Mackenzie fled to the US. Although two of Mackenzie's men were publicly hanged, the revolt was effective in that "responsible government" was granted and the united Province of Canada was created. Mackenzie was permitted to return in 1849.

A City of Neighbourhoods – Since World War II, the city has opened its doors to immigrants from around the world. Today Toronto benefits from a stimulating mix of cultures. **Kensington Market** *(Kensington Ave., east of Spadina and north of Dundas)* is the realm of the Portuguese and East Indian communities *(best time to visit is Mon–Sat mornings)*. One of the largest Chinese districts in North America, **Chinatown** *(Dundas St. from Elizabeth to Spadina)* is also vibrant with street vendors. The **Italian** districts *(College St. and St. Clair Ave., west of Bathurst)* evoke the mother country. **Greektown** *(Danforth Ave. between Coxwell and Broadview; ●Chester)* offers cafes, specialty shops and fruit markets featuring Greek food. The **India Bazaar** *(Gerrard St. E.)* offers restaurants, art, clothing, produce and street food from Southeast Asia. **Koreatown** *(Bloor St. W.)* is renowned for barbecue and karaoke. **Roncesvalles Village** is the place where the Polish community comes to shop and eat. Particularly active between Spadina and John Streets, **Queen Street West** has become a colourful area of trendy bistros, and boutiques.

CN Tower

Tourism Toronto

Toronto Today – **Dundas Square** *(Dundas and Yonge Sts.)*, which was opened with great fanfare in May 2003, has become Toronto's top visitor destination (www.ydsquare.ca). The centrepiece is an "urban beach," an array of 10 fountains that people can walk around or through. High-tech signage rather controversially surrounds the square, which is run as a business venture, with scheduled events. On the north-east corner of the intersection, **Toronto Life Square,** a $100 million entertainment and retail complex, carrying the name of a monthly lifestyle magazine, opened its first phase in 2007. Eventually, the complex will include retail shops, movie theatres, restaurants, bars and office space. On the exterior will be an enormous video screen (30x52ft, 9.8x15.9m), as well as 34 ancillary video panels displaying advertisements.

Another project that will define the city is a multimillion-dollar development of a somewhat derelict waterfront. Highlights of the mega-project include creating new city-core neighbourhoods, a waterfront park and promenade and, most significantly, reconfiguration of the elevated Gardiner Expressway, a 1950s eyesore that divides the city from its waterfront.

Toronto's natural harbour stretches 3km/2mi in length and 1.6km/1mi wide. Protected by offshore islands, it is one of the country's largest inland ports. Increased overland transport in the last decades, however, has resulted in decline in ship traffic. In 1972, the federal government set up Harbourfront to oversee converting the port area for cultural and residential use, a project that continues to this day, not without controversy. The City of Toronto proposed redevelopment, in 1999, of underutilized port lands; in 2000 the federal government pledged $1.5 billion for implementation. The newest parkland, opened in 2007, is the HTO Park at Queen Quay.

Toronto's extensive park system, tidy streets, cultural facilities, low crime rate and excellent public transport give the city a high position on any list of the world's most liveable cities. With a municipal population of nearly 2.6 million, the metropolis ranks among the continent's largest cities. As with all big cities, not everything is rosy. Toronto's downtown streets are often gridlocked, homelessness is visible and parking is expensive and often scarce. Still, Toronto is a great city to live in or to visit.

Entertainment and Festivals

The centre of English-language culture in Canada, Toronto boasts the Toronto Symphony and the Toronto Mendelssohn Choir at Roy Thomson Hall; popular concerts at the venerable (1894) Massey Hall; the Canadian Opera Company and the National Ballet of Canada at the Four Seasons Centre; contemporary dance (including the Toronto Dance Theatre) at the Harbourfront Centre's Premiere Dance Theatre and Enwave Theatre. The St. Lawrence Centre for the Arts, the Royal Alexandra and the Princess of Wales theatres, and the Elgin and Winter Garden Theatre Centre stage new and traditional plays and musicals.

Every fall the city hosts the Toronto International Film Festival, and summer brings a variety of outdoor entertainment. Several annual events draw visitors: the **Canadian National Exhibition** *(at the Exhibition Grounds late-Aug–Labour Day)*, reputedly the world's largest exhibition, now primarily a showcase for consumer goods; the **Metro International Caravan,** a festival of ethnic cultures *(mid-Jun)*; the **International Dragon Boat Festival,** 100 boat races in 2 days, with participants from around the world *(Jun)*; and **Caribana,** a West Indies festival of steel bands and floating nightclubs on the lake *(mid-Jul–early Aug)*.

Spectator sports include Toronto Blue Jays baseball, an annual harbour regatta *(Jul 1)*, horse shows *(Royal Agricultural Winter Fair)*, soccer and auto racing. Air Canada Centre (1999) is home to Toronto Raptors basketball and Maple Leafs ice-hockey teams.

Practical Information

AREA CODES

Since the Greater Toronto Area has several area codes, you will need to dial all 10 digits (area code plus the phone number) when making local calls. For more information: ☎800-668-6878 or www.bell.ca.

GETTING AROUND

BY PUBLIC TRANSPORTATION

The Toronto Transit Commission (TTC) operates an extensive public transit system of buses, streetcars and subway lines. Hours of operation: **Subway** Mon–Sat 6am–1:30am, Sun 9am–1:30am. **Buses and trams** Mon–Fri 5am–1:30am, reduced service weekends. Blue Night buses and trams daily 1am–5:30am. Fare $2.75 one way for unlimited travel with no stopovers. Exact fare required. Day Pass $9. Purchase tickets & tokens in subway stations or at stores displaying TTC ticket decal. Tokens 5 for $11.25, 10 for $22.50. Vending machines sell tokens in units of 1, 4 or 8. Free transfers between buses & streetcars. System maps & timetables available free of charge. Route information ☎416-393-4636 or www.ttc.ca.

BY CAR

Use of public transportation or walking is strongly encouraged within the city as streets are often congested and street parking may be difficult to find. Toronto has a strictly enforced tow-away policy. Motorists should park in designated **parking** areas which are identified by a sign with a green 'P'; there is a 3hr limit; public, off-street parking facilities are located throughout the city. For a free map and information about parking fees, call ☎416-393-7275. www.toronto.ca. Parking is serious enough to merit a website, www.greenp.com, devoted to finding parking lot space, parking services, and latest parking news.

Car rentals:
Avis ☎416-777-2847.
Hertz ☎416-979-1178.
National ☎800-227-7368.

BY TAXI

Co-op ☎416-504-2667. www.co-opcabs.com. Diamond ☎416-366-6868. www.diamondtaxi.ca. Beck Taxi ☎416-751-5555.

BY MOTORCOACH

Gray Line Tours ☎416-594-3310 or 800-594-3310. www.grayline.ca.

GENERAL INFORMATION

ACCOMMODATIONS

For a listing of suggested hotels, see Address Book. For **hotels/motels** contact Tourism Toronto (☎416-203-2600 or 800-499-2514 (Canada/US). www.torontotourism.com). Reservation services: Hotels.com ☎800-224-6835 (Canada/US) http://deals.hotels.com. Abodes of Choice B&B Assn. of Toronto, ☎416-537-7629. www.redtoronto.com. Downtown Toronto Assn. of B&B Guest Homes ☎416-410-3938. www.bnbinfo.com.

CITY PASS

CityPass offers six famous attractions (CN Tower, Royal Ontario Museum, Casa Loma, Ontario Science Centre, Toronto Zoo, Hockey Hall of Fame) at one price ($59) lower than the total of individual admission fees. ☎888-330-5008. http://citypass.com/city/toronto.html.

LOCAL PRESS

Daily: Toronto Star, Toronto Sun, Globe and Mail, National Post.
Weekly: L'Express (Francophone news).
Monthly: Toronto Life magazine, and free guides to entertainment, shopping, and restaurants (www.torontolife.com): Eye (www.eyeweekly.com), Now (weekly. www.nowtoronto.com), Where (monthly. www.wheretoronto.com).

ENTERTAINMENT

Consult the arts and entertainment supplements in local newspapers (Thursday edition) for schedules of cultural events and addresses of principal theatres and concert halls. Ticketmaster (☎416-870-8000 for concerts or 416-872-1111. www.ticketmaster.ca) sells tickets for theatre and the arts. For half-price, same-day tickets for theatrical, dance and musical events, contact www.totix. ca or ☎416-536-6468. Purchase tickets online or in person at T.O.Tix in Dundas

Square *(corner of Yonge and Dundas)* Tue–Sat noon–6:30pm. Full-price tickets are also available. Royal Alexandra and Princess of Wales theatres: ☎416-872-1212, *www.mirvish.com*. Useful Websites: www.torontolife.com (current events, restaurant and nightlife guide) and www.martiniboys.com (overview of trendy restaurants, clubs and pubs).

SPORTS

Toronto Blue Jays (baseball).Season Apr–Oct at Rogers Centre ☎416-341-1234. *http://toronto.bluejays.mlb*.com. **Toronto Maple Leafs** (ice hockey): season Oct–Apr at Air Canada Centre ☎416-815-5500 *(schedules)*, ☎416-872-5000 *(Ticketmaster). http://.mapleleafs. nhl.com.* **Toronto Argonauts** (football). Season mid-Jun–Nov at Rogers Centre *(*☎*416-489-2745 (schedules). www. argonauts.on.ca.* ☎*416-872-5000 (Ticketmaster).* **Toronto Raptors** (basketball): season Nov–Apr at Air Canada Centre ☎416-366-3865. *www. nba.com/raptors*.

USEFUL NUMBERS ☎

⬦ **Police: 911 (emergency) or 416-808-2222 (non-emergency)**
⬦ **Union Station** (VIA Rail) – *Front & Bay Sts*. Travellers Aid Society 416-366-7788. VIA Rail 1-888-842-7245.
⬦ **Metro Coach Terminal** – *610 Bay St.* 416-393-7911
⬦ **Toronto (Pearson) International Airport** – *416-766-3000.*
Terminal 1 & 2: 416-247-7678
Terminal 3: 416-776-5100
Toll Free: 866-207-1690
⬦ **Canadian Automobile Assn.:** 461 Yonge St. 416-221-4300
⬦ **CAA Emergency Road Service** (24hr): 416-222-5222
⬦ **Shoppers Drug Mart** (24hr pharmacy) *various locations:* 416-979-2424
⬦ **Post Office Station A** – *25 The Esplanade.* 416-979-8822
⬦ **Road Conditions** – 416-599-9090
⬦ **Weather** (24hr) – 416-661-0123

AFTERNOON TEA

Three historic hotels in downtown Toronto offer afternoon tea with traditional accompaniments: finger sandwiches, scones with clotted cream, pastries, petits fours and a wide selection of loose-leaf teas. At the sumptuous **Windsor Arms** hotel *(*✆ *see Address Book)*, afternoon tea is served at two daily sittings *(1pm* **&** *3:30pm)* and at 5:30pm Thu-Sun in the parlourlike Tea Room. The landmark **Le Royal Meridien King Edward Hotel** *(*✆ *see Address Book)* offers a gracious tea service in its majestic **Café Victoria** *(Tue–Sun 2pm-5pm).* An elegant space with high ceilings, ornate mouldings, brocade-covered banquettes, and striking floral arrangements, it's one of the oldest dining rooms in the city. Tea at the grande dame of hotels, **The Fairmont Royal York** *(*✆ *see Address Book)* is served in EPIC, a sleek, modern restaurant space. *(Sun–Fri 2:30pm–4pm, Sat 1pm–4pm).* A children's tea selection is available for little ones.

SHOPPING

Whether your taste is chic or a bit more edgy, you'll find what you're looking for in Toronto's many shopping districts. The upscale shops at **Bloor/Yorkville** *(Bloor and Cumberland Sts., Yorkville and Hazelton Aves.)* carry top designs—and the highest price tags. Offering everything from evening attire to funky weekend wear, **Yonge and Eglinton** caters to the yuppie crowd. Boutiques along **Queen Street West** *(west of Bathurst St.)* show off the latest fashion trends, while up-and-coming designers occupy **West Queen West** *(Bathurst to Shaw St.),* a bargain-filled bohemian hub where sophisticated buyers find haute couture at affordable prices. Finally, **College Street** *(Bathurst to Shaw St.)* attracts—what else?—college students and others who want cutting-edge clothes and gear. *For specifics, access www.torontotourism.com.*

SPAS

After a day of shopping or sightseeing, treat yourself to a trip to one of Toronto's many spas. The three cited here offer a full menu of services, including hair care. The newly renovated and expanded **Elizabeth Milan Hotel Day Spa** *(Arcade Level, Fairmont Royal York;* ☎*416-350-7500; www.elizabethmilan-spa.com)* offers professional treatments and services within a serene, Mediterranean-themed space, where the pace is deliberately slow. Skin care is a specialty and the Swedish massages are heavenly. Princess Margaret, the Duchess of York, Dame Edna and Jennifer Lopez are just a few of the celebrities who have been pampered here. With just seven treatment rooms, **The Spa at Windsor Arms** (☎416-934-6031; www. windsorarmshotel.com) is as intimate and exclusive as the hotel itself. One unusual treatment is Tui Na, a deep massage mixing Chinese and shiatsu techniques. The adjacent pool area with its poolside fireplace offers relaxation or invigoration. With an address in Crowne Plaza Toronto Centre, the **Victoria Spa** (225 Front St. W., 3rd floor; ☎416-413-9100; www.victoriaspa.com) ushers patrons into a calm space accented with Asian artifacts. Victoria offers a full range of aesthetics and therapeutic massages, plus a juice bar, for men and women. After your treatment, take a dip in the sparkling pool or sun on the deck beneath tall CN Tower.

The ●symbol indicates a subway station.

The Waterfront★★

Built largely on land reclaimed in the mid-19C to mid-20C for the city's growing port installations, the area south of Front Street contains Toronto's foremost landmarks—the CN Tower and Rogers Centre—and its largest lakefront revitalization, which today includes colourful shops, galleries, performance arenas, restaurants, sailing schools, a water park and an outdoor stage known as the Molson Amphitheatre, part of Ontario Place. *The grounds of both CN Tower and Rogers Centre can be reached on foot from Union Station by* **Skywalk,** *a large, glass-enclosed walkway containing eateries and souvenir shops.*

CN Tower★★★
301 Front St. W.; Entrance at Front and John Sts. ●Union, then via Skywalk. ✕&ⓄOpen June–Sept daily 9am–11pm. Rest of the year daily 9am–10pm (Fri–Sat 10:30pm). Hours may vary; call to confirm. ⓄClosed Dec 25. ☜$28. ☎416-868-6937. www.cntower.ca.

The city's most prominent landmark, this concrete structure reaches 180 storeys (over 553m/1,815ft in height), the tallest freestanding structure in the world. It attracts some 2 million visitors a year. In only 58 seconds visitors are "beamed up" 346m/1,136ft (nearly the height of the Empire State Building) in one of six exterior glass-front elevators to the **look-out level,** a seven-storey-tall, circular steel "turban." From its observation decks, **views**★★ of the city and suburbs, the lake and shoreline are superb (panels identify buildings and parks). One floor down, intrepid visitors can stand or sit on the **glass floor,** a section of thick glass panels that permit an impressive view 342m/1,122ft to the ground below. There's also **360 Restaurant** (reservations recommended; ☎416-362-5411), the world's highest revolving restaurant. The sweeping **views**★★★ of the cityscape and Lake Ontario from the **Skypod,** a windowed ring 447m/1,465ft above the ground, are spectacular. If visibility is good, Niagara Falls and Buffalo, 120km/75mi away, can be seen.

Rogers Centre★★
● Union, then via Skywalk. ✕&🅿☎416-341-2770. www.rogerscentre.com.

This huge, domed sports/entertainment complex next to CN Tower is home to American League baseball's Toronto Blue Jays. Designed by architect Roderick Robbie and engineer Michael Allen, the centre was built (1989) by a private consortium in partnership with local and provincial governments for over $570 million. The multipurpose stadium hosts rock concerts, conventions and trade shows as well as a variety of sports. Projecting from the Front Street facade 5m/16ft above street level, **Michael Snow's** 14 painted-fibreglass **sculptures** (The Audience) tower over arriving visitors. Rogers Centre boasts a 3ha/8-acre **retractable roof,** the 348-room **Renaissance Hotel** overlooking the playing field (☎416-341-7100 or 800-237-1512), a 150-seat cinema, several restaurants and underground parking.

Tourism Toronto

Harbourfront Centre

Harbourfront Centre★★

Info desk at York Quay Centre, 235 Queens Quay West. Access from York, Spadina and Bathurst Sts. ●Union or Spadina, transfer to 510 LRT to York Quay Centre. ✕♿🅿🕐Open mid-Apr–mid-Oct

daily 10am–11pm (Sun & holidays 9pm). Rest of the year Mon–Fri 9am–6pm, Sat–Sun 10am–6pm. Box office open Tues–Sat 1pm–6pm (8pm if evening performance).☎416-973-4000. www.harbourfront.on.ca.

A focal point of the city's cultural life, especially in summer, Harbourfront Centre is also the scene of year-round recreational, educational and commercial activities.

Queen's Quay Terminal (1927), with its imposing clock tower, accommodates airy offices, plush living spaces, fashionable boutiques and eateries, the 450-seat Premiere Dance Theatre and, on the fifth floor, the offices of the Toronto Convention and Visitors Assn. Nearby, **York Quay Centre** houses an art gallery, a crafts studio and summer theatre. Next is the **Power Plant Contemporary Art Gallery (A)** *(♿🕐open year-round Tue–Sun noon–6pm, Wed 8pm. 🕐Closed Mon except holidays open noon–6pm; ⬤$5; ☎416-973-4949; www.thepowerplant.org)*, the multipurpose **du Maurier Theatre Centre (B)**, with its glass-faceted foyer, evolved from a 1920s icehouse. The **concert stage (C)**, an open-air 1,750-seat concert facility, occupies the southwest corner of the quay. Sailing schools, nautical stores and restaurants are located at **Pier 4**, and the Marine Division of the Metro Police is based at John Quay. Just south of Pier 4 is **The Pier** 🄺🄸🄳🄶, a two-level interactive museum housing nautical exhibits,

GREEK ON DANFORTH

●Broadway, Chester or Pape. One of Toronto's most enjoyable walking neighbourhoods, the Danforth Avenue section known as Greektown *(www.greektowntoronto.com)* is lined with designer shops and restaurants, many with sidewalk patios. Popular eateries include **Myth** *(👝see Address Book)* and **Pappas Grill** *(440 Danforth Ave.; ☎416-469-9595; www.pappasgrill.com)*, best known for appetizers such as hummus and tzatziki dips and pizzas. **Romancing the Home** *(511 Danforth Ave.; ☎416-461-4663)* stocks hand-painted dishware or imports from Africa such as hand-crafted mirrors, raffia, animal-print pillows and Moroccan tapestries. Kids love **Suckers** *(450 Danforth Ave. ☎416-405-8946)*, a sweet shop brimming with candy, toys and premium ice cream. For great family fun, catch the annual **Taste of the Danforth** *(second weekend in Aug; www.toronto.com/tasteofthedanforth)*, which turns this busy thoroughfare into a pedestrian walkway bursting with live entertainment, food stalls, music and fashion shows.

a children's discovery zone and videos on Toronto and harbour history.

Toronto Islands★★

Ferries depart from Queen's Quay to three points in summer (Centre Island, Ward's Island and Hanlan's Point mid-Apr–mid Oct) and two in winter (Ward's Island and Hanlan's Point mid-Oct–mid-Apr). Wards Island year-round daily 6:35am–11:45pm, other islands hours vary, consult schedule.

$6 round-trip. ☎416-392-8193. www.toronto.ca/parks/island.

These islands function as Toronto's principal public parkland. Extending 6km/3.7mi from end to end, they offer expansive lawns, age-old shade trees, sandy beaches, marinas and splendid **views**★★ of downtown Toronto. Attrac-

tions on Centre Island include restaurants, cafes, a beach *(on the Lake Ontario side)*, a delightful theme/amusement park **Kids** for youngsters *(open late-Jun–Aug daily 10:30am–8pm; May & Sept call for hrs; ☎416-203-0405; www.centre-island.ca).* Visitors can explore the islands on foot or by bike *(motor vehicles prohibited on the islands; bike rentals available),* particularly **Algonquin** and Ward's Island, whose quaint roads lined with small, privately owned cottages have a decidedly rural charm. Near Toronto Island Airport on the islands' western end is **Hanlan's Point,** renowned for its **views** of the city *(a trackless train operates continuously between Centre Island and Hanlan's Point).*

The hour-long **Inner Harbour & Island Cruise** offers fine **views** of downtown

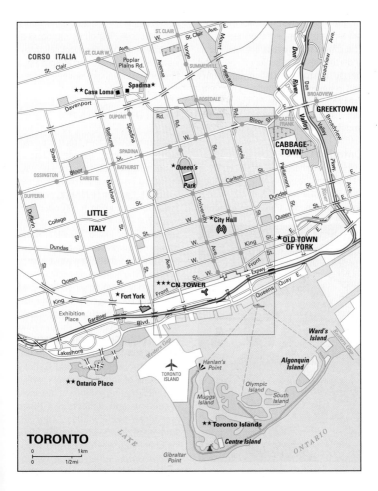

(departs from Pier 6, Queen's Quay West, York St. Jun–Aug daily every 30min 10am–6pm; April–May & Sept–Oct, daily every hour 10am–5pm; round-trip 1hr; ⊚$24; 🅿 *Toronto Harbour Tours:* ☎*416-869-1372; www.we-know-toronto.com).*

Fort York★

📷 *100 Garrison Rd. Access by Bathurst streetcar or by car: from Lakeshore Blvd. take Strachan St. just before Princes' Gate entrance to Exhibition Grounds, then right on Fleet St. and left on Garrison Rd. (under Gardiner Expressway).* 🅿 🕐 *Open late-May–Labour Day daily 10am–5pm. Rest of the year daily 10am–4pm (weekends 5pm)* 🕐 *Closed weekend before Christmas until Jan 2. ⊚$6.* ☎*416-392-6907. www. fortyork.ca.*

Constructed in 1793, Fort York was devastated in 1813 during American capture. It was rebuilt, but peace meant its military importance diminished.

The **officers' barracks** is furnished to show the lifestyle of senior officers of the period. Costumed staff conduct tours and in summer, stage military manoeuvres *(Jul–Aug)*. Events on Canada Day *(Jul 1)* and Simcoe Day *(Aug 1)* offer fife and drum, musketry and cannons.

Ontario Place★★

📷 *955 Lakeshore Blvd. W. Access from Exhibition Grounds.* ✗ ♿ 🅿 🕐 *Open Jul–Aug daily 10am–7pm. May–Jun & Sept call for hours. (Cinesphere* 🕐 *open year-round.) ⊚$33.50 ($17.75 grounds only).* ☎*416-314-9900. www.ontario place.com.*

This sprawling, innovative leisure complex designed by Eberhard Zeidler emerges from an extraordinary setting of lagoons, marinas and man-made islands on the lakefront bordering the Exhibition Grounds. With an emphasis on family entertainment and recreation, facilities include a water park, pedal and bumper boats, a water slide, mini-golf, helicopter rides, a children's village and restaurants.

Resembling a giant golf ball, **Cinesphere** features IMAX films on a screen six storeys high. The **Molson Amphitheatre** is used to stage a variety of musical productions. The **water park** has wading pools full of water jets.

In winter, **Holiday Dreams** *(*🅿🕐*late Nov–early Jan Fri–Sun only; call for hours; $12;* ☎*416-314-9900)* offers outdoor skating, a petting zoo, a riverboat cafe, movies at the Cinesphere and at 8pm Sat, a firework display.

Old Town York★

Although little dates from the 1793 plans of Lieutenant-Governor Simcoe, some structures date from the early 19C, including an active marketplace, the **South St. Lawrence Market** *(92 Front St. E. at Jarvis St.;* ●*King;* ✗ ♿ 🕐 *open year-round Tue–Thu 8am–6pm, Fri to 7pm, Sat 5am–5pm;* ☎*416-392-7120; www. stlawrencemarket.com)*, a cavernous brick building sheltering a two-storey food hall. The market is especially lively on Saturday morning when early-bird shoppers converge on fruit stands, bakeries, meat counters and delicatessens. The market encases the surviving portion of the **Second City Hall** *(1845-99)*. The former second-floor council chamber houses the **Market Gallery** of the City of Toronto Archives, which presents rotating exhibits of historical documents and artifacts *(♿ 🕐 open year-round Wed–Fri 10am–4pm, Sat 9am–4pm, Sun noon–4pm;* 🕐 *closed major holidays;* ☎*416-392-7604; www. toronto.ca/culture/the_ market_gallery. htm)*.

Ontario Tourism

Water park at Ontario Place

Directly across the street stands the **North St. Lawrence Market**, a bustling farmers' market with many specialty vendors, housed in a smaller building (✖️♿🕐*building open year-round; farmers' market only Sat 5am–5pm; antique stalls hours vary: check website for days and times;* ☎416-392-7219; *www.stlawrencemarket.com*). From the entrance there is a good view, to the west, of Toronto's **flatiron building,** the Gooderham (1892) on Wellington Street, against a backdrop of the towers of Brookfield Place.

Just behind the market via a charming walkway, the 1850 Neoclassical **St. Lawrence Hall** *(King and Jarvis Sts.)* is distinguished by its domed cupola. It now houses various commercial enterprises. Just opposite lies lovely St. James Park, a small manicured expanse that offers rest to passers-by.

Farther east is 🄺🄸🄳**Toronto's First Post Office**⋆ *(260 Adelaide St. E.;* 🕐*open year-round Mon–Fri 9am–4pm, weekends 10am–4pm;* 🕐*closed major holidays;* ☎416-865-1833; *www.townofyork. com*), opened in 1833. Costumed staff demonstrate quill-and-ink letter-writing. Kids can write and post a letter the old-fashioned way for $1.

Downtown

Containing the city's formidable financial core, Toronto's downtown exudes a sense of momentum and prosperity. Site of the country's leading banks; legal, insurance and brokerage firms; and the Toronto Stock Exchange, the area of King and Bay streets constitutes Canada's "Wall Street."

The skyscrapers are connected by an **underground city** of shops, eateries, banks and concourses extending eight blocks from Union Station and the Fairmont **Royal York Hotel** to City Hall, Eaton Centre and on up to Dundas Street. The PATH network of walkways, clearly marked, covers 10km/6mi.

One of the best-known and longest roads (1,896km/1,178mi) in Canada is **Yonge Street,** the city's east-west dividing line. Laid out by Simcoe in 1795 as a military route, this thoroughfare is lined

THE FIFTH

●*Broadway.* It has that Prohibition feel, but don't let the back-alley entrance fool you. **The Fifth Restaurant and Social Club** *(225 Richmond St. W.;* ☎416-973-3000), formerly known as Easy and the Fifth, is no cheap date. Housed in a renovated factory in the city's buzzing Entertainment District, this nightclub/restaurant with the air of an upscale loft, attracts young professionals (ages 25 to 45) for weekend drinks and dancing. The recently opened Black Betty rock n' roll lounge bar is somewhat relaxed, though still swish (better dress up!). **The Fifth ($$$)** is one of the city's best restaurants, with skirted chairs, white linens, live piano music and scrumptious French fare. In summer, enjoy your meal along with skyline views outside on **The Terrace,** a pretty rooftop patio. *Restaurant reservations are a must.*

with fancy boutiques, colourful flower stands, trendy restaurants, interesting stores and antiques shops.

Financial District⋆⋆

● *King or St. Andrew*
A stunning ebony-coloured ensemble covering an entire city block, the **Toronto-Dominion Centre**⋆⋆ was the first component of the current financial district. A fine example of the International style, the spartan black-glass towers, known locally as the T-D Centre, reflect the design of eminent 20C architect Mies van der Rohe, consultant for the project. The complex now includes five towers. The seven life-size bronze cows lolling contentedly on a grass patch adjoining the centre are by Saskatchewan sculptor Joe Fafard. Fronting Bay Street, the Ernst & Young tower (1992) incorporates the former Art Deco Stock Exchange Building (1937) within its base. On view throughout the centre are works by contemporary artists, predominantly Canadian.

The downtown abounds in other skyscrapers by noted architects, among them the adjacent **Royal Bank Plaza**⋆

Ontario Tourism

Roy Thomson Hall and the Financial District

(D), designed by Boris Zerafa. Completed in 1976, the 41-storey and 26-storey gold reflecting-glass towers are linked by a 40m/130ft-high glass-walled banking hall, entry point to the underground city. A suspended sculpture of 8,000 aluminum tubes, the work of renowned Venezuelan artist Jesus Rafael Soto, dominates the interior of the hall.

The tiered, aqua-glass towers of **Brookfield Place,** (formerly BCE Place) designed by Spanish architect Santiago Calatrava, abut a lower central building bisected into matching office wings by an elaborate arched, aluminum **atrium.** The complex is also the home of the 🅺🅸🅳🆂 **Hockey Hall of Fame**★ **(E)**. Here, the original Stanley Cup is on display in the stately, domed lobby (1886) of the former Bank of Montreal building. *(Take the escalator to lower level; ♿ ◷ open year-round Mon–Fri 10am–5pm, Sat 9:30am–6pm, Sun 10:30am–5pm; ◷ closed Jan 1 & Dec 25; ☜$13. ☏416-360-7765; www.hhof.com).*

Four buildings (1931 to 1972) form **Commerce Court,** a 57-storey stainless-steel tower, head office of the Canadian Imperial Bank of Commerce, designed by famed architect I.M. Pei.

Opposite Commerce Court, an "erector-set" canopy marks the entrance to the slender 68-storey **Scotia Plaza** (1988) by Boris Zerafa. It is distinguished by a V-shaped wedge at its summit.

First Canadian Place consists of a 72-storey white tower (1975) housing the Bank of Montreal and the 36-storey tower (1983) containing the **Toronto Stock Exchange (F)** *(✕♿🅿◷ open year-round Mon–Fri 8:30am–5pm; ◷ closed major holidays; ☏416-947-4670 or 888-873-8392; www.tsx.com).* Stock Market Place, a ground-level interactive **visitor centre,** offers mock trader terminals, free Internet access and a giant wall of TV panels showing investment information. Connecting the towers is a three-level plaza with elegant shops and an attractive water wall. Under Adelaide Street, the PATH walkway leads to a grouping of shops known as the Lanes and another called the Plaza Shops, which extend to Sheraton Centre.

Designed by Boris Zerafa, the multifaceted glass towers of **Sun Life Centre**★ (1984) frame the east and west sides of University Avenue at King Street. Near the entrance to the 28-storey east tower, an outdoor sculpture by Sorel Etrog suggests a massive wheel-based tool.

Roy Thomson Hall★★

60 Simcoe St. ●St. Andrew. ♿ ⬥ Visit by guided tour (1hr) only, year-round, call for hours. ☜$7. Reservations required. ☏416-593-4822. www.roythomson.com.

Resembling a large inverted bowl, this glass-sheathed concert hall, named for Canadian newspaper magnate Roy Thomson and designed by **Arthur**

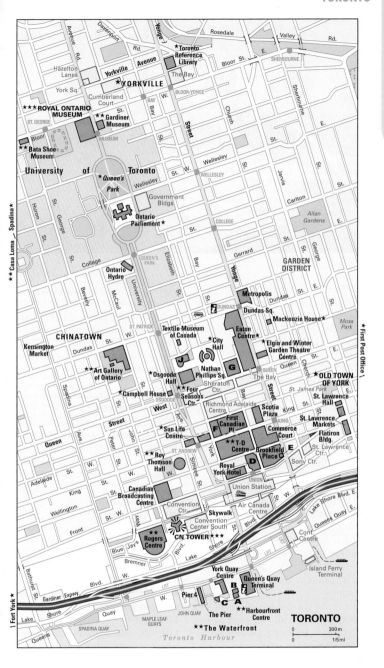

Toronto Harbour

TORONTO

0   300 m

0   1/5 mi

Erickson, dominates the corner of King and Simcoe streets. Home of the Toronto Symphony, the hall opened in 1982 and still retains its acoustical superiority. To insulate the performance area, a thick circular passageway with entry doors at intervals creates a "sound lock." Transparent at night when illuminated, the diamond-shaped exterior panels shimmer in daylight, their blue cast a reflection of the sky.

Ontario Tourism

Ice-skating at City Hall

On Front Street, south of Roy Thomson Hall, the concrete box-shaped 10-storey **Canadian Broadcasting Centre,** built in the Deconstructivist style in 1992, was designed by Philip Johnson.

City Hall Area★
●*Osgoode or Queen*
With its crescent-shaped towers and mushroom-like council chamber, **City Hall**★, completed in 1965, was the symbol of Toronto until supplanted by icons the CN Tower and Rogers Centre. The masterpiece by Finland's **Viljo Revell** remains a landmark nevertheless.
Spacious **Nathan Phillips Square** (named for a former mayor), with its wide, arch-covered reflecting pool, attracts crowds of ice-skaters in winter. The siting of Henry Moore's outdoor bronze sculpture *The Archer* on the grounds led to the sizable collection of his pieces in Toronto's Art Gallery of Ontario.
Occupying the east side of the square, **Old City Hall**★ **(G)**, designed by Toronto-born **Edward J. Lennox** (1855-1933), houses the provincial courts. Extending several blocks on Yonge Street between Queen and Dundas streets, **Eaton Centre**★ *(●Queen.* ✕&🄿◖*open year-round Mon–Fri 10am–9pm, Sat 9:30am–7pm, Sun noon–6pm; ☎416-598-8560; www.torontoeatoncentre.com)* is a five-level office/shopping complex designed by Eberhard Zeidler with trees,

plants, fountains and natural lighting. Note the aerial sculpture *Flight Stop* by Toronto's Michael Snow, a flock of soaring fibreglass Canadian geese.
The Hudson's Bay Company ("The Bay") store can be reached by a covered walkway across Queen Street.

Elgin and Winter Garden Theatre Centre★
189 Yonge St. Opposite Eaton Centre north of Queen St. ●*Queen.* &⬩◖*Visit by guided tour (1hr 30min) only, Thu 5pm, Sat 11am.* ⬩*$10. Box office Mon–Sat 11am–5pm, or until show time performance days.* ◐*Closed Dec 25.* ☎*416-314-2871. www. heritagefdn.on.ca.*
Reopened in 1989 after extensive restoration, this national historic site houses one of the few remaining double-decker theatres in the world. Designed by Thomas Lamb, the 1,500-seat Elgin and the 1,000-seat Winter Garden opened in 1913 and 1914 respectively as vaudeville, and later, silent-film houses. The Elgin theatre is reached through a gilded lobby of Corinthian pilasters and arched mirrors. A seven-storey marble staircase leads to the fanciful Winter Garden, with its ceiling of hanging beech boughs.

Mackenzie House★
82 Bond St. ●*Dundas.* ◐*Open May–Labour Day Tue–Sun noon–5pm. Sept–Dec Tue–Fri noon–4pm, weekends noon–5pm. Rest of the year weekends*

noon–5pm. ⊙*Closed major holidays.*
$4 (holidays $5.50). ☎*416-392-6915.*
*www.toronto.ca/culture/mackenzie_*
house.htm.

This 19C brick row house was the last
home of William Lyon Mackenzie, the
rebel leader and publisher. Rooms on
the three floors have been restored to
the 1850s period. In the modern annex
at the rear is a replica of his **print shop**
with a hand-operated flatbed press.

Osgoode Hall★

130 Queen St. W. ●Osgoode. Quiet is nec-
essary, since courts may be in session.
Guided tours (1hr) May–Aug Mon–Fri
10am & 2pm. ☎*416-947-3315 or 800-668-*
7380. www.lsuc.on.ca.

Home to the Supreme Court of Ontario
and the Law Society of Upper Canada,
this stately Neoclassical-style edifice is
set on expansive lawns west of Nathan
Phillips Square. Erected in 1867 allegedly
to keep cows out, an ornate cast-iron
fence isolates the judicial bastion from
the bustle of the city.

The two-tiered, arched interior courtyard induces admiration, as does the
magnificent **Great Library**—said to be
"perhaps the noblest room in Canada."
North of Osgoode Hall stands the provincial **Court House (J)**, with its circular rotunda and walkway to Nathan
Phillips Square.

Four Seasons Centre for the Performing Arts★★

145 Queen St. W. ●Osgoode Guided
tours (1hr) most Sat at 11:45am and noon
(check calendar on website for dates).
$7. Box office open Mon–Sat 11am–
7pm. ☎*416-363-8231. www.fourseasons*
centre.ca.

Opposite Osgoode Hall, on the south
side of Queen Street, rises Toronto's
long-awaited venue for the Canadian
Opera Company and the National Ballet of Canada. Opened in 2006, the new
performing arts centre was designed
by Canadian architect Jack Diamond.
The overwhelming aesthetics of the
multi-storey glass and structural-steel
lobby, called the City Room, are controversial, but the 2,071-seat R. Fraser
Elliott Hall offers excellent acoustics
and good sightlines from all seats in the
intimate horseshoe-shaped auditorium.
The small 150-seat Richard Bradshaw
Amphitheatre, named for the COC's
beloved general director (1944-2007),
is the venue for free concerts offered at
noon and early evening *(check website*
for schedule).

Campbell House★

160 Queen St. W. (University Ave. at Queen
St.) ●Osgoode. Visit by guided tour
(30min) only, mid-May–Labour Day
Tue–Fri 9:30am–4:30pm, weekends
noon–4:30pm. Rest of the year Tue–Fri
9:30am–4:30pm. ⊙Closed Jan 1 & Dec

Four Seasons Centre for the Performing Arts

25–26. ⌾$4.50. ☎416-597-0227. www. campbellhousemuseum.ca.

Once belonging to **Sir William Campbell** (1758-1834), chief justice of Upper Canada from 1825 to 1829, the Georgian brick mansion was built in 1822; it was moved to this site in 1972 from its location in historic York. The restored rooms contain some fine period pieces and surviving portraits of the Campbell family.

The headquarters of Canada Life Assurance Co. rise just behind Campbell House. A prominent landmark, the building is distinguished at night by its tower, the lights of which indicate the barometer reading.

Art Gallery of Ontario★★

317 Dundas St. W. ●St. Patrick. ✕&◯Open year-round Wed–Fri 10am–9pm, weekends 10am-5:30pm. ◯Closed Jan 1, Dec 25. ⌾$18. ☎416-979-6648. www.ago. net. ◉May be closed for renovation. In late fall 2008, the museum is scheduled to reopen; it closed in late 2007 to re-hang its collection.

Conceived by Toronto-born architect Frank Gehry, the AGO's massive $250-million expansion and renovation increase art-viewing space by 50 percent. Major elements of the transformation include a new glass-and-wood facade along Dundas Street, a four-storey south wing for exhibiting contemporary art, and a large gathering space with a two-storey museum store, a restaurant and a cafe, a lecture hall, a members' lounge and space for temporary exhibits. The project was propelled by the donation of nearly 2,000 works and $70 million by the late Canadian businessman Kenneth Thomson (Second Baron Thomson of Fleet). The donation includes Canadian and European paintings, Inuit sculpture and a remarkable collection of 75 medieval ivory carvings.

The gallery retains the world's largest public collection of works by renowned British sculptor **Henry Moore** (1898-1986). The permanent collection ranges from 15C European paintings to international contemporary art and includes Canadian art from the 18C to the present.

Henry Moore Sculpture Centre★★

The centre owns more than 1,000 of Moore's works, including 689 prints, 139 original plasters and bronzes and 74 drawings. The centre was designed by the artist to use natural light from the glass-panelled roof. At night, the effect of artificial lighting, with its interplay of shadows on the sculpted shapes, is stunning.

Permanent Collection★★

The **European Collection** covers the Old Masters, Impressionism and early-20C movements. Displayed in several galleries, the **Canadian Collection** features 18C to contemporary works.

Henry Moore Sculpture Centre, Art Gallery of Ontario

Ontario Tourism

Contemporary **Inuit art** on exhibit dates from 1910 to the present. Contemporary art and 20C art are displayed in galleries on both levels.

The Grange★
Entrance through art gallery's Agora restaurant and sculpture atrium.
This Georgian brick mansion (c.1817) was the home of lawyer, politician and Family Compact stalwart **Henry John Boulton** (1790-1870). In 1875 the Grange became the home of well-known scholar **Goldwin Smith,** Regius Professor of History at Oxford, who made it a centre of intellectual pursuits and progressive ideas. The mansion is meticulously furnished to give the aura of Family Compact days. Of special interest is the beautiful curved staircase in the entry hall. The basement contains kitchens typical of a 19C gentleman's house.
The residence faces lovely Grange Park *(open to the public via street access)*, from which visitors can appreciate the mansion's gracious facade.

Textile Museum of Canada
55 Centre Ave. ●St. Patrick. ♿⏰Open year-round daily 11am–5pm (Wed 8pm). ⏰Closed major holidays. ▱$12. ☎416-599-5321. www.textilemuseum.ca.
Occupying two floors of a high-rise hotel/condominium complex, the only Canadian museum devoted exclusively to textiles features traditional and contemporary works from around the world.

Queen's Park★

Based on E.J. Lennox's landscape scheme of 1876, this oval-shaped park is the setting for Ontario's Legislative Assembly (the provincial parliament) and nearby government buildings. To the west and east sprawls the **University of Toronto,** Canada's largest university, perhaps best known for its medical school where, in 1921, **Frederick Banting** and **Charles Best** succeeded in isolating insulin. To the south, the curved, mirrored, multi-storied headquarters building of **Ontario Hydro** (1975, Kenneth R. Cooper) rises above the surroundings.

COLLEGE STRIP
●*Bathurst, Queen's Park.* If you want to know where U of T and Ryerson students hang out, College Street *(between Bathurst and Shaw Sts.)* in Little Italy is the place. Quirky boutiques beckon during daylight hours, while lively clubs and pubs draw in late-night revellers. **Motoretta** *(no.554)* sells vintage Vespas in flashy colours along with related paraphernalia *(☎416-925-1818; www.motoretta.ca).* Diner-style **Café Diplomatico** *(no. 594)* is a combo coffee house/ice-cream haunt *(☎416-534-4637; www.diplomatico.ca; open Sun-Thu 8am–2am, Fri–Sat 8am–3am),* where latte lovers lay back on the outside patio. **Brasserie Aix** *(no. 584)* offers inspired French cuisine amid high-ceilinged elegance *(☎416-588-7377).* Streamlined **Xacutti** *(no. 503)* offers "new Indian" food in a hip setting *(☎416-323-3957).* To begin or end your evening, enter **Souz Dal** *(no. 636),* an intimate lounge specializing in flavoured martinis *(☎416-537-1883).*

The building has no furnace or heating plant; instead, energy given off by artificial lighting, equipment and people is stored in thermal reservoirs in the basement and recirculated.

Ontario Parliament★
●*Queen's Park. ✕♿⟲Guided tours (30min) leave from information counter at front doors, Victoria Day–Labour Day daily 9am–4pm. Rest of the year daily 10am–4pm. View legislature in session (call to ensure government is in session) from public galleries Mon–Wed 1:30pm–6pm, Thu 10am–noon, 1:30pm–6pm. ⏰Closed major holidays. ☎416-325-7500. www.ontla.on.ca.*
Dominating the south end of the park, the imposing sandstone 1893 **Legislative Building** (also called Parliament Buildings) typifies Richardsonian Romanesque architecture.
The ponderous exterior belies the interior's elegant beauty, particularly the white-marbled **west wing,** rebuilt after a fire in 1909, and the stately **legislative chamber,** with its rich mahogany and

sycamore. On view is the 200-year-old mace *(ground floor)*, a ceremonial gold "club" mandatory at House proceedings. Taken by the Americans during their 1813 assault on York, it was returned years later by President F.D. Roosevelt.

Gardiner Museum of Ceramic Art★★

111 Queen's Park (across from the Royal Ontario Museum). ✕ ♿ ⏰ *Open year-round Mon–Fri 10am–6pm (Fri 9pm), weekends 10am–5pm.* ⏰ *Closed Jan 1, Nov 20 & Dec 25.* 💳 *$12 (no charge Fri 4pm–9pm and 1st Fri of month).* ☎416-586-8080. www.gardinermuseum.on.ca.

Located in a modern granite building, this museum, the project of collectors George and Helen Gardiner, features pottery and porcelain from a variety of countries and cultures.

The Pottery Gallery *(ground floor)* show-cases works of the **Ancient Americas,** specifically from Mexico, and Central and South America, dating from 2000 BC to about AD 1500—primarily figurines, vessels and bowls of Olmec, Toltec, Aztec and other cultures. Also included is 15C and 16C **Italian majolica** and 17C English tin-glazed **delftware.**

The Porcelain Gallery *(2nd floor)* features **18C porcelains** of Du Paquier, Sèvres (characterized by bright yellows), the great English companies—Worcester, Derby, Chelsea—and others. Highlights are the Meissenware pieces. The Bell collection of blue-and-white Chinese porcelain, attractively presented in glass wall cabinets, contains close to 200 pieces.

The restaurant, called **Jamie Kennedy at the Gardiner** after its chef, opened in 2006 and has gained a considerable reputation.

Royal Ontario Museum★★★

● *Museum.*

Renowned for extensive research, this enormous museum, commonly referred to as the ROM, is housed in an H-shaped, five-floor building at Avenue Road and Bloor Street. Maintaining over 20 departments in art, archaeology and the natural sciences, the museum, known especially for its East Asian holdings, possesses a remarkable collection of six-million-plus artifacts and artworks from around the world.

The ROM continues to expand. Expected completion of its $270 million **Renaissance project** is 2009. Part of that project, the Michael Lee-Chin Crystal addition, designed by Daniel Libeskind, opened in mid-2007. It includes a new entrance, main lobby on Bloor Street West, seven permanent galleries and a restaurant. New galleries will open in 2008 and 2009.

▸ **Orient Yourself:** Located on the southwest corner of Bloor Street and Avenue Road, the ROM is best reached by foot or subway. Once inside, use the museum map for detailed orientation.

🅿 **Parking:** The closest municipal lot is at 9 Bedford Road *(one block west of Avenue Rd.)* and at 37 Yorkville Ave. *(east of Bay St.).* Metered parking is available on nearby streets but can be difficult to find.

🚫 **Don't Miss:** The Chinese collection, especially the Ming Tomb; the new Temerty Dinosaur Galleries in the Michael Lee-Chin Crystal addition, Level 2.

🕐 **Organizing Your Time:** Plan to spend at least 3–4 hours, but take a meal break at the Food Studio *(level B1)* or in the ROMkids Lunch Room *(level B1).*

Especially for Kids: The Hands-on Biodiversity gallery *(level 2)* and the Discovery gallery *(level 2).* Check "ROM Kids" on the website for current news.

Visit

100 Queen's Park. ✕ ♿ ⏰ *Open year-round daily 10am–5:30pm (Fri 9:30pm; Dec 24 & 31 4pm).* ⏰ *Closed Jan 1 & Dec 25.* 💳 *$20 (free Wed 4:30pm–5:30pm).* ☎416-586-8000. www.rom.on.ca. *Due to ongoing construction, the following galleries will not reopen until 2009: 20th Century Design, Byzantium, Rome, Nubia, Earth and Early Life, and Minerals and Gems.*

Ming Tomb

A 2008 reopening is planned for: Africa, the Americas and Asia, the Pacific, the Middle East, Textiles and Costumes and South Asia. The museum's floor plan, available at the information desk in the entrance rotunda, is most useful.

Level 1

The grand entrance **rotunda** is vaulted, with an exquisite domed **ceiling** of golden mosaic tessarae. Before entering the galleries, note the two **totem poles** in the stairwells. Crafted of red cedar by the Nisga'a and Haida peoples of British Columbia in the 19C, the poles are so tall that their upper sections can be viewed from the second and third floors. The taller pole depicts the family history of the chief who owed it. South of the rotunda lies the Sigmund Samuel Gallery, with its unequalled collection of Canadian art, historical artifacts and decorative arts; and the Daphne Cockwell Gallery, where exhibits trace First Nations culture and history.

The outstanding exhibit on this floor, in the Philosopher's Walk Wing, is the **Chinese collection,** one of the largest and most important of its kind outside China. Spanning nearly 6,000 years, the exhibits in this recently renovated space, date from the Shang dynasty 1523 BC (the Chinese Bronze Age) to the overthrow of the Qing or Manchu dynasty (1644-1911).

The celebrated **ROM Gallery of Chinese Architecture** contains, as its star attraction, the **Ming Tomb,** the only complete example in the Western world. It is reportedly the burial place of Zu Dashou, a 17C general who served the last Ming emperors and lived into the Qing period. Equally spectacular is a corner of a **17C Imperial Palace,** which visitors can walk around and enter. A new exhibit of artifacts traces the development of Chinese architecture from the 2C to the 17C.

The new **Joey and Toby Tanenbaum Gallery** groups a wealth of rare Chinese artifacts (tomb figures, bronze containers, jade carvings) into coherent exhibits illustrating China's history and culture. The **Matthews Family Court of Sculpture** contains 2,000 years of Buddhist sculpture, as well as pieces showing the influence of Islam, Judaism and Christianity.

Remarkable for its ink and colour clay wall paintings, the **Bishop White Gallery** simulates the interior of a Northern Chinese temple. Life-size polychromed and gilded statues of *bodhisattvas* (those enlightened, compassionate individuals destined for Buddha status) of the 12C-14C stand in the centre. **Korean and Japanese** art are presented in separate galleries in the Philosopher's Walk Wing. Among the most dramatic works in the gallery of **Korean Art** is an eight-panelled colour and ink painting on silk titled *One Hundred Boys at Play*.

The Herman Herzog Levy Gallery is devoted to changing exhibits of **East Asian** art drawn from the ROM's extensive collections, which include murals, monumental statues and a collection of small Buddhist and Daoist bronzes.

Level 2

Kids Natural history exhibits occupy this floor, the highlight of which are the magnificent, reassembled **dinosaurs** in authentic settings, newly installed in the James and Louise Temerty Galleries in the recently opened (2007) Michael Lee-Chin Crystal addition. The planned centrepiece is an enormous Barosaurus (late Jurassic, about 150 million years ago) discovered after much searching, in the fall of 2007—in the museum's own collection! When assembled, the largest dinosaur skeleton in Canada will be seen through the Crystal building's glass windows, seeming to overhang Bloor Street. Many of the collection's skeletons come from Upper Cretaceous rocks exposed in the badlands of the Red Deer River Valley in central Alberta. The glass atrium of the **Bird Gallery** is filled with Canadian geese, turkeys, owls, ducks and an assortment of smaller birds preserved in flight. The **Reptile Gallery** shows the remarkable diversity of these cold-blooded animals. The **Age of Mammals** is a new gallery containing enormous skeletons of Ice Age mammals, in an exhibit tracing development from the demise of the dinosaurs. The **Bat Cave** is a lifelike reconstruction of the St. Clair Cave in Jamaica, complete with hundreds of handmade bats.

Hands-On Biodiversity is a two-level interactive gallery that lets visitors crawl into a simulated wolf's den; identify leaves, sounds and tracks; and touch tusks, horns, bones, skulls and skins, among other activities. The **Discovery Gallery** is an innovative space with interactive exhibits for children, including costumes to try on.

Other galleries scheduled to open in 2008 and 2009 are the Schad Gallery of Biodiversity: Life in Crisis, and the Teck Cominco Suite of Earth Sciences Galleries, which will include the Inco Limited Gallery of Minerals (Dynamic Earth) and the S.R. Perren Gallery of Gold and Gems.

Level 3

This level, like Level 1, houses the ROM's World Culture galleries. The new Sir Christopher Ondaatje **South Asian** Gallery showcases textiles, jewellery, sculpture, arms and other artifacts, while the **Wirth Gallery of the Middle East** concentrates on developments in the **Middle East,** the cradle of civilization and modern religions.

The **Galleries of Africa: Egypt** exhibit depicts daily life via tools, utensils, jewellery and miniature figures. The section on **religion** includes coffins, animal mummies, canopic jars, the remarkably preserved **Antjau mummy** and the upright mummy case of a female musi-

---

Foot Notes

England's Edward II is credited with initiating the measurement of the "foot" in 1320. His own foot measured 36 barley corns; each corn was a third of an inch, making the total of 12 inches equal to one foot. In England in the 14C, the length of a shoe's pointed toe was regulated by law and depended upon the wearer's social status. The height of a shoe's heel also conveyed the social importance of the wearer. Thus the wealthy were, and still are, termed "well-heeled." The origin of calling someone a "square" is said to derive from the wearing of square-toed shoes long after they were in fashion.

Source: *Bata Shoe Museum*

"Shoes are such a personal artifact. They tell you about the owner's social status, habits, culture and religion. That's what makes them special."

Sonja Bata, founder, Bata Shoe Museum

cian. The **Punt wall reliefs,** sculptural casts from the temple of Queen Hatshepsut (1503-1482 BC), illustrate her trade mission along the Nile. The new **Gallery of Africa, the Americas and Asia Pacific** displays a great range of objects, many of which have been hidden away for years.

The **Gallery of the Bronze Age Aegean** showcases objects that pre-date the rise of classical Greece (3000-700 BC); Archaic, classical and Helenist marble sculpture, gold coins and decorated amphora are displayed in the **Gallery of Greece** (700-31 BC), The **Gallery of Ancient Cyprus** focuses on that corner of the Greek world (2200-30 BC).

The **Samuel European Galleries** concentrate on decorative arts from medieval times to the present. The **Lee Collection** assembles medieval and Renaissance wares of gold and silver. In the **Arms and Armour** gallery, armaments from medieval chain mail to modern-day weaponry can be seen. **Culture and Context** presents partial-room reconstructions, such as a Victorian parlour (1860-85). Art objects and furnishings from medieval times to the 20C are displayed in the South Wing.

Level 4

The new Patricia Harris Gallery of Textiles and Costume, opened in the Michael Lee-Chin Crystal addition in spring 2008, mounts changing exhibits of the ROM's extensive collection of costumes and textiles, ranging from ancient China through the present day. The display area permits visitors to see the back of woven textiles, and to see garments in three dimensions.

Additional Sights

Bata Shoe Museum★★

327 Bloor St. W. ●*St. George.* ♿ 🕐*Open year-round Mon–Sat 10am–5pm (Thu 8pm), Sun noon–5pm.* 🕐*Closed Good Friday, Dec 25.* ✎*$12. (no charge Thu 5pm–8pm).* ☎*416-979-7799. www.bata shoemuseum.ca.*

Housed in a five-storey building designed by renowned architect **Ray-**

mond Moriyama** to resemble a shoebox, this unique museum draws on its 12,500-piece collection to illustrate a 4,500-year history of shoemaking and mankind's footwear. It was opened in 1995 to house the collections of Sonja Bata, who began a worldwide search for footwear beginning in the 1940s.

Exhibits change three times a year. Shoes in the semi-permanent exhibit, titled "Footwear through the Ages," range from 3,550-year-old Theban funerary slippers and 1,500-year-old Anasazi sandals to Mahatma Gandhi's leather chappals (c.1940s) and Princess Diana's fuchsia kid pumps. Special exhibits are often themed and arranged by period, geographical location or ethnic group. On exhibit through November 2009, "Native North American Footwear" showcases some 90 pairs of shoes, including Cherokee and Woodlands moccasins, hard-soled beaded shoes worn by the Northern Cheyenne and deerskin Zuni wedding boots.

Yorkville★

●*Bay. www.bloor-yorkville.com.*

This upscale urban neighbourhood represents all that is chic in Toronto—and a remarkable transformation from the small village established by Joseph Bloor in 1830. Between Yonge Street and Avenue Road, **Yorkville Avenue** presents charming Victorian houses converted to expensive boutiques or trendy cafes sporting the latest architectural facades.

In York Square at the corner of Avenue Road and Yorkville Avenue, shops surround an interior brick courtyard where summer dining is alfresco. Behind the square lies posh Hazelton Lanes *(open during business hours)*, a labyrinthian shopping/office/condominium complex (1978) designed by Boris Zerafa. On the other side of Yorkville Avenue, Cumberland Court is a rambling enclosure of old and new shops, eateries and offices, with a passageway to Cumberland Street.

Toronto Reference Library★

789 Yonge St. ●*Bloor-Yonge.* ♿🕐*Open Mon–Thu 9:30am–8:30pm, Fri 9:30am–5:30pm, Sat 9am–5pm.* 🕐*Closed Sun.* ☎*416-395-5577. www.tpl.toronto.on.ca.*

ALL THE BEST

●Summerhill. 1101 Yonge St. ☎416-928-3330. www.allthebestfinefoods.com. In Sept. 2008, the shops will re-open in the renovated Scrivener Square development. Until then, the cheese and gourmet food store remains on Yonge St., while the bakery and party store are at 5 Scrivener Sq. **The Best's Bakery** sells a bounteous selection of berry crisps, tarts, cheesecakes, breads and pastries. The **Gourmet Foods and Cheese Store** offers ready-to-go food as well as an array of Canadian and imported cheese, exotic sauces and gourmet supplies. The **Party Store** sells snazzy table linen, candles, cutlery, wine coolers and picnic packs. When you tire of shopping, step next door into **Patachou** French pastry shop *(1095 Yonge St.; ☎416-927-1105)* for an invigorating cup of espresso, and perhaps take home a baguette.

An architectural gem designed by Raymond Moriyama, this massive 1973 brick and glass building contains Canada's most extensive public library with 4.5 million items and 50 miles of stacks on 5 floors. It is part of the vast Toronto Public Library system, which includes 99 branches.

Rising from a wide, light-filled centre, the tiered balconies are bordered by solid undulating balustrades. In a cozy corner on the fifth floor is a tiny room *(access from 4th floor)* brimming with the **Arthur Conan Doyle Collection**—famed Sherlock Holmes stories, Sherlockian criticism, Doyle's autobiography, historical novels, poetry and other writings. Worn Victorian furnishings complement mementos of the great detective's presence.

Casa Loma★★

1 Austin Terrace. ●Dupont, then climb steps. ✕ 🅿 *($2.75/hr)* 🕐 *Open year-round daily 9:30am–5pm (last admission 4pm).* 🕐 *Closes 1pm Christmas Eve; closed Dec 25.* ☜ *$16.* ☎ *416-923-1171. www.casaloma.org.*

This enormous sandstone castle, completed in 1914, was the lavish 98-room residence of prominent industrialist Sir **Henry Pellatt.** Maintained since 1937 by the Kiwanis Club, the medieval mansion is a popular tourist attraction.

Seven storeys in height, the castle boasts two towers—one open-air, the other enclosed—which offer good views of the city; secret passageways; and a 244m/800ft underground tunnel to the magnificent **carriage house** and stables. The palatial residence includes

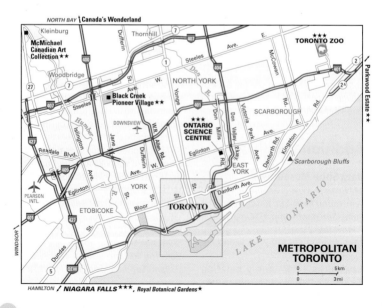

HAMILTON / **NIAGARA FALLS** ★★★, Royal Botanical Gardens ★

21 fireplaces, a **great hall** (22m/70ft ceiling), a marble-floor conservatory, an oak-panelled drawing room and a library for 10,000 books. Especially well appointed are the **Round Room** with its exquisite Louis XV tapestry furnishings, the **Windsor Room** and Lady Pellatt's suite.

Spadina Museum★

285 Spadina Rd. ●*Dupont, then climb steps.* ♿ 🚗 *Visit by guided tour (1hr) only, Apr–Labour Day Tue–Sun & holiday Mon noon–5pm. Sept–Dec Tue–Fri noon–4pm, weekends noon–5pm. Jan–Mar Sat noon–5pm.* ⊘*Closed Dec 25.* ⊚*$6 ($6.75 on holidays).* ☎ *416-392-6910. www.toronto.ca/culture/spadina.htm.*

The Spadina Museum is a historic house and garden that overlooks its 2.5ha/6-acre grounds in a fashionable residential district. The 50-room brick mansion was home to businessman **James Austin** and his heirs.

In 1866 Austin, a successful grocer who eventually headed Consumers' Gas and founded the Dominion Bank, acquired the estate. His son added the spacious billiard room in 1898 and in 1907, the terraces and porte-cochere. The third floor, with its hipped roof and pedimented dormers, was built in 1912.

Reflecting the grandeur of Victorian and Edwardian styles, the spacious **drawing room** with its matching striped seating, and the airy wicker-furnished **palm room** show the comforts the Austin family expected.

Metro Sights

Ontario Science Centre★★★

🔤*770 Don Mills Rd., 11km/7mi north of downtown (22km/14mi by car via Don Valley Pkwy. to Eglinton Ave.).* ●*Eglinton and then no. 34 Eglinton East bus (to Don Mills Rd. stop).* ✖♿🅿⊘*Open year-round daily 10am–5pm.* ⊘*Closed Dec 25.* ⊚*$18 ($25 with Omnimax).* ☎*416-696-1000. www.ontariosciencecentre.ca. Demonstrations and Omnimax films daily. For times and locations, check notice board at the bottom of escalator, level C.*

Cascading down the Don River ravine, this sizable complex, designed by Raymond Moriyama and opened in 1969, takes full advantage of its natural site. Starting in 2003, a $47.5 million renovation has modernized about a third of exhibit areas. Approaching the entrance, visitors are greeted by new landscaping, including concrete ramps softened by grass and shrubbery, and the FUNtain, a splashy water sculpture by Steve Mann that includes tubular "water organs" whereon visitors can play tunes by stopping water jets with their fingers. New major installations are *Cloud* by David Rokeby, which hangs from the ceiling of the entrance hall, and *Lotic Meander* by Stacy Levy, in the park area outside.

At the front entrance, the Omnimax Theatre shows 3-D films on subjects such as the ocean floor or hurricanes. On the next floor down, Level C, **Kid-Spark** attracts young children with its tactile exhibits such as a churning tub of water, a kids' supermarket (for honing math skills), or a sound studio where they can experiment with their own voices. The newly renovated **Space Hall** includes spectacular photos from the Hubble Telescope, a cloud chamber visitors can enter and the ever-popular self-piloted "rocket chair." On level E (the Mezzanine), the **Human Body** exhibit lets visitors see inside the body using digital imaging.

On Level D, the **Weston Family Innovation Centre,** opened in 2006, is geared toward teens and young adults with some 50 hands-on interactive exhibits that focus on film, video and music. The **Mindworks** exhibit examines how the mind functions, with games to test reasoning, communications and memory. **A Question of Truth** explores how scientific investigation is influenced by beliefs and preconceptions. **The Sport Hall** not only demonstrates how science influences sports, but lets visitors test their prowess with both virtual sports and a real climbing wall. In the **Living Earth** exhibit, visitors explore a limestone cave and experience an indoor rain forest, while the venerable **Science Arcade** offers humorous electricity demonstrations. Temporary exhibits occupy spaces throughout the building.

Toronto Zoo★★★

Kids *361A Old Finch Ave., in Scarborough. 35km/22mi northeast of downtown. ●Kennedy, transfer to bus 86A.* ✕♿🅿🕐*Open late May–Labour Day daily 9am–7:30pm. Jan–early Mar & early Oct–Dec daily 9:30am–4:30pm. Rest of the year daily 9am–6pm.* 🕐*Closed Dec 25. ☞$20. ☎416-392-5929. www.toronto zoo.com. Site map is available at the entrance. Begin by boarding the narrated shuttle, the Zoomobile (Jul–Labour Day daily 10am–7pm; rest of the year Mon–Fri 10am–6pm, weekends 10am–6pm; ☞$7 all-day pass), which provides a good overview of the main attractions. Disembark at the Serengeti station and continue on foot. ⚠Some animals may not be on display during new construction: check online for specific animals.*

Opened in 1974, this world-class zoological park features a remarkable variety of wildlife on 287ha/710 acres of tableland and forest. The 5,000 animals are divided into six "zoogeographic" regions: Africa, Australasia, Eurasia, the Americas, Indo-Malaya and Canada. Among the 460 species represented are numerous endangered or rare animals such as the Siberian tiger, the snow leopard, the Malayan tapir, the pygmy hippopotamus, the Indian rhinoceros and a small herd of extremely rare Central Asian Przewalski's horses. Designed by Raymond Moriyama, harmoniously integrated glass and wood pavilions provide shelter for animals unadapted to Canada's climate.

The renovated **Australasian Pavilion** reopened in spring 2008. It retains the ever-popular Komodo dragon couple, the kookaburra bird and the hairy-nosed wombat. A new Great Barrier Reef exhibit features coloured fish as well as sharks, seahorses and a live coral reef. The popular **Africa Pavilion,** abundant with tropical vegetation and exotic birds, is home to lowland gorillas and other primates as well as Canada's largest herd of African elephants.

Rides and special activities for kids ($5–$6) are available, such as camel and pony rides, Safari Simulator and face painting.

Black Creek Pioneer Village★★

Kids *1000 Murray Ross Parkway. 29km/ 18mi northwest of downtown. ●Yonge and Finch, transfer to Steeles bus no. 60.* ✕🅿🕐*Open Jul–Labour Day Mon–Fri 10am–5pm, weekends & holidays 11am–5pm. May–Jun & Sept–Dec Mon–Fri 9:30am–4pm, weekends & holidays 11am–4:30pm.* 🕐*Closed Dec 25, 26. $13. ☎416-736-1733. www. blackcreek.ca. Site plan is distributed at the entrance.*

Occupying 30 acres in a lovely country setting, this village is a re-creation of a 19C crossroads community representative of the Toronto area. It comprises 40 buildings, including 5 from the original farm established between 1816 and 1832 by Pennsylvania-German settlers, and a collection of 19C structures moved to the site.

Upon exiting the **orientation centre,** visitors enter mid-19C Ontario, among abundant greenery and dirt roads flanked by wooden sidewalks and split-rail fences. Highlights of the visit include the tinsmith shop; the **Stong farm;** the Half Way House, a spacious white inn with a two-tiered veranda; **Roblin's Mill,** a handsome four-storey water-powered stone gristmill; and the printing office, complete with a working flatbed press. Costumed guides demonstrate traditional 19C crafts and trades; vegetable gardens and farm animals complete the depiction of rural life in Ontario in the 1800s.

Excursions

Canada's Wonderland

Kids *Entrance at 9740 Jane St., in Vaughn. 30km/19mi north by Hwy. 400 and Rutherford Rd. Express "GO" bus from ●Yorkdale or York Mills.* ✕♿🅿🕐*Open early May–early Nov daily 10am (closing times vary). ☞Admission packages vary. Consult website or phone. ☎905-832-8131. www.canadaswonderland.com.*

This theme park features some 200 attractions, including rides, both thrilling and less so, with lots of activities for children. There is an outdoor wave pool with the 8ha/20-acre water park. Shows, events and concerts are offered on an on-going basis.

Mr. McGregor's House

10503 Islington Ave., Kleinburg. ☎*905-893-2508.* For a delightful afternoon tea, coffee break or lunch after visiting the McMichael gallery in the village of Kleinburg, enter this charming yellow house, named for the Beatrix Potter character, on the main street. McGregor's offers a bounty of tea cakes, cookies, tarts, fruit pies, nut breads, muffins, scones and other pastries—all labelled and set out on a large wooden table so guests can help themselves. An array of flavoured coffees and teas as well as juices and other beverages is also available. Eat inside in one of the whimsical dining rooms or outside at garden tables placed on the expansive backyard lawn, bordered with flowers and shaded by grand oaks.

McMichael Canadian Art Collection★★

10365 Islington Ave., in Kleinburg. About 40km/25mi north. Hwy. 400 to Major Mackenzie Dr., then west about 6km/4mi to Islington Ave., then north 1km/.6mi. ○✕&P *($5). Open year-round daily 10am–4pm (Sun until 5pm).* ○*Closed Dec 25.* ⊜*$15.* ☎*905-893-1121 or 888-213-1121 (Canada/US). www.mcmichael.com.*

Housed in log and fieldstone buildings among the wooded hills of the Humber Valley, this gallery features paintings by the first truly Canadian school—the **Group of Seven.** The gallery also owns a sizable collection of contemporary First Nations and Inuit art.

Though pioneer **Tom Thomson** (1877-1917) died before the group was formed, his influence was substantial. The original members were **Lawren Harris, A.Y. Jackson, J.E.H. MacDonald, Franklin Carmichael, Arthur Lismer, Freder-**ick Varley and **Frank Johnston.** Johnston left after the first exhibition; **A.J. Casson** joined the group in 1926. The group officially disbanded in 1932, but some members formed the Canadian Group of Painters, which had many of the same aims. In 1952 **Robert and Signe McMichael** bought land in rural Kleinburg, decorating their home with Group of Seven paintings. In 1965 they donated their famed collection and property to the province of Ontario. Subsequent gifts by such individuals as R.S. McLaughlin have enlarged the collection, which now totals some 6,000 works.

Examples of works by artists influenced by the seven, notably **Clarence Gagnon, Emily Carr** and **David Milne,** are also displayed. On exhibit upstairs are fine works by contemporary First Nations artists such as Clifford Maracle, **Norval Morrisseau, Daphne Odjig** and **Arthur Shilling.**

Spa Getaways

Hidden in the countryside an hour north of Toronto, **High Fields Country Inn & Spa (\$\$)** *(Concession 3, in Zephyr;* ☎*905-473-6132; www.highfields.com; check website for rates)* commands a hilltop overlooking Ontario's farmlands. A winding road leads to a large barn with horse pastures and the inn itself, complete with outdoor pool and tennis court. Paths groomed for guided nature walks or cross-country skiing thread the expansive property. The rambling main house holds overnight guest quarters, a dining area and treatment rooms. High Fields offers new-age techniques such as chakra and Japanese Reiki along with facials, wraps, massages and hydrotherapies. Breakfast, lunch and dinner **(\$\$\$)** are available.

Tucked away on 14 wooded acres in residential Port Hope, about an hour east of Toronto, **Ste. Anne's Country Inn & Spa, a Haldimand Hills Aveda Spa (\$\$\$\$\$)** *(175 Dorset St. W., in Grafton;* ☎*905-349-2493 or 888-346-6772; www.haldimand-hills.com)* welcomes guests to its grand porticoed mansion, appointed with Irish antiques, and surrounded by lushly landscaped grounds. Amenities include an outdoor pool, fitness room, sauna, chef-staffed kitchen, and dining room that affords a view of Lake Ontario. Body treatments include facials, manicures, pedicures, hydrotherapies, massages, wraps and exercise sessions.

Oshawa★★

POPULATION 152,000 – MAP P 108

Lying on the north shore of Lake Ontario, Oshawa is the centre of Canada's automobile industry. The industrial city is part of the Golden Horseshoe, a 60km/100mi horseshoe-shaped arc that stretches from Oshawa, east of Toronto, south and west to Hamilton, and wherein about a quarter of the country's manufacturing is based.

- **Information:** Tourist Information Centre, 2 Bloor St. E. *(corner Bloor & Simcoe Sts.)*. ☎905-725-4523 or 800-667-4292. www.oshawa.ca.
- ▶ **Orient Yourself:** Oshawa is on the north shore of Lake Ontario, 39km/24mi east of Toronto. Its downtown hub focuses on the vicinity of King Street and Simcoe Street South. A major shopping mall, Oshawa Centre, sits at the corner of King Street and Stevenson Road.
- P **Parking:** All the sights mentioned below have designated parking.
- ☺ **Don't Miss:** The Canadian Automotive Museum, for rare cars.
- ⏱ **Organizing Your Time:** Allow 4hrs to visit the museums, beginning with the automotive museum, which opens at 9am. End the morning at Parkwood estate, where you can eat lunch in either the garden or the greenhouse teahouse *(advance reservations required; ♿ see below)*.
- ♿ **Also See:** SOUTH CENTRAL ONTARIO

A Bit of History

Fur-Trading Hub – In the mid-18C, the French founded a trading post near Oshawa Creek to facilitate continued fur trade with the area's Mississauga Indians. Settlement took hold, and the village was eventually named Oshawa, an Ojibwa word meaning "across the other side of the stream or river."

Oshawa Today – In 1924 Oshawa attained city status. Today its fine harbour serves as one of the country's ports-of-entry. The downtown core is experiencing rejuvenation, enhanced by a number of building **murals** begun in 1995 *(contact the tourist office for a murals brochure or access a map online at www.oshawa.ca)*. Acres of parkland and three creeks thread the urban terrain, com-

Parkwood National Historic Site's Formal Garden

Butterill/Ontario Tourism

plemented by walking trails and paved bicycle paths. The city's name has long been synonymous with industrialist and philanthropist **Robert S. McLaughlin** (1871-1972), who furthered his father's carriage business. Attracted especially to its railroad and harbour facilities, the senior McLaughlin relocated to Oshawa in 1876. McLaughlin's carriage company eventually became the Canadian division of car-maker General Motors. The General Motors Centre, Oshawa's downtown entertainment venue, hosts the city's hockey team games as well as concerts and other citywide events.

Sights

Canadian Automotive Museum★

99 Simcoe St. South. ○*Open year-round Mon–Fri 9am–5pm, weekends 10am–6pm.* ○*Closed Dec 25.* ⬡*$5.* ☎*905-576-1222. www.oshawa.ca*

The history of the automobile industry in Canada is explained by means of photographs, illustrations, models and of course, by actual vehicles. Dating primarily from 1898 to 1981, about 70 automobiles, in mint condition, are on display, including the 1903 Redpath Messenger built in Toronto, the 1912 McLaughlin Buick and the 1923 Rauch and Lang electric car.

Robert McLaughlin Gallery

72 Queen St., Civic Centre. ✕&○*Open year-round Mon–Fri 10am–5pm (Thu 9pm), weekends noon–4pm.* ○*Closed Jan 1, Dec 24–26. Contribution requested.* ☎*905-576-3000. www.rmg.on.ca.*

Originally built in 1969, the expanded gallery was designed by noted Canadian architect Arthur Erickson in 1987. Part of the Civic Centre, the building features a dramatic skylight atrium and overlooks pleasant gardens.

Inside, the works of the **Painters Eleven,** a group of Toronto abstract artists who united in the 1950s are highlighted. Drawing on the gallery's permanent collection of some 6,800 works, the changing exhibits feature mainly contemporary Canadian art.

Additional Sight

Parkwood National Historic Site★★

270 Simcoe St. North. 4km/2.5mi north of Hwy. 401. ✕🚂🍴*Visit by guided tour (1hr) Jun–Sept Mon–Sun 10:30am–4pm. Rest of the year Tue–Sun 1:30pm–4pm.* ○*Closed major holidays.* ⬡*$7 (no charge to visit the gardens).* ☎*905-433-4311. www.park woodestate.com.* ⬡*Advance reservations are required for lunch or afternoon tea at the teahouse.*

This gracious, imposing residence was completed for Robert S. McLaughlin in 1917. He converted his father's carriage business into a motor company, and used an American engine in his famous **McLaughlin Buick.** In 1918 he sold the company to the General Motors Corp. of the US, but remained chairman of the Canadian division, whose main plant is in Oshawa.

Tastefully appointed, the house contains priceless antiques from all over the world. Every room has furnishings of the finest woods and fabrics created by skilled craftsmen. Tours take in 30 of the 55 rooms in the **mansion.** Architecturally, the mansion's exterior reveals a composite of classical revival styles, including Neoclassical and Georgian Revival. The three-storey, L-shaped house boasts five chimneys, an indoor swimming pool, squash court, bowling alley, pipe organ and even a barber shop. Principal rooms on the ground floor include a sunroom, billiard room, dining room and library. The second floor's main rooms are McLaughlin's bedroom suite, the master suite (all major bedrooms have a private bathroom) and an art gallery. A third floor side wing held the servants' quarters. In the basement were the laundry and a built-in vault. Amenities, luxurious at the time, included an electric elevator, a built-in vacuum cleaner and an inter-room telephone system.

The house is set on 12 acres of beautiful **gardens** (○*open free-of-charge summer through fall).* Originally created in the 1920s, they contain mature trees, manicured lawns, statuary and fountains. The pleasant **teahouse** is set beside a long pool with fountains.

Burlington

POPULATION 164,415 – MAP P 108

Founded on lands granted to Britain's Iroquois ally Joseph Brant, Burlington is a pleasant city with lovely neighbourhoods, extensive parks and in the vicinity of the lake, very expensive houses. The city has taken advantage of its long waterfront to develop a recreational area featuring parkland, hiking trails, restaurants and entertainment venues. The 740km/444mi Waterfront Trail extending from Brockville to Niagara-on-the-Lake runs along the shore, providing 23km/14mi of cycling in the city.

- **Information:** Visitor Centre, 414 Locust St. ☎905-634-5594 or 877-499-9989. www.tourismburlington.com.
- **Orient Yourself:** Burlington lies at the far western end of Lake Ontario, beneath the cliffs of the Niagara Escarpment, on the north side of Burlington Bay, which is called Hamilton Harbour by citizens of the city to the south. The city centre sits mostly south of the Parkway Belt and Highway 407. The downtown core stretches out from Brant Street—anchored by Upper Canada Plaza (on the lakeside), home to City Hall, and Brant Plaza—and from Elizabeth Street. A walking tour map of downtown is available at the visitor centre.
- **Parking:** Limited metered parking (3hrs max) is available in lots along the waterfront; there is also a parking garage at the Visitor Centre on Locust Street.
- **Don't Miss:** Discovery Landing, the glass pavilion that is the heart of the waterfront development; the Royal Botanical Gardens shared with Hamilton (♿ *See Hamilton*).
- **Organizing Your Time:** Lunch at Discovery Landing overlooking the lake is a pleasant addition to your tour. Hamilton is only 2.2km/1.3mi away via the Skyway Bridge.
- **Also See:** NIAGARA PENINSULA

Discovery Landing

Sights

Discovery Landing

1340 Lakeshore Rd. ✕ 🕐*Open daily 7am–10pm (observatory open 10am–10pm)* 🚶*Tours of the waterfront can be booked by calling* ☎*905-335-7600, ext. 7391. http://cms.burlington.ca.*

The centrepiece of Burlington's $17.4 million waterfront renewal project is the tall glass rectangle by the Baird Sampson Neuert architectural firm of Toronto. It overlooks the lake and the Rotary Centennial Pond, a reflecting pool in the summer and a popular skating rink in the winter *(for ice conditions call* ☎*905-634-7263)*. From a glass tower called the observatory, visitors can view Lake Ontario's many moods, some of them stormy. Discovery Landing also houses a restaurant, a cafe and information displays.

The **Brant Street Pier,** at the eastern edge of the waterfront, is scheduled to open in 2008, and will provide another spectacular point from which to view lake activity.

Joseph Brant Museum

1240 North Shore Blvd. E. 🕐*Open year-round Tue–Fri 10am–4:30pm, Sun 1pm–4:30pm.* 👜*$4.* ☎*905-634-3556 or 888-748-5386. www.museumsofburlington.com.*

Completed in 1938, this spacious, two-storey clapboard house is a reconstruction of the dwelling built in 1800 by Capt. **Joseph Brant** *(⌖see sidebar).* A Mohawk from New York State, Brant led the Six Nations warriors supporting the British in the American War of Independence. Reviled south of the border as a blood-

Portrait of Joseph Brant

Joseph Brant Museum

thirsty marauder, he was welcomed at the war's end to Canada and granted vast tracts of land, including the land which Burlington occupies. Exhibits describe Brant's life as well as Iroquois and local history. Brant memorabilia shares space with an extensive collection of Victoriana, which would surely have puzzled him.

Ireland House at Oakridge Farm

2168 Guelph Line. 🕐*Open year-round Tue–Fri 10am–4:30pm, Sun 1pm–4:30pm.* 👜*$4.* ☎*905-332-9888 or 800-374-2099. www.museumsofburlington.com.*

This restored homestead, with many original furnishings, gives an excellent idea of how British immigrants settled into Ontario. Completed in 1837 the house has been restored to show life at various periods throughout the 19C. The grounds offer an especially pleasant stroll, and have facilities for picnics.

Joseph Brant

The Mohawk war chief Joseph Brant (1743-1807) arrived here in 1800, after years of battles and conspiracies involving the British, the Americans, the French and fellow First Nations. He had met both King George III and George Washington, and had visited London and Paris. The British granted him 1,396ha/3,450 acres more or less to keep him in sight. But during the American Revolution, he had proven an energetic ally, convincing the Six Nations of New York to join the British. Defeated, many of the warriors fled their ancestral land in 1784 for Grand River, now Brantford.

Today Brant is remembered as Burlington's first citizen with several community facilities named in his honour, such as the Joseph Brant Museum, the Joseph Brant Memorial Hospital and Joseph Brant Day, a family festival held in August.

Hamilton ★

POPULATION 504,559 – MAP P 87

The city of Hamilton lies at the extreme western end of Lake Ontario. It has a fine landlocked harbour bounded on the lakeside by a sandbar. A canal has been cut through the bar to enable ships of the seaway to reach port with their loads of iron ore for Hamilton's huge steel mills, which have given the city its title of Steel City. The sandbar is crossed by the Skyway Bridge, part of the Queen Elizabeth Way (QEW), which connects Toronto with Niagara Falls. Hamilton is set on the Niagara Escarpment, which swings around the end of Lake Ontario at this point, rising steeply to 76m/250ft in the city. Known locally as "the mountain," it provides pleasant parks and views.

- **Information:** Tourist Office, 34 James St. S. ☎905-546-2666 or 800-263-8590. www.tourismhamilton.com.
- ▶ **Orient Yourself:** Hamilton lies southwest of Toronto. The city centre is situated south of the harbour; the botanical gardens are located to the north. Look at the map that follows to orient yourself.
- **Parking:** Parking meters are enforced Mon–Sat 8am–6pm. Meter fees are $0.50 to $1/hr. There are also 19 lots and 2 covered garages.
- **Don't Miss:** The Royal Botanical Gardens offer lovely landscapes and pleasant restaurants.
- **Organizing Your Time:** Hamilton deserves at least a day of your time.
- **Especially for Kids:** The African Lion Safari Park.
- **Also See:** NIAGARA PENINSULA

Sights

City Centre★

Downtown Hamilton has *(along Main St. between Bay and James Sts.)* several attractive buildings, in particular City Hall; the Education Centre; the Art Gallery; and Hamilton Place, a cultural centre with two theatres. A few blocks west sits **Hess Village**★ *(junction Hess and George Sts.)*, a district of older homes converted to fashionable boutiques, restaurants and cafes.

Also in the vicinity is the **farmers' market** *(55 York Blvd.; ♿ ⊙ open year-round Tue & Thu 7am–6pm, Fri 8am–6pm, Sat*

Hamilton's Art Gallery

Hamilton Tourism

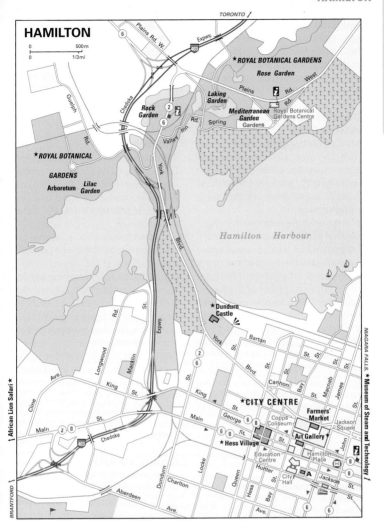

HAMILTON

0 ———— 500 m
0 ———— 1/3 mi

★ ROYAL BOTANICAL GARDENS
Rose Garden

Laking Garden

Rock Garden

Mediterranean Garden
Royal Botanical Gardens Centre
Gardens

★ ROYAL BOTANICAL
GARDENS
Arboretum   Lilac Garden

Hamilton   Harbour

★ Dundurn Castle

★ CITY CENTRE

Farmers' Market
Copps Coliseum
Art Gallery
★ Hess Village
Education Centre
Hamilton Place
City Hall

African Lion Safari ★ | BRANTFORD

NIAGARA FALLS. ★ Museum of Steam and Technology /

6am–6pm; ☎905-546-2096), one of Ontario's largest indoor markets, selling the produce of the Niagara Peninsula.

Art Gallery★

123 King St. W. ♿✕⏰Open year-round Tue–Wed noon–7pm, Thu–Fri noon–9pm, Sat–Sun noon–5pm. ⏰Closed Mon except holidays. ☜$12. ☎905-527-6610. www. artgalleryofhamilton.on.ca.

This distinctive concrete structure stands across a plaza from City Hall. Beginning in 2003 the building underwent an $18 million overhaul; the newly refurbished gallery reopened in 2005. Its attractive interior is open and airy,

with wooden ceilings. Changing exhibits from the permanent collection of more than 9,000 works of European, Canadian and contemporary art are displayed, as well as visiting shows.

Whitehern Historic House and Garden (A)

41 Jackson St. W. ☜⚬⚬Visit by guided tour (1hr) only mid-Jun–Labour Day Tue–Sun 11am–4pm. Rest of the year Tue–Sun 1pm–4pm. ⏰Closed Jan 1 & Dec 25–26. ☜$6. ☎905-546-2018. www.my hamilton.ca.

In small but pleasant gardens surrounded by Hamilton's city centre, this

Georgian-style house was the residence, until 1968, of three generations of the McQuesten family, who inspired such projects as the Royal Botanical Gardens and the Niagara Parkway. It contains the original furnishings.

Dundurn National Historic Site★

610 York Blvd. ✕🕐🍽Visit by guided tour (1hr) only, Jul–Labour Day daily 10am–4pm. Rest of the year Tue–Sun noon–4pm. 🕐Closed Jan 1, Good Friday & Dec 25. 💳$10. ☎905-546-2872. www.myhamilton.ca

This grand stone house, with its Neoclassical portico entry, stands on a hill in Dundurn Park, which provides a good **view** of Hamilton bay and the city. A showplace of 19C privilege, it illustrates the wealth and power of the Family Compact. The residence was completed in 1835 by Sir **Allan Napier MacNab,** a member of the Family Compact who served as prime minister of the Province of Canada from 1854 to 1856.

Of particular interest is the basement, the domain of an army of servants needed to run a house of this magnitude in the mid-19C (McNab died in debt, however).

Additional Sights

Royal Botanical Gardens★

680 Plains Rd. W. ✕🕐RBG Centre open daily 10am–dusk. Outdoor gardens open May–mid-Oct. 🕐Closed Dec 25, Jan 1. 💳$8. ☎905-527-1158. www.rbg.ca. Free shuttle bus May–Oct.

These gardens occupy 900ha/2,223 acres of land at the western tip of Lake Ontario. Much of this area is natural parkland with walking trails *($1/hr trailhead fee).* Several featured gardens are worth seeing *(car required).* From the Royal Botanical Gardens Centre, the **Mediterranean garden** can be visited. This conservatory houses vegetation from the five regions of the world that have a Mediterranean climate (the Mediterranean Rim, Southern Africa, Australia, California and Chile). The nearby **Larking garden** abounds in irises and peonies *(May-Jun)* and herbaceous perennials *(May-Oct).* Farther afield, the **rock garden**★ is a whirl of colour in summer, with its flowering plants and shrubs set amid water and rocks. In the arboretum *(return along York Blvd. and turn right),* the **lilac garden** is especially lovely in late May and early June.

Museum of Steam and Technology★

900 Woodward Ave. Just south of Queen Elizabeth Way (QEW). 🕐Open Jun–Labour Day Tue–Sun 11am–4pm. Rest of the year Tue–Sun noon–4pm. 🕐Closed Jan 1, Dec 25-26. 💳$6 adult. ☎905-546-4797. www.myhamilton.ca.

Hamilton's former water-pumping station, completed in 1859, now provides a rare example of 19C steam technology. Architecturally interesting with its arches and cast-iron Doric columns, the engine house contains two Gartshore steam-powered beam engines in full working order. They once pumped as much as 5 million gallons of water a day, until replaced in 1910. The boiler house has displays on the use of steam power and a working model of the beam engines.

Excursion

African Lion Safari★

🧒Safari Rd., in Cambridge. 32km/20mi northwest via Hwy. 8, then right onto Rte. 52 North after Rockton and left on Safari Rd. ✕♿🕐Open late Jun–Aug daily 10am–5:30pm. Early May–Jun & Sept–early-Oct daily 10am–4pm. 💳$27.95. (off-season $23.95) ☎519-623-2620 or 800-461-9453 (US/Canada). www.lionsafari.com.

Visitors drive their own cars through various enclosures of African and North American free-roaming animals, numbering some 1,000 in more than 100 species. The monkey jungle contains about 100 African baboons that will climb over your car and steal any removable part they can. You will also see zebras, a white rhino, a giraffe, an ostrich and several large cats. There's also a boat ride on Safari Lake and a train ride around the grounds *(11am daily;15min).*

For the best little places, follow the leader.

Looking for the latest news on today's best hotels and restaurants? Pick up the Michelin Guide and look for the Bib Gourmand and Bib Hotel symbols. With 45,000 addresses in Europe, in every category and price range, the perfect place to dine or stay is never far away.

MICHELIN
A better way forward

NIAGARA PENINSULA

The Niagara Peninsula is an isthmus lying between the southern shore of Lake Ontario and Lake Erie's north shore. The 56km/35mi-long Niagara River runs along its eastern end, dividing Canada from the US. Roughly halfway along its course from Lake Erie to Lake Ontario, the river plunges over an immense cliff, creating one of the world's great natural wonders, Niagara Falls. Between Port Weller and Port Colborne, the 45km/28mi-long Welland Canal bisects the peninsula, enabling large vessels to pass from lake to lake. A moderate climate, fertile soil and miles of shoreline make the region a prime tourism destination and fruit-growing area, famous for its wine industry. The cities of Niagara Falls and St. Catharines and towns like Fort Erie and Niagara-on-the-Lake are rich in history and beauty. Heritage buildings, pleasant inns, wineries and the Shaw Festival draw visitors from far and wide.

The peninsula's singular feature is the **Niagara Escarpment,** over which the falls tumble. Formed 390 million years ago, this hard dolomite ridge of rock extends 725km/453mi in Ontario from near the falls west through the Bruce Peninsula, between Lake Huron and Georgian Bay. The escarpment has been designated a UNESCO World Biosphere Reserve, which means its ecosystem is monitored and protected. The escarpment fosters the moderate climate that enables vineyards to grow. The lakes influence the region's temperatures. On the peninsula warm weather, sometimes 30°C/86°F, lasts through September, making the area ideal for recreation.

The mid-17C saw the eradication of the region's aboriginal people, the Neu-trals, by the Iroquois, who as fur-traders, established few settlements in the area. The name Niagara derives from an Iroquois word meaning "the strait." Loyalists fleeing the US settled here after the American Revolutionary War; Niagara-on-the-Lake was briefly the capital of Upper Canada. By the 1800s British immigrants populated the peninsula. Hydroelectricity generated by the falls eventually supplanted water-powered mills and industries in St. Catharines and Niagara Falls. In the 19C successive canals were created to connect the two Great Lakes. Today's **Welland Canal** is part of the St. Lawrence Seaway. The **War of 1812** raged briefly across the US/Canada frontier; historic forts and monuments to heroes stand today.

©John Carvalho/iStockphoto

Niagara Falls

Address Book

For dollar-sign categories, see the Legend on the cover flap.

WHERE TO STAY

$ HI-Niagara Falls – *4549 Cataract Ave., Niagara Falls.* ☎*888-749-0058. www.hostellingniagara.com. 88 beds.* A 20min walk away from the Niagara Falls, this hostel is located downtown, near the bus and train stations. The modern building offers both 6- and 8-bed dormitory or family rooms, as well as private rooms. Kitchen, laundry, wireless Internet, bike rental.

$$ Brock Plaza Hotel – *5685 Falls Ave., Niagara Falls.* ☎*800-263-7135. www. niagarafallshotels.com/brock. 233 rooms.* ✕🛏🅿. To experience old-fashioned Niagara Falls, stay at this fully renovated dowager, opened in 1929, with its fabulous views of the falls from most (but not all—be sure to check) guest rooms. Its location is right in the middle of the honky-tonk excitement that the Parks Commission has removed from the park itself. Marilyn Monroe stayed here while filming *Niagara*.

$$ Jordon House and $$$ Inn on the Twenty – *3751 Main St., Jordon.* ☎*905-562-9591. www.jordonhouse.ca; www.innonthetwenty.com. 42 rooms.* ✕🅢🅿. This accommodation consists of two addresses about 5min apart on foot. The 28-room Inn on the Twenty occupies a renovated sugar warehouse, and the rooms are vaguely retro. The 14-room Jordon House hotel once housed a coach stop; its rooms have a spare, modern decor. The charming village of Jordon, just south of Lake Ontario, contains lots to see within strolling distance. The QEW expressway will whisk you to the falls in 30min. **On the Twenty Restaurant ($$$)**, overlooking Twenty Mile Creek, serves breakfast to overnight guests *(not included in the rate)* and is open to the public for lunch and dinner. The hotel will arrange wine-tour packages. Cave Spring Cellars, just across the street, offers tours and tastings. Some treatments at Spa on the Twenty incorporate grape-based products.

$$ South Landing Inn – *21 Front St. S., Queenston.* ☎*905-262-4634. www. southlandinginn.com. 23 rooms.* ✕🅿 The original inn, built in the early 18C, accommodated tourists visiting Niagara Falls. The old building, now extensively renovated, holds five rooms, while the 1987 annex has another 18 rooms, with balconies. Quarters are clean and comfortable, although not very Victorian. Breakfast *($5)* is served in a sunny, wood-panelled room.

$$$ Keefer Mansion Inn – *14 St. Davids St. W., Thorold.* ☎*905-680-9581. www. keefermansion.com. 10 rooms.* ✕🅿 Close enough to the falls to serve as a vacation base, this 120-year-old Victorian mansion, owned by the town of Thorold, exudes both authenticity and modern convenience. Rooms are furnished in dark mahogany with lots of curlicues, but a light touch in the paintwork and soft furnishings avoid oppressiveness. The **restaurant ($$$)** offers a reasonably-priced three-course menu and a four-course tasting menu. Dishes include seared cod with green cabbage ragout, or tenderloin with scalloped pumpkin and potato gratin; the desserts are tempting, but try the cheese selection with a local wine.

$$$ Niagara Falls Marriott Fallsview – *5685 Falls Ave., Niagara Falls.* ☎*800-263-7135. www.niagarafalls marriott.com. 432 rooms.* ✕🛏🅢🅿 One of Niagara Falls' several Las Vegas-style luxury high rises, this modern, 23-storey resort hotel overlooks the falls and offers easy access to downtown entertainment. Rooms overlook the falls or the river, and family suites are available. With windows directly onto the falls, the second-floor **Terrapin Grille ($$$$)** *(reservations* ☎*905-357-7300 x4235)* is open for three meals a day. The dinner menu features standard fare (desserts are the best item), but the service and views make dining here a delightful experience.

$$$ Shaw Club Hotel & Spa – *92 Picton St., Niagara-on-the-Lake.* ☎*800-511-7070. www.shawclub.com. 30 rooms.* ♿ P Spa ⬛. Situated across from the Shaw Festival Theatre, this gracious hotel offers top-notch service and ambience. Rooms are serenely decorated, with Zen-like bathrooms, as well as ipod stations and plasma TVs. **Zee's ($$$)** restaurant focuses on Canadian dishes, like Ontario lamb and Quebec duck. In Shaw's on-site spa, indulge yourself in a maple-butter body wrap.

$$$$ Pillar and Post – *48 John St., Niagara-on-the-Lake.* ☎*905-468-1362. www.vintage-hotels.com/niagara-on-the-lake. 122 rooms.* ✕ ⬛ Spa P This hotel occupies a (much renovated) 1890 canning factory. Rooms, many with 4-poster beds, provide the comfort of home, and the public areas are sunny, and reposeful. Afternoon tea is a treat. The 100 Fountain Spa is ultra-modern, with a saltwater pool. The **Cannery and Carriages Restaurant ($$$$)** offers inventive dishes such as grilled caribou tenderloin with dried cherry sauce or grilled salmon with a honey and olive oil glaze. Try the lemon mousse in an oatmeal crust with pecans for dessert. The selection of Niagara wines is remarkable.

WHERE TO EAT

$ Elements on the Falls – *6650 Niagara Pkwy., Niagara Falls.* ☎*905-354-3631. www.niagaraparks.com.* ♿ P **Canadian.** This restaurant, owned by Niagara Parks, is located on the second floor of the Table Rock Centre, a renovated 1926 castle-like building directly over the viewing platform for Horseshoe Falls; the view is majestic. The restaurant reopened in spring 2008 after a makeover and has improved menus. Reservations are essential, but window seats cannot be reserved.

$ McFarlane House Tea Garden – *15927 Niagara Parkway, Niagara-on-the-Lake.* ☎*905-468-3322. www.niagaraparks.com. Closed mid-Sept–early May.* **Light Fare.** The Tea Garden in this historic 1800 farmhouse (☞*$4.50)* offers light refreshments to be enjoyed on the spot, or carried off for picnics in the surrounding park.

$ Riverview Market Eatery and $ Edgewaters Tap and Grill – *6345 Niagara Pkwy., Niagara Falls.* ☎*905-356-2217. www.niagaraparks.com.* ♿ P *Reservations suggested. Closed Dec. 25.* **Canadian.** Both of these eateries run by Niagara Parks occupy Queen Victoria Place, a heritage building across from the American Falls. The Riverview on the lower level offers healthy cafeteria meals: sandwiches, wraps, salads, pasta. In good weather, there's patio dining. Edgewaters serves simple fare such as hamburgers, salads steaks and chicken dishes. Its location overlooking both falls is hard to beat.

$$ Old Winery Restaurant – *2228 Niagara Stone Rd., Niagara-on-the-Lake.* ☎*905-468-8900. www.theoldwineryrestaurant.com.* **Italian.** The atmosphere at this restaurant recalls an Italian trattoria, and the menu features pizza and pasta as well as main fare featuring grilled meat. Located near the Jackson Triggs Winery, it's a convenient place to dine before the theatre or to take a break from wine touring.

$$$$ The Charles Inn – *209 Queen St., Niagara-the-Lake.* ☎*866-566-8883. www.charlesinn.ca.* **Contemporary.** Sitting close to the Shaw Festival theatre, this restaurant is set in the early-Victorian dining room of a gracious inn. The menu is limited but creative and features dishes such as butternut squash risotto, grilled pickerel from the lake, boneless saddle of rabbit with smoked bacon and prawns. Try the white-chocolate crème brûlée for dessert or sample the local cheese accompanied by Niagara wines. An elegant afternoon tea is also served.

$$$$ Skylon Tower – *5200 Robinson St., Niagara Falls.* ☎*905-356-2651 or 800-814-9577. www.skylon.com.* **Canadian.** For lunch or dinner 236m/775ft above the falls in a revolving room (one revolution per hour), come to the Skylon Tower. It's hard to beat the view, particularly at night when coloured lights play off the waters. The menu is unambitious, but the food is nicely prepared and presented: the staff clearly realize that this is a special occasion for every diner. *Reservations essential.*

Niagara Falls★★★

MAPS P 96, P97, P98

About halfway along its course from Lake Erie to Lake Ontario, the Niagara River suddenly plunges over an immense cliff, creating one of the world's great natural wonders. Niagara Falls themselves straddle the US-Canada border. The **American Falls** on the US side of the river are 300m/1,000ft wide and more than 50m/160ft high. The Canadian or **Horseshoe Falls** (named for their shape) are nearly 800m/2,600ft wide, about the same height, and contain 90 percent of the water allowed to flow down the river. It is these Horseshoe Falls that people think of as Niagara. Although many cataracts in the world are higher than Niagara, the terrific water flow (much reduced today by hydroelectric diversion) and the relatively accessible location have drawn visitors for centuries.

- 🛈 **Information:** Tourist Office, 5400 Robinson St. ☎905-356-6061 or 800-563-2557. www.niagarafallstourism.com. The Niagara Parks Commission www.niagaraparks.com.
- ▶ **Orient Yourself:** The Skylon tower offers an excellent view of the region. Use the maps that follow to get your bearings in the area.
- 🅿 **Parking:** Free parking at Niagara Parks locations outside the main falls-Queen Victoria park area. $10 (summer) Rapids View lot. $12 (May–Jun & Sept–Dec) Falls lot; Jan–Apr $6. Use the People Mover (🕭 *see Practical Information*).
- 👁 **Don't Miss:** See the falls after dark when they are illuminated. There are also fireworks displays in summer and winter; for details, contact the Tourist Office. Drive at least one way along the Niagara Parkway.
- 🕐 **Organizing Your Time:** Allow a minimum one full day for the falls plus half a day (4hrs) for the Excursions.
- 🄺🄸🄳🅂 **Kids:** Scary but fun, White Water Walk captures the full force of the falls. The butterfly conservatory in the botanical gardens makes a relaxing visit. For a rainy day, investigate the IMAX Theatre's *Niagara: Miracles, Myths and Magic* (www.imaxniagara.com).
- 👌 **Also See:** TORONTO AREA

A Bit of Geography

In geological terms, the falls are not old. At the end of the last Ice Age, some 10,500 years ago, the waters of Lake Erie created an exit channel for themselves over the present-day Niagara Escarpment into the old Lake Iroquois (ancestor of Lake Ontario). Today, the Niagara River has cut a gorge some 11km/7mi back from the edge of the escarpment at Queenston to the present position of the falls. In another 15,000 years or so, the gorge will extend back about four miles into softer rock that will erode faster. The falls will probably be replaced by a series of rapids. Eventually, the gorge will erode back to Lake Erie and the falls will cease entirely.

A Bit of History

The first European to view the falls, in 1678, was French Récollet priest **Louis Hennepin** (1626-1705), who heard such a thunderous noise that he followed the river upstream to discover its source. While spectacular to view, the falls prevented shipping between lakes Erie and Ontario. The opening in 1829 of the **Welland Canal,** now part of the St. Lawrence Seaway, provided a link to the Erie Canal in New York and promoted the cross-border trade that has contributed to both countries' prosperity. Today the river's water volume varies by hour and season. Major power developments divert up to 75 percent of the water above the falls. In winter so much water is diverted that the falls partially freeze—a spectacular sight.

Practical Information

AREA CODES

The area codes for the Niagara Falls area are 289 and 905 on the Canadian side and 716 on the New York side. For local calls within each area code, you need only dial the 7-digit number.
For more information: ☎800-668-6878 or www.bell.ca.

GETTING THERE AND GETTING AROUND

BY AIR

The Niagara Falls area is served by three airports:
Lester B. Pearson International Airport (YYZ) in Toronto is 125km/78mi from Niagara Falls; you can shuttle via Niagara Airbus. (☎800-268-8111 from the 416/905 area codes, or 905-677-8083; www.niagaraairbus.com ;$72 one-way).
Buffalo International Airport (BUF) on the NY side is 40km/25mi from the falls; take the Airport Shuttle Service to Niagara Falls ON (☎800-551-9365 or www.buffaloairporttaxi.com; $40 one-way).
Hamilton International Airport (YHM) (☎905-679-1999 or www.flyhi.ca) is the closest Canadian airport. WestJet and Air Canada Jazz provide regular domestic service. Niagara Airbus (☎800-268-8111 or www.niagaraairbus.com) provides transport by private car to Niagara Falls.
Avis (☎800-272-5871 or www.avis.com), Hertz (☎800-263-0600 or www.hertz.com), National (☎888-227-7368 or www.nationalcar.com) car rental services have counters at the airports.

BY RAIL

The **VIA Rail** train station is located near Whirlpool Bridge (4267 Bridge St., Niagara Falls; ☎888-842-7245 or www.viarail.ca) VIA Rail also provides service to St. Catharines and to Niagara-on-the-Lake.
The **Amtrak** station is located 27th St. and Lockport Rd., Niagara Falls NY (☎800-872-7245; www.amtrack.com)

BY CAR AND PEOPLE MOVER

Niagara Falls is served by major highways out of Toronto (130km/81mi via the Queen Elizabeth Way) and Buffalo NY (27km/17mi on Interstate 190, and over the Peace Bridge). Some 18 free parking lots operated by Niagara Parks are located at attractions away from the central falls/ Victoria Park area, while several small free parking/picnic areas can be found along the Niagara Parkway. Pay parking lots are found near the falls: the **Falls Parking Lot,** near Table Rock Centre and Horseshoe Falls, is open year-round and charges an all-day fee (*$18*). The **Rapidsview Parking Lot,** which takes RVs, is on the Niagara Parkway and charges $10 a day; it is open mid-May to mid-Oct, weekends Apr to mid-May. The **Floral Showcase Parking Lot** charges $4 an hour (maximum 4 hours) from Apr to Oct, no charge the rest of the year. The **Fraser Hill Parking Lot,** behind the Floral Showcase, charges $12, or $6 after Jan 1. From the Rapidsview lot, a free shuttle goes to Table Rock Centre, from which you can take **People Mover Buses** (*$7.50 all-day*) from Apr to Oct to all the Niagara Parks attractions (👁 see NIAGARA FALLS). The loop is 30km/17mi, and you can get off and on the bus as often as you like.

BY BUS

Greyhound Bus (☎800-661-8747. www.greyhound.ca) has several daily departures for Niagara Falls from the Toronto Bus Terminal (610 Bay St. ☎416-393-7911), $46 round trip, 2hrs. The Niagara Falls bus terminal is conveniently located downtown (4555 Erie Ave. ☎905-357-2133). Service between Buffalo and Niagara Falls is also frequent, $10 round trip, 35min.
Within the city, the **Falls Shuttle,** operated by the Niagara Transit Commission, whisks you efficiently around two circuits, the Red Line (downtown) and the Blue Line (Fallsview Loop). $2.25 (exact fare required). All-day tickets are sold at hotels, the bus terminal or on the shuttle itself.

BUS TOURS

For many visitors, guided bus tours provide a less hectic means of seeing sights, especially during the summer high season. Many hotels will make necessary arrangements with tour operators. Tours of the Falls area, as well as of Niagara wine country, Niagara-on-the-Lake, the Welland Canal and historical sites are available from **Greater Niagara Falls Information Centre:** ☎877-370-6009. www.niagarafallsontario.com. **Niagara Falls Tours** arranges a host of programs, by bus, van, boat, airplane and helicopter; hotel pick-up is an added perk; ☎888-880-8091; www.niagarafallstours.net. **Gray Line** offers several tours; ☎800-594-3310; www.grayline-niagarafalls.com. For tours in red double-deck buses, contact **Double Deck Tours:** ☎905-374-7423. www.doubledecktours.com. The company has a booth at Maid of the Mist Plaza.

GENERAL INFORMATION

ACCOMMODATIONS AND VISITOR INFORMATION

The **Niagara Parks Commission** operates four welcome centres: Table Rock, Maid-of-the-Mist, Clifton Hill (Clifton Hill and Falls Ave) and Murray Street (near Victoria Place) and Fallsview *(open from 9am, Jun to Aug)*. The **Greater Niagara Information Centre** at 5615 Stanley Ave., Niagara Falls *(☎877-370-6009; www.niagarafallsontario.com)* offers maps, information and discounts on many hotels and sightseeing tours For a listing of suggested hotels, ⓒsee *the Address Book*. For a complete list of accommodations, contact the **Niagara Falls Visitor and Convention Bureau** *(Niagara Falls Tourism, 5400 Robinson St., Niagara Falls ON, L2G 2A6; ☎800-563-2557; www.niagarafallstourism.com)*; the **Niagara Falls Economic Development Corp.** *(Tourism Niagara, 2201 St. David's Rd., PO Box 1042, Thorold ON, L2V 4T7; ☎800-263-2988; www.tourismniagara.com)* or contact the **Niagara Parks Commission** *(Niagara Parks ☎877-642-7275; www.niagaraparks.com)*. For bed-and-breakfast accommodation, contact the **Bed & Breakfast Assn. of Niagara Falls** *(www.bbniagarafalls.com)*, which lists 20 B&Bs, several conveniently close to the falls and downtown, others in more serene locations. For **Niagara-on-the-Lake,** contact the Chamber of Commerce: ☎905-468-1950. www.niagaraonthelake.com. For small hotels, contact the Niagara-on-the-Lake Bed and Breakfast Assn.: ☎866-855-0123; www.bba.notl.on.ca, which lists some 200 establishments.

DISCOUNT PASSES

Ask at one of the Niagara Parks Welcome Centres or at the Greater Niagara Information Centre about the **Niagara Falls and Great Gorge Adventure Pass,** available in summer, which provides admission to four major attractions (Journey Behind the Falls, Maid of the Mist, Butterfly Conservatory and White Water Walk), all-day transport on the People Mover bus and the Falls Incline Railway, and discounts to Niagara Heritage Trail, Whirlpool Aero Car and other attractions for $39.95. The **Winter Magic Pass** provides admission to Journey Behind the Falls, the Butterfly Conservatory, the Aviary and Niagara Skywheel plus discounts on other tickets (but no transport) for $27.99. For details: www.niagaraparks.com.

ACCESSIBILITY

The following attractions are accessible to wheelchairs: the Butterfly Conservatory, Journey Behind the Falls, White Water Walk, Maid of the Mist, Sir Adam Beck Power Tours and the Floral Showcase. In addition, Niagara Parks restaurants, gift shops and restrooms are accessible. The heritage buildings, such as Old Fort Erie, the Laura Secord Homestead and the McFarland House, are accessible on the ground floors only. Wheelchairs can be rented at Table Rock Welcome Centre *($15/day)*. Go online for more information: www.accessibleniagara.com

WINE COUNTRY TOURS

Many of the bus tour companies operating out of Niagara Falls offer tours of Niagara Peninsula wine country, with stops at three or more wineries. If you are a serious oenophile, check the **Niagara-on-the Lake** website, www.niagaraonthelake.com, for a list of wineries and specialized tours. The **Ontario Wine Council,** 110 Hannover Drive, Suite B205, St. Catharines ON, L2W 1A4; ☎905-684-8070, http://winesofontario.org, provides comprehensive information on the industry including lists and links to wineries, self-guided tours, maps and background info. The **Canadian Vitners' Assn.,** Suite 200-440

Laurier Ave. W, Ottawa ON, K1R 7X6, ☎613-782-2283, provides information on the industry. For a non-driving tour, catch **VIA Rail** from Toronto to either St. Catharines or Niagara Falls, then transfer to a van for a tour of four wineries, plus lunch *($155, transport and lunch included)*. Contact www.trainpackages. ca or Niagara World Wine Tours, 92 Picton St., Niagara-on-the-Lake ON,

L0S 1J0, ☎800-680-7006, http://niagara worldwinetours.ca. The company also offers **cycling tours of wineries.** Steve Bauer Bike Tours *(PO Box 22037, RPO Glenridge, St. Catharines ON, L2T 4C1. www.stevebauer.com; ☎905-704-1224)* organizes scheduled half-day and daylong vineyard tours on bicycles as well as customized tours.

The Province of Ontario and the State of New York have created beautiful parks full of flowers on both sides of the river adjacent to the falls, while the twin cities of Niagara Falls—Ontario and New York State—supply bright lights and lively amusement, mostly family-oriented.

Sights

Operated by the Niagara Parks Commission, the **People Mover** *buses stop at more than 20 attractions along the Niagara Pkwy. from the falls to Queenston Heights Park. Buses run every 20min mid-Apr–Oct. Hours of operation vary; check online at www.niagaraparks.com or 877-642-7275 (Canada/US). Tickets available at main terminal, 7369 Niagara Pkwy. (southwest of the falls) or in summer, from People Mover booths along the* parkway. ☞$7.50 (unlimited boarding all day; includes Falls Incline Railway).

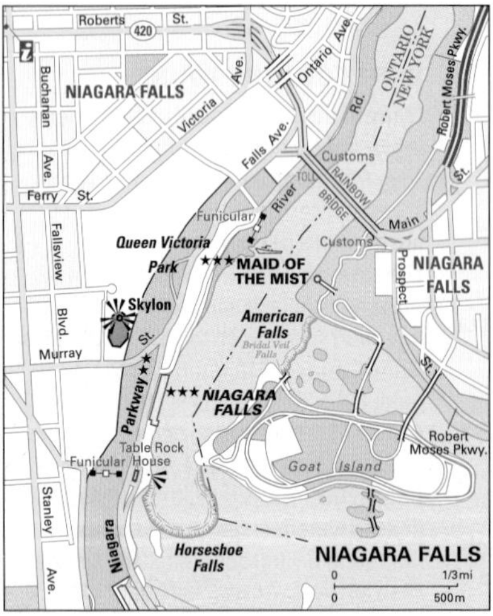

The Falls★★★

The falls can be viewed from the riverbank level, from the water level at the bottom of the cataract and from the summit of various viewing towers.

The Walk from Rainbow Bridge to Table Rock★★★

About 1.6km/1mi. From Rainbow Bridge visitors can wander along the bank beside the river, passing **Queen Victoria Park**. The American Falls are in view, and it is possible to stand on the brink of Horseshoe Falls at Table Rock. In Table Rock House, elevators descend to enable visitors to walk along **tunnels** to see the curtain of falling water (&♿⏰open daily 9am, closing hrs vary; ⏰closed Dec. 25; ☞$12 ($9 mid-Dec–Apr). ☎877-642-7275 Canada/US; www.niagaraparks.com).

Maid of the Mist★★★

Access from River Rd. Elevator & boat ride (weather permitting). ♿⏰*Departs from Maid of the Mist Plaza Apr–late Oct daily 9am or 9:45am, closing hours vary.* ⏰*Closed Oct 24 until ice-free. Round-trip 30min.* ☞*$14.50. Maid of the Mist Steamboat Co. Ltd.* ☎*905-358-5781. www.maid ofthemist.com.*

This boat trip is memorable and wet *(visitors are equipped with raincoats and hoods)*. The boat goes to the foot of the Horseshoe cataract.

Map: NIAGARA FALLS — showing Roberts St., 420, Ontario Ave., Robert Moses Pkwy., Victoria Ave., Falls Ave., River Rd., NIAGARA FALLS, Buchanan Ave., Ferry St., Fallsview Blvd., Murray, Queen Victoria Park, Skylon, Funicular, Customs, Rainbow Bridge, Main, Prospect, NIAGARA FALLS (NEW YORK), MAID OF THE MIST★★★, American Falls, Bridal Veil Falls, NIAGARA FALLS★★★, Parkway, Table Rock House, Funicular, Goat Island, Robert Moses Pkwy., Stanley Ave., Niagara, Horseshoe Falls, NIAGARA FALLS. Scale: 1/3mi, 500m.

The View from Above★★★

Three towers in Niagara Falls provide a spectacular elevated view of the cataract. The best view is from the **Skylon** (*5200 Robinson St.* ✕ ♿ 🕐 *open Jun–Oct daily 8am–midnight; rest of the year daily 9am–10pm.* 💲*$12;* ☎*905-356-2651; www.skylon.com*), ascended by exterior elevators known as yellow bugs.

Additional Sights

Niagara Parkway (North)★★

This road follows the river to its junction with Lake Ontario. From the falls the parkway passes under Rainbow Bridge, through a pleasant residential area and past the Whirlpool Bridge.

White Water Walk★★

🧒 🕐 *Open daily Apr–late fall, 9am–closing hrs vary.* 🕐*Closed winter.* 💲*$8.50.* ☎*877-642-7275 (Canada/US). www.niagaraparks.com.*

Visitors on this walk (formerly called Great Gorge Adventure) take an elevator that descends to the bottom of the gorge. There visitors can see some of the world's most hazardous water thundering, roiling and rising into huge **rapids**.

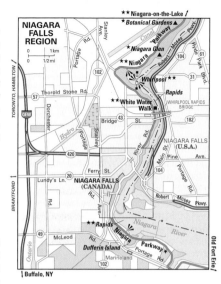

The Whirlpool★★

Weather permitting. 🕐*Open early Mar–Jun daily 10am & Jul–late Nov 9am; closing times vary.* 💲*$11.* ☎*877-642-7275 Canada/US. www.niagaraparks.com.*

A colourful antique Spanish aerocar crosses the gorge high above the river, with excellent **views**★★ of the water as it swirls around the whirlpool and the rocky gorge. Thompson's Point scenic look provides a fine **view**★.

Niagara Falls

©Kenneth Cheung/iStockphoto

Niagara Glen★

There is a view of the river from above. Trails lead to the water's edge (*15min to descend, 30min to ascend*).

Niagara Parks Botanical Gardens★

✕ ♿ ◷*Open year-round daily dawn–dusk. ◷Closed Dec 25. ☎877-642-7275 (Canada/US). www.niagaraparks.com.* Beautiful plantings of flowers, shrubs and trees are maintained by students of the Niagara Parks Commission School of Horticulture. The **rose garden** is particularly lovely in early June. The 1,022sq m/11,000sq ft **Kids butterfly conservatory** shelters some 2,000 butterflies in climate-controlled comfort (◷*open mid-Jun–Labour Day daily 9am–9pm; rest of the year closing times vary; ◷closed Dec 25; ◎$11*).

About 1.6km/1mi from the botanical gardens, across the river on the US side, the immense **Robert Moses Generating Station** can be seen. Farther on, the **Sir Adam Beck Generating Station** is visible on the Canadian side. These two large stations use water diverted from the river above the falls to generate electricity.

Just after the power stations, be sure to note the large **floral clock**.

Queenston Heights★

◷ *Open daily year-round.*

These heights are part of the Niagara Escarpment and were once the location of Niagara Falls. Today they are a pleasant park that provides good views of the river. In the park stands a monument to Gen. Sir **Isaac Brock,** a British military hero of the War of 1812. The heights were captured by the Americans during the war. Brock was killed while leading the successful charge to recapture them. Now Brock's statue overlooks them from the top of his monument.

Excursions

Queenston★

14km/8.5mi north of the falls.

Filled with attractive houses and gardens, this village lying north of the falls sits at the foot of the escarpment. It is the site of the Battle of Queenston Heights, which took place during the War of 1812. A stone memorial recalls Gen. Sir Isaac Brock, who died in the battle. Many local places are named for this war hero.

Laura Secord Homestead

29 Queenston St. ⸺⸺Visit by guided tour (30min) only, Jul–Labour Day daily 11am–5pm. Early May–Jun Mon–Fri 9:30am–3.30pm, weekends 11am–5pm. Sept–early Oct Wed–Sun 11am–5pm. ◎$4.50. ☎877-642-7275 (Canada/US). www.niagaraparks.com.

In 1813 Laura Secord walked 30km/19mi from her home in enemy-held Queenston to warn the British of a surprise attack planned by the Americans. Forewarned, the British won a great victory at the subsequent Battle of Beaver Dams.

Her rather plain house has been beautifully restored by the candy company named after this Canadian heroine.

NIAGARA FALLS
EXCURSIONS

Niagara Parkway (South)★
32km/20mi south to Fort Erie.
Rushing along at 48km/h/30mph, Niagara River is impressive, revealing its **rapids**★★ as it prepares to plunge over a cliff. **Niagara Parkway (South)**★ crosses to **Dufferin Island,** where a pleasant park (*open year-round;* ☎*877-642-7275; www.niagaraparks.com*) has hiking trails, streams and a swimming area. The river slowly becomes a broad, quietly flowing stream.
At the city of **Fort Erie,** the Peace Bridge crosses the river to the large American city of **Buffalo.** There are good **views**★ of the Buffalo skyline.

Old Fort Erie
350 Lakeshore Rd., in Fort Erie. ✕*Open early May–early Oct daily 10am–5pm. Rest of the year, call for hours.* *$9.* ☎*905-871-0540. www.niagaraparks.com.*
The first fort was built by the British in 1764. The present structure is a reconstruction (1937) of the third fort built on this site; the star-shaped stone stronghold is set at the mouth of Lake Erie. In 1814, during the War of 1812, it was the scene of bloody fighting between British and American soldiers. Students in early-19C uniforms perform manoeuvres and serve as guides.

St. Catharines★
POPULATION 131,989 – MAP P 98

Surrounded by fruit orchards and vineyards, St. Catharines is known as the Garden City for its 405ha/1,000 acres of lovely public parks; its downtown core possesses many heritage buildings, some 800 in all. Brock University, which offers a degree in winemaking, is located here. Sited at the northern entrance to the Welland Canal, the city has long been a manufacturing and shipping centre. The lively harbourfront area known as Port Dalhousie, terminus to the early Welland Canal, boasts 19C lighthouses, restaurants and a waterside walkway. It has hosted the Royal Canadian Henley Regatta *(Aug)* since 1903. Settled by Loyalists granted free land after the American Revolution, the city served as an end point in the 1850s for the Underground Railroad, the network of safe houses that led escaped African-American slaves to safety in Canada.

- **Information:** Visitor Information Centre, 1932 Welland Canal Parkway. ☎800-305-5134. www.stcatharines.ca/tourism.
- **Orient Yourself:** Major commercial arteries downtown are St. Paul and King Streets *(www.stcathdowntown.com).* Yates Street and Queen Street hold heritage districts, and the village of Port Dalhousie hugs Lake Ontario's shore. A brochure is available for self-guided walking tours of these heritage areas *(call ☎905-984-8882, ext. 244).*
- **Parking:** The downtown area, built along old Indian trails, is short on parking space; parking limit at meters is 3hrs. Parking at the museum is free.
- **Don't Miss:** The St. Catharines Museum at Lock 3, Port Dalhousie.
- **Also See:** SOUTHERN ONTARIO

Sights

British Methodist Episcopal Church National Historic Site
92 Geneva St. *Visit by appointment only; contact Ada Summers at* ☎*905-984-6769 (Harriet Tubman Centre for Cultural Services).* ☎*905-682-0993. www.pc.gc.ca or www.freedomtrail.ca.*

Completed in 1855, this small white stucco church had a dramatic history as a terminus of the Underground Railway. **Harriet Tubman,** the "Black Moses," who rescued some 200 slaves including her parents, was a church member and lived on North Street, near the church. The St Catherine's Museum

Dutka/Ontario Tourism

The Royal Canadian Henley Regatta

hosts an exhibit, *Follow the North Star*, which explains the history.

St. Catharines Parks

Recreation and Community Services. ☎*905-688-5601, ext. 1927.* *www.stcatharines.ca.*

In the downtown area, **Montebello Park,** covering 2.6ha/6.5acres at the corner of Lake and Ontario streets, was designed by Frederick Law Olmstead, who created Central Park in New York City and Mount Royal in Montreal. Also in the downtown area, the 49ha/122-acre **Burgoyne Woods,** on Edgewood Road, offers nature trails, sports facilities and picnic areas. The 8.5ha/21acre **Ontario Jaycee Gardens,** a horticultural park, lies near Port Dalhousie and contains ruins of the third Welland Canal. Situated near Lake Ontario is the 6ha/15acre **Happy Rolph's Bird Sanctuary,** where migrating and native birds can be spotted; a [Kids]**petting farm** is open seasonally *(*⊙*open May–mid-Oct)*. The **Walker Arboretum,** sited on a former private estate in the centre city *(109 St. Paul Crescent)*, sits in a protected microclimate that permits exotic plantings; meandering paths lead to the Rodman Hall Arts Centre, housed the 1863 mansion *(*⊙*open Jul–Sept Tue–Sun noon–5pm;* ⊙*closed major holidays;* ☎ *905-684-2925; www.brocku.ca/rodmanhall)*.

St. Catharines Museum at Lock 3★

Welland Canal Centre, 1932 Welland Canal Pkwy. (take Rte. 81, Queenston St., and turn right on the pkwy.). ✕⚙🅿⊙*Open year-round daily 9am–5pm, .* ⊛*$4.25.* ☎*800-305-5143. www.stcatharineslock3 museum.ca.*

This modern museum, from which you can view huge ocean-going ships passing through the present-day Welland Canal, details the great engineering feat undertaken over nearly two centuries. The exhibit *Follow the North Star* describes the town's role as a terminus of the Underground Railway.

Additional Sight

Port Dalhousie

From downtown St. Catharines, follow Ontario St. north to Lakeport Rd., turn left and continue to the harbour. ☎*905-937-4783. www.portdalhousie.com.*

Once the terminus of three successive Welland Canals, beginning in 1820, Port Dalhousie contains lovely Victorian buildings, as well as two 19C lighthouses along its harbourfront. The **Harbour Walkway** *(entrance at Main St., between Lock & Dalhousie Sts.)*, between Lakeside Park and East and West Piers, takes in the historic section of the old town.

Niagara-on-the-Lake ★★

POPULATION 13,839 – MAP P 98

One of Canada's prettiest and most historical towns, Niagara-on-the Lake was founded as the first capital of Upper Canada by Lt. Gov. John Graves Simcoe in 1792. Then called Newark, its prominence was short-lived however; in 1796 the capital, was moved to York (now Toronto), which was thought easier to defend. This move was prescient, since the Americans burned the town in 1813 during the War of 1812. Like St. Catharines, the town became a terminus of the Underground Railway. Since the mid-19C, Niagara-on-the Lake has been a vacation centre famed for its orchards, vineyards, charming inns, spas, gardens and, since 1962, the celebrated Shaw Festival.

- **Information:** Visitor and Convention Bureau, 26 Queen St. (lower level). ☎905-468-1950. www.niagaraonthelake.com.
- **Orient Yourself:** Queen Street is the town's main thoroughfare. The Historical Museum offers walking tours of the historic district, which is bounded primarily by Front, Centre, Wellington and Simcoe Streets.
- **Parking:** On-street parking is limited in the historic district *(access a parking map at www.niagaraonthelake.com)*. Five municipal parking lots in the area provide the best solution.
- **Don't Miss:** A stroll around downtown, noting the 19C Greek Revival architecture; a play at the Shaw Festival *(Mar–Nov)*. For a picnic on the lawn before a theatre performance, or a take-away lunch to enjoy on a bike ride along the Niagara Parkway, stock up on sandwich fixings, salads, fruit and such from Hendrick's Valu-Mart *(130 Queen St.; ☎905-468-7731; www.valu-mart.net)*.
- **Also See:** TORONTO AND AREA

Sights

Town Centre★

The old town centre was named a National Historic District in 2004 because of its well-preserved early-19C buildings, which Parks Canada considers among the best in Canada. Pleasant shops, restaurants, teahouses, hotels and the **Niagara Apothecary,** an 1866 pharmacy (♿🕐*open May–Labour Day daily noon–6pm; Sept–mid-Oct weekends only noon–6pm; www.niagaraapothecary.ca)* line a wide, main thoroughfare, **Queen Street★,** with the Clock Tower Cenotaph at its centre. Many beautiful old houses have been converted to inns.

The **Historical Museum** *(43 Castlereagh St. 🕐open May–Oct daily 10am–5pm; rest of the year daily 1pm–5pm; 👓$5;*

Wine Country

The Niagara Peninsula is home to nearly 60 wineries, half of which can be found in the vicinity of Niagara-on-the-Lake. Many of these wineries offer public tours of their facilities and tastings of their products. Two celebrated Canadians, hockey-great Wayne Gretzky and comedian-film star Dan Aykroyd, are involved in the wine business and recently announced plans to break ground in the area for new namesake wineries. Among the major festivals held in the peninsula throughout the year are the Niagara Ice Wine Festival *(Jan)*, the Niagara New Vintage Festival *(mid-Jun)* and the Niagara Wine Festival *(Sept)*. For self-guided driving tours of the wineries, access winesofontario.org, which has downloadable maps of the wine routes and links to the specific wineries in the area. 🚗It's best not to visit more than four wineries a day; take your time to enjoy the facilities and the scenery as well. For more details and packaged tours, 👣see Wine Country Tours in the Practical Information section.

Jeff Speed/Ontario Tourism

Niagara-on-the-Lake Town Centre

☎905-468-3912; www.niagarahistorical. museum.), a 1907 brick building that is Canada's first historical museum, has a remarkably varied collection of portraits, photos and possessions of local figures. It offers walking tours of the Historic District (☞$5).

Shaw Festival Theatre

10 Queen's Parade. Box office: ☎800-511-7429. www.shawfest.com.

Niagara-on-the-Lake is home to the **Shaw Festival,** a season *(Mar–Nov)* of theatrical performances featuring the works of the Irish playwright **George Bernard Shaw** (1856-1950), his contemporaries, and plays set in his era. It was founded in 1962 to revitalize a struggling local economy. The choice of Shaw as the festival's guiding spirit was propitious. The first summer performances in 1962 comprised an eight-week run of Shaw's *Don Juan in Hell* and *Candida*, organized by a local lawyer and playwright, Brian Doherty. Shaw's plays have always been popular. He lived to be 94 years old, through times even more tumultuous than Shakespeare's: two world wars; three monarchs; fascism; communism; the advent of electricity, telephones, automobiles, airplanes and

birth control. In addition, many great playwrights were his contemporaries, and his times still inspire plays.

The festival now occupies three venues. The smaller c.1916 Royal George *(85 Queen St.)* and c.1840 Courthouse *(26 Queen St.)* theatres are architectural jewels, while the splendid 850-seat Festival Theatre was opened by Queen Elizabeth II in 1973.

Fort George★

River Rd. near the theatre. ♿ ⏰*Open Apr–Oct daily 10am–5pm, Nov weekends only 10am–5pm.* ☞ *$11.* ☎*905-468-4257. www.friendsoffortgeorge.ca or www. pc.gc.ca.*

Built by the British in the 1790s, this fort (reconstructed) served as a headquarters for the British Army in Southern Ontario in the War of 1812 and was the scene of fierce fighting. Killed in the Battle of Queenston Heights, Gen. Sir Isaac Brock was initially buried here. Self-guided tours include the barracks, powder magazine, kitchen and blockhouse. Costumed staff demonstrate activities of the period. Musket and cannon drills as well as fife and drum corps music are performed in summer *(Jul–Aug)*.

Welland Canal★★

MAP P 98

Navigation of large watercraft between lakes Ontario and Erie was blocked by the great falls and rapids of the Niagara Escarpment until canals and locks were built in the 19C. The first canal, completed in 1829, extended from Port Dalhousie (now in the town of St Catharines) to Port Robinson on Chippewa Creek; its 40 locks were made of oak timber. Masonry was used for the next two canals, completed in 1853 and 1887. Part of the 3,700km/2,300mi St. Lawrence Seaway system, the present Welland Canal, which entered service in 1932, is the fourth; it measures 45km/28mi long and connects Port Weller on Lake Ontario with Port Colborne on Lake Erie.

🛈 **Information:** Information Services, the St. Lawrence Seaway Management Corp., 202 Pitt St., Cornwall. www.greatlakes-seaway.com.

▶ **Orient Yourself:** The Welland Canal Parkway is a good way to view the enormous ships as they rise up to Lock 7, the highest point on the canal. The parkway is accessible by car, by bike or on foot.

Sights

The Drive along the Canal★★

About 12km/9mi from Lake Ontario to Thorold on the Welland Canals Pkwy. (formerly Government Rd).

There are fine views of the huge ships on the seaway negotiating seven of the eight locks of this section. The canal's eight locks raise ships a total of 99m/326ft—the difference in the levels of the two lakes; it takes a ship about eight hours to navigate the canal.

Just north of the lift bridge at Lock 3 in St. Catharines, the visitor centre (🛈*see ST. CATHARINES)* includes a convenient **viewing platform** of the seaway from which you can see ships manoeuvring entry into the canal. At Lock 7 in Thorold, there is a tourist centre from which visitors can watch great ships rise up to the highest point on the canal after passing through locks 4, 5 and 6, the famed Flight Locks *(Lock 7 Tourist Centre, 50 Chapel St. S., Thorold; ☎888-680-9477; www.thoroldtourism.ca).* In **Port Colborne** visitors can watch ships pass through the town's business district; the best observation point is Lock 8 Park, with its large viewing platform *(Tourism assistant, 296 Felden Ave., Port Colborne; ☎905-834-1668; www.portcolborne.com/tourism).*

Pamela Delaney/Michelin

Welland Canal

SOUTHERN ONTARIO

Because Ontario is so immense, many people consider southern Ontario to be any place south of Lake Nipissing. However, the southern part of the province has, in fact, several distinct regions that each merit a leisurely visit. The south-ernmost area, bounded Guelph in the northwest to Goderich on the shores of Lake Huron, then south to London and Lake Erie, is a favourite with tourists. Lying just outside the industrial powerhouse of the Golden Horseshoe, southern Ontario is one of the most prosperous regions in Canada, with highly productive farmland, high-tech industries, a modern manufacturing sector and in London, a well-established financial sector based on insurance. A major part of the area's strength comes from its fine universities, which spin off new businesses and provide professional expertise. Still, a large portion of the economy depends on tourists drawn by the beautiful countryside watered by meandering rivers, mild climate, historical associations, cultural events (especially theatre) and small towns vying to be the prettiest in Canada.

Protected by three of the Great Lakes and by the Niagara Escarpment, the area benefits from relatively long, warm sum-mers (around 22°C/72°F), while winter temperatures hover just below 0°C (under 32°F). Precipitation is generous, and river levels rise in spring as melt-water rushes from the snowbelt just to the north towards the St. Lawrence. The placid Thames, which runs through London, is a torrent in the spring, with a water flow ten times greater than in late summer. The glaciers that retreated 10,000 years ago left rich soils as well as sandy valleys from the shores of the proto-Great Lakes, along which run riv-ers such as the Grand near Brantford.

The southern Ontario area was sparsely settled until the 1820s, when English, Scottish and Irish immigrants began moving in. Around the Kitchener area, Mennonites from Pennsylvania and Ger-man Lutherans bought up farmland and developed manufacturing industries and breweries. The farming economy required weekly markets to sell produce as well as hotels and restaurants to serve farmers and buyers; several of these markets and inns survive to this day, notably around Kitchener. Unlike areas farther east, towns here did not experi-ence the violence of the War of 1812, and only a few early settlers, notably the Iro-quois who settled Brantford and former

Daffodil Garden of Hope, Niagara-on-the-Lake

Pamela Delaney/Michelin

Practical Information

AREA CODES

The area codes for southwestern Ontario are 519 and 226. For local calls, dial all 10 digits (area code plus the number, but without the 1-prefix for long distance). For more information: ☎1-800-668-6878 or www.bell.ca.

GETTING AROUND

BY AIR

London International Airport (YXU) (1750 Crumlin Rd., London. ☎519-452-4015; www.londonairport.on.ca) is served by Northwest Airlines (links to Detroit MI), Air Canada Jazz (links to Toronto, Ottawa and Montreal) and WestJet (links to Winnipeg and Calgary). Car Rentals: Avis (☎800-879-2847 or www.avis.com) Hertz (☎800-263-0600 or www.hertz.com) National (☎800-227-7368 or www.nationalcar.com) and Enterprise (☎800-736-8222 or www.enterprise.com) car rental services have counters at the airports.

Region of Waterloo International Airport (YKF) (4881 Fountain St. N., Breslau. ☎519-648-2256; www.waterlooairport.ca) is served by Northwest Airlines (links to Detroit MI), WestJet (links to Calgary) and Bearskin Airlines (links to Ottawa). Car Rentals: Avis (☎888-897-8448 or www.avis.com) Hertz (☎800-263-0600 or www.hertz.com) and National (☎800-227-7368 or www.nationalcar.com) car rental services have counters at the airports.

BY TRAIN

The **VIA Rail** train serves Brantford, Guelph, Kitchener-Waterloo, London and Stratford. (☎888-842-7245 Canada/US; www.viarail.ca).

BY BUS

Greyhound Bus (☎800-661-8747; www.greyhound.ca) provides scheduled bus service to Brantford, Guelph, Kitchener-Waterloo, London and Stratford. Several local bus companies provide regional transportation.

GENERAL INFORMATION

ACCOMMODATIONS AND VISITOR INFORMATION

The **Southern Ontario Tourism Organization** (www.soto.on.ca) offers information on attractions, accommodations, events and maps.

Ontario Tourism Marketing Corp. (10th floor, Hearst Block, 900 Bay St., Toronto; ☎800-668-2746; www.ontariotravel.net) offers useful information on Southwestern Ontario.

For information on First Nations sites and activities, contact the **Aboriginal Tourism Assn. of Southern Ontario** (34 Merton St., Ottawa; ☎877-746-5658; www.ataso.ca).

For Bed and Breakfast accommodation, contact the **Waterloo Region Bed & Breakfast Assn.** (73 George St., Waterloo ON; www.bbwaterlooregion.ca) and **Huron Tourism Assn.** (Courthouse Square, Goderich; ☎800-280-7637; www.ontarioswestcoast.ca) as well as the tourist information offices listed under each Sight heading.

FARMERS' MARKETS

Goderich – South side of Court House Park. ☎519-524-5356. www.goderich.ca. Mid-May–mid-Oct, Sat 8am-1pm. A farmers' market selling local produce, flowers, fish and meat products and crafts.

Guelph – 2-4 Gordon St. (Intersection Waterloo & Gordon Sts.). ☎519-822-1260. http://guelphfarmersmarket.com. Year-round Sat 7am-noon. Farm produce, meat, cheese and eggs, crafts, health foods, honey, maple syrup.

Kitchener – 300 King St. W, Kitchener. ☎519-741-2287. www.kitchenermarket.ca. Year-round Sat 7am-2pm & late May-early Oct Wed 8am-2pm.

London – 130 King St., London. ☎519-439-3921. www.coventmarket.com. Outdoor market May-Nov Thu & Sat 8am-1pm. Indoor Market year-round Mon-Thu & Sat 8am-6pm, Sun 11-4pm.

St. Jacobs – At Weber St. N. and Farmers' Market Rd., north of Waterloo. ☎519-747-1830. www.stjacobs.com. Year-round Thu

& Sat 7am-3:30pm, Jun-Labour Day Tue 8am-3pm, Jun-Dec Sun 10am-4pm.

SHOPPING

Martins Fruit Farm – *1420 Lobsinger Line, RR#1, Waterloo.* ☎519-664-2750. *www.martinsapples.ca.* Just down the road from the St. Jacobs Market, this apple emporium in the midst of an orchard sells some 16 varieties of apples as well as apple products such as jelly and cider. Each variety has its specific use and season, depending on its keeping qualities.

Southworks Outlet Mall – *64 Grand Ave. S., Cambridge.* ☎519-740-0380. *www.southworks.ca.* This outlet mall, with some 30 shops, is located in an old foundry dating to 1847, which closed only in 1987. Bits of the old industrial construction, such as overhead cranes, are still in evidence. There is also an antiques market on the premises.

LEISURE ACTIVITIES

Upward Bound Ad-Ventures Hot-air Balloons – *Suite 224, 425 Hespeler Rd, Cambridge.* ☎519-651-2859. *www3. sympatico.ca/upwardboundadventures.* Balloon rides over the countryside around Elora last about 90min for up to six passengers. Prices from $195-$225 per person.

Yuk Yuks Comedy Clubs – *340 Wellington Rd., London.* ☎519-936-2309; *1 King St. W., Kitchener.* ☎519-893-5233. Also clubs in Barrie, Hamilton, Mississauga, Niagara Falls, Ottawa, Toronto, and Windsor. www.yukyuks. com. For a look at what Ontario finds funny, visit one of these cabaret-style clubs where you can chuckle or on amateur night, sample new talent *(admission limited to 19 years old and older, or 16-18 year olds accompanied by an adult; reservations suggested).*

Address Book

⚘*For dollar-sign categories, see the Legend on the cover flap.*

WHERE TO STAY

$ The SGH Residence – *130 Youngs St., Stratford.* ☎519-271- 5084. *www.sgh residence.ca.* ▱⚖. Attached to Stratford General Hospital, this residence offers cheerfully decorated dormitory-style or single rooms, each with a sink, vanity and small refrigerator. Amenities include kitchenettes on each floor and coin-operated laundry facilities. Rates include breakfast, served in the hospital cafeteria. The courtyard holds a swimming pool and lounge chairs.

$$ Stone Willow Inn – *940 Queen St. E., St. Marys.* ☎519-284-4140 or 800-409-3366. *www.stonewillow.com. 25 rooms.* ✖▣. A country inn with modern facilities and a moderate price, located close to Stratford in the pretty limestone town of St. Marys. The on-site restaurant, **Mrs. B's Country Style Dining ($$)** unpretentiously serves breakfast, lunch and dinner. A small terrace overlooks the garden.

$$ Norfolk Guest House – *102 Eramosa Rd., Guelph.* ☎519-767-1095. *www. norfolkguesthouse.ca. 6 rooms.* ▣⚖.

In the historic downtown of Guelph, this lovely late-19C red brick and stone house boasts six bedrooms, each decorated in a different whimsical but attractive style, with more traditional main rooms. Complimentary breakfast, with home-made bread and muffins, is served in the elegant dining room; or if you stay in one of the two suites, in your room.

$$$ Bentleys Lofts and Annex – *99 Ontario St., Stratford ON.* ☎519-271-1121 or 800-361-5322. *www.bentleys-annex.com. 12 rooms.* ✖▣. No quaint Elizabethan touches here, these rooms offer sleek modern lines and electric fireplaces. The six loft suites, which have extra beds for families, have all the amenities, while the six annex rooms over the restaurant, are simply luxurious. **Bentley's Bar and Restaurant($$)**, open from 11am to 2am, offers good pub grub such as steaks, pizza and shepherd's pie.

$$$ The Little Inn of Bayfield – *26 Main St., Bayfield.* ☎519-565-2611 or 800-565-1832. *www.littleinn.com. 28 rooms.* ✖▣⬛. A former coach stop, this charming inn, operating since 1832, offers guests the simplicity of times past coupled with modern amenities such as whirlpools and working fireplaces. Rooms are individually decorated with country antiques. The airy **dining room ($$$)** is open to the public year-round. Menus change frequently to reflect the freshest seasonal produce from Huron County. A typical summer menu might include a rack of lamb, citrus-glazed pork tenderloin, or Lake Huron fish with new potatoes. Extensive wine list. The Inn operates a renowned **cooking school** where classes are integrated into a relaxing spa vacation; reserve dates early.

$$$$ Touchstone Manor – *325 St. David St., Stratford.* ☎*519-273-5820. www.touchstone-manor.com. 4 rooms. Closed Dec–May.* 🅿🚭. Lords and ladies of the manor will feel at home in this 1938 stone Georgian Revival house set on a wide lawn just outside the downtown core. The spacious bedrooms are decorated in restrained Victorian style with dark wood furniture and feather duvets. The parlour's comfortable chairs, fireplace and high windows invite relaxation before or after the theatre. A delicious cooked breakfast, included in the room rate, is served in the elegant dining room. No children, no pets.

WHERE TO EAT

$ Café Milagro's – *1271 Commissioners Rd. W., London.* ☎*519-473-0074.* **Canadian.** Fortify yourself at this small, Euro-style bistro, open for breakfast, lunch and casual dining. Popular lunch choices at this former coffeehouse-turned-restaurant are burgers, quiches and wraps. Dinner offerings include chicken, pork, beef and even Asian dishes. Sidewalk seating is available.

$ The Desert Rose Café – *130 Metcalfe St., Elora.* ☎*519-846-0433. Closed Nov-Mar.* **Vegetarian.** This restaurant serves vegetarian food in a casual atmosphere. Savour soups, salads or sandwiches inside or on the patio out back.

$ E.J.'s at Baden – *39 Snyder's Rd. W., Baden.* ☎*519-634-5711. www.ejsatbaden.com.* **German.** In the village of Baden, west of Kitchener, this restaurant, built as a hotel in 1874, dishes up pork schnitzel, baby back ribs, steaks, seafood and locally produced Oktoberfest sausage as well as pub grub.

15 beers on tap in one of the country's oldest taverns.

$ Kennedy's Restaurant – *1750 Erb's Rd. W., St. Agatha.* ☎*519-747-1313, or 800-250-5953. www.kennedycatering.ca.* **Pub Fare/German.** This old-fashioned Irish pub is known for its rolled ribs, roasted and stuffed with savoury dressing. Other dishes include schnitzels, cabbage rolls, and liver and onions. Also traditional pub fare like bangers and mash, fish and chips or shepherd's pie.

$ Olde Heidelberg Restaurant and Brew Pub – *3006 Longsinger Line (RR#15), Heidelberg.* ☎*519-699-4413. www.oldhh.com.* **German.** This 1860 stagecoach stop near the St. Jacob's market serves traditional German fare such as wiener schnitzel, sauerkraut and pork. Photos of dishes posted on the wall help diners make their selection. Chicken, fish and beef can also be ordered. The pub is popular for its Bavarian-style lager beer brewed on-site.

$$ John Peel Restaurant – *48 Dalhousie St., Brantford.* ☎*519-753-7337. www.johnpeel.ca.* **Steakhouse.** A culinary fixture here since 1974, this restaurant offers fine dining in a downtown setting. John Peel's steak entrées include filet mignon and New York sirloin, while the fish menu often features salmon, orange roughy and shrimp. The wine list numbers upwards of 150 selections. Hot apple beignets with ice cream or crème caramel tempt diners for dessert.

$$ Michael's on the Thames – *1 York St., London.* ☎*519-672-0111. www.michaelsonthethames.com. No lunch Sat-Sun.* **International.** Try Michael's enclosed sunroom overlooking the river, where oysters Rockefeller or mussels meuniere are a prelude to main courses such as rack of lamb, pork tenderloin, or veal osso buco. Flambéed desserts are prepared tableside.

$$ Villa Cornelia – *142 Kent St., London.* ☎*519-679-3444. www.villacornelia restaurant.com. Closed Sun.* **Canadian.** The menu at this romantic 1892 Queen Anne house offers meat and fish entrées with a few surprises like Russian blini with smoked salmon or seafood Normandy (shrimp, scallops, monkfish and salmon) with pasta. Desserts include pavlova and lemon chiffon torte.

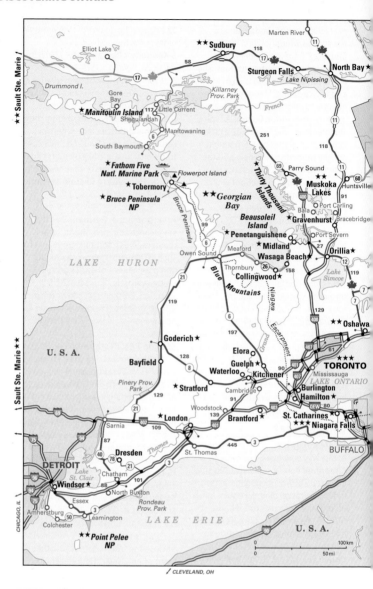

$$$ Benmiller Inn & Spa – *81175 Benmiller Rd., Goderich.* ☎*519-524-2191 or 265-1711. www.benmiller.on.ca.* **Contemporary.** The modern, creekside Ivey Dining Room of this spacious country inn serves produce from Huron County farms and perch from Lake Huron, as well as salmon and seafood. Try the braised lamb shanks, or the filet mignon with seasonal vegetables. Desserts highlight local fruits in tarte Tatin or cherry clafoutis. The wine list features Ontario wines, particularly Pelee Island wines. On the property, built around a 19C woollen mill, are 57 guest rooms.

$$$ Elora Mill Inn – *77 Mill St., Elora.* ☎*519-846-9118. www.eloramill.com.* **Contemporary.** Within the inn's large dining room within this restored 19C mill, guests can hear the rush of the river's waterfall below. The small, carefully selected menu features local seasonal produce for such dishes as roast duck

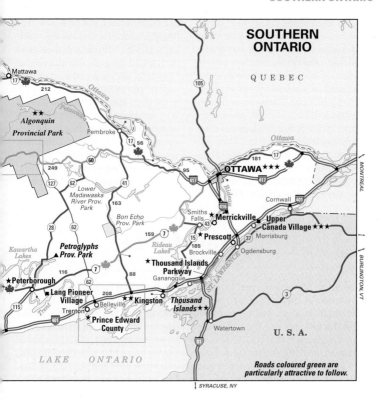

SOUTHERN ONTARIO

QUEBEC

Mattawa

Ottawa

Petawawa

★★
Algonquin
Provincial Park

Pembroke

Ottawa

OTTAWA ★★★

Cornwall

Lower
Madawaska
River Prov.
Park

Bon Echo
Prov. Park

Smiths
Falls ★ **Merrickville**

Upper ★★★
Canada Village

Morrisburg

Petroglyphs
Prov. Park

Rideau
Lakes

★ **Prescott**

Brockville   Ogdensburg

Kawartha
Lakes

★ **Thousand Islands**
Parkway

Gananoque

★**Peterborough**

★ **Lang Pioneer**
Village

Belleville ★★ **Kingston** *Thousand*
Islands ★★

Trenton

★ **Prince Edward**
County

Watertown

U.S.A.

LAKE   ONTARIO

MONTREAL

BURLINGTON VT

Roads coloured green are
particularly attractive to follow.

SYRACUSE, NY

with leeks and prunes. The cheesecake with seasonal berries is worth the wait. On the premises are 32 guest rooms with colourful bed quilts and antique furnishings.

$$$ Olde School Restaurant – *687 Powerline Rd., 2km off Hwy. 403, Brantford.* ☎*519-753-3131 or 888-448-3131. www.theoldeschoolrestaurant. ca. No lunch Sat. Sun brunch.* ♿ 🅿 **Canadian.** This 19C brick school building is awash in Victorian details such as stained-glass windows and ornate lighting fixtures. It is a bit out of the way, toward the town of Paris, but the Queen visited in 1997. Dining areas sport names such as Principal's Room and Teachers' Lounge. The menu is resolutely conventional, with some Greek dishes as well as fish, chicken, lamb, beef main courses.

$$$$ Church Restaurant – *70 Brunswick St., Stratford.* ☎*519-273-3424. www.churchrestaurant.com. Closed off-season. Tue-Sat dinner only, Sun lunch & dinner.* **French.** This is a former church, with tables set under the vaulted ceiling. Menus are sophisticated with items such as poached skate, roast loin of red deer, or pork barbecues. Early sittings at 5pm and a prix-fixe option expedites matters for theatre-goers. Upstairs, a bistro, **The Belfry ($$)** *(Tue-Sat lunch & dinner, closed Sun & Mon)* offers the same high standard with a simpler fare.

$$$$ The Old Prune – *151 Albert St., Stratford.* ☎*519-271-5052. www.old prune.on.ca. Closed Mon & mid-Oct-mid-May. No lunch Tue.* **French.** Four dining rooms overlook a reflecting pool. An intriguing menu, with a prix-fixe option for theatre-goers, might include a warm duck-breast salad or lamb with wild leeks. There is also a vegetarian menu. Save room for desserts like warm chocolate cake or pineapple carpaccio.

slaves freed by the British, were Loyalists from the US. Towns grew up along navigable rivers, later supplanted by railways, creating historic town centres reflecting all aspects of Victorian architecture and waterside parks so pleasant to visit today. The towns of Guelph and Goderich were actually planned on drawing boards by a development company and laid out in perfect harmony. Others, such as Stratford, were set up with nostalgic references to British or, in the case of Kitchener (formerly Berlin), German antecedents. Weathered to a butter colour, the limestone that furnished stone for so many 19C buildings was quarried in outcroppings found throughout the area. Old quarries, as Elora or St. Mary's, are now small lakes used for recreation.

In the years leading up to the US Civil War, fugitive slaves arrived via the Underground Railway. True to the prevailing tendency, African-Canadians set about making "model" towns at the Pierpoint Settlement at Garafraxa, near Guelph, and the Dawn Settlement near Dresden.

Brantford ★
POPULATION 90,192 – MAP P 108

Named for Six Nations chief Joseph Brant, this manufacturing city, located on the banks of the Grand River, is also famous as the family home of inventor Alexander Graham Bell and birthplace of hockey great Wayne Gretzky. Once a manufacturing centre, Brantford saw its major industries, based on farm equipment, collapse in the late 20C; the sleepy downtown area still reflects economic distress. Recently, Ontario's strong economy has brought in new employment, while residents have striven to develop tourist attractions and beautify the city; floral plantings abound. Named a Canadian Heritage River, the Grand offers canoeing, kayaking and rafting adventures. Nearby Paris, at the confluence of the Grand and the Nith rivers, is a pretty town with old stone houses most recently seen in the Oscar-nominated film Away from Her.

- **Information:** Tourist Centre, 399 Wayne Gretzky Parkway, ☎519-751-9900 or 800-265-6299. www.visitbrantford.ca.
- **Orient Yourself:** The Grand River meanders through town, northwest to southeast, paralleled most of the distance by the Trans-Canada Trail, which is groomed for walking, cycling and jogging. Colborne, Dalhousie and West streets, as well as Brant Avenue, are the principal downtown arteries leading to the bridge across the Grand.
- **Don't Miss:** The Alexander Graham Bell Homestead offers fascinating displays about the invention of the telephone.
- **Organizing Your Time:** Brantford is about an hour's drive from Toronto, and about the same distance to Niagara Falls. Allow one day to leisurely visit the sights.
- **Especially for Kids:** Wayne Gretzky Sports Centre.
- **Also See:** NIAGARA PENINSULA.

A Bit of History

Brantford stands on land given to the Six Nations Indians in 1784 by the British government as a reward for their support during the American Revolutionary War. Led by Capt. **Joseph Brant** (1743-1807), some 2,000 Iroquois and Loyalists fled north in 1784 after the Revolution; their fierce warfare had made them much reviled in the US. Brant, whose Mohawk name was Thayendanegea, meaning "he places two bets," was born in present-day Ohio and grew up in New York state. When Brant was still a young boy, his sister Molly became the mistress, then the wife, of the British superintendent of Indians, Sir William Johnson. When about 13 years old, Brant fought under Sir William during the French and Indian War. When Brant was 19, Sir William sent him to a school for Indians that later became Dartmouth College, furthering development of the strange amalgam of high literacy, aristocratic English manners, Anglican beliefs and bone-chilling ferocity that made him such an enigma. Thanks also to Sir William, Brant became a Freemason, giving him useful contacts among both English and Americans. Brant visited England, where he made a favourable impression and was in turn much impressed by British power.

Due to his exertions, a significant number of Iroquois, who had planned to stay neutral during the Revolution, threw their weight to the British. Raids led by Brant and his British associate Col. John Butler of Butler's Rangers terrorized American communities; he was implicated in several massacres. After the war, Brant lived in lavish comfort at Burlington Bay, keeping slaves and educating two sons at Dartmouth. He worked hard to promote his people and their land claims with British authorities. His prestige was so great that George Washington (a fellow Mason) hired him as an intermediary in negotiations with tribes in the Ohio Valley (Brant reneged). After his death a bronze statue of him was erected in Brantford in 1886. Although he normally wore English clothes, he sat for portraits in Mohawk garb: a painting of Brant by George Romney hangs in the National Gallery in Ottawa.

Brant sold some of his land at Brantford to English settlers in the belief they would teach farming to the Mohawks. In 1830 settlers purchased the remaining land and the Indians moved south of the river, to what is now the Six Nations Reserve. Named for Brant, the town of Brantford was incorporated in 1847. The Indian reserve to the south is the scene in August of the **Six Nations Native Pageant** (Wahhdekah). *For information, contact Indigenous Culture and Media Innovations, Ohsweken;* ☎*519-445-1418; www.icmi.ca.* The downtown **Sanderson Centre** (88 Dalhousie St.; ☎*519-758-8090 or 800-265-0710; www.*

sandersoncentre.ca), a restored vaudeville house, presents touring productions as well as local theatre.

Sights

Myrtleville House Museum
34 Myrtleville Dr. ♿ 🕐*Open Apr–Dec Mon–Fri 9am–4pm. Jul–Aug also open Sat–Sun 1pm–4pm. Rest of the year Tue–Fri 9am–4pm.* 🕐*Closed major holidays.* ☞*Guided tours on request.* ☜*$4.* ☎*519-752-0396. www.myrtleville.ca.*

For a close look at how a prosperous farm family lived over four generations, visit this remarkably preserved farm, now located within the town of Brantford. The Georgian house was constructed in 1837 by Allan and Eliza Good, immigrants from Ireland, who named it after Mrs. Good's ancestral home. It was occupied by their descendents for some 140 years, and turned over to Heritage Canada with all the furnishings intact. The family had moved in 1913 into a new house nearby, so the homestead reflects the 19C quite well. The 2.2ha/5.5 acre site includes several outbuildings, and on summer weekends the guides wear period costumes.

Wayne Gretzky Sports Centre
254 N. Park St. ♿ 🕐*Open year-round. Public swims Tue & Thu 7am–8:30pm, Fri 7:30am–9:30pm, weekends 2pm–5pm.* 🕐*Closed major holidays.* ☜*$4.50. Open to non-members.*

🧒 Named for one of Canada's hockey superstars, this modern recreational centre boasts a 65m/214ft swimming pool and a "torpedo tube" waterslide, as well as a fitness centre, arenas, hockey stadium and other facilities. The pool is an especially popular place for children to cool off in summer.

Woodland Cultural Centre
184 Mohawk St. ♿ 🕐*Open year-round Mon–Fri 9am–4pm, weekends 10am–5pm.* 🕐*Closed major holidays.* ☜*$5 (museum).* ☎*519-759-2650. www.woodland-centre.on.ca.*

The centre houses a research library on First Nations history, and maintains a **museum** that presents an interesting

Wayne Gretzky

Born in Brantford, Ontario, **Wayne Gretzky** (b. 1961) is revered as the National Hockey League's greatest player. A backyard ice skater at age two, first coached by his father in hockey, he went on to become the youngest player and highest scorer in the 1977 Junior World Cup championship. He was the NHL's first player to average over two points a game. For four seasons in the 1980s, he led his team, the Edmonton Oilers, to victory in Stanley Cup competitions. In the 1981-82 season, he established an NHL record for regular-season scoring: 92 goals, 120 assists, 212 total points. For seven consecutive years, he was awarded the leading NHL scorer trophy. He won the NHL's most valuable player trophy eight years in a row. It is evident that his native city adores him: Wayne Gretzky Parkway, the Wayne Gretzky International Hockey Tournament held annually here, and the Wayne Gretzky Sports Centre are all named in his honour.

collection of native art and artifacts. Note in particular the Iroquoian pipes and beaded Ojibway pouches with their intricate floral designs. A highlight is the Constitution of the League of Five Nations (1452), made of shell beads and string. The re-created interior of a 19C long-house and related displays depict the way of life of the Eastern Woodlands Indians, of which the Six Nations Indians are a part. Exhibits of contemporary First Nations art are held throughout the year. A short drive away stands the oldest Protestant church in Ontario, **Her Majesty's Royal Chapel of the Mohawks** *(301 Mohawk St; ⟨⟩. ⟨⟩Open July–Labour Day daily 10am–5:30pm, May–Jun & Sept–Oct Wed–Sun 10am–5pm; ⟨⟩contribution requested; ⟨⟩519-756-0240; www. mohawkchapel.ca).* This Anglican chapel was originally built in 1785 as part of the Crown's compensation to Mohawks who had supported Britain during the American Revolution; the tombs of Capt. Joseph Brant and his son John lie in the churchyard. The church has been much altered but retains its beauty; each of the stained glass windows (1959-1962) illustrates an event in Mohawk cultural history. The church still possesses original items given the Mohawks by Queen Anne in 1712, transported here from New York state after the Revolution.

Bell Homestead National Historic Site★

94 Tutela Heights Rd. From downtown, take Colborne St. W. across Grand River, turn left on Mt. Pleasant St. and left again on Tutela Heights Rd. ⟨⟩Visit by guided tour (45min) only. ⟨⟩Open year-round Tue–Sun 9:30am–4:30pm. ⟨⟩Closed Jan 1 & Dec 24-26. ⟨⟩$5. ⟨⟩519-756-6220. www.bellhomestead.on.ca.

Pamela Delaney/Michelin

Bell Homestead National Historic Site

In 1870 Alexander Graham Bell (1847-1922), scion of a distinguished family of elocution experts, left Scotland with his parents, who settled in Brantford. After a short stay in their home, young Alexander left for Boston, where his success at teaching deaf pupils (his father's profession) to speak was so remarkable that he soon opened his own school and lectured at Boston University. While trying to reproduce sounds visibly for his deaf pupils, he discovered how to transmit and receive speech along an electrified wire. Based on this discovery he developed the telephone, an idea he conceived in Brantford in 1874 while visiting his parents. The first "long distance" call was made from his parents' home in Brantford when Bell, in Paris, Ontario *(about 11km/7mi away)*, was able to hear his father's voice. His telephone received a US patent on March 7, 1876.

Set on the high banks of the Grand River, the Bell house (1858) has been a museum since 1910 (Bell and his family were among the first museum visitors). With its covered veranda, it is furnished much as it would have been in Bell's day, with many original pieces. There is an interesting display on his life, inventions and research.

Next door stands a smaller clapboard structure moved to this spot from the centre of Brantford. Bell's father, Melville Bell, and a friend, Thomas Henderson, launched the Bell Telephone Company of Canada in 1877, from this house, which now serves as a telephone museum. Inside, there is a 1920s telephone exchange, as well as many old phone models.

Also on the grounds is a small teahouse where visitors may enjoy a light lunch, afternoon tea or morning coffee (open Tue–Sun 10am–3pm).

Guelph ★

POPULATION 114 943 – MAP P108

Located northeast of the urban agglomeration of Kitchener-Waterloo-Cambridge, Guelph is not only a prosperous city but is also one of Canada's most pleasant places to live. Lovely Victorian architecture and beautiful green spaces are abundant. Founded in 1827 as headquarters of the Canada Company, the town was designed by the development firm's Canadian superintendent. A Scottish novelist, John Galt envisioned a romantic European setting of streets radiating from the Speed River. The limestone used in many of the buildings comes from nearby quarries. The town benefited from a railroad and quickly grew into a prosperous manufacturing centre with an innovative local government. Today, many businesses have moved to malls on the outskirts, leaving the city centre relatively tranquil. The University of Guelph is known particularly for its agriculture and veterinary science schools.

- **Information:** Visitor Information Centre, 42 Wyndham St. N, Suite 101B. ☎519-873-1445 or 800-334-4519. www.visitguelphwellington.ca.
- **Orient Yourself:** The old city on the west bank of the Speed River centres on St. George's Square; the structured layout resembles that of a Renaissance town, with city blocks of varying dimensions. At the confluence of the Speed and Eramosa rivers lies a lovely area of parks, gardens, bridges and walking trails.
- **Parking:** Downtown on-street parking is free for a maximum of two hours per day, Monday to Saturday. For longer-term stays, six paying municipal parking lots lie in the city centre.
- **Don't Miss:** Guelph Walkabout Tours are short, self-guided strolls around the city's major sights, while driving tours take you around historic Wellington County. Maps are available at the Visitor Information Centre.
- **Organizing Your Time:** Allow one day minimum to enjoy Guelph, concentrating in the downtown section of the city.

Guelph City Hall

Pamela Delaney/Michelin

A Bit of History

A roundabout tribute to the British royal family, the name Guelph derives from the Guelf family, ancestors of the Hanover family from which the present House of Windsor is descended. The city likes to call itself the Royal City.

The site of the present-day town was known as a neutral zone to aboriginal tribes, who canoed down the Speed River to trade. The first non-aboriginal settlers, arriving in the 1820s, were African-American former slaves led by Richard Pierpoint, a Senegalese who had served with Butler's Rangers during the American Revolutionary War. The Pierpoint Settlement at Garafraxa, near present-day Fergus, gradually dispersed after Pierpoint's death in 1838.

Lt. Col. John McCrae, author of Canada's most celebrated poem, *In Flanders Fields*, was born and raised in Guelph.

Downtown

The Guelph Arts Council, *127 Wyndam St. N., Suite 404,* conducts **guided walking tours** *(2hr)* on selected Sundays *(Apr–Oct 2pm; ➣$3)* ☎519-836-3280; *www.guelpharts.ca.*

Planner John Galt set aside land so no religious denomination would feel slighted. As a result, **stone churches** built in versions of Gothic Revival abound; Guelph is sometimes called the City of Churches. The most spectacular edifice is the large twin-spired Catholic **Church of Our Lady Immaculate** *(28 Norfolk St.),* started in 1874 but completed only in 1926.

Grand 19C houses, often designed in the Italianate style by local architect John Hall Jr., stand on the streets around St. George's Square, notably between Macdonnell and Norwich streets. The limestone **Albion Hotel** *(49 Norfolk St.),* built 1856, has a colourful history as a tavern and smuggling centre; it now houses a restaurant. At 25 Waterloo Avenue, **Beaver Hall** (1864) is an Italianate construction with a touch of the Moorish; it now holds a real estate agency.

The **Civic Museum,** a remarkable three-storey 1850s limestone structure, features exhibits on local history and events *(6 Dublin St. S.; ⏱open year-round daily 1pm–5pm; ⏱closed Dec 24–26; ➣$4, or $6 combined with McCrae House, described below; ☎519-836-5280; www.guelph.ca/museum).*

Public buildings were meant to be grandiose: the Renaissance Revival **City Hall** *(59 Carden St.),* dating from 1856 and the Scottish castellated **Wellington County Courthouse** *(74 Woolich St.)* dating from 1842-44), are still impressive. The **Dominion Public Building** *(138 Wyndam St. N.)* was built in 1936-38 in the Modern Classicism style as a post office; it is now a Wellington County office building.

At the **Macdonald Steward Art Centre** *(358 Gordon St.;* ⏰*open year-round Tue-Sun noon-5pm;* 🎫*suggested contribution $10;* 🅿 ☎*519-837-0010; www.msac.uoguelph.ca)* hangs what is purported to be the only portrait painted of Shakespeare in his lifetime. It descended in the family of an Ottawa resident, and portrays a ginger-bearded young man. For a change of setting, stroll down **Quebec Street,** lined with boutiques and other shops.

Sight

McCrae House National Historic Site
108 Water St. ⏰*Open Jul–Nov daily 1pm–5pm. Rest of the year Sun–Fri 1pm–5pm.* ⏰*Closed Dec 24–Jan 1.* 🎫*$4 (joint admission to McCrae House and Civic Museum $6).* ☎*519-836-1482. www.guelph.ca/museum.*

This modest c.1857 cottage, set in a flower garden, is the birthplace of Lt. Col. **John McCrae** (1872-1918), a surgeon who wrote the elegiac poem *In Flanders Fields,* shortly after burying a comrade killed at the second battle of Ypres during World War I. Published in *Punch* magazine December 8, 1915, the poem touched a chord internationally and launched the red poppy that people still purchase on Remembrance Day. McCrae died of pneumonia and is buried in France.

Several rooms are decorated to reflect the 1870s. The dining room contains early 20C furnishings belonging to the McCrae family. The Memorial Gardens on the site include a bronze book, the open pages of which feature McCrae's poem.

Kitchener–Waterloo

POPULATION 302,143 – MAP P 108

Orderly and clean, these twin industrial cities in Southern Ontario reflect their German heritage. The first immigrants were Mennonite farmers from Pennsylvania, who hewed out of wilderness the prosperous farms on which the area developed. Later German immigrants brought a range of business and manufacturing skills, creating the diverse economy still evident today. Thanks in large part to its concentration of universities—the University of Waterloo, Wilfrid Laurier University and the nearby University of Guelph—the area (which includes the town of Cambridge) is a hub for high-technology and knowledge-based industries. The Canadian Innovation Centre *(www.innovationcentre.ca),* spun from a UW program, helps people with bright ideas develop sound businesses that have kept the economy resilient.

- **Information:** Kitchener-Waterloo Tourism, 200 King St W., Kitchener. ☎519-745-3536 or 800-265- 6959. www.kwtourism.ca.
- **Orient Yourself:** The area is a cluster of big and small towns. Kitchener and Waterloo are separate cities that, together with the town of Cambridge, form an urban agglomeration. The county is also called Waterloo. King Street (Dundas Street in Cambridge) connects all three towns. For helpful interactive maps, go to the city website www.kitchener.ca.
- **Parking:** Parking at the farmers' markets is free.
- **Don't Miss:** The farmers' markets in Kitchener and nearby St. Jacobs. If you are here in autumn, enjoy Oktoberfest *(see below).*
- **Organizing Your Time:** Allow 2 days, including a half day for Elora.
- **Especially for Kids:** The Elora Quarry swimming hole has ice-cold water.
- **Also See:** TORONTO AND AREA

A Bit of History

The area was first settled around 1806 by some 20 Mennonite families from Lancaster County, Pennsylvania, attracted by low land prices and promises of religious tolerance. The Mennonites, of Swiss-German origin, spoke a form of Low German and their presence attracted other German-speakers, mostly Lutherans, who brought manufacturing and business skills. By 1834, there was a Lutheran church. They named their thriving town Berlin in 1833; the township of Waterloo was named after the 1815 victory over Napoleon. By 1836, these German settlers had set up an English-language school for their children. When World War I broke out, anti-German sentiment was rife across Ontario and the name Berlin was considered unpatriotic. Townspeople voted in June 1916 to rename the town Kitchener, after General Lord Kitchener, the Boer War hero recently drowned at sea.

Part of the German heritage is a tradition of breweries, hotels and inns. Since farmers had to come to town for markets, the hospitality industry got an early start and is still going strong. At year-round **farmers' markets** (*see Practical Information*) in Kitchener and nearby St. Jacobs, German specialties are for sale. Every fall there is a nine-day **Oktoberfest** featuring Bavarian food and drink, oom-pah-pah bands and dancing *(Oktoberfest Inc., 17 Benton St., Kitchener; ☎519-570-4267 or 888-294-4267; www.oktoberfest.ca)*. In late May the towns of Kitchener, Cambridge and St. Jacobs hold regional **quilt shows,** auctions, demonstrations and sales events; year-round, quilts are sold in local stores and at farmers' markets.

Sights

Woodside National Historic Site
528 Wellington St. N., Kitchener. ◑Open mid-May–Dec 23 daily 10am–5pm. ◑ Closed Dec 24–mid-May. ⬤ $4. ♿(partial)☎519-571-5684. www.pc.gc.ca. Standing in an attractive park, this low-lying brick Victorian house was the boyhood home of **William Lyon Mackenzie**

The Mennonites in St. Jacobs Country

The first settlers in this area, the **Mennonites** were members of a Protestant sect that grew out of the Anabaptist movement (whose members believed in adult baptism) during the reformation of 16C Europe. The Mennonites were persecuted in Europe and began coming to America in the early 18C. Many emigrated to Pennsylvania, but during the American Revolution the group's commitment to nonviolence (members refused to serve in any army) made them unpopular. Some Mennonites moved North with the Loyalists, settling in the Kitchener area. Old Order Mennonites eschew electricity, modern machinery, cars and telephones. They can sometimes be seen in the country north and west of Kitchener-Waterloo, driving horse-drawn buggies that display a fluorescent triangle on the back as a safety precaution. Mennonite men wear black suits and wide hats; the women wear ankle-length black dresses and small bonnets. To learn more about Ontario's Mennonites and their way of life, catch the 13min video (⬤$4) and related exhibits at the visitor centre in St. Jacobs *(1406 King St. N.; ☎519-664-3518; www.stjacobs.com)*. Contact the centre about tours of the Mennonite country. Please remember that Mennonites are not a tourist attraction; they want to stay separate from "English" life.

Joseph Schneider Haus Museum

Pamela Delaney/Michelin

King (1874-1950) prime minister of Canada 1921-30 and 1935-48. Built in 1853 the house has been restored to reflect the period of King's residence from 1886 to 1893. He wrote that his childhood at Woodside with his three siblings and beloved dog "left the most abiding of all impressions;" in view of King's decidedly eccentric personality, this statement invests the house with added interest. The influence of his grandfather, the rebel newspaperman and political leader William Lyon Mackenzie, is of particular note.

In a theatre located in the basement, an audiovisual presentation *(14min)* provides an introduction, and there is an excellent **display** on King's life and association with Woodside. On holidays the house is decorated to reflect how the King family would have celebrated in the late 19C.

Joseph Schneider Haus Museum

466 Queen St. S., Kitchener. ⓞ*Open Jul–Aug Mon–Sat 10am–5pm, Sun 1pm–5pm. Mid-Feb–Jun & Sept–Dec 24 Wed–Sat 10am–5pm, Sun 1pm–5pm.* ⓞ*Closed Dec 25–mid-Feb.* ⌑*$2.25.* ☎*519-742-7752. www.region.waterloo.on.ca.*

This Georgian frame house was built about 1816 by Kitchener's founder, Joseph Schneider. It is restored and fur-nished to the period of the mid-1850s. An added wing displays decorative arts and German folk art. Special events and seasonal activities such as sheep shearing and quilting parties reflect the family's Mennonite roots.

Doon Heritage Crossroads

Kids*About 3km/2mi from Hwy. 401. Take Exit 275 and turn north. 10 Huron Rd., Kitchener.* ⌑ⓞ*Open May–Labour Day daily 10am–4:30pm. Rest of Sept–late-Dec Mon–Fri 10am–4:30pm.* ⌑*$7.* ☎*519-748-1914. www.region.waterloo.on.ca.*

Many authentic buildings have been moved to this site to depict a small rural Waterloo village c.1914, on the eve of World War I, with staff costumed accordingly. Doon Heritage Crossroads encompasses some 20 historic buildings as well as gardens and farm animals, including breeds such as the Canadienne cow, now rare.

The visitor centre's orientation video *(8min)* incorporates vintage photographs from the sight's archival collection. Costumed interpreters demonstrate daily activities typical of rural life. Originally constructed c.1820, the two-storey frame house at the **Peter Martin Farm,** has been restored to its 1914 appearance and permits an overview of Mennonite family life.

Pamela Delaney/Michelin

Elora Mill Inn on the Grand River

Excursions

Elora

About 37km/23mi northeast via Regional Rds. 22 and 18. ℹ️*Visitor centre, 5 Mill St.* ☎*519-846-9841. www.elora.info.*
In this charming 19C mill town on the banks of the Grand River, stone buildings house quaint shops and restaurants. Elora's spectacular attraction is its 21m/70ft **gorge,** above which perches the Elora Mill Inn, a five-floor former feed and lumber mill. The inn's lounge and patio and several guest rooms overlook the thunderous falls of the river as it meets the gorge. In summertime villagers enjoy a dip in the cold waters of the **Elora Quarry** 🅺, just east of the village *(318 Wellington Country Rd. 18;* ☎*519-846-5234;* 🕐*open mid-Jun– Labour Day;* 👟*$4.25).* The Elora Festival *(33 Henderson St.;* ☎*519-846-0331; www. elorafestival.com;* 🕐*mid-Jul–early Aug),* is a popular celebration of classical and contemporary music.

Castle Kilbride National Historic Site

60 Snyder's Rd. E., in Baden. About 20km/ 12mi southwest via Rte. 6 (Highland Rd. W.), then Rte. 1 (Synder's Rd. E.). 🕐*Open Jul-Aug Tue-Fri 10am-4pm, weekends 1pm-4pm. Apr-Jun & Sept-Dec Tue-Sun 1pm-4pm, Mar weekends only 1pm-4pm.* 🕐*Closed Jan-Feb.* 👟*$6.* ☎*800-469- 5576. www.castlekilbride.ca.*
This Italianate villa, built in 1877 by Scottish immigrant James Livingston, is difficult to miss: the towering two-storey structure made of yellow brick stands on a knoll, a square windowed cupola topping its hipped roof. The upper-storey windows are tall and narrow, with an elaborate crown. The ground floor entrance is flanked by a matching pair of bay windows. The castle's designation as an historic site is entirely due to its period architecture. Remarkably, when the township purchased the house in the early 1990s for a museum, people who had bought the original furnishings at an auction gave them back so they could be displayed in the museum.
Adorned with many trappings of the Victorian era, the castle's interior features trompe l'oeil frescos and elaborate woodwork and plasterwork. The majority of furnishings are original to the mansion. Visitors enter the main hall, graced with Corinthian columns. The library holds several paintings, and the parlour and dining room are divided by intricate wood spoolwork crafted in the early 1900s.

Stratford ★

POPULATION 30,461 – MAP P 108

This community is home to the annual Stratford Festival, a major repertory theatre event occupying four theatres that attracts people from all over North America. Though the focus is Shakespearean, the festival offers a wide variety of drama and music as well as behind-the-scenes tours, lectures and workshops. The town itself was founded in the 19C by British immigrants and given the name Stratford after the name of a local hotel, already a landmark. The river, then called the Little Thames, was re-named the Avon. The town became a prosperous railway centre, and its major industry was furniture-making. Today the principal businesses are manufacturing and tourism.

- **Information:** Stratford Tourism Alliance, 47 Downie St. ☎519-271-5140 or 800-561-7926. www.welcometostratford.com. In summer, a visitor centre on York Street near the Music Theatre offers information and maps.
- ▶ **Orient Yourself:** The core downtown, where three of the four theatres sit, occupies the east side of the Avon River, mostly around the intersection of Ontario and Downie streets. The Festival Theatre stands farther northeast, in beautiful Queens Park edging the river.
- **Parking:** The Tourism Alliance (*see above*) issues a one-day free-parking pass to visitors. Parking lots at the Festival Theatre (*$8*) and at the Tom Patterson Theatre are reserved for theatre-goers only. There are 800 metered spaces downtown, but no overnight parking on city streets.
- **Don't Miss:** Take in a play and stroll one of the lovely gardens.
- **Organizing Your Time:** Plan to spend 2 days in Stratford, including an evening performance. Book well ahead for your hotel, restaurant and theatre tickets.
- **Also See:** TORONTO AND AREA

A Bit of History

The festival is said to have had its beginnings in 1832 when one William Sargint called his establishment on the Huron Road to Goderich the Shakespeare Inn. The community that grew around the hostelry adopted the name of the birthplace of the famous English dramatist and renamed the river the Avon. In 1952, local journalist **Tom Patterson** dreamed of creating a festival to celebrate the

Downtown Stratford

Pamela Delaney/Michelin

Pamela Delaney/Michelin

Festival Theatre

works of the Bard, the town's name-sake. From modest beginnings in a tent a year later, the festival has grown to its present seven-month season *(May-Nov)* in four theatres, which are named the Festival *(55 Queen St.)*, the Tom Patterson *(111 Lakeside Dr.)*, the Avon *(99 Downie St.)* and the Studio *(34 George St. E.)*, as well as various summer music venues. The festival draws a yearly attendance of nearly 500,000. Offerings in the past have ranged from Shakespeare's *Hamlet* and *As You Like It* to Molière's *Tartuffe,* Oscar Wilde's *The Importance of Being Earnest* and Gilbert and Sullivan extrava-ganzas.

For performance schedule and reserva-tions, contact the Stratford Festival box office: ☎519-273-1600, or 800-567-1600 (Canada/US); or go online to www. stratfordfestival.ca.

The festival offers educational pro-grams for serious buffs. Among them are: **Meet the Festival,** held in the Tom Patterson and Studio theatres, which brings actors and other theatre personnel together with the public for informal hour-long discussions *(Wed and Fri Jul-Aug & Sat in Sept; times and guest names published each Jun).* **After-show discussions** are held on Fridays in July and August and on Thursdays in September at the Festival and Studio theatres. **Pre-show lectures** are given in the Festival Theatre. *Call ☎800-567-1600 to reserve your place. No charge.* When ordering your ticket, ask about **Backstage Tours,** which take in the costume warehouse and the Arthur Meighen Garden. *(times vary; $7).*

Summer Music

From late July to mid-August, central Stratford resounds with music of every pos-sible variety, from jazz to opera to military band marches. Concerts are held in the Victorian-style Stratford City Hall, in churches and in city parks. *For tickets or general information, contact Stratford Summer Music ☎519-273-1600 or 800-567-1600. www. stratfordsummermusic.ca.*

Stratford's Swans

Swans were introduced to the Avon in 1918. The white swans are Mute Swans (although they aren't mute). The black swans come from Australia. Visitors are asked not to feed the swans bread, which the swans find indigestible. Instead, buy popcorn ($1 a bag) at the Information Centre on York Street.

Ontario Tourism

Sights

Festival Theatre

55 Queen St., in Queens Park. ♿✖️🅿️ *($8)* ☎️*800-567-1600. www.stratfordfestival.ca.*
Reflecting the tent of its origin, the building resembling a circus "big top" contains an apron, or thrust, stage, surrounded by audience seating for 1,838 on three sides. This modern interpretation of the Elizabethan stage used in Shakespeare's day was revolutionary in the 1950s (but much copied since) because no elaborate scenery could be used and no member of the audience was more than 20m/65ft from the stage.

The theatre is set at the edge of a pleasant park that stretches down to the river, dammed at this point to form **Victoria Lake,** the home of many swans (⚓*see sidebar).* Before evening performances in the summer, the beautifully manicured lawns and the small island in the lake are dotted with picnicking theatregoers. At intermission audience members wander among the formal flower beds and over the lawns surrounding the theatre.

Stratford Gardens

🏛️*Tourism Stratford offers a map showing a walking tour of six gardens.*
Lovely public gardens are part of the Stratford experience. At the Festival Theatre is the **Arthur Meighen Garden,** a profusion of blooms that visitors can admire on their own, on a Backstage Tour or on garden tours *(Jun–Aug Tue–Fri 10am). Book ahead at the Festival Theatre, 55 Queen St.;* ☎️*519-273-1600.*

Just west of the Festival Theatre, **Queens Park** *(55 Queens Park Dr.;* ☎️*519-271-0250 x243)* embraces grassy lawns, picnic areas and a band shell for musical performances.

The **Burnham Woods Arboretum** *(*☎️*519-271-5140)* located at the corner of Martin and William streets on the west side of the river within Queens Park, offers a leafy retreat.

On the opposite bank, on Lakeside Drive, **Meadow Rue Corner** contains a series of small gardens of indigenous plants, linked by a winding trail.

Millennium Park, on Romeo Street, is a fanciful space with ponds, fountains, sculptures and ornamental flowerbeds. It lies near **Confederation Park,** a Japanese-inspired space with a small waterfall and shade trees, next to the Gallery Stratford.

The **Shakespeare Gardens,** near the Huron Street Bridge, next to the Perth County Courthouse, display the exuberant blooms and roses associated with English herbaceous beds. *Free public tours are offered Jul-Aug Mon at 2pm & Thu at 9:30am.*

For a stroll in the woods not far away, the **T.J. Dolan Natural Area** on John Street lies along the Avon River.

About 11km/7mi outside Stratford, the **Wildwood Conservation Area** *(RR2 in St. Mary's;* ☎️*519-284-2931)* includes wetlands, 20km/12mi of hiking trails, a small lake and a campground. While there, visit the pretty town of **St. Marys,** whose Victorian buildings are constructed of limestone quarried in the present-day lake. *(www.townofstmarys.com).*

Goderich ★

POPULATION 7,604 – MAP P 108

This town was founded in 1828 as the terminus of the Huron Road, a right-of-way built in the early 19C to encourage settlement of southern Ontario. It was named after Lord Goderich, then British prime minister. The town is uncommonly pretty, with wide, tree-lined residential streets radiating like the spokes of a wheel from a central octagonal **square**, surrounded by shops and restaurants. On a visit, Queen Elizabeth II called Goderich "the prettiest town in Canada," an opinion disputed by many other contenders, but the town has the undoubted advantage of a lovely harbour and beaches on the western shore of Lake Huron, with spectacular sunsets. Like Guelph, Goderich is a planned town built by John Galt and the Canada Company along the lines of Renaissance towns in Europe. The principal industry is the Sifto Canada Inc. salt mine, the world's largest, but tourism has long been a major source of income.

- **Information:** 57 West St. ☎519-524-6600, or 800-280-7637. www.goderich.ca.
- ▶ **Orient Yourself:** The town sits on a bluff above the point where the Maitland River joins Lake Huron, midway between Port Elgin and Sarnia. Eight principal streets radiate from Court House Square; West Street and the Square itself compose the heritage districts.
- **Don't Miss:** Take time to stroll and admire the large houses and three beaches; the Information Centre offers maps for self-guided walking tours; as well as for bicycle trails; the Tiger Dunlop Nature Trail; and the Maitland Trail, a footpath along the Maitland River.
- **Organizing Your Time:** Allow at least a day to see the sights of Goderich and the waterfront.
- **Especially for Kids:** The Huron Historic Gaol and harbour tugboat tours.
- **Also See:** GEORGIAN BAY

Aerial view of the town square

Courtesy of Gordon Strathdee

Sights

The Waterfront
Follow West St. from Court House Sq. A walking-tour brochure is available at the Information Centre.

Goderich's harbour has been an active one, particularly since 1984 when dredging deepened the lake to provide entry for full-cargo vessels. About 100 large freighters visit the harbour every year, loading rock salt from the mine as well as loading and delivering grain. Small craft berth at the city marina and a fleet of tugboats service entering and exiting freighters. [Kids] *Tugboat harbour tours (30min; $5) are conducted May–Sept; for details, contact MacDonald Marine ☎519-524-9551. www.mactug.com.*

In warmer weather, residents and visitors alike are drawn to the three sandy public beaches, the snack bars, and the extensive **boardwalk** that links swimming, windsurfing and sailing areas.

Huron County Museum★
110 North St. ♿ ⏱ *Open May–Dec Mon–Sat 10am–4:30pm, Sun 1pm–4:30pm. Rest of the year Mon–Fri 10am–4:30pm, Sat 1pm–4:30pm.* ⏱ *Closed Sun Jan–Mar.* *$5 ($7.50 museum & gaol).* ☎519-524-2686. www.huroncounty.ca/museum.*

The museum, part of which is housed in the 1856 Central School, was originally the project of an avid local collector, Joseph Herbert Neill (1884-1969). It has since been considerably enlarged and modernized. Agricultural implements, military artifacts, and furniture are on view over two floors, as well as exhibits relating to John Galt and the Canada Company, which developed the area in the early 18C. Paintings by Huron County artists hang in a gallery.

Huron Historic Gaol National Historic Site★
[Kids] *181 Victoria St. N.* ⏱ *Open early May–late Oct Mon–Sat 10am–4:30pm, Sun 1pm–4:30pm.* ⏱ *Closed Nov–mid-May.* *$5 ($7.50 museum & gaol).* ☎519-524-6971. www.huroncounty.ca/museum.*

This unusual 150-year-old octagonal stone structure housed the county jail (gaol is the British spelling) from 1841 to 1972; it was built as a modern, humane

Huron County Museum

Pamela Delaney/Michelin

facility during a period of prison reform in Britain and North America; from 1901, the prison governor lived in a house attached to the outer wall.

Visitors may enter the cells, library, kitchen, laundry room and outdoor yards. The top floor of the gaol served as the courtroom, where penalties were handed out. The adjoining governor's house, which is furnished with wooden furniture and modern amenities of the day, may be toured.

Excursion

Bayfield
21km/13mi south by Hwy. 21. Chamber of Commerce: ☎519-565-5900. www.villageofbayfield.com.

This small village near Lake Huron has a short but colourful main street, shaded by tall trees and brimming with interesting shops, restaurants, lodgings and places of worship. The **Little Inn of Bayfield,** a former coach stop, has welcomed overnight guests since the 1830s (*26 Main St.; www.littleinn.com*). It and the **Red Pump Inn** (*21 Main St.; www.theredpumpinn.com*) both have dining rooms open to the public. There's a trendy yet historic feel to Bayfield, devoid of urban sprawl. In pleasant weather people browse in the shops or relax at the outdoor tables in front of several restaurants. Surrounding tree-lined residential streets are pleasant.

London ★

POPULATION 352,395 – MAP P 108

London lies on rich farmland, upon which its wealth was originally based. It developed a thriving insurance industry (London Life, Canada Trust), breweries (Labatt, Carling) and eventually a university, now the University of Western Ontario, one of Canada's most distinguished. The economy is also supported by a modern manufacturing sector, a strong service sector, and research and development. Today London is a bustling metropolis fraught with traffic, but expansive green spaces, like Springbank Park, and quiet tree-lined residential streets with attractive houses can still be found.

- **Information:** Tourist Office, 696 Wellington St. South. ☎519-661-5000 or 800-265-2602. www.londontourism.ca.
- ▶ **Orient Yourself:** The **downtown** core has suffered from migration of business to the perimeter; but the John Labatt Centre *(99 Dundas St.; ☎519-667-5700; www.johnlabattcentre.com)*, a venue for hockey games and concerts, has livened up the downtown night scene. **Woodfield Village,** a 19C residential district in the old town, has Victorian houses, many built in a characteristic butter-yellow brick. London enjoys expansive green spaces, notably 78ha/193 acre **Springbank Park,** a hub of outdoor activity west of the downtown core. In summer you can get your bearings with a tour on a red double-decker bus operated by Tourism London *(138 Wellington St.; ☎519-661-5000 or 800-265-2602)*.
- **Parking:** Parking in the downtown core and on the campus can be difficult. In city parking lots, time limits are strictly enforced. Museum London has a spacious parking area *($1.25/hr)*.
- **Don't Miss:** Western Ontario University offers tours of its attractive campus: ☎559-661-2100. www.welcome.uwo.ca.
- **Organizing Your Time:** Two days is the minimum amount of time needed to enjoy the sights of London. Allow one day for the Sights and one day for the Excursions.
- **Especially for Kids:** Storybook Gardens in Springbank Park and Fanshawe Pioneer Village.
- **Also See:** WINDSOR

A Bit of History

In 1792 **John Graves Simcoe,** lieutenant-governor of Upper Canada (now Ontario), set aside a 405ha/1000-acre site for a provincial capital. He considered the existing administrative centre, Niagara-on-the-Lake, too close to the American border. Simcoe named the site for the British capital, calling the river on which it stood the Thames. However, approval of the choice of capital from higher authorities was never forthcoming, and **York** (now Toronto) received the honour instead.

At the time, the territory was occupied largely by Ojibwa Indians, a distant branch of the Algonquins. The city was finally laid out in 1826, as British immigrants flooded into the area, while road and railway links insured commercial prosperity.

Sights

Museum London★★

421 Ridout St. N. ✖ ♿ 🅿. ⏰*Open Jun-Labour Day Tue–Sun 11am–5pm (Thu til 9pm). Rest of the year Tue–Sun noon–5pm.* 💲*Contribution requested.* ☎519-661-0333. www.londonmuseum.on.ca.

Set in a park overlooking the river Thames, this spectacular museum is remarkable chiefly for its design by Toronto architect Raymond Moriyama. Opened in 1980 the structure comprises concrete barrel vaults covered by alu-

Museum London

minum and baked enamel. Each vault contains skylights—Moriyama's answer to the problem of providing indirect natural lighting without damaging the art. The result is a series of airy and spacious galleries where changing exhibits are displayed.

Selections from the permanent Canadian collection of 18C, 19C and contemporary works are on view, including portraits by London's native son Paul Peel, who maintained a studio on Richmond Street. The historical galleries display artifacts and photos of the city's past. The museum's bright modern restaurant, **On the Fork ($$)** *(lunch & dinner Wed–Sat; ☎519-850-3675; www.onthefork.com)*, overlooks the Thames River and offers a reasonably-priced menu of salads, and main courses such as pan-roasted skate on a bed of fennel, or roast duck with risotto; Sunday brunch is a treat.

Eldon House★

481 Ridout St. N. ⏲Open Jun–Sept Tue–Sun noon–5pm. Jan–Apr Sat–Sun noon–5pm, May & Oct–Dec Wed–Sun noon–5pm. ☜$6 (by donation Sun & Wed). ☎519-661-0333. www.london museum.on.ca.

Just north of a series of restored Georgian houses stands London's oldest house, constructed in 1834 by John Harris, a retired British naval captain, and his wife, Amelia. The large and elegant frame residence is completely surrounded by a veranda. A centre of social and cultural activities, the house was occupied by the same family until 1959, when it passed to the city with all its contents.

Its furnishings reflect a refined way of life at a time when most pioneer settlers lived in log cabins. The library and drawing room are particularly noteworthy.

Springbank Park

Springbank Dr.

This 140ha/300-acre green space bordering the Thames River is a hub of outdoor activity west of the downtown core. There are picnic facilities, ball fields, playground areas for children and miles of walking trails. Join city dwellers for a stride along Maurice Chapman Walkway at the water's edge, and ride the park's merry-go-round or mini-train *(☜$1.50; ⏲closed Nov–Apr)*. The park's highlight is **Storybook Gardens**★ *(1958 Storybook Lane; ⏲open May–Oct daily 10am–5pm; rest of the year Fri–Sun 10am–5pm; ☜$3.50; ☎519-661-5770; www.story book.london.ca)*, an assortment of fanciful constructions based on nursery rhymes that house animals, and games for youngsters. Other highlights in Storybook Gardens, to the delight of kids of all ages, are a water park, an

Pamela Delaney/Michelin

Storybook Gardens in Springbank Park

island for pirates, a farm with barnyard animals and an enchanted forest sheltering peacocks, owls, hawks and other birds.

Excursions

Fanshawe Pioneer Village★

Kids 2609 Fanshawe Park Rd. E., in Fanshawe Conservation Area. 15km/9mi northeast of downtown London. ✕ ◷Open Mid-May–mid-Oct Tue–Sun and holiday Mon 10am–4:30pm. ⊛$5. ☎519-457-1296. www.fanshawepioneer village.ca.

This reconstructed 19C village is set in a large park beside Fanshawe Lake, a reservoir constructed to control flooding by the river Thames. The village contains several houses and shops, a church, a fire hall, and an Orange Lodge, the social centre of the community. A Protestant fraternity founded in Ireland in 1795 and named for William III (of Orange), the militantly Protestant **Orange Order** had considerable influence in the founding of Ontario.

Costumed guides lend life to the village, and visitors can shop at the Denfield General Store, which operated in the village from 1877 to 1952. The Lochaber Presbyterian Church holds a Gaelic bible.

Ska-Nah-Doht Iroquoian Village and Museum★

8449 Irish Dr. in Longwoods Road Conservation Area. 32km/20mi southwest by Hwy. 401, then Hwy. 402, Exit 86. ♿◷Open mid-May–Labour Day daily 9am–4:30pm. Rest of the year Mon–Fri 9am–4:30pm. ◷Closed holidays. ⊛$3. ☎519-264-2420. www.lowerthames-conservation.on.ca. ◔Insect repellent recommended.

This village is a re-creation of the type inhabited by Iroquois in Ontario some 1,000 years ago, when they lived by hunting and by intermittent farming. The native people cultivated the land, trapped animals and fished to sustain themselves.

The park visitor centre at the entrance features audiovisual programs and displays. Housed in the Longwoods Resource Centre, the **museum** features interactive exhibits illustrating the culture and history of the Iroquois, as well as artifacts uncovered during area excavations.

Approaching the **village** (bear right), you will see large deer traps made of stakes and an above-ground burial site. The village is surrounded by a wooden palisade with a complicated entrance to make it easy to defend. Inside, three long-houses where the families lived, a primitive sauna called a sweat lodge, drying racks for smoking meat, stretching racks for hides, storage pits and a fish trap give visitors a glimpse of daily life. Many of the exhibits are hands-on, offering visitors an opportunity to grind corn or tend a fire.

In the fields outside the palisade, corn, squash and tobacco crops are grown. Archaeological digs on-site have revealed new artifacts (displayed in the museum) and insights into aboriginal culture.

Dresden

POPULATION 2,700 - MAP P 108

The country around this small manufacturing centre was first settled by black slaves who fled the US for freedom in British North America. **Josiah Henson** (1796-1883), a slave for 41 years, escaped with his family to Canada via the Underground Railway, arriving in Ontario with his family in 1830. In 1841 he moved to the Dresden area, where other fugitive slaves had settled. He helped establish the Dawn Settlement as a refuge for other fugitives and founded one of Canada's first industrial schools. Unable to write, Henson dictated the story of his life (The Life of Josiah Henson—Formerly a Slave), which so impressed **Harriet Beecher Stowe** that she used him as the model for her influential 1852 novel Uncle Tom's Cabin, which fanned anti-slavery sentiment in the US and helped spark the Civil War.

- ⓘ **Information:** www.dresden.ca.
- ▶ **Orient Yourself:** A self-guided walking tour of Dresden and the Dawn Settlement can be downloaded from the town website.
- Ⓟ **Parking:** There is self-parking at the historic site .
- ⊙ **Don't Miss:** Uncle Tom's Cabin.
- ⊙ **Organizing Your Time:** Allow at least two hours to tour the site and view the exhibits.
- ⊙ **Also See:** WINDSOR

Sight

Uncle Tom's Cabin Historic Site★

29251 Uncle Tom's Rd.,1.6km/1mi west off Hwy. 21. ♿⊙Open mid-May–Oct Tue–Sat 10am–4pm, Sun noon–4pm (Jul–Aug open daily). $6.25. ☎519-683-2978. www.uncletomscabin.org.

This collection of wooden buildings, on the site of the Dawn Settlement, includes the **Rev. Josiah Henson's house** (Uncle Tom's Cabin), a simple church of the same era as the one in which he preached, and a fugitive slave's house as well as outbuildings such as a sawmill and a smokehouse. In the interpretive centre, items and documents, such as posters advertising slave sales, recall the era of slavery. Exhibits tell Henson's story. His grave is located on the premises.

Rev. Josiah Henson's House

Kopman/Ontario Tourism

WINDSOR AND LAKE ERIE

This area, which encompasses the city of Windsor and Essex County, offers a combination of big-city excitement and rural idylls in a green and prosperous peninsula at Canada's southernmost point. The effect of two lakes (Lake Erie to the south and Lake St. Clair to the north) and the wide Detroit River moderates the climate, making summers the warmest in Ontario (average high in July 28°C/82°F), and extending the growing season to 212 days, the longest in the country. Local residents like to point out that Essex County lies on the same latitude as Northern California or Tuscany and that, as in these sunny climes, vineyards and fruit orchards flourish.

While it is true that the rich soil left by retreating glaciers is famously productive, much of the fruit and vegetable crop (notably tomatoes) grows under glass or plastic, the largest such greenhouse industry in North America—some 607ha/1,500 acres. These crops can be seen, particularly around Leamington. Country roads south of Windsor lead through small towns such as LaSalle, Amherstburg, Malden Centre and Kingsville, which encompass a historic British fort, an important Underground Railway stop, a noted bird sanctuary, an island winery and other attractions. At the tip of a pointed peninsula in Lake Erie lies renowned birding site Point Pelee National Park, which draws ornithologists and birding enthusiasts from all parts of the globe. Southwest of Point Pelee, Pelee Island sits within Lake Erie; accessible by ferry, the island draws visitors to its beaches, provincial nature reserve and large winery.

Lake Erie is the southernmost, fourth-largest and shallowest (mean depth 19m/62ft) of the five Great Lakes. To the east, it flows into the Niagara River, which tumbles over Niagara Falls; to the west, it receives water from Lake Huron, via the Detroit River. The Canada/US boundary runs through the centre of the lake. Because of the dense population and intensive agriculture on both shores of the lake, it had become severely polluted by the 1970s, with speculation that

Aerial view of Windsor

CVB Windsor, Essex County & Pelee Island

Practical Information

AREA CODES

The area codes for this region are 519 and the new 226, being introduced gradually. For local calls, dial all 10 digits (area code plus the number, but without the 1-prefix). The area code for downtown Detroit is 313. For more information: ☎1-800-668-6878 or www.bell.ca.

GETTING AROUND

BY AIR

Windsor Airport (YQG) (3200 Country Rd. 42; ☎519-969-2430; www.windsor-airport.net) is served by Air Canada Jazz (several daily links to Toronto).

The following car rental services have counters at the airport: Avis (☎800-879-2847 or www.avis.com), Budget (☎800-268-8900 or www.budget.com), Enterprise (☎800-261-7331 or www.enterprise.com), National (☎800-227-7368 or www.nationalcar.com).

Detroit Metropolitan Wayne County Airport (DTW) (☎734-247-7678. www.metroairport.com) is served by major US and international airlines including Air Canada. The following car rental services have counters at the airport: Alamo (☎800-327-9633 or www.alamo.com), Avis (☎800-331-1212 or www.avis.com), Budget (☎800-527-0700 or www.budget.com), Dollar (☎800-421-6878 or www.dollar.com), Enterprise (☎800-325-8007 or www.enterprise.com), Hertz (☎800-654-3131 or www.hertz.com) and National (☎800-227-7368 or www.nationalcar.com).

BY TRAIN

The **VIA Rail** train travels from Toronto through London to Windsor. The station address in Windsor is 298 Walker Rd. (☎888-842-7245 Canada/US; www.viarail.ca).

BY BUS

Greyhound Bus (☎800-661-8747; www.greyhound.ca) provides scheduled bus service to Windsor. The depot is at 44 University Ave. E. in Windsor. **Transit Windsor,** the city bus line, operates a Tunnel Bus link to downtown Detroit leaving from the Windsor International Transit Terminal (300 Chatham St. W.; $2.45 one-way). You can bring carry-on luggage and must pass customs. Check details at www.citywindsor.ca.

GENERAL INFORMATION

ACCOMMODATIONS AND VISITOR INFORMATION

The **Convention and Visitors' Bureau of Windsor Essex County and Pelee Island** (333 Riverside Dr. W., Windsor; ☎519-255-6530 or 800-265-3633; www.visitwindsor.com) offers information on the area, with printable and interactive maps. It also operates a kiosk at Casino Windsor (☎519-258-7878 or 800-991-7777; www.harrahs.com/casinos).

Southern Ontario Tourism Organization (www.soto.on.ca) offers information on attractions, accommodations, events and maps.

Ontario Tourism Marketing Corp. (10th floor, Hearst Block, 900 Bay St., Toronto; ☎800-668-2746; www.ontariotravel.net) offers useful information on Southwestern Ontario.

For information on First Nations sites and activities, contact the **Aboriginal Tourism Assn. of Southern Ontario** (34 Merton St., Ottawa; ☎877-746-5658; www.ataso.ca).

WINERIES

The northwest shore of Lake Erie is Ontario's newest vineyard region.

The **Southwest Ontario Vintners' Assn.** (☎519-676-5867; www.swovintners.com) provides a map of vineyards and contact information for all of its 13 members as well as a listing of special events, such as concerts, receptions, vintage tastings and other events open to the public.

WALKING TOURS

The city of Windsor has managed to preserve a large number of heritage buildings clustered along streets in planned communities laid out a century ago and ideal for walking. Detailed self-guided walking tours of Walkerville and Ford City as well of Victoria Avenue, old Sandwich and heritage gardens are available from the Convention and Visitors Bureau, or go to the city website, www.citywindsor.ca , click on History of Windsor, then on Walking Tours for maps and detailed descriptions of many of the buildings seen on the tours. Or

contact the Planning Department, *Suite 404B, 400 City Hall Square E., Windsor ON N9A 7A6;* ☎*519-255-6543.* Guided tours are offered in summer: contact the Visitors Bureau.

Address Book

For dollar-sign categories, ⓒ see the Legend on the cover flap.

WHERE TO STAY

$ University of Windsor Alumni Hall and Conference Centre – *401 Sunset Ave., Windsor.* ☎*519-253-300 ext. 7074. https://web4.uwindsor.ca. Available May 2-Aug 22.* ⓒ✕🅿🖵
Student housing available in summer includes single rooms with bed and shared washroom, suites with two bedrooms, kitchenette and bath, or five-bedroom townhouses with full kitchen and bath. Breakfast included. The rooms are comfortable, with wireless Internet access; laundry facilities, snack bar and fitness centre on the premises. The suites are located in the Conference Centre near the Ambassador Bridge; 30 townhouses are situated in the Clarke Residence, located across the street.

$ The Tin Goose Inn – *1060 East West Rd., Pelee Island.* ☎*519-733-6900 or 877-737-5557. www.vintagegoose.com. 8 rooms. Closed Oct–Apr.* ✕🅿🖵
This island inn, belonging to the same owners as the mainland Vintage Goose Inn, offers a nostalgic glimpse of the slower summer vacations of days past. Guests share bathrooms (not too difficult—there are 6 of them) and a narrow, screened front porch. Cottages have private baths. The inn is a bit isolated: you will need a bike or a car to reach restaurants. A continental breakfast is included in the room rate. The **dining room ($$)** opens for dinner *(Fri–Sat only)*, serving a prix-fixe meal with such dishes as brie coated in cocoanut, chicken breast poached with pears or Lake Erie pickerel as well as delicious desserts: try the apple tarte with caramel sauce. Reservations advised.

$$ Best Western Seacliffe Inn – *388 Erie St. S., Leamington.* ☎*519-324-9266. www.seacliffeinn.com. 29 rooms.* ✕ⓒ🅿🖵. For much of its 100-year history, this nautically themed inn served Lake Erie sailors desperate for a dry bed. Now, after extensive renovation, the inn welcomes tourists drawn by the scenery and migrating birds. Uncluttered rooms are individually decorated and boast a gas fireplace. Open to the public year-round, the **dining room ($$)** serves contemporary meat and seafood dishes in the lounge or on the patio overlooking the harbour.

$$ Radisson Riverfront Hotel – *333 Riverside Dr. W., Windsor.* ☎*519-977-9777 or 888-201-1718. www.radisson. com. 207 rooms.* ✕🅿🖾
Location is the great advantage of this modern high rise, which offers spectacular views of the Detroit River. The hotel is close to downtown restaurants, the Casino Windsor, riverside parks, the Detroit-Windsor Tunnel and the Ambassador Bridge. Guest rooms are spacious and each has a desk with high-speed Internet access. Amenities include a fitness centre, indoor pool and two restaurants.

$$ Windsor Inn on the River – *3857 Riverside Dr. E., Windsor.* ☎*519-945-2110 or 866-635-0055. www.windsorinnon theriver.com. 5 suites.* 🅿🖵
This three-storey 1890 white frame house, built as a retreat from the city, is now a comfortable bed and breakfast inn close to downtown. The wide lawn leads to the nearby 19km/12-mi linear riverside park, and the view extends to Alexander Park and Belle Isle. Suites, with baths, are furnished in period style, but without fussiness; some have oak floors and a fireplace. The breakfast, included in the rate, is served in the dining room or in fine weather,

on the veranda. Guests may request picnic baskets.

$$$ Vintage Goose Inn and Spa – *31 Division St. S., Kingsville.* ☎*519-733-5070 or 877-737-5557 . www.vintagegoose. com. 6 rooms.* 🅂🅟🄰 🄿 🛏. This 1887 house stands on wide grounds with flower gardens and old trees. The sunny guest rooms, some with private entrances, are decorated in the manner of a Victorian dollhouse. A copious breakfast, included in the rate, is served in the dining room. The adjoining spa offers a full package of treatments for men and women, including volcanic mud or seaweed wraps. The inn arranges tours of area wineries, with dinner at **Jack's Dining Room ($)** just a block away (👐*see Where to Eat*).

WHERE TO EAT

$ Dominion House Tavern – *3140 Sandwich St., Windsor.* ☎*519-971-7400.* **Pub Fare.** This c.1880 structure with Tudor-style half-timbering is a local institution in the old Sandwich district. Since its inception, the landmark hostelry has not wavered in its vocation. When the courthouse stood nearby, judges and officials lunched here; today students favour it, perhaps due to its convenient (think late night) hours of Mon–Sat 11:30am 2am, Sun from 4pm. Enjoy the likes of steak braised in Guinness topped with puff pastry, or a Scotch egg and fish and chips.

$ Jack's Dining Room – *24 Main St. W., Kingsville.* ☎*519-733-6900; www. jacksdining.com.* **International.** Located one block from the Vintage Goose Inn, Jack's is a cozy restaurant and pub named with a nod to noted conservationist and area resident Jack Miner (👐*see Jack Miner Bird Sanctuary*). The extensive menu offers a melange of seafood, Italian, Greek, Canadian and even Russian favourites, plus concoctions with clever names such as Old Hen, Canadian Club Barbeque, and Prickly Pear Pasta. The signature Kingsville perch dinner is borrowed from the Vintage Goose's repertoire: pan-grilled, locally caught perch filets in garlic-dill breading, served with caper-dill aioli.

$ Taloola Cafe – *386 Devonshire Rd., Windsor.* ☎*519-254-6652.* **Canadian.** Pause here at this quasi-New Age cafe during your tour of the Walkerville garden city for a light meal and a glass of Essex County wine. The pretty redbrick building in which the cafe is housed is typical of the commercial structures within this historic district. The Taloola is open for breakfast, lunch and dinner. Buckwheat crepes come with a choice of fillings; salads with fresh vegetables and fruit are served with a tortilla. Many menu items are vegan. Live music is offered Saturday evenings.

$$ Mamo Bistro – *5880 Wyandotte St. E., Windsor.* ☎*519-948-0693. www. mamobistro.com. Closed Sun & Mon.* **Contemporary.** Mamo's offers a sophisticated, imaginative dinner menu, which chef-owner Ryan Odette changes often. The choices are not extensive, but each dish is unusual: instead of chicken, you will find duck or quail, and the fish is whatever is freshest at the market. Bring your own wine; the corkage is free weekdays, $15 on weekends. The bistro's location is a block up from Riverside Drive East.

$$$ La Casalinga – *653 Erie St. E., Windsor.* ☎*519-258-9979. www.lacasalinga1. com. Dinner only. Closed Mon.* **Italian.** It's not mere whimsy that Erie Street is known locally as Via Italia: the excellent Italian eateries and shops here have spawned the sobriquet. La Casalinga offers an extensive menu of traditional foods, with antipasti that's not to be missed. *Secondi piatti* such as osso bucco, seafood risotto, and agnello (lamb rack) are served as well as a variety of pasta dishes. A popular cooking school also operates on the premises.

$$$ Caldwell's Grant – *269 Dalhousie St., Amherstburg.* ☎*519-736-2100. www. caldwellsgrant.com.* **Contemporary.** This austere two-storey building, dating from 1836, has a rip-roaring history and its own private ghost. Present-day dining, however, is an entirely relaxing experience in the modern dining rooms with wood flooring and exposed brick walls, or on the stone-floored terrace in fine weather. The menu stresses seafood and fresh fish in creative combinations as well as a variety of excellent steaks. For dessert, try the pecan bread pudding.

Cars in Canada

For most Canadians, Windsor evokes automobile manufacturing. After Henry Ford set up the first American plant here in 1904, Chrysler and General Motors also created Canadian subsidiaries, but most manufacturing took place in the US, resulting in a massive Canadian trade deficit. The 1965 Canada-US Automotive Agreement (Autopact) in effect created one automobile market across the two countries. Although abolished in 2001 as the World Trade Organization found it discriminatory, Autopact forever changed Canadian industry. Today, parts and assembled vehicles flow back and forth across the border; parts and assembly shipped totaled some $88.5 billion in 2006, and Canada is the world's third largest automobile exporter, after the US and Japan. Chrysler Canada is headquartered in Windsor. General Motors Canada is headquartered in Oshawa where it operates major assembly and manufacturing plants, as well as at St. Catharines and at Ingersoll (a smaller plant in partnership with Suzuki). Ford Canada, headquartered in Oakville, has assembly plants in Oakville and St. Thomas, as well as parts manufacturing plants in Windsor. Other companies with assembly plants in Canada are Honda (Alliston, near Toronto) and Toyota (Cambridge).

it might fill up. However, agreements between Canada and the US have resulted in far cleaner water. The fishing industry has recovered to become the largest of all the Great Lakes (some 20,000 tonnes annually). Yellow lake perch served in lakeside restaurants is highly regarded.

The origins of Windsor lie in a French Jesuit mission to the Hurons, who were living here when the French arrived; today a French heritage is still much in evidence. While the hinterlands of Essex County, settled by Loyalists, boast resolutely British place names, many street names of Windsor are French and a French-speaking presence remains in the city. Particularly after World War II, Italian immigrants flooded the city to work in automobile factories: Erie Street is popularly called Via Italia. Other ethnic groups, notably Arabic and Chinese. have grown in size in recent years, drawn by manufacturing jobs but also by opportunities in small business. This ethnic diversity has given the city lively restaurants, ethnic festivals, and specialty shops. Essex County also has an important place in the history of the Underground Railroad that spirited fugitive slaves from the US to Canada. The John Freeman Walls Historical Site in Lakeshore and the North American Black Historical Museum in Amherstburg bear testimony to this period.

Ambassador Bridge

Ontario Tourism

Windsor ★

POPULATION 216,473 – MAP P 108

Like its American twin city on the north side of the Detroit River, the city of Windsor is associated in most people's minds with automobile manufacturing. In addition, Windsor's enviable location as a seaport (thanks to the St. Lawrence Seaway) and railway hub close to major US cities has contributed to making it one of Canada's busiest ports of entry: about one-third of all US/Canada trade crosses at Windsor. Although an industrial city, Windsor retains greenery and livable neighbourhoods as well as a respected university, lively cultural institutions, parks and many historic sites. A remarkable number of late 19C and early 20C buildings—Ford City and Walkerville are planned communities—are well preserved. Across the river, Detroit boasts major US sports teams and cultural institutions such as the Detroit Institute of Arts. These attractions draw conventions and tourists, another major economic activity in the area. Every year a two-week **International Freedom Festival** is celebrated *(Jun–Jul)* to include the national holidays of both countries: July 1st (Canada) and July 4th (US).

- **Information:** Convention and Visitors Bureau, 333 Riverside Dr. W., Suite 103. ☎519-255-6530 or 800-265-3633. www.visitwindsor.com.
- ▶ **Orient Yourself:** For a detailed street map of greater Windsor, go online to www.visitwindsor.ca/pdfmaps. The city of Windsor lies on the south side of the Detroit River opposite the American city of Detroit. The Ambassador Bridge and the Detroit-Windsor Tunnel connect the cities. The principal downtown arteries in Windsor are Ouellette, Walker and Lauzon streets, which run north-south, while Wyandotte, Tecumseh and E.C. Row run east-west. A 19km/12mi recreational trail called Riverside follows the south shore of the river, offering scenic views of the Detroit skyline.
- **Parking:** US quarters are accepted at parking meters and pay/display machines. Check parking signage very carefully. Overnight parking is prohibited on certain streets.
- **Don't Miss:** Dieppe Gardens, a place to watch ships pass in the St. Lawrence Seaway.
- **Organizing Your Time:** It's best to reserve one day for downtown attractions and a second day for the Ojibway Prairie Complex and Excursion (call in advance to confirm opening hours or make appointment).
- **Especially for Kids:** The Nature Centre at Ojibway Prairie Complex.
- **Also See:** NIAGARA PENINSULA

A Bit of History

Windsor is the oldest continuously settled town in Ontario. The area around the Detroit straits was first settled by the French, who began exploring the region in the 17C. In 1701 **Antoine de la Mothe Cadillac** built a post on the north side of the Detroit River, Fort Pontchartrain, which became the headquarters of the French fur trade in the Great Lakes/Mississippi River area. A Jesuit mission to the native Huron population was set up in 1748 south of the river. Shortly afterwards, French settlers began arriving, as the government of New France sought to counter British inroads; the layout of streets in present-day Windsor reflects the Québec system of *rangs*, long strips of land running perpendicular to the river providing access to transport. Captured by the British in 1760, Fort Pontchartrain was handed over to the Americans after the Revolutionary War, and the Detroit River became the international border. Soon afterwards, Loyalists and French who wished to remain in Canada began farming south of the river, and the little mission became known as Sandwich. In the 1820s the opening of the Erie and Welland canals created opportunities for agricultural commerce. In 1836 the town of Windsor, a name evoking British ties, was incorporated; it eventually absorbed Sandwich. Railroad lines arrived later in the century, and in 1857 the first major industry was begun: the **Hiram Walker Distillery,** maker of Canadian Club whiskey. The Walker family, practicing 19C paternalism, set up an impressive planned garden community still much in evidence today as Walkerville. **Henry Ford** set up the first automobile plants in Windsor in 1904 to serve the Canadian market, followed by other major manufacturers. The Canada-US Autopact of 1965 gave a huge impetus to an already flourishing industry.

Recent reverses in the auto industry have affected the city, but the economy has proved resilient due to a strong base in other industries, many of them spin-offs from auto-making, such as aerospace, high-tech manufacturing, R&D, pharmaceuticals, agribusiness, food processing, education and tourism. It is a testament to the city of Windsor that most people who work here choose to live near their jobs: a large proportion walk to work. City walking paths and beaches are numerous, many offering scenic views of the Detroit River and of lakes St. Clair and Erie. Windsor is backdropped by the charming hinterland of Essex County with its inns and spas, prosperous market farms and vineyards.

Sights

Dieppe Gardens★
Open daily year-round.
The outstanding attraction of this park, which stretches several blocks along the river, west of the main thoroughfare *(Ouellette Ave.)*, is its **view★★** of the Detroit skyline across the water. The gardens are also a good vantage point from which to watch the huge ships of the seaway. The park was named for the Essex Scottish Regiment of Windsor, which participated in the disastrous August 19, 1942, Dieppe Raid in France, the precursor to D-Day. Monuments and historical plaques in the park recall

moments in local history. Note the three **Jesuit pear trees,** a rare variety grown from graftings taken from ancient trees planted by the area's first settler, Charles Chauvin, in 1749.

Art Gallery of Windsor★
401 Riverside Dr. W. ✕⬥⏱Open year-round Wed 11am–8pm, Thu–Fri 11am–9pm, weekends 11am–5pm. ⏱Closed Dec 25–26 & Dec 31–Jan 1. ⬤$3. ☎519-977-0013. www.agw.ca.
Devoted to Canadian art, the Art Gallery of Windsor (AGW) collects and showcases the works of local, regional and national artists. The gallery had its beginnings in 1943 when it exhibited art in the lavish, Edwardian-style Willistead Manor, former residence of Hiriam Walker's second son *(⬤see below)*. The present contemporary building, into which the gallery moved in 2001, enjoys a fine setting overlooking the Detroit River.

With particular strengths in late-19C Canadian painting and modernist works from the early 20C, the permanent collection numbers more than 3,000 works and dates from 1750 to the present; it encompasses sculpture, prints, photographs and videos as well as drawings and paintings. Collection highlights include paintings by the Group of Seven, Emily Carr and Cornelius Krieghoff. The AGW's ongoing exhibit entitled *Art for Canada: An Illustrated History* is an encyclopedic look at the country's art from primitive beginnings to 1930; works from the gallery's collection are exhibited on a rotating basis. Temporary and touring shows are also featured at the AGW.

Willistead Manor
1899 Niagara St. ⬥Visit by guided tour (30min) only, Jul–Aug Sun 1pm–4pm (last tour 3:30pm). Sept–Nov & Jan–Jun first & third Sun of month 1pm–4pm. Dec Sun 1pm–4pm & Wed 7pm–9pm. ⏱Closed Jan 1, Easter Sun & Dec 24–26. ⬤$5. ☎519-253-2365. www.willistead manor.com.
This lavish Tudor-style mansion, designed by Detroit architect Albert Kahn, was built in 1906 for Edward Chandler Walker, second son of Hiram Walker,

who founded of the eponymous distillery. The estate was named for Edward's late elder brother, Willis. The limestone was quarried in nearby Amherstburg, and Scottish masons were brought over to cut it. Occupied only a few years, the 36-room manor was deeded to the city in 1921, and for a period housed the Art Gallery of Windsor. The handsome rooms represent a romantic notion of English aristocratic life.

Willistead was the culminating dwelling in the garden city of **Walkerville,** founded in 1858 by Hiram Walker. The city was organized along workplace hierarchy, with terraced houses for workers, semi-detached houses for management and clergy, and mansions situated around St. Mary's Anglican Church (1983 St. Mary's Gate) for the upper classes. Starting in the 300 block, a stroll down **Devonshire Road** passes well-preserved houses and public buildings; other buildings of significance sit on adjoining streets. Workers' residences are concentrated in the 800 block of **Monmouth Road,** the 700 block of **Walker Road** and the 600 block of **Argyle Road.** The city has prepared a self-guided tour brochure (©see Walking Tours in Practical Information).

François Baby House

254 Pitt St. W. ©Open late-May–late-Sept Tue–Sat 10am–5pm, Sun 2pm–5pm, Rest of the year Tue–Sat 10am–5pm. ☎519-253-1812. www.windsorpublic library.com.

The François Baby [pronounced Bah-bee] House was built 1812 in the French style on a long narrow strip of land fronting on the river (for access to transport). The stone farmhouse served as headquarters for, successively, American and British forces during the War of 1812. In 1838 the Battle of Windsor took place in the farm's orchard during the Upper Canada Uprising.

The structure now houses the **Windsor Community Museum,** which hosts a comprehensive permanent exhibit on the history of Windsor. A number of hands-on displays include a model of the Ambassador Bridge that visitors can cross.

Nearby, the **Duff-Baby Mansion** *(221 Mill St.; ©open by appointment only: contact Windsor Community Museum ☎519-253-1812; www.windsorpubliclibrary. com)* was built by fur trader Alexander Duff in 1798, and purchased in 1807 by a prominent French Canadian, James (Jacques) Bâby. This dwelling is the oldest house in southwestern Ontario. Administered by the Ontario Heritage Trust *(www.heritagefdn.on.ca)*, the two-storey white house incorporates French architectural elements such as a steeply pitched roof (four aligned dormers top the roof above the entrance) and a timber wall frame filled in with brick; yet its dimensions suggest an adaptation of Georgian-style houses typical of North America. Provincial offices now occupy the house. The former carriage house serves as an interpretation centre with exhibits.

Additional Sight

Ojibway Prairie Complex

5200 Matchette Rd. From downtown, take Sandwich St. southeast to Ojibway Pkwy., which edges Ojibway Park. Matchette Rd. is one block east. ©Open May–Nov daily 10am–5pm. Rest of the year Thu–Tue 10am–5pm. ☎519-966-5852. www.ojibway.ca.

This vast 127ha/315-acre green space in southeast Windsor, just 10 minutes from the city centre, includes four parks administered by the city as well as a provincial nature reserve. Many rare plants and animals have been observed here, including remains of the prairie that once extended across Essex County. The area was somewhat miraculously preserved from development because of the failure of a series of major development projects; in 1958 the city purchased the site.

The **Kids ☝ nature centre** features natural history displays and live exhibits with snakes, turtles or other animals. Walking trails crisscross the complex, and the park's naturalist often leads tours. Some 244 species of birds have been sighted here, including the rare northern bobwhite and western meadowlark;

but the greater prairie chicken has not been recorded here since 1897.

Excursion

John Freeman Walls Historic Site

859 Puce Rd., in Lakeshore. About 48km/30mi east of Windsor. Take Exit 28 from Hwy. 401; go north 2km/1mi. ⏲ *Open late-Jun–mid-Aug Mon–Fri 10am–5pm. Mid-May–mid-Jun & late-Aug–Oct by appointment. Call in advance to confirm hours.* ⬤ *$6.* ☎ *519-727-6555. www.under groundrailroadmuseum.com.*

This outdoor museum is a collection of buildings relating to the Underground Railway and the life of John Walls (1813-1909), in particular. He escaped from plantation slavery in North Carolina to Canada via the famed Underground Railway. After his escape, Walls added "Freeman" to his name. John's descendants, including a great-great grandson (a Windsor resident), established and operate this site.

Visitors can view Walls' two-storey 1846 log cabin, where he and his wife, Jane King Walls (1822-1910), raised their nine offspring; a 1798 log cabin moved to the site; a chapel; a flat-bed rail car and a caboose; and the family cemetery, where some 40 relatives and fugitive slaves are interred, including John Walls, who lived to age 96.

Essex County

MAP P 108

With some 166,000 residents, Essex County, sprawling over 1,720sq km/688sq mi, is the second-most populated county in the province. Over the next 10 years, the county is expected to grow considerably—no surprise, given its beautiful beaches, peaceful views of Lake Erie and Lake St. Clair and moderate climate. From Riverside Drive in Windsor, the Detroit River Heritage Parkway follows County Road 20 south through LaSalle to Amherstburg and on to Malden Centre, where County Road 50 continues east to Kingsville. Plaques and markers en route underscore the significance of the county's 402km/250mi coastline in Canadian/US history.

Attractions such as Fort Malden and the North American Black Historical Museum revisit the past and support a growing tourism industry. Conservation Areas and Jack Miner's sanctuary near Kingsville afford serious bird-watching. Today farmland and rural pastures are interspersed with wineries in Amherstburg, Kingsville, Ruthven and Pelee Island; the county's greenhouse farms account for three-fourths of Ontario's greenhouse vegetable production. In summer the Kingsville ferry plies the waves of Lake Erie to take vacationers to Pelee Island for relaxation and recreation. While it doesn't offer the historical interest or many attractions of the Lake Erie coast, the Lake St. Clair shore offers beaches, bird-watching and recreation sites.

🛈 **Information:** The Convention and Visitors' Bureau of Windsor Essex County and Pelee Island. ☎519-255-6530 or 800-265-3633. www.visitwindsor.ca.

▶ **Orient Yourself:** Essex County is Canada's southernmost county; its southern edge borders Lake Erie. Pelee Island is the most southerly inhabited point in all of Canada.

👁 **Don't Miss:** In summer, take the ferry from Kingsville to Pelee Island to enjoy its natural wonders.

⏲ **Organizing Your Time:** The drive should take a half day, but allow a total of two days to leisurely enjoy the attractions along the way.

👶 **Especially for Kids:** Fort Malden and Jack Miner's Bird Sanctuary.

👣 **Also See:** NIAGARA PENINSULA

Driving Tour

From Amherstburg to Kingsville

56km/35mi via Rte. 20 & Rte. 50.

Amherstburg

25km/15mi south of Windsor via Rtes. 2 & 20. Tourism centre (seasonal): 116 Sandwich St. N. ☎519-736-8230 (seasonal) or 519-736-0012. www.amherstburg.ca.
This small town grew from initial settlement around a British fort established near the mouth of the Detroit River at Lake Erie in 1796, Fort Amherstburg. The community served as an entry point into Canada for escaping slaves on the Underground Railroad.

North American Black Historical Museum

277 King St. ♿ ⊙Open May–Oct Tue–Sun noon–5pm. Nov–Dec Sat–Sun 1pm–5pm. ⊜$5.50 ☎519-736-5433 or 800-713-6336. www.blackhistoricalmuseum.com.
A national historical site, this modern museum (renovated in 2001) is constructed around the Nazrey African Methodist Episcopal Church, built by freed slaves.

Exhibits include the history of slavery in North America and the Underground Railroad, but the most interesting displays describe the achievements of African-American and Canadian inventors, businesspeople and military units, augmented by photographs, posters and documents.

Fort Malden National Historic Site★

[Kids] *100 Laird Ave. ♿ ⊙Open May–Labour Day daily 10am–5pm, Sept–Oct Mon–Fri 1pm–5pm, weekends 10am–5pm. ⊜$4. ☎519-736-5416. www.pc.gc.ca.*
Occupying a 4.5ha/11-acre **site** overlooking the seaway, this fort was originally constructed by the British after the War of 1812 to defend against possible American attack. An earlier British post, **Fort Amherstburg**, was built in 1796 at the mouth of the Detroit River where it meets Lake Erie. No longer in existence, Fort Amherstburg served as the base of British operations against the Americans during the War of 1812. The Upper Canada Rebellions, spearheaded by **William Lyon Mackenzie** in Toronto, re-energised Fort Malden, as soldiers were stationed here to repulse possible attacks by rebels and their American supporters. As a result, much needed modifications and repairs were undertaken at the fort from 1838 to 1839. Few remnants of the original Fort Malden remain, however.

In the **visitor centre,** a video *(6min)* explains the fort's role in the War of 1812 and the Rebellions of 1837-1838. Visitors can tour the remains of the earthworks (c.1840) and a barracks restored to its 1819 state. The **interpretation centre** holds military displays that include an example of Mackenzie's rebel flag.

Firing demonstrations at Fort Malden

Fisher/Ontario Tourism

Jack Miner

Born in Ohio, at the end of the Civil War, Jack Miner moved with his family to the Kingsville area when he was 13 years old. To earn income, he became a professional trapper and hunter during his formative years. His accomplishments as a trailblazing conservationist are many: he established one of the first organizations to protect game, initiated waterfowl reserve management with the founding of his sanctuary, and began the banding of migratory birds (he personally banded some 90,000 ducks and geese in his lifetime). His tagging practices led to legislative restrictions on the hunting of waterfowl. During his career as a champion of conservation, he lectured, authored books, won several awards and was recognized internationally.

▶ *Follow Rte. 20 south, then east for a total of about 20km/12mi to Rte. 50. Turn right on Rte. 50 and go 2km/1mi to reach the beach.*

Malden Centre

At junction of Rte.20 with Rte.50.
This hamlet sits at the crossroads of two rural routes. Take the time to stroll Lake Erie's sandy shore and climb the tower at the **Holiday Beach Conservation Area** *(6952 Country Rd. 50; ⏱open year-round daily 7am–9pm; $8/vehicle; ☎519-736-3772; www.erca.org)* to watch for migrating birds over the marshlands of Big Creek. In autumn the area is visited by thousands of raptors such as hawks, falcons and eagles on their flight over the Detroit River to warmer points south.

▶ *Continue east on Rte.50 for approximately 18km/11mi. This quiet road through the flat farmland that borders Lake Erie offers occasional vistas of the lake as well as opportunities to view marshland birds and colourful market gardens.*

John R. Park Conservation Area★

915 County Rd. 50. ⏱Open Mar Mon–Fri 11am–4pm. May–Oct Sun–Thu 11am–4pm. Dec Sun–Fri 11am–4pm. Rest of the year Tue–Thu 11am–4pm. ⏱Closed major holidays. ⊚$4.50. ☎519-738-2029. www.erca.org.
This well-preserved farmstead edging the waters of Lake Erie belonged to John Richardson Park (1801-80) who moved from New England and bought 46ha/114acres in Essex County. As Park and his brothers prospered from their successful shipping company, he built the Classical Revival-style house, lavish for the times, in 1842. He and his wife, Amelia, raised their six children here.

Opened as a museum in 1978 and administered by the Essex Region Conservation Authority, the homestead features several outbuildings, including an ice house, barn, forge, smokehouse and sawmill. The main house illustrates the luxuries enjoyed by an upper-class family in the 19C as seen in handsome wood furnishings, rich fabrics and household goods. Note the piano, desk and tall case clock downstairs. The spacious kitchen features a large working fireplace. Upstairs bedrooms are simply furnished. In spring the gardens are abundant with heirloom crops, and animals are housed at the farmstead in summer.

▶ *Continue east on Rte.50 for approximately 16km/10mi to Kingsville, following Rte. 50 as it curves north to Rte. 20. Turn right on Rte. 20, then left on Rte. 29 (Division Rd.). Turn left on Rd. 3 West.*

Jack Miner Bird Sanctuary★

Kids *2km/1.5mi north of Kingsville town centre via Rte. 29 (Division Rd.), then left on Rd. 3 West. ⏱Open year-round Mon–Sat 8am–5pm. ⏱Closed Dec 25. ☎519-733-4034. www.jackminer.com.*
Founded by renowned conservationist **Jack Miner** (1865-1944), this sanctuary, one of the earliest in Canada, is a well-known stopping place for wildfowl on their seasonal migration.
The best time to visit is November and early December when an estimated 10,000 geese and ducks land to feed. A small museum on the premises houses Miner memorabilia.

Jack Miner Bird Sanctuary

Ontario Tourism

▶ *Return to Kingsville, following Rte. 29 (Division St. S.) south to the waterfront. Turn left on Park St. and right on Ferry St. Ferry terminal is located on Ferry St. in Kingsville.*

Pelee Island

Municipality of Pelee Island, 1050 West Shore Rd., ☎519-724-2931. www.pelee. org. ⊘Bottled water is advised. The car ferry M.V. Jiimaan makes the 1hr30min one-way crossing from Kingsville from *early spring to late fall. ♿🅿. For schedules, contact Pelee Island Transportation ☎519-733-4474 (Kingsville). Reservations Owen Sound Transportation Co. ☎800-661-2220. www.ontarioferries.com.*

Once a centre for rum-running and smuggling, this 4,000ha/10,000-acre island at the southwest end of Lake Erie is now a retreat for those seeking relaxation. In summer the local population of 300 swells to some 1,500. Bicycles are the preferred island transport

Lake St. Clair

Northern Essex County lies along Lake St. Clair, tucked between lakes Huron and Erie; much smaller than the other Great Lakes, it has a surface area of 962sq km/430sq mi, compared to Lake Superior's 82,400sq km/31,820sq mi. The Michigan-Ontario border runs down its centre, with about two-thirds of the surface within Canada. The shallow lake averages only 3m/10ft deep, and must be dredged often to permit passage of big ships. Where the St. Clair River, which drains Lake Huron, enters Lake St. Clair, a large wetland delta has formed. The Canadian portion is within the Walpole Indian Reservation (Chippewa, Potawatomi, Ottawa tribes). Pollution similar to Lake Erie's is being tackled by an US/Canadian alliance. The lake was named by French explorers in 1679 in honour of St. Claire of Assisi, founder of the Poor Claires religious order, on whose name day they arrived here.

A drive eastwards from Windsor along County Road 2, which lies within the town of Lakeshore and passes through many small communities, leads past two wetlands known for bird-watching: **Ruscom Shores Conservation Area,** near Deerbrook, with a 1km/.6mi trail, and **Tremblay Beach Conservation Area,** some 10km/6mi farther on, with a swimming beach. At Tremblay Beach, turn south on County Road 37, then west on County Road 46 to the **Big O Conservation Area,** which, in early May, lies on a major flyway for migratory birds. East on CR46 stretches the **Roscom Tilbury West Conservation Area,** a 63-acre park offering fishing, hiking and campgrounds. Continuing east on County Road 2, you reach **Lighthouse Cove;** the reassembled 200-year-old lighthouse is one of the oldest on the Great Lakes.

(rentals opposite the ferry docks). At Lighthouse Point Provincial Nature Reserve is a stand of deciduous forest, and the Stone Road Alvar Conservation Area is a limestone plain unique in the province, with rare plants. The Pelee Island Bird Observatory offers views of migrating birds. The **Pelee Island Winery** offers tours (mid-May to mid-Oct; Kingsville; ☎519-733-6553 or 800-597-3533; www.peleeisland.com). But soybeans, wheat and other crops are grown on the island as well as grapes. Sandy beaches, restaurants, a bakery, a co-op, a summer theatre and other pleasures make this island a tourist paradise.

Point Pelee National Park★★

MAP P 108

Situated on a pointed peninsula extending into Lake Erie south of Windsor and near the Michigan border, this national park is one of Canada's smallest national parks, but each year 300,000 visitors come to see it . Due primarily to the efforts of naturalist W.E. Saunders, of London, Ontario, and renowned conservationist Jack Miner, the small triangular expanse was designated a national park in 1918. For most visitors, birds are Point Pelee's major attraction. Well known to ornithologists across the continent, its location at the convergence of two major flyways, its extension into Lake Erie and its lack of cultivation have combined to foster large bird populations. Point Pelee is a UNESCO designated Wetland of International Significance. Two-thirds of the park consists of freshwater marshes. The park is one of the few places where the true deciduous forest of eastern North America still exists. The southernmost tip of the Canadian mainland possesses a unique plant and animal life, largely due to its latitude of 42°N, the same as that of Rome. A tiny island just off Fish Point Provincial Nature Reserve, part of Point Pelee National Park, is Canada's farthest point south.

- 🛈 **Information:** Visitor Centre, 407 Monarch Lane, Leamington. ☎519-322-2365 or 888-773-8888. www.pc.gc.ca.
- ▶ **Orient Yourself:** The park lies 10km/6mi south of Leamington, Ontario. Access a colour map of the park online at www.pc.gc.ca. The park **visitor centre** is located 7km/4mi south of the park entrance, on the park's west side. Eight walking trails of 4km/2.5mi or less are clearly marked. Beaches with visitor facilities lie along the western border of the park. The end point of the park is known as The Tip.
- 🅿 **Parking:** There are several designated parking areas. ⚠Warning: cars parked on the roads are towed. A free shuttle, operating every 20min (Apr–Oct), runs from the visitor centre to the tip of the park and back.
- 👁 **Don't Miss:** In the visitor centre, check the visitor log of sightings and buy a Checklist of Birds to keep track of birds you see. ⚲Binoculars recommended.
- 🕓 **Organizing Your Time:** You need a full day to enjoy this park. Activities include hiking, fishing, canoeing, bicycling (bicycle & canoe rentals available), swimming and in winter, cross-country skiing and ice-skating. Consider bringing a canoe or kayak, or renting one on-site.
- Kids **Especially for Kids:** The children's room in the visitor centre.

A Bit of Geology

Flora – The peninsula took its shape 10,000 years ago when wind and lake currents deposited sand on a ridge of glacial till under the waters of **Lake** **Erie**. Today the ridge is covered with as much as 60m/200ft of sand. The sandbar continues under the waters of the lake for some distance, creating a hazard for shipping. The sand spit itself is mantled with a lush forest of deciduous

Bergeron/Ontario Tourism

Boardwalk over the marshland in Point Pelee National Park

trees (there are few evergreens). White sassafras flourishes alongside hop trees, sumac, black walnut, sycamore, shagbark hickory, hackberry and red cedar. Beneath them, many species of plants thrive, including the prickly pear cactus with its yellow flower.

An Ornithologist's Paradise – Spring and fall migrations can be spectacular: as many as 100 species have been sighted in one day. Some 380 species have been recorded in the park, approximately 100 of them remaining to nest. September is the month of the southern migration for the **monarch butterfly.** Visitors can see trees covered with these beautiful insects.

Visit

✗ ঐ ◷ *Park open Apr–Oct daily 6am–10pm (open 5am during May migration). Rest of the year daily 7am–7pm.* ◐ *$7.80/day.* ☎ *519-322-2365. www.pc.gc.ca. For recorded information on migration, weather conditions and events* ☎ *519-322-2371.*
The park visitor centre is 7km/4mi south of park entrance. ঐ. ◷ *Open Jul–Labour Day daily 9am–7pm, May–mid-May daily 7am–5pm, Jun & Sept daily 10am–6pm, Oct & April daily 10am–5pm. Rest of the year weekends only 10am–5pm.*

The **visitor centre** provides a good introduction to the park through its exhibits, theatre programs and publications, including trail guides, available in the on-site bookstore; there is a **special room** Kids for children to preview the park's treasures. Excellent flora and fauna displays together with an interesting account of the park's creation can be viewed. Visitors should watch the video presentation *(15min),* which provides an overall orientation. Check the day's recording in the visitor log of sighted bird species.
From the visitor centre, two trails, **Tilden Woods Trail** *(1km/.6mi)* and **Woodland Nature Trail** *(2.75km/1.7mi)* lead to a wet forest, savannah and other park habitats. At the tip, visitors can observe birds across the lake beginning their southern migration in the fall.
Paths lead in both directions along the park's 19km/11mi of fine sandy beaches (⊘ *swimming prohibited at the tip; swimming beaches are accessible from the picnic areas).* An 1840s house and barn are focal points of the **DeLaurier Trail** *(1km/.6mi),* along which interpretive panels and artifacts provide a brief history of the area's settlement.
Marshland between the sandbars can be toured by a **boardwalk** *(1km/.6mi),* where two lookout towers provide good **panoramas**★ of the marsh. Resident muskrats, turtles and fish as well as birds can be seen.

KINGSTON AND THE THOUSAND ISLANDS

The St. Lawrence River, as it leaves the eastern end of Lake Ontario, harbours a number of islands—1,864 of them in fact, but known collectively as the Thousand Islands. Of varying sizes, these islands—most of them forested—are a magnet for recreation, especially water sports, as well as summer cottages. The lovely mainland city of Kingston sits opposite Wolfe Island, the largest of the Thousand Islands. Abundant with tree-lined streets, parks and 19C heritage buildings, Kingston serves as the gateway to the islands. Rural charm survives in the countryside, notably in Prince Edward County—a large headland to the west, connected to the mainland by an isthmus. Since the building of a canal across the land link, the headland, bounded on the east and north by the Bay of Quinte, is now referred to as an island. Here a vibrant tourist industry has developed in recent years. Pleasant inns, spas and restaurants serve visitors from Ottawa and Toronto, and a burgeoning wine industry has taken root along the southern portion of the county, where Lake Ontario ensures a relatively mild climate. Lighthouses dot the coast—sentinels of a two-century maritime tradition of Great Lakes shipping. The St. Lawrence Seaway runs along the southern shore of the river, and myriad pleasure craft can be viewed, along with ocean-going freighters. Leisurely cruises among the Thousand Islands in the St. Lawrence constitute one of the area's great attractions.

A billion years ago, this area was part of a great mountain range taller than the Himalaya; after erosion, the remains constitute rolling hills such as the knoll on which Kingston's Fort Henry sits. The limestone that characterizes local architecture is quarried from the beds of ancient tropical seas that once lay here. Just east of Kingston, the **Frontenac Axis,** an 80km/50mi extension of the rocky Precambrian Canadian Shield that covers the north of the province, cuts through Gananoque [Gan-ah-KNOCK-kwee] across the farmland and crosses the St. Lawrence to form the granite outcroppings known as the Thousand Islands, and on towards the Adirondack Mountains in New York state.

Some of the Thousand Islands

Onatrio Tourism

Practical Information

AREA CODES

The area code for this region, which includes Ottawa, is 613. For local calls, dial all 10 digits (area code plus the number, but without the 1-prefix). For more information: ☎1-800-668-6878 or www.bell.ca.

GETTING AROUND

BY AIR

Kingston Airport (Norman Rogers Airport) (YGK) *(1114 Len Birchell Way; ☎613-389-6404; www.cityofkingston. ca/residents /transportation/airport)* is served by Air Canada Jazz (several daily links to Toronto). Avis *(☎613-531-3311 or 800-879-2847. www.avis.com)* has a rental-car counter at the airport.

Kingston lies about 2hrs from Ottawa International Airport (◖see *Practical Information for Ottawa).*

BY TRAIN

VIA Rail travels from Toronto to Ottawa through Kingston, with links to destinations across Canada. The station address is 1800 John Counter Blvd. in Kingston. *(☎888-842-7245 Canada/US; www.viarail.ca).*

BY BUS

Greyhound Bus/Voyageur *(☎613-547-4916 or 800-661-8747; www.greyhound. ca)* and **Coach Canada** *(☎705-748-6411 or 800-461-7661; www.coachcanada. com)* provide scheduled bus service to Kingston. The depot is at 1175 John Counter Blvd. in Kingston *(☎613-547-4916).*

BY FERRY

The ferry to **Wolfe Island** operates all year long and is free of charge; the crossing takes 20min. The ferry accommodates 55 cars and 330 passengers. When there is no ice, the ferry operates from Maryville Dock; when there is ice, or in low water conditions, the ferry moves to Dawson Point Dock. The first ferry leaves Wolfe Island at 5:45am, and the last ferry leaves Kingston at 2am. For information: ☎613-548-7227 or www.wolfeisland.com/ferry.

Horne's Ferry, operating since 1802 between Hinkley Point, (Wolfe Island) and Cape Vincent, New York *(☎613-385-2402; in New York ☎315-783-0638),* shuttles cars and passengers 8am to 7:30pm daily May to late fall. Car and driver $12, each passenger $2. You must pass customs and immigration.

The **Glenora Ferry** (a continuation of Highway 33) runs year-round daily from 6am to 1:15 am, every half hour, connecting Adolphustown with Picton; the service is free *(Ontario Ministry of Transportation; ☎613-476-2641; http:// kingston.cioc.ca)*

GENERAL INFORMATION

Kingston Tourist Information Office, 209 Ontario St., Kingston (across from City Hall). ☎613-548-4415 or 888-855-4555. www.tourism.kingston canada.com.

1000 Islands Tourist Office, in Lansdowne. ☎315-482-2520 or 800-847-5263.www.visit1000islands.com.

Prince Edward County Chamber of Tourism and Commerce, 116 Main St., Picton. ☎613-476-2421. www.thecounty.ca.

For information on First Nations sites and activities, contact the **Aboriginal Tourism Assn. of Southern Ontario** 34 Merton St., Ottawa. ☎877-746-5658. www.ataso.ca.

WINERIES

For information on Prince Edward County's wineries, contact **Taste the Country** *(289 Main St., Bloomfield Town Hall, Lower Level, Bloomfield; ☎613-393-2796 or 866-845-6644; www. tastetrail.ca).* Inquire about the self-guided tour, which includes inns and restaurants as well as wineries.

The **Carmela Estates Winery** also operates a restaurant, The Vines, mid-May to Aug *(1886 Greer Rd., Wellington; ☎613-399-3939 or 866-578-3445; www.carmelaestates.ca)*

The **County Cider Company** *(County Rd. 8, Picton; ☎613-476-1022; www. countycider.com),* located just off the

Loyalist Parkway (Hwy. 33), produces a range of ciders, including sparkling varieties and ice cider. The company offers tours and a small restaurant serves light lunches; in fine weather, you can sit outside and enjoy a view of Lake Ontario.

MARKETS

The Kingston Market in Market Square, operating since 1801, offers produce and crafts for sale on Tue, Thu and Sat, 6am–6pm and antiques and crafts on Sun 6am–6pm. ☎613-546-4291, ext. 3150. In winter, the square also holds a public skating rink.

TOURS

To see Kingston in comfort, try the 50min city tour on a **Confederation Tour Trolley.** Departures every hour daily July–Aug 10am–7pm. Labour Day–early Oct 10am-2pm; mid-May–Jun 10am–5pm. 209-211 Ontario St., Kingston. ☎613-548-4453 or 888-855-4555.

The 90min **Haunted Walk** tours of the city or of Fort Henry, always after dark, show you what should not be seen by mortal eye! The ticket booth is located at 200 Ontario St., in the lobby of the Prince George Hotel, open Thu–Sat noon–5pm. ☎613-549-6366. www. hauntedwalk.com. City tour $12.50, Fort Henry $14.50. ♿ Wheelchair accessible with assistance.

You can download a 40min **audio tour** of the old city at no charge at www. kingstonaudiotours.com. Inquire at the Tourist Information Office about guided tours by accredited guides.

The **Kingston General Hospital,** a National Historic Site, offers tours of its original 19C building (which briefly served as Canada's Parliament), as well as the early 20C Fenwick Operating Theatre and the Nurses' Residence, with lively tales of epidemic-fighting. Tickets available at Museum of Health Care (Ann Baillie Building, 32 George St., Kingston). $5. Tours depart from museum mid-May–Labour Day Tue–Sat at 11am, 1pm and 3pm. ☎613-548-2419.

The **Kingston Waterfront Walkway,** 8km/5mi long, begins at King Street West at the entrance to the Rideau Canal, passing several landmarks, including the Penitentiary , Macdonald Park and the Martello towers, Market Square and Place d'Armes. A walk takes about 2hrs. Download a map and guide at www.cityofkingston.ca/pdf/recreation /waterfrontpathwaybrochure.

Around **Picton,** in Prince Edward County, railroad beds have been turned into recreational pathways. A **bicycle path** follows the Loyalist Parkway (Hwy. 33) across the county.

Address Book

For dollar-sign categories, ♿ see the Legend on the cover flap.

WHERE TO STAY

For additional accommodations, ♿ see Prince Edward County below.

$ Alexander Henry B&B – Berthed at the Marine Museum, 55 Ontario St., Kingston ☎613-542-2261. www.mar museum.ca. 47 on-board cabins. Closed mid-Sept–mid-May. ⌑. This former icebreaker plied the waters of the Great Lakes for over 25 years. In 1985 the ship was converted to a very basic bed-and-breakfast accommodation and has since hosted 60,000 overnight guests. Cabins come with double or single beds (most singles are bunk beds); most cabins include a sink, but only four VIP

cabins have private toilets, showers and views. Included in the room rate are a continental breakfast served in the officers' mess and admission to the adjacent Maritime Museum of the Great Lakes.

$ Maple Rest Heritage House – Sandbanks Provincial Park, 3004 County Rd. 12, Picton. ☎519-826-7290 or 888-668-7275. www.ontarioparks. com. 4 bedrooms. 🅿. Fully furnished, this two-storey Victorian heritage house is maintained by the province on the sandbanks of Prince Edward County. It is conveniently located near trails, beaches and all park facilities. The master bedroom has a whirlpool tub. The fully equipped kitchen and bathroom are modern, and some furniture is antique. There's a front porch, a spacious screened-in rear porch and a sundeck. Amenities include a gas fireplace, TV and telephone. Vehicle passes for two cars are included in the rate.

$$ Hotel Belvedere – *141 King St. E., Kingston.* ☎*613-548-1565 or 800-559-0584. www.hotelbelvedere.com. 20 rooms.* 🅿️ 🛏️. This well-situated hotel, built in 1880, exudes Edwardian elegance throughout. The antiques-appointed sitting room is done in muted beige tones. Fireplace- and duvet-equipped guest quarters—some with whirlpool tub, all with private bath—occupy three floors. A complimentary continental breakfast is included in the rate. On the inviting terrace are umbrella-shaded tables, potted urns and seasonal plantings.

$$ Frontenac Club Inn – *225 King St. E., Kingston.* ☎ *613-547-6167. www. frontenacclub.com. 13 rooms & suites.* 🅿️ 🛏️. Once a branch of the Bank of Montreal, this 1845 limestone building, located downtown, also served as an officers' club. Beautifully restored, it offers comfort and style in a contemporary setting. Sunny, spacious guest rooms, each individually decorated, are appointed with uncluttered touches of Victoriana; some rooms have high ceilings and gas fireplaces, all have desks. Several bathrooms have claw-foot tubs; some have Jacuzzis. A complimentary breakfast is included in the room rate.

$$ Rosemount Inn and Spa – *46 Sydenham St. S., Kingston.* ☎*613-531-8844 or 888-871-8844. www.rose mountinn.com. Two-night minimum on weekends. 10 rooms, 1 suite.* 🅿️ 🆂🅿🅰 🛏️. Guests at this stately Italianate stone house (c.1848) enjoy its wicker-furnished porch, lovely gardens, gourmet breakfasts and convenient walking distance to the downtown core. All bedrooms have ensuite bathrooms (one with a cast-iron tub) and ceiling fans. Some rooms feature four-poster beds, others have brass beds. A formal breakfast comes with the room rate, and complimentary afternoon tea is served in the living room.

$$ Trinity House Inn – *90 Stone St. S., Gananoque.* ☎*613-382-8383. www. trinityinn.com. 8 rooms & apartment.* 🅿️ ✕ 🛏️. Just off the main street, this 1859 two-storey brick mansion offers comfortable rooms with package plans, including a B&B rate. One suite has a Jacuzzi tub. The **dining room ($$)** offers a classic French menu featuring lamb, duck and beef dishes with local produce. The back garden is landscaped with water features, flower plantings and statuary. Complimentary breakfast served on a glassed-in porch overlooking the garden and use of a computer are included in the room rate. The apartment has a kitchenette.

$$$ Claramount Inn and Spa – *97 Bridge St,. Picton.* ☎*613-476-2709 or 800-679-7756. www.claramountinn. com. Two-night minimum on weekends mid-May–mid-Oct. 10 suites.* 🅿️ ✕ 🆂🅿🅰. This handsomely restored 1906 Colonial Revival mansion is painted in bright yellow with white trim. The inn incorporates original architectural features,

Claramount Inn and Spa, Picton

Ontario Tourism

such as leaded windows and elaborate fireplaces. Bedrooms are appointed with period furniture but have modern amenities such as soaking tubs and flat-screen TVs. Spa facilities include a saltwater pool; a range of treatment packages is available. **Clara's ($$$),** directed by chef Michael Hoy, offers contemporary cuisine such as venison with herb potato rosti and onion jam, or a yellow fin tuna salad; in fine weather, guests dine on the veranda.

$$$ Devonshire Inn on the Lake – *24 Wharf St., Wellington.* ☎ *613-399-1851 or 800-544-9937. www.devonshire-inn. com. Two-night minimum most weekends. 6 rooms, 1 suite.* 🅿✕▨
Located near Sandbanks Provincial Park and several wineries, this gracious inn offers tranquil, well-appointed guest rooms; some bathrooms have Jacuzzi tubs. Creative cuisine based on French classics is served in the **dining room($$$)**. In particular, side dishes are a delightful surprise. Try the pheasant flavoured with vanilla and served with couscous and baby vegetables or the Cornish hen with roasted garlic pomme puree, haricot vert and tomato tarte tatin. A buffet-style hot breakfast of eggs, pancakes or quiche with bacon or sausage comes with the room rate.

$$$ Gananoque Inn and Spa – *550 Stone St. S., Gananoque.* ☎ *613-382-2165 or 800-465-3101. www.gananoque inn.com. 51 rooms, 6 suites.* 🅿✕ Spa
This hotel has welcomed guests since the 1890s. Five buildings include two century-old houses with suites. Rooms are comfortably furnished; some feature a fireplace or Jacuzzi or balcony overlooking the water. Guest bathrobes are provided. The spacious light-filled **dining room ($$)** has a terrace overlooking the water. The French cuisine is inventive: roast pork or lamb with tri-coloured potatoes and relishes. A variety of treatments are available at the spa.

$$$ Merrill Inn – *343 Main St., Picton.* ☎ *613-476-7451 or 866-567-5969. www. merrillinn.com. 13 rooms. Two-night minimum stay in summer.* 🅿✕▨
This high-Victorian 1878 mansion with three pointed gables and elaborate gingerbread trim dominates Picton's

Main Street. Inside, guest rooms are modern with patterned bedspreads and decorated in colours that invite repose. The **restaurant ($$$)** is justly celebrated for chef Michael Sullivan's contemporary cuisine featuring local seafood like mussels and yellow perch, as well as quail and lamb, county wines and cider. A breakfast buffet and afternoon refreshments are included in the room rate. The inn arranges sleigh rides, winery tours and other outings.

WHERE TO EAT

$–$$$ Fort Henry – *1 Fort Henry Dr., Kingston.* ☎*613-530-2550 or 800-882-6704. www.foodandheritage.com. Closed Sept–Jun.* **Canadian.**
On Wednesdays during July and August here at the historic fort, visitors can dine before watching the Sunset Ceremony performance by the Fort Henry Guard. Served by waiters in red mess uniforms, the three-course meal *($60)* is followed by reserved seating for the ceremony. A simple barbecue meal *($10)* is followed by general seating for the show. Dinners *($25)* without admission to the performance are offered every evening during July and August in the Officers' Dining Rooms. On the last Saturday in July, dinner *($65)* is offered prior to the Fort Henry Tattoo performance. *Reservations (except for the barbecue) essential.*

$ The Island Grill – *1222 Main St., Wolfe Island.* ☎*613-385-2157. www. wolfeislandgrill.com. Closed Dec. 31-Jan31.* **Canadian.** Catch the ferry from Kingston to Wolfe Island (🄲 *see By Ferry above)*, just offshore, for a relaxed meal at the Island Grill. Serving breakfast, lunch and dinner, the restaurant sits near the ferry dock and its seating overlooks the St. Lawrence River. A variety of sandwiches, wraps and burgers is available at lunch. Dinner offerings include rib-eye steak or fish (haddock) and chips. Try the fruit strudel wrap for dessert (fruit-filled tortilla with ice cream). There's a kids' menu and live music some evenings.

$$ Chez Piggy – *68-R Princess St., Kingston.* ☎*613-549-7673. www.chez piggy.com.* **International.** Housed in a restored livery stable built of limestone, the Pig, as it is affectionately known, offers lunch, dinner and Sunday brunch, served indoors or on the popular garden patio at umbrella-shaded tables. The eclectic menu offers a world tour of food: patrons can have New England fish chowder followed by baked ricotta-filled manicotti ala Bolognese at lunch and Vietnamese spring rolls succeeded by lamb tajine in a squash hot pot with ptitim salad for dinner. A three-course prix-fixe meal is offered every evening. The restaurant's delicious breads come from the owners' bakery, Pan Chancho (44 Princess St.; ☎613-544-7790; www. panchancho.com), next-door.

$$ Le Chien Noir Bistro – 69 Brock St., Kingston. ☎613-549-5635. www.lechiennoir.com. **French.** Sitting near Market Square, this bistro serves up honest French fare for lunch, dinner and weekend brunch, incorporating provincial stand-outs such as Alberta steak frites, Prince Edward Island mussels, Atlantic salmon or Quebec duck. One surprise: a gourmet version of poutine, the Québécois snack staple. Patrons may choose to dine in the intimate, exposed brick interior or outdoors at sidewalk seating or the large patio in fine weather.

$$ General Wolfe Hotel – 1237 Hwy. 96, Wolfe Island. ☎613-865-2611 or 800-353-1098. www.generalwolfehotel.com. **French.** Situated three blocks from the ferry dock, this waterside hotel fronts a busy marina. Opened as in inn around 1860, the hostelry offers an impressive selection of classic French dishes in its rather vast dining room, which seats more than 300 patrons. Main courses might include pheasant stuffed with chestnuts, coquilles St. Jacques, duck à l'orange or chateaubriand for two with fresh vegetables. Wine pairings are suggested for all dishes. A four-course table d'hôte menu includes coffee or tea. There is also a casual restaurant, and the inn has nine simply furnished bedrooms (**$**) for overnight guests.

$$ Milford Bistro – 3048 County Rd. 10, Milford. ☎613-476-0004 or 866-576-0004. www.milfordbistro.com. Closed seasonally. **Contemporary.** This pleasant eatery, sitting near a pond, offers contemporary cuisine at lunch and dinner, with an emphasis on local ingredients and charcoal broiling. For dinner, start with the chilled beetroot soup, and move on to the barbecued sirloin with potato skins stuffed with cheese from the nearby Black River Cheese Factory. For dessert the fresh berries in ice cider incorporates County Cider Company's flagship beverage, and the bistro features an extensive list of local as well as imported wines.

$$$ Casa Domenico – 35 Brock St., Kingston. ☎613-542-0870. www.casadomenico.com. **Italian.** Open for lunch and dinner, this fine-dining restaurant serves a varied and often unexpected version of traditional Italian dishes. Antipasti offerings include ravioli alla Silvio, a mix of goat cheese and artichoke ravioli with brown butter, honey mushrooms, tomatoes, spinach and balsamic vinegar. One of the tempting pastas is the Cappasanta: linguine, king crab, scallops, mushrooms, red pepper, spinach in a tomato lobster bisque sauce. A variety of fish, lamb, beef and duck are served as second courses. Friendly dining room with exposed masonry walls.

$$$ Ristorante Luigina – 354 King St. E., Kingston. ☎613-530-3474. www.luiginarestaurant.com. Dinner only. Closed Sun. **Contemporary Italian.** Luigina is the namesake female in this chef-owner pair from Fabriano, Italy, who turn out classic Italian cuisine with a contemporary touch using fresh and imported ingredients. Cheery rooms on three floors exude a warm, Old-World ambience in which to enjoy dishes such as veal scaloppini in a porcini mushroom sauce or even braised rabbit. Panna cotta and tiramisu enrich the dessert menu.

NIGHTLIFE

Thousand Islands Playhouse – 185 South St., Gananoque. ☎613-382-7020 or 866-382-7020. www.1000islandsplayhouse.com. Season runs May–Sept. Located on the waterfront just around the corner from the Gananoque Inn, this two-level playhouse holds not one, but two theatres. For more than 25 years, the Springer Theatre has entertained residents and visitors alike in its intimate space. In 2004 the Firehall Theatre was added, enabling the playhouse to double its seasonal offerings. Both repeatedly fill all seats with diverse productions of new and classic plays, children's theatre, concerts and stand-up comedy presentations.

Kingston Brewing Company – *34 Clarence St., Kingston. ☎613-542-4978. Open year-round Mon–Sat 11am–1am, Sun 11:30am–12:30am.* Behind the Victorian storefront, this brewing company offers a variety of house-crafted beers.

Tir nan Og Irish Pub – *200 Ontario St., Kingston. ☎613-544-7474. Open year-round Sun–Tue 11am–1am, Wed–Sat 11am-2am.* This Irish pub in the landmark Prince George Hotel offers Irish beer, food and song.

SHOPPING

Earth to Spirit Trading Company – *340 King St. E., Kingston. ☎613-536-5252. www.earthtospirit.com.* Exquisite fair-trade baskets, jewellery, masks, sculpture, art glass, metal works, African pottery, hand-carved wood and many other crafts from around the world are for sale in this classy, gallery-style emporium.

A-1 Clothing Ltd. – *358 King St. E., Kingston. ☎613-548-8732 or 877-948-8732. www.aoneclothing.com.* This packed corner store near City Hall has been an institution for more than 65 years. Outdoor adventurers, especially the city's many sailing enthusiasts, stock up here on outdoor gear, footwear and rugged clothing for hiking, backpacking, camping, climbing, windsurfing, sailing and other sports. Several recognized brand names are carried. Step inside for high-tech hiking poles, Swiss army knives, heavy-duty rain suits, fleece liners, Gortex jackets and other sporting accoutrements.

Wilton Cheese Factory – *RR2 Wilton, Odessa. ☎613-386-1223. www.wiltoncheese.com.* The interior of the factory shop at this long-time cheese-making facility resembles an old-time general store, with a counter and shelves lined with merchandise. Offerings include Colby, havarti, Gouda, feta, Swiss, Jarlesberg and creamed cheese. The company specialises in aged cheddar, in particular, or flavoured with multiple ingredients.

LEISURE

Dolce Bella Spa – *8 Cataraqui St., Kingston. ☎613-544-1166 or 877-424-4417. www.dolcebellaspa.com.* Housed within a restored woollen mill with exposed beams and redbrick walls, this polished day spa overlooks the Cataraqui River, the first hint that serenity rules here. Patrons are pampered from head to toe with a range of spa treatments for men and women, including hydrotherapy, contouring and massage. A full-service hair salon, sunless tanning, and half-day and full-day packages (including a gourmet lunch) are available.

Ahoy Rentals – *23 Ontario St., Kingston. ☎613-539-3202. www.ahoyrentals.com.* For messing about in boats, this company is a full-service operation. Here you can rent sailboats, kayaks, canoes or bicycles, or even take a sailboat cruise with an experienced skipper. Sailing and kayaking initiation courses are also offered.

The first European explorers in this area were led by Samuel de Champlain around 1615. A French fur-trading post, Cataraqui, established in 1673, is recalled by the name of the river that flows through Kingston. After abandoning the site due to unfriendly Iroquois, the French returned in 1695 to build a mighty fortress, Fort Frontenac, recalled in local place names including the county and a provincial park. When New France fell to the British, the fort was abandoned. Today visitors can see its curtain wall at Place d'Armes in Kingston. In 1783 the British negotiated with the local Mississauga Indians, a branch of the Ojibway, for land to give to Loyalists and Hessian mercenaries displaced by the American Revolution. The first settlers encountered thick woods that they quickly cut down for farms. Despite an early burst of economic activity thanks to the Rideau Canal, the area never developed the major industry that characterizes Ontario's Golden Horseshoe to the west.

Kingston ★★

The lovely city of Kingston hugs the north shore of Lake Ontario at the point where the St. Lawrence River leaves the lake in a channel full of islands. This onetime capital of the Province of Canada owes its political and economic development to its location at the junction of the lake and the river. One of the main shipbuilding centres on the Great Lakes in the 19C, Kingston remains a water-focused city; it is widely known today as a centre for water sports, especially sailing, windsurfing and river cruising. The Canadian Olympic Training Regatta is held here every August. The former colonial stronghold is also home to several military colleges, such as the **Royal Military College** (Fort Frederick), the Canadian Army Staff College and the National Defence College. Fort Henry, a 19C British stronghold, lies across the LaSalle Causeway, open for tours. The historic city comprises a compact cluster of 19C buildings, many of them constructed of limestone: some 700 buildings in Kingston have landmark designations.

- **Information:** Tourist Office, 209 Ontario St. ☎613-548-4415 or 888-855-4555. www.cityofkingson.ca/visitors.
- **Orient Yourself:** Use the map in this chapter to orient yourself. Downtown Kingston is arranged around Market Square and the waterfront. Princess and Brock streets are the principal thoroughfares. Ontario Street follows the harbour; the LaSalle Causeway connects the west and east banks of the Catarqui River.
- **Parking:** Meters operate in downtown Kingston Mon–Sat 9.30am–5.30pm, 2hr limit, $1.50 per hour. In city parking lots with attendants, the first hour is free.
- **Don't Miss:** Walk around the downtown area and surrounding old residential area to see lovely 19C limestone buildings.
- **Organizing Your Time:** There are many good inns and hotels in the downtown area, within walking distance of the sights.
- **Especially for Kids:** Fort Henry.
- **Also See:** SOUTH CENTRAL ONTARIO

A Bit of History

A French fur-trading post called Cataraqui was founded on the site of the present city in 1673. In 1695 the mighty fortress named Frontenac was erected here by the French; it was abandoned in 1758 after it fell to the British. In 1783, following the American Revolutionary War, the British obtained land from local Mississauga Indians to distribute to Loyalists and to the Hessian (German) mercenaries who had formed a substantial part of the British Army in North America. Called Kingston, the settlement they established soon became an important British naval base and dockyard, and a fort was built to protect it during the War of 1812. After the war Kingston's significance increased with the building of the Rideau Canal, opened in 1832, and of a stone fortress,

Fort Henry. Kingston served as capital of the Province of Canada from 1841 until 1843, when government shifted to Montreal. Yet Kingston remained a vital military centre and important port. However, development of railways in mid-century took business away from the port, which proved too shallow for bigger ships. Instead of becoming a manufacturing centre, Kingston developed around its military establishments, commercial activity and Queen's University.

While tenaciously preserving its past, Kingston continues to keep abreast of the times. Its performing arts centre since 1966, the historic Grand Theatre (1879) has been overhauled to serve the public as a state-of-the-art performance venue. The city has constructed a mammoth sports and entertainment complex downtown. Recently opened, the **K-Rock Centre** *(1 Barracks St.; ☎613-650-5000; www.kingstonrsec.com)* serves as the home of the city's hockey team, the Kingston Frontenacs, as well as a venue for basketball, concerts, ice shows and theatrical performances. An outdoor ice-skating rink recently opened in Market Square, and the newly built Kingston Multiplex Community Centre features four National Hockey League regulation ice rinks.

Sights

Historic District

Above the harbour, in Confederation Park, looms the dome of the handsome **City Hall**★, considered one of the finest 19C classical buildings in Canada; at its back lies Market Square, opened in 1801, where a $6 million renovation was completed in 2008 and an ice-skating rink added outdoors. Other notable buildings are the **Court House**★ with a small dome similar to that of City Hall; the **Cathedral of St. George,** which is reminiscent of Christopher Wren's London churches; the **Grant Hall** building of Queen's University; and some of the buildings of the Royal Military College. The central Market Square is a heritage conservation district.

On the waterfront, the Flora Macdonald Conservation Basin (named for a prominent federal politician), with a 400-slip marina for sailing and power boats, and Portsmouth Olympic Basin (built for the 1976 Olympic Games) offer views of pleasure craft. The Olympic basin, with its 300-slip marina, hosts the annual training regatta.

Marine Museum of the Great Lakes★

55 Ontario St. ◯Open mid-May–early Oct daily 10am–4pm. Early Mar–late May & mid-Oct–end Oct Mon–Fri 10am–4pm. ◯Closed major holidays. ☞$6.50. ☎613-542-2261. www.marmuseum.ca.
Set in old shipbuilding works beside Lake Ontario, this museum has displays on sail and steam vessels that have plied the Great Lakes. An interesting shipbuilders' gallery explains various construction methods, and a special section is devoted to Kingston's shipbuilding days. There are audiovisual presentations and changing exhibits on various aspects of marine life. The museum's largest artifact, the ship *Alexander Henry,* is permanently berthed nearby. Launched in 1958, the ship served as an ice-breaker on the Great Lakes for more than 25 years. Retired in 1985, the vessel was converted into a bed-and-breakfast lodging a year later and is still welcoming overnight guests today *(see Address Book).*

Pump House Steam Museum

23 Ontario St. ◯Open mid-Jun–Labour Day Wed–Sun noon–4pm. ☞$4. ☎613-542-0543. www.cityofkingston.ca.
Kingston's 1849 pumping station has been restored to pay tribute to Canada's steam age. Among the many machines and scale models are two enormous steam pumps once used in the pump house, restored to their condition in 1897.

Canada's Penitentiary Museum

555 King St. W. ◯Open May–Oct Mon–Fri 9am–4pm, weekends and holidays 10am–4pm. Rest of year, open by appointment. ☞Contribution suggested. ☎613-530-3122. www.penitentiarymuseum.ca.
The museum is housed in "Cedarhedge," once the warden's elegant Italianate limestone residence (1873), designed by penitentiary architect Henry H. Horsey. In its heyday, Cedarhedge had extensive grounds tended by squads of inmate labourers; today the view over the bay is still spectacular.

The museum holds exhibits describing the social history of the penitentiary movement, conceived as a reform of brutal jails. Exhibits include two reconstructed cells, one Victorian and one modern (1990), and 19C restraint and punishment devices that would today be considered torture.

Agnes Etherington Art Centre

University Ave. at Bader Lane, Queen's University. ◯Open year-round Tue–Fri 10am–4:30pm, weekends & holiday Mon 1pm–5pm. ☞$4. ☎613-533-2190. www.aeac.ca.

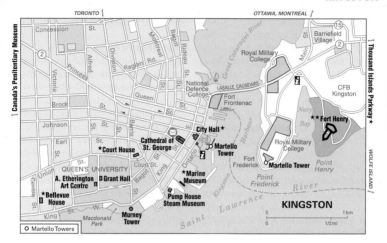

The older part of this art centre occupies a Neo-Georgian house bequeathed by a local arts grande dame. The space has been much expanded, notably by an $8 million refit in 2000, which added eight galleries in a modern addition. Comprised of 14,000 objects, the permanent collection includes a small number of remarkable 17C Dutch paintings of the Rembrandt school, an excellent assemblage of West African art, and a good selection of Canadian and Inuit decorative art.

Murney Tower

West of harbour, at King W. & Barrie Sts. ○*Open mid-May–Labour Day daily 10am –5pm.* ⊛*$3.* ☎*613-544-9925. www.kings tonhistoricalsociety.ca or www.pc.gc.ca.* This squat stone tower in a pleasant park beside the lake dates to 1848. A National Historic Site, it is one of Kingston's Martello towers. It is in good repair with fine stonework and vaulting. Inside, living quarters of the garrison have been re-created, and the gun platform with its 15kg/32-pound cannon on a circular traverse can be seen.

Bellevue House

Pamela Delaney/Michelin

Bellevue House★

35 Centre St. ♿ ⏰*Open Jun–Labour Day daily 9am–6pm. Apr–May & Sept–Oct daily 10am–5pm.* ⏰*Closed Good Friday & Easter Monday.* ◉*$3.90.* ☎*613-545-8666. www.pc.gc.ca.*

This somewhat exotic Italian-styled villa—with its red, finial-crowned roof, square tower, heavy wood balconies and columned porch—contrasts sharply with Kingston's traditional stone buildings. When completed c.1840, it caused a sensation and for a short time (1848 to 1849), served as the residence of Canada's first prime minister, **Sir John A. Macdonald** (1815-91). A Scot by birth, Macdonald spent much of his youth in Kingston and opened his first law office in the city in 1835. He went on to enter provincial politics, becoming one of the chief architects of Canadian Confederation in 1867. During his terms in office (1867-73, 1878-91), the building of the Canadian Pacific Railway was the realization of one of his dreams.

Now a National Historic Site, the house is handsomely furnished to reflect Macdonald's time of residence. In the visitor centre there are exhibits and an introductory film *(8min).*

Additional Sight

Fort Henry★★

Kids *County Rd. 2, east of downtown.* ✕⏰*Open mid-May–Sept daily 10am–5pm.* ◉*$12.50.* ☎*613-542-7388. www. forthenry.com or www.pc.gc.ca.*

Completed in 1837, this large, exceedingly strong stone fortress is set on a peninsula above Lake Ontario. Its main defences face inland, expressly to guard the land approach to the naval dockyard at Point Frederick. The water approaches were covered by Martello towers built later. Having never been attacked, the fort eventually fell into decay. Restored in 1938 and now a National Historic Site, it is best known for the **Fort Henry Guard,** a troop of trained students who re-create the life of the 19C British soldier, guide visitors around the storerooms and quarters, and perform military manoeuvres. In particular, the **garrison parade** *(daily)* should not be missed. *For a meal at the fort,* ♿ *see Address Book.*

The Thousand Islands★★

MAP P 109

As it leaves Lake Ontario, the St. Lawrence River is littered, for an 80km/50mi stretch, with 1,864 islands. One of the oldest vacation areas in northeastern North America, the islands attract Americans and Canadians to their sparkling waters and pink granite rocks. Some are large and lushly forested; others small with a few ragged pines; others are barren—mere boulders worn smooth by retreating glaciers. All of them are of Precambrian rock, the remnants of the **Frontenac Axis,** which links the Canadian Shield with the Adirondacks of New York state. The international border passes among them. Many islands are occupied by houses that can be viewed from passing cruise ships, while parks and towns lie on the larger islands. A spectacular 13km/8mi suspension bridge, the 1000 Islands Bridge, crosses from Ivy Lea on the Canadian side to Collins Landing in the US, connecting Hwy 401 in Canada to Interstate 81 in the US. For the very brave, there is a pedestrian walkway on the US side of the bridge.

> 🛈 **Information:** 1000 Islands Tourist Office. ☎315-482-2520 or 800-847-5263. www.visit1000islands.com.

> ▸ **Orient Yourself:** The islands dot the St. Lawrence River as it leaves Lake Ontario at the lake's eastern end. The US/Canada border winds among the islands. Wolfe Island, opposite the city of Kingston, is the largest of the Thousand Islands.

> 🜁 **Don't Miss:** Take a cruise around the islands.

Boldt Castle on Heart Island

🕐 **Organizing Your Time:** Allow one full day to see the islands. If you plan to visit an American island, be sure to carry proper documents 👁 *see Know Before You Go in the Planning Your Trip section.*

Visit

Boat Trips★★

Several companies offer cruises among the islands in summer. These relaxing passages through the maze of islands afford views of trees, rock and water interspersed at times with summer houses. Dwellings range from small shacks on rock islets to the palaces of Millionaires' Row on Wellesley Island. The huge ships of the St. Lawrence Seaway, which follows the American coast, can be seen alongside private cruisers, yachts and canoes. On the 3hr cruises, a stop can be made at Heart Island to visit **Boldt Castle,** built by a German immigrant at great cost but never finished *(located in the US; for document requirements, 👁 see Know Before You Go). Cruises range from 1hr to 3hrs in duration and cost between $16.50 to $70 (for dinner cruises).* **From Kingston:** *Kingston 1000 Islands Cruises ☎613-549-5544 or 800-848-0011. www.1000islandscruises. ca.* **From Gananoque** *or* **from Ivy Lea:** *Gananoque Boat Line ☎613-382-2144 or*

888-717-4837. www.ganboatline.com. **From Rockport:** *Rockport Boat Line ☎613-659-3402 or 800-563-8687. www. rockportcruises.com.*

Thousand Islands Parkway★

Begins 3km/1.8mi east of Gananoque at Interchange 648 (Hwy. 401). 37km/23mi to Interchange 685 (Hwy. 401), south of Brockville.
This scenic drive follows the shore of the St. Lawrence, offering many good views. **Skydeck** *(👍🕐open mid-April–Oct daily 9am–dusk; ✺$9; ☎613-659-2335; www.1000islandsskydeck.com)* on Hill Island provides a fine **view**★ of the islands *(take bridge to island, toll $2; do not enter US).*
At Mallorytown Landing is the visitor centre for **St. Lawrence Islands National Park** *(2 County Rd. 5, Mallorytown; 👍🕐open daily mid-May–early Oct 10am–4pm; 🅿$7/day; ☎613-923-5261; www.pc.gc.ca).* Beside the visitor centre, a hut enclosed the remains of the wreck of an early 19C gunboat.

Prince Edward County ★

POPULATION 23,763 – MAP P 109 AND P 155

Lying on the northeast shore of Lake Ontario southwest of Kingston, Prince Edward County occupies a 700sq km/270sq mi landmass connected to the mainland by a small isthmus at the far northwest end. The Bay of Quinte, which is really a long arm of Lake Ontario, wraps around the northern side. Highway 33, also called the Loyalist Parkway, crosses the peninsula from the northwest through the principal town of Picton and continues northeast to Amerstview, near Kingston; within the county, a bicycle path runs the entire length of the highway.

A graceful resort town, Picton welcomes weekenders with its inns, spas and fine restaurants as well as art galleries and entertainment. Sandy beaches stretch along the 800km/496mi shoreline, cut by deep bays. Within the county are 6 lakes, 4 provincial parks, 3 national wildlife areas and 9 lighthouse sites. Marinas, with opportunities for fishing, diving and sightseeing charters, abound. Some 40 vineyards, 13 wineries and orchards as well as old farms, some dating from the early 19C, dot the green landscape. For outdoor enthusiasts, there are opportunities for biking, hiking camping, boating, and diving among the many shipwrecks along this sometimes treacherous coast of Lake Ontario.

- **Information:** Chamber of Tourism and Commerce, 116 Main St., Picton. ☎613-476-2421. www.thecounty.ca.
- ▶ **Orient Yourself:** There are only three land routes (all exiting Highway 401) and one ferry to Prince Edward County. The Glenora Ferry crosses from Adophustown to Picton (& *see Practical Information for schedules*). Since Picton Township includes the county, many businesses give their address as Picton, even though they may be in another town altogether.
- **Don't Miss:** Tour two or three wineries and stay at a local inn; visit one of the parks or museums.
- **Organizing Your Time:** Allow a minimum 2 days. To visit the wineries, follow the Taste Trail (www.tastetrail.ca).
- **Also See:** OTTAWA REGION

View from County Cider Company estate

Ontario Tourism

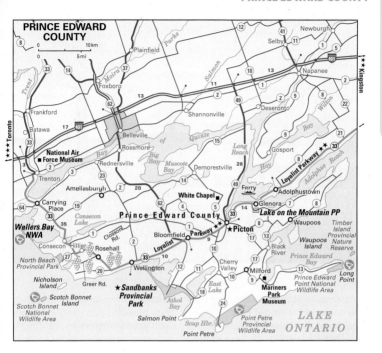

A Bit of History

According to legend, when the first settlers arrived in the 1780s, the area was so thickly wooded that children who wandered off forest paths were never seen again. Settlers quickly turned the forest into rolling farmland. Picton, incorporated as a town in 1837, was named, in a burst of patriotism, for General Sir Thomas Picton, Wellington's second-in-command, who died at the Battle of Waterloo; another town was named for the Iron Duke himself. Sir John A. Macdonald, united Canada's first prime minister and a Kingston native, practiced law in Picton from 1833 to 1835. During Prohibition in the US, the county enjoyed a lively rum-running commerce, which then served Ontario when the province also experimented with enforced temperance. Near Picton, just off Highway 49, stands the **White Chapel,** dating from 1809 (☎613-476-8080), reputedly the oldest Methodist church in Ontario.

Sights

Loyalist Parkway★★

Take Exit 525 off Hwy. 401 (.6km/1mi north of Trenton). Distance: 100km/62mi to Amherstview, near Kingston.

From the mainland, **Highway 33,** called the Loyalist Parkway, crosses the isthmus at Carrying Place and winds through Price Edward County through the main town of **Picton**★, passing small villages and bucolic countryside. It runs along a stretch of Lake Ontario shore near Wellington and on to Adolphustown on the other side of the Glenora Ferry before continuing northeast toward Kingston. En route look out over the long sand spit of the **Wellers Bay National Wildlife Area** (♿access prohibited due to unexploded bombs at former weapons range). On the southern stretch, near Rosehall, cluster five **wineries** that offer tours: Rosehall Run, Carmela Estates and Norman Hardie (all along Greer Rd. west of Hwy.33); and Sandbanks Estates and By Chadsey's Cairns (both along Hwy. 33 south of Rosehall, but west of Wellington). To visit the wineries, access www.

Ontario Tourism

Taste Trail sign post

tastetrail.ca. Stop to see the dunes of **Sandbanks Provincial Park**★ (⏳*see below*), **south of Bloomfield.** Museums along the way include the **Rose House Museum** in Waupoos *(3333 County Rd. 8, Waupoos; ⏰open Jul–Aug Tue–Sun & holiday Mon 10am–4:30pm; May–Jun & early Sept weekends 10am–4:30pm; ✎contribution suggested; ☎613-476-1159; www.pec.on.ca).* This 1804 farmstead gives a glimpse of what must have been a rather grim life.

Ameliasburgh Historical Museum
517 County Rd. 19, Ameliasburgh. ✕ ⏰*Open mid-May–early Oct Fri–Wed 10am–4:30pm. www.pec.on.ca/ameliasburghmuseum. ✎$4. ☎613-968-9678.*
In this re-created pioneer village, buildings from the 19C, including a log cabin, are grouped around an 1868 stone church. Working displays include farm out-buildings and animal pens, a dairy and a blacksmith forge. A small tearoom offers light meals.

Sandbanks Provincial Park★
From Main St. (Hwy.33) in Bloomfield, take Stanley St. east to Country Rd. 12 south to the park. ☎613-393-3319. www.ontarioparks.com. 549 campsites. ⏰Open year-round. ✎Vehicle permit $9, walk-in $2.
Located in the far south shore, off Highway 33, the park offers hiking, boating,

canoeing, fishing, camping and boating *(rentals available).* Vast stretches of sandbanks provide not only an opportunity to swim at the beaches, but a chance to observe delicate plant life. The **Restaurant on the Knoll ($$)** sits just outside the park, overlooking West Lake *(1642 County Rd. 12; ☎613-393-2063 or 800-724-2393; www.isaiahtubbs.com/dining.htm).* The attached **Isaiah Tubbs Hotel ($$)** has 70 guest rooms, including two-level lakeside suites.

Regent Theatre
224 Main St., Picton. ♿⏰*Box office open Mon–Sat 10am–4pm. ☎613-476-8416 or 877-411-4761. www.theregenttheatre.org.*
This 1922 Edwardian opera house, now a venue for theatre, musical performances and movies, has become the centre of Prince Edward County's cultural life. The interior, which seats an audience of 351, has been thoroughly updated while retaining its vintage charm.

Macaulay Heritage Park
Church & Union Sts., Picton. ⏰*Open Jul–Aug daily 10am–4:30pm. Mid-May–Jun & Sept–mid-Oct daily 1pm–4:30pm. ✎$4. Museum ☎613-476-3833; House ☎613-476-3836.*
This municipal park includes the Church of St. Mary Magdalene (now the county museum), a cemetery, a pretty garden and the restored c.1830 Georgian

Macaulay House and carriage house of the Rev. William Macaulay (1794-1874), who laid out the original village of Picton and chose its name. In summer months, costumed volunteers show visitors around this interesting park, illustrative of early life here.

Mariners Park Museum

2065 County Rd. 13 at Country Rd. 10, near Milford. ☎613-476-8392. www.pec.on.ca. ⏰*Open Jul–Labour Day Tue–Sun 10am–4:30pm (open holiday Mon), May–Jun & Sept weekends 10am–4:30pm.* ✎*Contribution suggested.*

This intriguing museum is devoted to Great Lakes sailors, many of whom came from Prince Edward County. Displays include a lighthouse that operated until 1965. Sailors worked even in winter, when they hauled goods across the ice.

Lake on the Mountain Provincial Park

Country Rd. 7, off Hwy. 33, near Glenora. ☎613-393-3319. www.ontarioparks.com. ⏰*Open daily year-round.* ✎*Vehicle permit $9, walk-in $2.*

This beautiful park sits on a hilltop near Picton, along Route 7 near the Glenora Ferry. It centres on a lake formed in a rare doline, or sinkhole, created when underlying limestone collapsed. The lake's great depth and lack of an apparent source caused the Mohawks to believe it was sacred. Visitors and local residents bring picnics and swimming gear and enjoy views over the Bay of Quinte. Housed in a limestone structure, the **Lake on the Mountain Resort ($$)** offers a great **view**★ of the lake, delicious Canadian fare at lunch or dinner and eight guest cottages. *(County Rd. 7, Picton. ☎613-476-1321; www.lakeonthemountain.com).*

Excursion

National Air Force Museum (Trenton)

Take Hwy. 33 to the mainland to Hwy. 401. Head east, take Exit 526 from Hwy 401 (Trenton) and follow signs to Quinte West. ⏰*Open May–Sept daily 10am–5pm. Rest of the year Wed–Sun 10am–5pm. ☎613-965-7223 or 866-701-7223. www.airforcemuseum.ca.*

This modern museum, located near a major air base, offers an overview of the social history of the Canadian Air Force as well as an open-air park where some 16 aircraft are displayed. Indoor exhibits detail Canada's role in the Royal Flying Corps and the Royal Air Force during World War I, the Canadian Air Force from 1920 until the integration of the Canadian Forces in 1968 and the makeup of Canada's Air Force today. A restored WWII Halifax bomber is one of the highlights of the aircraft on view.

Opiola/Ontario Tourism

Sandbanks Provincial Park

OTTAWA REGION

Chosen as Canada's capital by Queen Victoria and laid out by a French architect, Jacques Gréber, Ottawa sits on the south bank of the **Ottawa River,** at the point where it meets the **Rideau River** from the south and the **Gatineau River** from the north. The capital city lies due west of Montreal, about 160km/100mi upstream from the confluence of the Ottawa and St. Lawrence rivers. The Ottawa River marks the boundary between the provinces of Ontario and Quebec, but the National Capital Region spans the river, encompassing a large area that includes Gatineau, Quebec.

The city has emerged as a national cultural centre second only to Toronto, with innovative museums and galleries, two highly regarded orchestras, an opera company and a lively theatre scene. Thanks in large part to the National Capital Commission, Ottawa is an exceptionally beautiful city. Although the federal government remains the major employer, the regional economy—based on high-tech, life sciences and knowledge industries—provides high-quality jobs. Ottawa has more engineers, scientists and PhDs per capita than any city in the country, and is one of the world's leading R&D centres. The tourism and hospitality industry, film and television production and an agricultural sector are major contributors to the prosperity of the region. In the countryside, 19C mill towns such as Merrickville and Prescott, many with Victorian architecture still intact, have found a second vocation in tourism.

Geologically, Parliament Hill is a limestone bluff emerging from the bed of an ancient tropical sea. The gently rolling Gatineau Hills are the remains of a huge mountain range that, a billion years ago, extended into the Laurentians and was the highest the earth has ever seen. Ottawa's climate offers four definite seasons. Extremes range from 33°C/91°F in summer to -40°C/-40°F in winter (colder than Moscow!), although average temperatures are far more moderate. Snow-

Parliament Hill at dusk

MacDonald/Ontario Tourism

Practical Information

AREA CODES

The area code for this region, including Ottawa, is 613. For local calls, dial all 10 digits (area code plus the number, but without the 1-prefix). For more information: ☎1-800-668-6878 or www.bell.ca.

GETTING AROUND

BY AIR

Ottawa International Airport (YOW) *(1000 Airport Pkwy. Private, Ottawa; ☎613-248-2000; www.ottawa-airport. ca)* is served by Air Canada Jazz, other Canadian airlines and principal US airlines, with scheduled non-stop flights to cities across Canada and the US as well as to London (Heathrow) and to Montego Bay *(Oct–Apr)*. **Car rental** companies serving the airport are: Avis *(☎613-739-3334. www.avis.com)*, Budget *(☎613-521-4844. www.budget. com)*, Enterprise *(☎613-248-0005. www. enterprise.com)*, Hertz *(☎613-521-3332. www.hertz.com)*, and National Alamo *(☎613-737-7023. www.alamo.com)*. For information on hotel shuttles: ☎613-260-2359 or www.yowshuttle.com. **Taxi** dispatch: ☎613-523-1234; an average fare to downtown (about 20min away) is $25. For limousine service: ☎613-523-1450 or 888-901-6222. **Public transit** (bus 97) is available at Post 14 at the level 1 Arrivals area. Minimum purchase 2 tickets *($1.90; purchase on bus or at Ground Transportation Desk, level 1 Arrivals)*.

BY TRAIN

VIA Rail station address is 200 Tremblay Rd., Ottawa. *(☎888-842-7245 Canada/US; www.viarail.ca)*. Trains connect to Montreal, Toronto and other points in Canada. City bus 95 serves the station. The **taxi** cab ride downtown costs about $15.

BY BUS

The **Central Bus Depot,** for inter-city bus connections, is located at 265 Catherine St., Ottawa *(☎613-238-5900)*. **Voyageur-Colonial** *(☎613-238-6668)*, which is owned by **Greyhound** (www. greyhound.ca), provides service to Quebec and to eastern points in Ontario. Greyhound serves the western directions. Voyager-Colonial also operates day-trip buses to Montreal and the Thousand Islands.

PUBLIC TRANSPORTATION

The municipal **bus service** in Ottawa is operated by OC Transport *(1500 St. Laurent Blvd., Ottawa. ☎613-741-4390 or www.octranspo.com)* Bus fares are $0.95 each, or 10 for $9.50. You can buy tickets on the bus (exact fare only), at sales centres located in the stations at Rideau Centre, Lincoln Fields, St Laurent or Place d'Orléans, or at one of some 300 vendors located in shops across the city.

The O-Train is a **light rail transit** (LRT) train travelling on an 8km/5mi track and serving five stations between Greenboro in south Ottawa to Bayview in the north. Tickets ($2.25) can be purchased from machines on the station platforms.

GENERAL INFORMATION

VISITOR INFORMATION

Ottawa Tourist Office: 130 Albert St., Suite 800, Ottawa. ☎613-237-5150 or 800-363-4465. www.ottawatourism.ca.
National Capital Commission Visitor Infocentres are located at 50 Rideau St., Customer Service, 1st level, Rideau Court and at 90 Wellington St. (across from Parliament Hill) and at Gatineau Park, 33 Scott Rd., Chelsea in the province of Quebec. ☎613-239-5000 or 800-465-1867. www.canadascapital.gc.ca.
Rideau Canal National Historic Site: ☎613-263-5170 or 800-230-0016, www. pc.gc.ca/rideaucanal for information on tours of the canal.

Upper Canada Village: 13740 Country Road 2, in Morrisburg. ☎613-543-4328 or 800-437-2233. www.uppercanada village.com.

Merrickville and District Chamber of Commerce: 446 Main St. W., Merrickville. ☎613-269-2229. www. realmerrickville.ca.

DISCOUNTS

Several Ottawa museums participate in a discount program called the **Canada's Capital Museum Passport,** which offers 50% off the admission fee to 10 museums. Valid for 7 days from your first museum visit, the passport costs $30 ($75/families). It is sold at the Capital Infocentre, 90 Wellingston St., and at the participating museums. For details, www.virtualmuseum.ca/passport/index.html.

PRESS

Daily: *The Ottawa Sun, The Ottawa Citizen, Le Droit.* Arts/culture/entertainment information in the Saturday editions. **Specialty:** *The Hill Times* (weekly, federal politics), *Frank* (biweekly, satirical), *Ottawa Xpress* (online www.ottawaexpress.ca entertainment news).

TOURS

Around About Ottawa *(☎613-599-1016; www.aroundaboutottawa.com)*: Professionally guided 2hr walking tours cover 2km/1.24mi around the city's centre, Mon–Fri. Four different tour routes are offered. You can sign up as an individual or a group. ☞$15 per person; reservations required.

Gray Line Bus Tours *(265 Catherine St., Ottawa; ☎613-565-5463 or 800-297-6422; www.grayline.ca)*: The Hop On, Hop Off Tour starts at the corner of Sparks and Elgin any time from 10am to 3pm. You can stay on the double-decker red bus or trolley for the full 1hr30min narrated tour, or hop off to see a place and rejoin the tour any time within the next two days. ☞$28.30.

River Boat Trip *See the Sights section.*

LEISURE

National Arts Centre – *53 Elgin St., Ottawa. ☎613-947-7000 or 866-850-2787. www.nac-cna.ca.* ✕♿🅿

The **NAC Orchestra,** under music director Pinchas Zuckerman and conductor laureate Mario Bernardi, and the **Ottawa Symphony Orchestra** perform in Southam Hall. The NAC hosts Canada's leading ballet companies as well as classical and contemporary companies from around the world. **Opera Lyra** *(www.operalyra.ca)* presents four operas during its season in Southam Hall. Often there are free noontime concerts. On the light-hearted side, enjoy Broadway shows, improvisational theatre (a Canadian specialty) and festivals. In addition, **Le Café** draws raves for its fine Canadian lunch and dinner cuisine *(see Where to Eat).*

Great Canadian Theatre Company – *1233 Wellington St. W., Ottawa. ☎613-236-5196. www. gctc.ca.* ✕♿🅿 Housed in the new spectacular 262-seat, $12-million Irving Greenberg Theatre Centre, this English-language company promotes Canadian plays, particularly new material, and well as the international repertoire.

Ottawa Senators – Ice hockey. Season October to early April at Scotiabank Place, Kanata *(for individual tickets: Capital Tickets ☎613-599-3267 or 877-7883267; www. capitaltickets.ca)* www.senators.nhl.com; www2.scotiabankplace.com.

MARKETS

ByWard Market, Ottawa, is open May–mid-Oct daily 6am–6pm. Rest of the year daily 8am–5pm. Closed Jan 1 & Dec 25. ☎613-562-3325. www.bywardmarket.com.

The Prescott Market, in Prescott, is located at the Clock Tower parking lot, King and Centre Sts. Open mid-April–Dec Tue–Thu, & Sat 7am–7pm. ☎613-925-2812.

---

fall is abundant: the canal becomes the world's longest skating rink and resorts in the Gatineau Hills welcome skiers. Other seasons provide opportunities for cycling, swimming, boating and rafting down the Gatineau River.

Settled by loggers and mill operators, Ottawa and the surrounding area developed with the **Rideau Canal**, a 202km/126mi waterway extending from Ottawa to Kingston intended as a transport system secure from possible American attack. Its commercial use was quickly supplanted by railroads in the mid-19C, but the canal has had a resurgence as a venue for recreation. In June 2007, UNESCO designated it a World Heritage Site.

Address Book

For dollar-sign categories, see the Legend on the cover flap.

WHERE TO STAY

$ Hostelling International Ottawa – *In Ottawa Jail, 75 Nicholas St., Ottawa.* ☏*613-235-2595 or 866-299-1478.* *www.hihostels.ca. 154 beds.* ⓟ
Housed in the 1863 Carleton County Gaol near ByWard Market, this hostel offers beds in renovated jail cells, as well as dormitories and semi-private rooms. Rooms for couples are available, as are laundry facilities, lockers, Internet access and it is said, ghosts. Historic tours show off the gallows and the cells.

$$ A Rose on Colonel By B&B – *9 Rosedale Ave., Ottawa.* ☏*613-291-7831.* *www.rosebandb.com. 3 rooms.* ⓟ ⌂
This 1925 redbrick abode in a quiet, tree-filled neighbourhood is only steps away from the Rideau Canal. There's a private entrance for guests. Airy rooms are individually appointed: two overlook the canal; the third is shaded by a 200-year-old oak tree. Coffee, tea and hot chocolate are available 24/7 in the lounge. Included in the rate are breakfasts of waffles, or eggs, or French toast or other staples, with the option of being served in bed.

$$ Auberge The King Edward – *525 King Edward Ave., Ottawa.* ☏*613-565-6700 or 800-841-8786. www.bbcanada. com/464.html. 3 rooms.* ⓟ ⌂
Asymmetrical turrets and bull's-eye windows characterize this Victorian terrace house in Sandy Hill. The restored interior features mouldings, archways, fireplaces and bay windows. Spacious guest quarters feature 3m/10ft ceilings, antique furnishings, air-conditioning and wireless Internet. Two rooms have private balconies. Framing the grounds is a cast-iron fence built in the 1870s to deter the neighbours' cows and pigs. A full breakfast is included in the rate.

$$ Gasthaus Switzerland Inn – *89 Daly Ave., Ottawa.* ☏*613-237-0335 or 888-663-0000. www.gasthausswitzer landinn.com. 22 rooms.* ⓟ ⌂
Located in the Sandy Hill neighbourhood east of the city centre, this heritage limestone house (1832) sits adjacent to Ottawa University and

close to cinemas and theatres. Guests enjoy well-lit rooms with duvets, large windows, wireless Internet and possibly a working fireplace. A hearty complimentary breakfast includes Swiss Bircher-Muesli (see recipe on Website), a nutritious cold cereal made with yogurt, oats and lots of fruit. In summer, enjoy breakfast in the garden amid a host of flowering plants.

$$ McGee's Inn – *185 Daly Ave., Ottawa.* ☏*613-237-6089 or 800-262-4337. www. mcgeesinn.com. 12 rooms.* ⓟ ⌂
This sprawling brick mansion (1886) in Sandy Hill was built for John McGee, brother of Thomas D'Arcy McGee, a father of Confederation assassinated in Ottawa in 1868. Two themed bedrooms—one with a canopy bed—have gas fireplaces and double Jacuzzis. Every guest room has a small fridge, air-conditioning, Internet access and cable TV. Complimentary breakfasts of eggs Benedict or omelettes or crepes, served with sausage, are generous.

$$ Millisle B&B – *205 Mill St., Merrickville.* ☏*613-269-3627. www.bbcanada. com/millislebb. 5 rooms.* ⓟ ⌂
Housed in an impressive 1840s Victorian pile with a turret-capped wraparound porch, this tree-shaded inn offers common-area rooms furnished to the period. Bedrooms, some with four-poster beds, manage to be both charming and modern. All guest rooms come with ensuite bathrooms, some of which feature claw-foot tubs. The cooked breakfast is ample, and you can enjoy a gourmet dinner upon request.

$$ Wolford House B&B – *826 County Rd. 23, Merrickville.* ☏*613-269-3112.* *www.bbcanada.com/wolfordhouse.* *3 rooms.* ⓟ ⌂. This accommodation sits on spacious grounds in the countryside just outside town. Expansive lawns and well-tended gardens centred on a gazebo cover the property. Interior rooms in the modern house are tastefully appointed with Colonial-style wood furniture and accents. Guest rooms feature pine-wood furniture, patterned bedspreads and ensuite bathrooms. The hot breakfasts are scrumptious; orange French toast is the house specialty.

$$$ Hotel Indigo – *123 Metcalfe St., Ottawa.* ☎*613-231-6555 or 877-846-3446. www. hotelindigo.com. 106 rooms.* ✕♿🅿*(fee)*⌇. Opened in 2007 as an InterContinental Hotel Group property, this stylish boutique hotel resides near Sparks Street Mall in the redbrick building formerly occupied by the Hotel Roxborough. Completely renovated, the structure encases Indigo's sleek lobby, with its soaring atrium; five floors of guest rooms, each with flat-screen TV and mini-fridge; a 24/7 fitness centre; and indoor pool. Catering to business travellers, the hotel features such amenities as a business centre, wireless Internet, an ATM and complimentary daily newspaper. The on-site restaurant serves breakfast, lunch and dinner.

$$$ Lord Elgin Hotel – *100 Elgin St., Ottawa.* ☎*613-235-3333 or 800-267-4298. www.lordelginhotel.ca. 355 rooms & 4 suites.* ✕♿🅿⌇. Named for James Bruce, 8th Earl of Elgin and governor general of British North America from 1847–54, this Ottawa institution near Confederation Square is well located for sightseeing and shopping. Opened in 1941 and later expanded, the hotel has air-conditioning and extensive fitness facilities with an indoor pool, whirlpool and sauna. Standard guest rooms are decorated with pastel fabrics and blond furnishings and include a complimentary daily newspaper. The on-site restaurant, **The Elgin Café ($$$)**, offers international cuisine in its bright, contemporary dining room.

$$$ Sam Jakes Inn and Spa – *118 Main St. E., Merrickville.* ☎*613-269-3711 or 800-567-4667. www.samjakesinn.com. 33 rooms.* ✕🅿🅂. This lodging is sited within an 1861 Victorian stone mansion, built by an Irish immigrant and department store owner. The inn has been meticulously renovated with 1860s-style furnishings and many modern conveniences; six suites have fireplaces. Separate buildings hold luxury suites and a conference centre. The Village Spa offers a variety of treatments. The inn's **restaurant ($$$)** serves contemporary cuisine with Swiss accents (lots of rösti variations); the menu indicates which products are procured from within 175km/100mi of Merrickville.

$$$ Upper Canada Guest House – *adjacent to Upper Canada Village, 13740 Country Rd. 2, Morrisburg.* ☎*613-543-4328 or 800-437-2233. www.uppercanadavillage.com/ghouse.htm. 2-night minimum stay Jun–Aug. $1,470 week.* 🅿. Families and groups of up to six people will find solitude at this two-storey, late-19C farmhouse, which rents out as a complete accommodation. Modern amenities include a fully equipped kitchen, TV, two bathrooms, washer and dryer, screened-in porch and carport for two vehicles. Its location on a grassy point that juts into the wide St. Lawrence River assures excellent views.

$$$$ Fairmont Château Laurier – *1 Rideau St., Ottawa.* ☎*613-241-1414 or 800-441-1414. www.fairmont.com. 429 rooms.* ✕♿🅿⌇. Named after former Canadian prime minister Sir Wilfrid Laurier, this massive limestone structure, castlelike in appearance, has been an Ottawa landmark since 1912. The hotel enjoys an enviable location next door to Parliament. Immense leaded-glass windows pierce the oak-panelled lobby and adjoining rooms. Guest rooms have been renovated with luxurious furnishings; some rooms boast views of Parliament Hill and the Rideau Canal. Services include babysitting. A highlight is the indoor pool with its cushy chaise longues. **Wilfrid's ($$$)**, a favourite local meeting spot, serves regional Canadian cuisine.

WHERE TO EAT

$ Blue Cactus – *2 ByWard Market, Ottawa.* ☎*613-241-7061. www.blue cactusbarandgrill.com.* ♿ **American Southwestern.** Sample some of Ottawa's best margaritas or the house-blend Sangria, or choose from a selection of nine regional micro-brewed beers while you ponder the large menu at this marketside cafe. Start with the ever-popular Blue Cactus nachos, then brave the Voodoo Chicken with searing Creole mustard sauce or try the house specialty: sizzling fajitas. In summer, the floor-to-ceiling windows become patio-style doors.

$ Roses Café – *523 Gladstone Ave., Ottawa.* ☎*613-233-5574.* **Indian.** Popular with locals, this cozy eatery features spicy Southern Indian cuisine and specializes in *dosas* (a type of semolina pancake stuffed with spiced meats and vegetables). There is also an Indian restaurant on Wellington called Roses, which leads to confusion; it's good, too.

$ Yang Sheng – *662 Somerset St. W., Ottawa.* ☎613-235-5794. **Chinese.** This casual eatery is always crowded with a local Asian clientele, students among them. Yang Sheng's spicy cuisine includes dim sum, and ample servings of delicacies like hot and sour soup, barbecued duck and spicy Szechwan eggplant.

$ Zak's Diner – *14 ByWard Market Sq., Ottawa.* ☎613-241-2401. *www.zaksdiner. com. Open 24 hours.* **American.** A trip down nostalgia lane, Zak's offers up the 1950s, complete with juke box, Formica surfaces, blue-upholstered booths and retro ads cluttering the walls. A great place to bring kids. The menus (breakfast, lunch, dinner) are fortunately a big step up from '50s cuisine, with spinach and chicken salads, a variety of tortilla wraps, and multifarious burger and sandwich options (including the Reuben sandwich and Philly cheesesteak). For a blast from the past, try one of the blue-plate specials: yes, meatloaf and gravy, liver and onions, hot beef or chicken sandwiches.

$$ Canal Ritz – *375 Queen Elizabeth Dr., Ottawa.* ☎613-238-8998. *www.canalritz. com.* ♿ **Italian.** Patrons can literally paddle here by canoe, tie up at the dock (or else walk or cycle to the restaurant along the bike paths) and drop in at this renovated boathouse perched on a bend in the Rideau Canal. The floor-to-ceiling windows and a summertime patio place diners seemingly atop the canal. The Ritz specialty is oven-baked thin-crust pizza, but people come here more for the view than for the food.

$$ Feleena's – *742 Bank St., Ottawa.* ☎613-233-2010. *www.feleenas.ca.* **Mexican.** A favourite in the Glebe district—an upscale neighbourhood near downtown with great boutique shopping—Feleena's offers a comfortable adobe-toned interior with Diego Rivera-style murals. The menu is resolutely authentic, but with a few dishes, such as the salmon with cilantro or the tasty vegetarian enchilada, to appeal to the less adventurous palate. Try the *pechugo de pollo,* chicken breast stuffed with goat cheese and peppers in a creamy cilantro sauce, or opt for the classic enchilada, tamale, burrito or quesadilla served with a variety of stuffings. On weekends, brunch starts at 11:30am. In the summer, lounge on the terrace with a margarita.

$$ Festival Japan – *149 Kent St., Ottawa.* ☎613-234-1224. *www.festival japan.ca. No lunch weekends.* **Japanese.** With its traditional setting of screens, polished wood and bamboo, this restaurant is a relaxing place in Ottawa's busy centre. The menu is extensive and includes all principal types of Japanese food, from sushi to sukiyaki, including an assortment of Japanese noodles. Served alone or in combinations with other dishes, the tempura is good, with a delicate crust. For a bit of adventure, the grilled water eel has an unusual, chewy texture, and the marinated grilled squid is delightful. In particular, the fish dishes are nicely presented.

$$ Merlot Rooftop Grill – *100 Kent St., in Marriott hotel, Ottawa.* ☎613-783-4212. *www.merlotottawa.com.* **Canadian.** Located on the 29th floor of the Marriott hotel, this revolving restaurant offers lovely views of Ottawa at sunset. The food is good as well: Atlantic salmon filet in a whiskey and molasses glaze, served with a melted leek and Yukon gold potato spring roll. The specialty is grilled meat such as Alberta beef tenderloin in a balsamic tomato and thyme compote served with gratin potatoes, or the buffalo tenderloin with a blackberry-cinnamon chutney and a wine reduction. Sunday brunch (*10:30am-2pm, $31, reservations essential*) is a feast of hot dishes and salads as well as breakfast fare.

$$ Willard's Hotel – *Queen St., in Upper Canada Village, Morrisburg.* ☎613-543-3735. *www.uppercanadavillage.com. No dinner.* **Canadian.** This two-storey white-frame structure, constructed in 1785, is a popular dining spot in the village. Authentic 19C fare is served to visitors by staff in 1850s period costumes at lunch (*11am–5pm*) and tea time. Dishes such as pan-fried perch and sirloin steak smothered in wine-rich gravy issue forth from the busy kitchen.

Homemade apple pie, bread pudding and lemon syllabub are good choices for desert. Tea *(11am–5pm)* is served on the shaded veranda or in the parlour. *Reservations recommended.*

$$$ Le Café – *In National Arts Centre, 53 Elgin St., Ottawa. ☎613-594-5127. www.nac-cna.ca.* **Canadian.** Overlooking the Rideau Canal, this upscale restaurant is known for its well-presented regional Canadian cuisine, created by renowned chef Kurt Waldele. The menu features foods from all over the country, such as Alberta Angus sirloin steak, Atlantic salmon, Ontario double pork chops, Quebec apple cider, and Newfoundland screech rum cake. In summer, patrons enjoy the airy patio and the passing parade of "canalites."

$$$ Empire Grill – *47 Clarence St., Ottawa. ☎613-241-1343. www.empiregrill.com.* **Contemporary.** A patio spilling out onto bustling market streets in summer, an Art Deco-style martini bar and comfortable indoor booths entice diners to linger at this friendly, relaxed restaurant. The focus here is on aged Alberta Angus beef such as filet, rib-eye, T-bone, strip-loin steaks, grilled to perfection. Fish, chicken, veal, seafood and other dishes are also on the menu as well as sharing platters. The Empire offers a weekend brunch.

$$$$ Beckta Dining & Wine – *226 Nepean St., Ottawa. ☎613-238-7063. www.beckta.com. Dinner only. Closed some holidays.* **Contemporary.** Inventive cuisine has made this upscale restaurant the local trendsetter: the Rolling Stones dined here. Chef Michael Moffatt spotlights game, fish and beef from Canada: bison striploin, Nunavut wild char, Canadian bouillabaisse and Alberta beef tenderloin, for example. Products are fresh, often organic, so winter menus stress root vegetables, while summer menus highlight what's garden-fresh. Niagara and Okanagan wines are included in the extensive wine list. Beckta is located in a two-storey redbrick Victorian a few blocks south of Parliament Hill.

$$$$ Juniper Kitchen and Wine Bar – *245 Richmond Rd., Ottawa. ☎613-728-0220. www.juniperdining.ca. No lunch weekends.* **Contemporary.** Despite its down-home name, this is an upscale eatery on the cutting edge of culinary inventiveness. The focus is New Canadian cuisine that is seasonal and obtained as close at hand as possible. Try the Lamb Two Ways: one coated in herbs and peppercorns and roasted, the other braised and served with a Pernod and fennel seed sauce. The vegetarian option might be Chinese-inspired crepes rolled with wild mushrooms braised in ginger and sesame and roasted sweet peppers, in a *hoisin* sauce. Desserts are just as interesting: prune and brandy crème brûlé, for example. The wine cellar is extensive, with bottles from all major regions and some unexpected (Austrian whites). *Reservations recommended.*

NIGHTLIFE

Heart and Crown – *67 Clarence St., Ottawa. At Parent in ByWard Market. ☎613-562-0674. www.irishvillage.ca.* This Irish pub serves shepherd's pie and Guinness beef stew in a lively, casual setting. A total of 16 taps promise a wide selection of brews. In summertime the pub's outdoor tables afford great people-watching in the heart of the market. Wednesday through Saturday enjoy live Celtic music.

D'Arcy McGee's Irish Pub – *44 Sparks St. Ottawa. ☎613-230-4433. www.ottawa.darcymcgees.com.* The high-gloss wood interior, with detailed scroll-work around the bar, was hand-carved in Ireland for authenticity's sake. Draft beer and a fine array of Irish whisky, cognac, bourbon, port, Cuban cigars and, well, plenty of craic (good times and fun) complement the corned beef and cabbage. Entertainment Wed and weekends: Celtic, blues, whatever.

The Manx Pub – *370 Elgin St., Ottawa. At the corner of Frank St. ☎613-231-2070.* This small pub is located below street level in a redbrick row house. A magnet for students and professors, the place features cozy booths and dark oak flooring. Single-malt scotch is a house specialty, though there's an excellent variety of beer, cider and microbrews. Imaginative pub fare such as wild mushroom ragout and quesadillas.

Ottawa ★★★

POPULATION 808,391
MAPS PP 169 AND 176

Situated at the convergence of the Ottawa, Rideau and Gatineau rivers, this seat of national government charms visitors with its handsome waterways, expansive parklands, miles of bicycle paths, colourful springtime tulips and the world's longest skating rink: the Rideau Canal. Although the region was known to the Outaouais Indians (from whom the city gets its name) and visited by French explorers, there was little settlement in the area until 1800. The building of the canal, completed in 1832, spawned a thriving community. By the mid-1830s the town had become the hub of Ottawa Valley's squared-timber industry. Although still a centre for forestry and for the rich agriculture to the south, Ottawa is chiefly a city of government. High rises contain government departments and ministries, the most dominant being **Place du Portage** across the river in Gatineau, Quebec. As many Québécois work in Ottawa but live in Québec, French is even more present in Ottawa than the statistics indicate. The capital area is bilingual, with 50 percent of the population speaking English, 32 percent French; many people speak more than one language.

- **Information:** Ottawa Tourism, 130 Albert St., Suite 800, Ottawa. ☎613-237-5150 or 800-363-4465 or www.ottawatourism.ca.
- **Orient Yourself:** Refer to the maps in this chapter to get your bearings. The Parliament Buildings are located in a large park on the south shore of the Ottawa River, an area bounded to the south by Wellington Street and to the east by the Rideau Canal. South of Wellington Street lies the heart of Ottawa's tourist area, with museums, the Sparks Street Mall, the National Arts Centre, the Rideau Centre shopping mall, the Byward Market (a hub of shops and eateries) and many hotels, churches and shops. The Sandy Hill neighbourhood sits east of the city centre. The city of Gatineau lies across the Ottawa River in the province of Quebec.
- **Parking:** No public parking is permitted on Parliament Hill. Pay lots and metered parking are available in the downtown area south of Wellington Street. Many museums and other sights provide parking lots (where parking is often free-of-charge), as do hotels.
- **Don't Miss:** The trails and parks where you can walk or bicycle and enjoy spectacular views, particularly along the Rideau Canal. Other than your own interests, use the Michelin star ratings to decide what museums to visit; for discounted admission information, access www.virtualmuseum.ca/passport/index.html.
- **Organizing Your Time:** To do the capital justice, reserve 5 to 7 days here. Ottawa's spectacular natural setting is best appreciated through the Scenic Drives (see below), such as Ottawa River Parkway and Rideau Canal drive, which take at least two hours.
- **Especially for Kids:** The Canada Agriculture Museum, where kids can pet rare breeds of domesticated animals, the Canadian Museum of Nature and the Canada Science and Technology Museum.

A Bit of History

The First Settler – In the winter of 1800, American **Philemon Wright** travelled by oxcart on frozen waterways from New England and harnessed the **Chaudière Falls** to power gristmills and sawmills on the Quebec side of the river. He felled white pine and floated the first raft of squared timber to Quebec in 1806, launching what was to become a vast industry.

☺ A Bit of Advice ☺
Visiting Parliament Hill

Since Parliament Hill's tourist activities are numerous during peak season *(mid-May to Labour Day)*, it is advisable to stop first at the large white tent (**Info-tent**) located between Centre Block and West Block for a schedule of the day's events.(🕐*open mid-May–Labour Day 9am–5pm & til 8pm weekdays late Jun–Labour Day)*. Information is also available at the National Capital Commission's **Capital Infocentre** at 90 Wellington Street *(corner Metcalfe St.;* 🕐*open early-May–Labour Day daily 8:30am–9pm; rest of the year daily 9am–5pm;* ⊘*Closed Jan 1 & Dec 25–26;* ☎*613-239-5000 or 800-465-1867; www.canadascapital.gc.ca)*. Another useful website for your visit is www.parl.gc.ca, Parliament's official website, with up-dates on Senate and House sessions.

Parliament Hill is "guarded" by the Mounties—members of the Royal Canadian Mounted Police, attired in their famous ceremonial uniforms of stetsons, red tunics, riding breeches, boots and spurs *(summer only)*. Regiments of Foot Guards wearing bearskin caps, scarlet tunics and blue trousers are also stationed on the Hill in summer. Resembling the ceremony held outside Buckingham Palace, a **Changing of the Guard★★** is performed in summer *(late Jun–late Aug 9:45am)* and a seasonal, bilingual **sound and light show** *(30min)* presents Canada's history (♿🕐*9:30 & 10:30pm mid-Jul–mid-Aug, 9pm & 10pm mid-Aug–Sept.; in case of rain, show may be cancelled)*. During the holiday season, a Christmas lights show is held nightly *(mid-Dec–mid-Jan;* ☎*613-239-5000)*.

The Rideau Canal – The War of 1812 exposed the dangers of using the St. Lawrence as a military communications and supply route from Montreal to Upper Canada. Ships were vulnerable to perilous rapids and gunfire from the US. After the war the **Duke of Wellington** sent men to Canada to look for a safer passage. The route selected followed the Ottawa, Rideau and Cataraqui rivers and a series of lakes to reach the Royal Navy base at Kingston on Lake Ontario. Construction of the canals and locks necessary to make the route navigable was entrusted in 1826 to Lt.-Col. **John By** of the Royal Engineers, who established his base at the present site of Ottawa, named Bytown. By 1832 the canal system was completed, but its cost was so great that By returned to England unemployed and penniless. By 1849, a lock system had rendered the St. Lawrence River's rapids harmless, resulting in reduced commercial traffic on the canal, whose route was less direct. By the end of WW II the canal's original role was greatly diminished, but gradually it found new use as a waterway for pleasure craft. In 2007 the Rideau Canal was designated a UNESCO World Heritage Site, as North America's best-preserved slackwater canal.

Lumbertown – The completion of canal construction did not signal the end of Bytown's boom. Using the power of Chaudière Falls, residents built sawmills on the Bytown side of the Ottawa River. Having never been used militarily, the Rideau Canal blossomed briefly as a means of transporting the lumber south to the US. Bytown became a rowdy centre for lumberjacks and rivermen skilled at negotiating the rapids.

Westminster in the Wilderness – The 1850s saw great rivalry among Montreal, Toronto, Kingston and Quebec City over selection as the capital of the newly united Canada. The government asked **Queen Victoria** to decide the issue. She chose Bytown, which had hastily changed its name to Ottawa, after a local Algonquin-speaking Indian tribe, as a more suitable appellation for a capital. The choice did not please everyone: "the nearest lumber village to the north pole" wrote Torontonian **Goldwin Smith**. Despite such quips, the parliament buildings were begun in 1859 and completed enough by 1867 to be used by representatives of the new confederation.

Ottawa Today – A city of parks, scenic roads and bicycle paths, Ottawa is also a city of flowers, especially in May when thousands of tulips bloom—a gift from the Dutch, whose future queen spent the war years in Ottawa. It is a city that has capitalized on the cause of its founding—the **Rideau Canal.** Flanked by tree-lined drives, this waterway is a recreational haven: canoeing, boating, jogging, strolling, biking in summer, and ice-skating and cross-country skiing in winter, when little "chalets," set on the ice, offer food and skate rentals. The canal can be followed its entire 202km/126mi length to Lake Ontario through picturesque countryside with lovely lakes. Ottawa boasts other scenic roads that follow the Ottawa and Rideau rivers.

Finally, Ottawa is a cultural centre, with the greatest number of museums of any Canadian city, and a fine selection of art and music, dance and drama at the **National Arts Centre.** The latest addition to the city's arts scene is the dazzling new **Irving Greenberg Theatre Centre,** home to the Great Canadian Theatre Company and an art exhibition space (*see Leisure in Practical Informa-*

tion). The city is particularly lively in February during the winter festival titled **Winterlude,** in May for the **Canadian Tulip Festival,** and from late June to early July, when **Canada Day** is celebrated in style on Parliament Hill.

In 2001 the City of Ottawa absorbed 12 former municipalities to become a megacity, overseen by one mayor, one city manager and nearly two dozen city executives.

Parliament Hill and Area★★

Parliament Hill is immediately identifiable by its three imposing Gothic-Revival style parliament buildings. **East Block,** with its whimsical windowed tower that looks like a face, and **West Block,** both designed by Strent and Laver, were completed in 1865. The **Parliamentary Library,** designed by Thomas Fuller and Chilion Jones, was finished only in 1876. **Centre Block,** originally designed by Fuller and Jones, was officially opened in 1866 but rebuilt in 1920 after most of it was destroyed by a fire in 1916. The **Peace Tower** at its centre was added in

Foot Guards Regiment in the Changing of the Guard, Parliament Hill

1927 as a monument to Canadians killed since Confederation. Today Centre Block contains the Houses of Parliament—the Commons and the Senate. West and East blocks contain the offices of senators and members of Parliament. All three buildings are open for public tours.

Parliament Hill dominates the northern side of **Confederation Square,** a triangular-shaped "island" that serves as the centrepiece for several of the capital's historic and cultural institutions. In the middle of the square stands the towering granite archway of the **National War Memorial (1),** which was dedicated in 1939 by King George VI. Neighbouring "the Hill," as it is familiarly known, is **Château Laurier** (*see Address Book*) a distinguished hotel recognizable by its turrets and steeply pitched copper roofs. The government conference centre stands opposite. Bordering the southern tip of Confederation Square is the National Arts Centre.

Sights

Approached from Wellington Street, Parliament Hill seems to belie its name. Canada's Parliament actually stands on a bluff overlooking the Ottawa River and must be viewed from that angle to appreciate its designation.

Ottawa River Boat Trip★★
Departs from Ottawa locks mid-May–mid-Oct daily 11am, 2pm, 4pm; evening cruises late Jun–Labour Day 7:30pm. Cruise departs from Gatineau dock 30min earlier. Round-trip 1hr 30min. $18. Paul's Boat Lines. ✕ ♿ ☎613-225-6781. www.paulsboatcruises.com.
This is an excellent trip, especially at dusk, affording close-up views of Parliament Hill, the Rideau Falls and the houses along Sussex Drive overlooking the river, in particular the prime minister's residence. The sheer size and force of the Ottawa River are impressive.

Parliament Buildings★★
Dominating Parliament Hill, Ottawa's parliament buildings, largely constructed with Nepean sandstone, house Canada's Senate, House of Commons and Parliamentary Library, which are open for guided tours. In addition, the offices of country's prime minister, party leaders and other government officials are located here.

Centre Block★
Visit by guided tour (45min) only, mid-May–Labour Day daily 9am–8:30pm. Rest of the year daily 9am–4:30pm. Times vary if Parliament in session. Closed Jan 1, Jul 1 & Dec 25. ♿ ☎613-239-5000 or 800-465-1867. www.canadascapital.gc.ca.
The original 1866 structure served as the first Parliament building. The current building dates to 1927, rebuilt over 11 years after the 1916 fire. Tours enable visitors to enter the Senate, the House of Commons and the **Parliamentary Library**. Parliamentary proceedings are open to the public if the House or Senate is in session *(for schedule, access www.parl.gc.ca)*. Each sitting begins with the **Speaker's Parade.**

Separately, the 92m/302ft **Peace Tower,** fronting Centre Block, can be ascended by elevator for a fine **view**★ of the sprawling capital from the campanile's observation deck. The tower contains a room commemorating Canada's fallen war heroes and a 53-bell carillon, which is featured in regularly scheduled concerts *(Jul–Aug weekdays 2pm–3pm; rest of the year weekdays noon–12:15pm).*

Parliamentary Library★★
Built over 17 years, from 1859 to 1876, the library is a separate building, linked to Centre Block by a corridor; its solid iron doors saved the library from destruction by the 1916 fire, the only part of the original Centre Block structure to escape damage. Modelled on the reading room of the British Museum, the circular Gothic-Revival style structure boasts flying buttresses and leaded glass windows. The interior features wood-panelling and a cherry, oak and walnut parquet floor, which replicates the original, damaged in a 1952 fire. Completed in 2006, a four-year renovation includes new copper roofing for the library's three roofs.

East Block★
Visit by guided tour (45min) only, Jul–Labour Day daily 10am–6pm. Closed

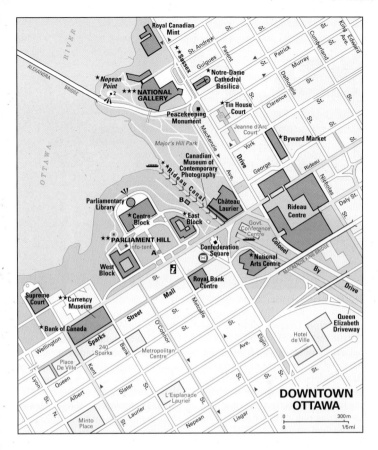

DOWNTOWN OTTAWA

0 — 300m
0 — 1/5mi

Jul 1. ♿☎*613-239-5000 or 800-465-1867.
www.canadascapital.gc.ca.*
The interior of this mid-19C building
has been restored to its 1872 appearance. Some of the offices have been
authentically furnished to represent
their occupants at the time: Prime Minister Sir John A. Macdonald; his Quebec
colleague and fellow Father of Confederation Sir George-Étienne Cartier; the
governor general, Lord Dufferin; and the
Privy Council. In summer students role-
play these historical figures to enliven
the visit.

The Grounds
In front of the parliament buildings is a
low-lying fountain called the **Centennial Flame (A)** because of the natural
gas always burning at its centre. Symbolizing the first 100 years of Confederation,
it was lit at midnight on New Year's Eve,
1966. Around the flame the 13 shields of

Canada's provinces and territories are
displayed, with the date they entered
Confederation.
The walk around Centre Block is pleasant, affording **views**★ of the river and
of Gatineau, which rapidly changed
from an industrial centre to a federal
government annex containing large
office complexes. A notable collection
of statues, many by Quebec sculptor
Louis-Philippe Hébert (1850-1917),
commemorates Canadian prime ministers, as well as Queen Victoria and
Queen Elizabeth II.

Rideau Canal★★
*Between Parliament Hill and Mayor's
Hill Park at Ottawa River.*
In 2007 this 202km/126mi-long canal,
with a total of 45 locks, was designated
a UNESCO World Heritage Site. It is
the only early 19C canal on the continent still functioning along its original

Tour boats on the Rideau Canal

Obrien/Ontario Tourism

route—from Ottawa south to Lake Ontario via Kingston's harbour. Built for military purposes (*see A Bit of History*), the canal has been reborn as a recreational waterway. In summer, a variety of small craft ply its waters; in winter, the frozen canal waters form one long ice-skating rink with heated huts and on-site food stands.

From Wellington Street visitors can descend into the small gorge where the Rideau Canal begins. Eight **locks** raise boats from the Ottawa River to the top of the cliff. There is also a **boat trip** on the canal. *Departs from Rideau Canal Dock, behind Conference Centre, mid-May–mid-Oct daily 10am, 11.30am, 1.30pm, 3pm, 4:30pm. Late Jun–Labour Day cruises also at 7pm & 8:30pm. Round-trip 1hr 15min. $16. Paul's Boat Lines. 613-225-6781. www.paulsboat cruises.com.*

Beside the locks stands the **Old Commissariat Building (B)**, completed by Colonel By in 1827 as a military supply depot. The historic structure now houses the **Bytown Museum,** with a display on the canal builders *Open mid-May–early Oct daily 10am–5pm (8pm Jul–Aug), April–mid-May & Sept–Oct Thu–Mon 10am–2pm. Rest of the year by appointment only. $6. 613-234-4570. www.bytownmuseum.com.*

Above the canal, and next to Château Laurier, the **Canadian Museum of Contemporary Photography,** an affiliate of the National Gallery (*temporarily closed for construction; exhibits take place at the National Gallery of Canada; 613-990-8257; http://cmcp.gallery.ca).* South of Wellington and facing the canal, the handsome **National Arts Centre**★ contains theatres and a celebrated cafe with an outdoor terrace located beside the waterway (*visit by 45min guided tour only, leaving from main lobby Jul–Aug, Tue, Thu & Sat 11am & 2pm; $2; 613-947-7000; www.nac-cna.ca).* Across the canal stands the Rideau Centre, a hotel, convention and shopping complex.

ByWard Market★

Open May–mid Oct daily 6am–6pm. Rest of the year daily 8am–5pm. Closed Jan 1 & Dec 25. 613-562-3325. www.byward-market.com.

Stretching over several blocks, this colourful market (primarily indoors in winter) has existed since 1846. From spring to fall there are stalls of flowers, fruit and vegetables. The ByWard Market Building holds restaurants, craft shops and coffeehouses.

Tin House Court★

This pleasant cobblestone square, bordered by stone buildings and graced by a fountain, is home to Art Price's 1973 sculpture, once part of the actual facade of tinsmith Honoré Foisy's whimsical house. When Foisy's house was demolished, Price restored the facade and the city erected it in testament to Foisy's mastery of his craft. The courtyard is a favourite haunt of Ottawans, who curl up on the grass to read or eat sandwiches.

To the south, across Clarence Street, Nunavut artist Pauta Saila's bronze sculpture of a dancing bear energizes cobblestoned Jeanne d'Arc Court.

Notre-Dame Cathedral Basilica★

385 Sussex Dr. ◷*Open Mon 11:30am–6pm, Tue–Sat 9am–6pm, Sun 8am–8pm.* *Guided tours available.* ♿ 🅿 ☎613-241-7496. www.notredameottawa.com.
The city's oldest church, this basilica with twin spires is a Roman Catholic cathedral built between 1841 and the 1880s. Note the gold-leaf statue of the Madonna and Child between the steeples.

The fine **woodwork** of the interior was carved in mahogany by Philippe Parizeau. Around the sanctuary there are niches containing statues of the prophets, patriarchs and apostles crafted in wood by Louis-Philippe Hébert, which have been painted to look like stone.

To the right of the basilica, there is a statue of Joseph-Eugene Guigues, the first bishop of Ottawa, who was responsible for the cathedral's completion.

Peacekeeping Monument

Across the street, and adjacent to the basilica, is a prominent memorial to Canadians who have served as international peacekeepers. Titled *The Reconciliation,* the monument was dedicated in 1992.

It features two male and one female bronze figures in military dress. They look toward a grove, the symbol of peace, their backs to the detritus of war lying between converging granite walls.

Nepean Point★

Situated high above the river beside Alexandra Bridge, this point offers a splendid **view**★★ of Parliament Hill, Gatineau and the Gatineau Hills across the river. Overlooking the river facing west is a statue of **Samuel de Champlain (2),** who paddled up the Ottawa River in 1613 and 1615.

Sparks Street Mall

South of Parliament Hill, this pleasant pedestrian mall with trees, seating and cafe tables between the shops. Note the **Royal Bank Centre** and at the opposite end of the mall, the attractive **Bank of Canada**★, designed by Arthur Erickson and opened in 1980. Set within a 12-storey court, this Neoclassical building is now flanked by two 12-storey towers of solar-tinted glass and oxidized copper. In the court are trees, shrubs, a pool and the Currency Museum (♿ *see below*).Outside the east tower in a small park stands a bronze sculpture by Sorel Etrog titled *Flight* (1966).

Supreme Court

301 Wellington St. *Visit by guided tour (30min) only, May–Aug daily 9am–5pm. Tours continual throughout day. Sept–Apr Mon–Fri 9am–5pm. Book tour in advance.* ♿☎613-995-4330 or 866-360-1522. www.scc-csc.gc.ca.
Created in 1875, but not "supreme" until 1949 (when appeals to England's Judicial Committee of the Privy Council were abolished), Canada's Supreme Court occupies a building with green roofs overlooking the Ottawa River. The court itself consists of nine judges, five of whom constitute a quorum. Visitors can listen to a hearing of an appeal if the court is in session, and see the building's interior.

Additional Sights

Rideau Hall
♿*See Scenic Drives.*

Royal Canadian Mounted Police Rockcliffe
♿*See Scenic Drives.*

The Museums★★★

As befits a capital city, Ottawa has a number of fine museums, many of which are national museums and therefore large and comprehensive in scope. Several are concentrated within walking distance of one another in the city core. Others, such as the Aviation Museum and the Agriculture Museum, are on the outskirts of the city proper. For discounted admission fees, *⚲see Discounts in Practical Information for information about Canada's Capital Museum Passport.*

National Gallery of Canada★★★

380 Sussex Dr. 🕐*Open May–Sept daily 10am–5pm (Thu 8pm). Rest of the year Tue–Sun 10am–5pm (Thu til 8pm).* 🕐*Closed Jan 1, Good Friday & Dec 25.* 🎫*$9. (special exhibits additional fee)* ✕🅿♿☎*613-990-1985 or 800-319-2787. www.gallery.ca.*

This magnificent glass, granite and concrete building (1988, Moshe Safdie), capped by prismatic glass "turrets," rises on the banks of the Ottawa River across from the Gothic-Revival parliament buildings. Its bold beauty, light and airy exhibit spaces, and tranquil interior courtyards provide a unique setting for the vast national collections.

Canadian Art

Level 1. This collection is displayed in a series of galleries arranged to trace the development of Canadian art. Both the **garden court,** with its colourful plantings, and the restful **water court** add grace and beauty to the transition from gallery to gallery. In the centre is the reconstructed chapel of the Convent of Our Lady of the Sacred Heart (1888) featuring decorative fan-vaulted ceiling, cast-iron columns and carved woodwork. Other highlights include the Croscup Room murals, painted in Nova Scotia in the mid-19C; early Quebec religious art, including Paul Jourdain's gilt tabernacle and Antoine Plamondon's *Portrait of Sister Saint-Alphonse;* the works of Paul Kane and Cornelius Krieghoff; Lucius O'Brien's *Sunrise on*

the Saguenay; paintings by Tom Thomson and the Group of Seven, Emily Carr, David Milne, Marc-Aurèle Fortin, Jean-Paul Lemieux, Alfred Pellan *(On the Beach)*, Goodridge Roberts, Guido Molinari and Claude Tousignant. Modern and contemporary works are also featured, including those by Paul-Émile Borduas, Harold Town, Jack Shadbolt, Michael Snow, Yves Gaucher, Mary Pratt and Joyce Wieland.

Galleries devoted to Inuit art *(ground floor)* feature work by artists such as Janet Kigusiuq, Jessie Oonark, Charlie Ugyuk and Pudlo.

European and American Art

Level 2. Among the highlights of the National Gallery's impressive and comprehensive collection of European art are Simone Martini's *St. Catherine of Alexandria,* Lucas Cranach the Elder's *Venus,* Rembrandt's *The Toilet of Esther,* El Greco's *St. Francis and Brother Leo Meditating on Death,* Bernini's fine bust of Pope Urban VIII and Benjamin West's *Death of General Wolfe* (the original of this much-reproduced painting). Impressionists are well represented as are such 20C masters as Fernand Léger *(The Mechanics)*, Pablo Picasso and Gustav Klimt. American artists Clyfford Still, Jackson Pollock, Andy Warhol, George Segal, Donald Judd, David Smith and Barnett Newman *(Voice of Fire)* are among those represented in the American art collection.

Sculpture on view in the Asian Galleries dates from the third century AD to the present.

Exhibited on both floors, the National Gallery's extensive collection of contemporary art encompasses video, film, painting, sculpture and installation. Artists represented in the collection include Lucian Freud, Alex Janvier, Brian Jungen, Philippe Parreno and Douglas Gordon.

Other Museums

Canadian Museum of Civilization★★★ (Quebec)

(Musée canadien des Civilisations) *100 Rue Laurier, Gatineau QC.* 🕐*Open Jul-Labour Day daily 9am-6pm (Thu-Fri 9pm). May-Jun & rest of Sept-mid-Oct daily 9am-*

6pm (Thu 9pm). Rest of the year Tue–Sun 9am–5pm (Thu 9pm). ✆$10 *(supplemental fees for IMAX theatre, Canadian War Museum & special exhibits).* ✕ ♿ 🅿 *($10 maximum/day)* ☎819-776-7000 *or 800-555-5621. www.civilization.ca.*

Inaugurated in 1989, this sizable museum is dedicated to the history of Canada and to the art and traditions of native cultures and ethnic groups. The sweeping curves of the two large buildings designed by **Douglas Cardinal** evoke the emergence of the North American continent and its subsequent moulding by wind, water and glaciers. The **Canadian Shield Wing** houses administrative offices and conservation laboratories, while the **Glacier Wing** provides 16,000 sq m/177,600 sq ft of exhibit halls.

In the **grand hall** six cultural regions of the Canadian Pacific Coast are illustrated through the wooden houses of village chieftains and majestic totem poles rising to the ceiling. In the **Canada Hall,** artifacts and reconstructed buildings recreate 1,000 years of Canadian heritage. The delightful **children's museum** encourages young people to explore the world, from a Mexican village to a Pakistani street. A costume room, puppet theatre, games section and art studio complete the exhibit.

In the IMAX Theatre, a seven-storey IMAX screen and dome provide unparalleled 180-degree viewing for 295 spectators.

Canada Aviation Museum★★★

Rockcliffe Airport, 11 Aviation Pkwy. 🕐*Open May–Labour Day daily 9am–5pm. Rest of the year Wed–Sun 10am–5pm.* 🕐*Closed Dec.25.* ✆$6. ✕ ♿ 🅿 ☎ *613-993-2010 or 800-463-2038 (Canada only). www.aviation.technomuses.ca.*

This enormous triangular-shaped building recalls the three-sided pattern of numerous airfields built in the country during WWI. Opened in 1988 the museum is devoted to the history of aviation from pioneer days to the present, with special emphasis on Canadian contributions.

Inside, there is a replica of the *Silver Dart,* the first aircraft to fly in Canada. There are fighters and bombers used in both

world wars: a Spad 7, a Sopwith Snipe, Hawker Hurricane, Supermarine Spitfire and a Lancaster Bomber. Early "bush" float planes include the De Havilland Beaver, first flown in 1947. The **RCAF Hall of Tribute** honours men and women of the Royal Canadian Air Force.

Canadian Museum of Nature★★

240 MacLeod St. 🕐*Open May–Labour Day daily 9am–6pm (Wed & Thu 8pm). Rest of the year Tue–Sun 9am–5pm (Thu 8pm). Open during holiday and spring break Mon.* 🕐*Closed Dec 25 & 2nd week in Jan.* ✆$5. (No charge Sat before noon). ✕ ♿ 🅿 ☎*613-566-4700 or 800-263-4433. www.nature.ca. Due to ongoing renovations, half the museum (east and central portions) is closed until 2010.*

Occupying the entire building since 1989, this comprehensive museum is devoted to the earth's geological history and the origin of life. In 2006 renovations were completed to the west wing and a new south wing constructed. Newly refurbished and reopened galleries are the fossil, bird and mammal galleries. Compelling exhibits include an outstanding display on **dinosaurs,** with complete reconstructions of skeletons; lifelike dioramas of **birds in Canada;** and dioramas of **Canadian mammals** include the musk-ox of Northwest and Nunavut territories, the pronghorn of Saskatchewan, British Columbia's grizzly bear and the moose of New Brunswick. **Plants** are the focus of a gallery that includes medicinal varieties. Children will enjoy the hands-on **Discovery Zone** where they can examine specimens, and watch movies *(30min)* about nature.

Currency Museum★★

In Bank of Canada complex, 245 Sparks St. ♿🕐*Open May–Sept Mon–Sat 10:30am–5pm, Sun 1pm–5pm. Rest of the year Tue–Sat 10:30am–5pm, Sun 1pm–5pm.* 🕐*Closed major holidays.* ☎613-782-8914. *www.currencymuseum.ca.*

This museum presents the history of money from early China, Greece, Rome, Byzantium, Medieval and Renaissance Europe to its introduction and use in North America. The development of Canadian money is illustrated with wampum, the card money of New

France, Hudson's Bay Company tokens, the first banknotes and other examples. The exhibit on counterfeiting reveals interesting complicity of governments in this ancient practice.

Canada Science and Technology Museum★★

Kids *1867 St. Laurent Blvd.* Open May–Labour Day daily 9am–5pm. Rest of the year Tue–Sun 9am–5pm. Closed Dec 25. *$7.50.* ✕ ♿ 🅿 ☎613-991-3044.www.sciencetech.technomuses.ca.

The flashing beacon of the old Cape North (Nova Scotia) lighthouse marks the museum's location. Visitors can tour the lighthouse and see outdoor exhibits such as an Atlas rocket and a steam locomotive.

Displays inside concentrate on transportation. The hall of **steam locomotives** is impressive because of the sheer size of the vehicles. Exhibits on early automobiles (1900-30) in Canada and the ocean liner *Titanic* are also featured. Other sections of the museum are devoted to such themes as communications, computers, physics, astronomy and the exploration of space and Canada's contributions in particular.

Canadian War Museum★★

1 Vimy Place. Open Jul–Labour Day daily 9am–6pm (Thu & Fri 9pm). May–Jun & Sept daily 9am–6pm (Thu 9pm). Rest of the year Tue–Sun 9am–5pm (Thu 9pm). Closed Dec 25. *$10. (No charge Thu after 4pm).* ✕ ♿ 🅿 ☎819-776-8600 or 800-555-5621. www.warmuseum.ca.

This museum, newly designed in 2005, traces the history of war in Canada through its vast permanent collection of one million artifacts, vehicles, artillery, art and photographs.

Five themed galleries showcase state-of-the-art exhibits describing the nation's military conflicts from aboriginal warfare and frontier skirmishes through the Boer and World Wars to modern peacekeeping efforts and today's military technology. In silent tribute, **Memorial Hall** holds the headstone of a WWI Unknown Soldier. In Regeneration Hall, a model of Walter Allward's sculpture *Hope* from the Vimy Memorial in France symbolizes a future without war.

Paths over the museum's roof allow superb **views**★ of the Ottawa River. The on-site Military History Research Centre (open May–mid–Oct Mon–Fri 9am–4:30pm; rest of the year Tues–Fri 9am–4:30pm; closed major holidays; ☎819-776-8652) preserves important national collections documenting Canada's military history.

Royal Canadian Mint

320 Sussex Dr. Visit by guided tour (40min) only, mid–May–Labour Day Mon–Fri 9am–7pm, weekends 9am–5:30pm. Rest of year Mon–Sun 9am–5pm. Closed Jan 1, Dec 25. *$5, weekends $3.50.* Reservation recommended. ♿ ☎613-993-8990 or 800-276-7714. www.mint.ca.

Canada's circulating money is created at the branch of the Royal Canadian Mint in Winnipeg. Commemorative and collector (numismatic) coins are made at this Ottawa location.

The spacious modern exhibit area cuts through the original 1908 stone building, with displays on the history of money and on the Ottawa mint's production of commemorative and collector coins. One of the most interesting parts of the tour is a look into the mint's business as a gold and, since 2006, silver refinery. The mint's prize product is a coin made of Canadian-mined gold that is 99.999% pure, the highest level of purity yet achieved. Tours include a video (10min) about the mint's role and observation of the manufacturing, inspection and packaging processes.

Canadian Ski Museum

1960 Scott St. Open year-round Mon–Sat 9am–5pm, Sun 11am–5pm. Closed Dec 25. *Contribution suggested.* ☎613-722-3584. www.skimuseum.ca.

Archival photographs and equipment depict the history of the sport. The museum's growing collection, including donations by Canada's famed skiers, comprises clothing, masks, poles and other equipment, medals, trophies, even ski waxes and some 500 pairs of skis (some vintage skis more than 150 years old). A Hall of Fame features history's great Canadian skiers.

Laurier House★

335 Laurier Ave. E. ⟶Visit by guided tour (1hr) only, mid-May–early Oct daily 9am–5pm. Rest of year Mon–Fri 9am–5pm. ⊙Closed Easter holidays. ⟋$4. ☎613-992-8142. www.pc.gc.ca.

This yellow brick house with a veranda pays tribute to three Canadian prime ministers. In 1897 Canada's first French-speaking prime minister, **Sir Wilfrid Laurier,** in office from 1896 to 1911, moved into the house. After his death, Lady Laurier willed the house to Canadian prime minister **William Lyon Mackenzie King,** grandson of the rebel William Lyon Mackenzie. King resided here until his death in 1950.

The tour includes King's library, bedroom, dining room and two rooms with Laurier memorabilia as well as a reconstruction of the study of **Lester Bowles Pearson,** 1957 Nobel Peace Prize winner and prime minister from 1963 to 1968. Pearson did not live in the house, but the photographs and political cartoons in his study are fascinating.

In summer *(Sun, Jul-Aug 1pm & 3pm),* the Parks Canada Players present a 1940s-style radio broadcast from the house, with refreshments served on the veranda. *Call for reservations.*

Canada Agriculture Museum★

Kids Building 88, Prince of Wales Dr., on grounds of the Central Experimental Farm. Main exhibition area: ⊙open Mar–Oct daily 9am–5pm; ⊙closed Nov–Feb. Barns: ⊙open year-round 9am–5pm. ⟋$6. ☎613-991-3044 or 866-442-4416. www.agriculture.technomuses.ca.

This museum is housed in a barn dating from the 1920s. The machinery displayed, the techniques, even the smells, evoke farming in times past. Old breeds of sheep, cattle, pigs and horses can be seen. *(⟶guided tours of animal barns year-round; ☎613-991-3053).* Seasonally, visitors can take wagon rides on the premises *(Jun–Sept Wed–Sun; ⟋$2.50).* The 425ha/1,050-acre **Central Experimental Farm** is the headquarters of Canada's Agriculture and Agri-Food department. On the grounds are splendid ornamental gardens. There is also a tropical greenhouse and a large arboretum bordering the Rideau Canal

(& P grounds open year-round daily dawn–dusk; greenhouse open year-round daily 9am–4pm; ☎613-759-6900).

Billings Estate Museum★

2100 Cabot St. ⊙Open mid-May–Oct Wed–Sun noon–5pm. ⟶Guided tours Wed–Sun noon–5pm. ⟋$4.50. & P ☎613-247-4830. www.friendsofbillings estatemuseum.org.

This attractive clapboard house with dormer windows is the oldest frame house in Ottawa, and a National Historic Site. Built in 1829 by Braddish Billings, the dwelling was inhabited by four generations of his family before becoming a city property in 1975.

The refurbished rooms are full of artifacts, photographs and furniture relating to all four generations. There's also an explanation of the architectural styles of the estate.

Scenic Drives★★

Ottawa is well known for its lovely drives beside the river, along the canal and in the Gatineau Hills to the north.

Sussex Drive and Rockcliffe Parkway★★

8km/5mi from Confederation Square. This drive winds along the river and through the prestigious residential area of Rockcliffe. After passing the Notre Dame Basilica and the Canadian War Museum, watch on the right, after the Macdonald-Cartier Bridge to Gatineau, for a dark glass and concrete modern structure—the **Lester B. Pearson Building,** which houses the Department of Foreign Affairs and International Trade. The road then crosses the Rideau River to Green Island past **Ottawa's former city hall** (designed by Moshe Safdie, architect of the National Gallery).

Rideau Falls★

P Park beside the French Embassy. On both sides of Green Island, the Rideau River drops over a sheer cliff into the Ottawa River. The falls are said to resemble a curtain, hence their name, which means "curtain" in French. To

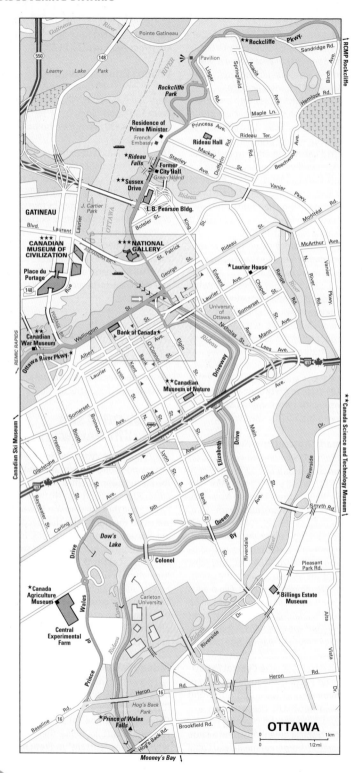

OTTAWA

see the second set of falls, visitors can cross the first set by a bridge. There are good views of the Ottawa River and Gatineau.

Along Sussex Drive, the entrance to the official residence of Canadian prime ministers, **24 Sussex Drive,** is seen on the left. Hidden among the trees, the stone house overlooks the river and is best viewed from the water. Around the corner is the gate to **Rideau Hall,** official residence of the governor general, set amid landscaped grounds that can be visited (🕐 *open Apr–mid-Oct daily 8am–8pm; rest of the year daily 8am–5pm;* ☎613-991-4422 or 866-842-4422). There are ⚲**tours** *(45min)* of the residence *(Jul–Labour Day daily self-guided 10am–1pm or guided 1pm–4pm; May–Jun weekends 10am–4pm; Sept–Oct & Feb weekends noon–4pm; other times, by reservation:* ☎866-842-4422; *www.gg.ca).* The road then passes through **Rockcliffe Park** via a one-way route. On the return there are good views of the river. Farther on, however, there are excellent **views**★★ from a covered pavilion of Pointe Gatineau on the Quebec shore and of the Gatineau Hills. The steepled church in Pointe Gatineau is St. François de Sales, built in 1886.

Rockcliffe is an area of large stone mansions, tree-lined streets and lovely gardens. The drive ends at **RCMP Rockcliffe** (Royal Canadian Mounted Police), where members of the famous **musical ride** and their horses are trained. When the troop is not on tour *(generally May–Oct),* the horses can be seen in training (🕐*May–Aug daily 9am–3:30pm; Sept Mon–Fri 9am–3:30pm; rest of the year Tue & Thu 10am–2pm;* ♿☎613-998-8199; *www.rcmp-grc.gc.ca or www.canadas capital.gc.ca).*

Rideau Canal Driveways★

Each drive is about 8km/5mi from Confederation Square.

The **Queen Elizabeth Driveway** follows the canal's west bank; the **Colonel By Drive** parallels the east bank. The University of Ottawa is soon passed on the left. Later on, Carleton University is also seen. At **Dow's Lake,** where the canal

Winter on the Rideau Canal

Ontario Tourism

widens out, canoes and paddleboats can be rented. At this point the two drives diverge, the Colonel By continuing along the canal, the Queen Elizabeth entering the Central Experimental Farm. From Colonel By Drive, there are views of Prince of Wales Falls and the Rideau Canal locks before the drive ends at Hog's Back Road.

Prince of Wales Falls★
Free parking in Hog's Back Park.

Mooney's Bay marks the end of the Rideau Canal; thereafter, the Rideau River is navigable. After leaving the bay the river drops over these falls and rushes through a small gorge. The result of a geological fault that exposed the underlying formations and strata, the falls are particularly impressive in the spring thaw. The dam was built by Colonel By in 1829. Mooney's Bay *(access from Riverside Dr.)* is one of Ottawa's main recreational areas.

Ottawa River Parkway★

1km/7mi from Confederation Square.
Wellington Street passes the parliament buildings and the Supreme Court, and becomes the parkway south of Portage Bridge. The drive beside the Ottawa River offers lookout points for the Remic Rapids. The best view is from **Bate Island**★ *(take Champlain Bridge to Gatineau and exit for island).* The parkway continues, affording other good viewpoints.

Upper Canada Village★★★

MAP P 109

Reflecting life in the 1860s in rural Ontario, this 27ha/66-acre living museum is among the finest restoration projects in North America. Lying in an area settled by Loyalists after the American Revolution, the village was created in the late 1950s when plans were made to flood some 20,000 acres of farmland during construction of the St. Lawrence Seaway and the control dam at Cornwall. More than 500 houses, churches, offices, shops and other structures were moved to higher ground to preserve them. Today some 40 of these heritage buildings can be visited in Upper Canada Village. The site is located in Morrisburg, on the St. Lawrence, upriver from Cornwall and southeast of Ottawa.

Access – *11km/7mi east of Morrisburg. From Hwy. 401, take Exit 758 (Upper Canada Rd.) and travel south. Turn left onto Country Rd. 2 and continue east 2km/1.25mi to the village.* ☐*The parking lot is just past Crysler Farm Battlefield Park.*

- **Information:** Upper Canada Village, 13740 Country Rd. 2, Morrisburg. ☎613-543-4328 or 800-437-2233. www.uppercanadavillage.com.
- **Orient Yourself:** To make most efficient use of time, pick up a map of the village from the admissions building. The area behind the admissions gate extends along two principal streets *(Queen & Albert Sts.)*, on a north-south axis, with several cross streets. There are three on-site restaurants: Village Cafe *(near entrance)*, Harvest Barn Restaurant *(Albert St.)* and Williard's Hotel *(Queen St.)*.
- **Parking:** Leave your car at the large parking lot near the entrance.
- **Don't Miss:** Beach's sawmill to see water-powered sawing of logs into boards; draft horses and oxen being used at Loucks Farm.
- **Organizing Your Time:** Plan to spend 3–4 hours, but one- and two-hour tours are possible.
- **Especially for Kids:** The costumed interpreters include children, so visiting kids can interact with children their own age.
- **Also See:** KINGSTON AND THE THOUSAND ISLANDS

Visit

Open mid-May–early-Oct daily 9:30am–5pm. Horse-drawn transportation (free) on premises. $17.95 ☎613-543-4328 or 800-437-2233. www.upper canadavillage.com.

Upon entering this bustling rural "community," visitors are transported back to the 19C. Costumed "inhabitants" walk the sawn boardwalks or travel about by horses on sandy roads. They quilt, make cheese and bread, operate the mills and complete farm chores, among other activities. Much of the livestock is rare: breeds seldom seen today, such as the Canadian horses that haul the touring wagons and coaches, and the massive red Devon oxen that pull the field plows. Visitors may choose to see the sights from the waterside perspective of the village canal by boarding the horse-drawn scows (flat-bottomed boats).

The progression from hastily erected log shanties in pioneer days to later substantial dwellings of brick and stone is readily apparent. Note in particular the elegant refinement of the **Robertson House,** a middle-class residence; the solid prosperity of the **Loucks Farm,** in contrast to the tenant farm; and luxury of **Crysler Hall** with its Greek-Revival architecture. There are also churches and schools, a village store, a doctor's surgery, a print shop and a tavern. Loaves of bread baked in a large brick oven at the village baker can be purchased in the gift shop.

In the heart of the village stands the white clapboard, two-storey **Willard's**

Upper Canada Village

Hotel, where patrons may enjoy an 1850s-style meal. (&see *Address Book*). Built in 1785 as the residence of a German-born Loyalist from New York, the house also served as an inn. In the 1830s the property was purchased by John Willard, who operated a tavern in Montreal. Today the hotel reflects the time of its heyday in the 1850s, when it was a lively inn and dining establishment.

The **sawmill,** flour mill and **woollen mill** operate on water power and show the trend toward industrialization. The flour mill features a steam engine that dates to 1865.

A **children's activity centre,** housed in a large barn, offers educational activites.

Nearby Attractions

Battlefield Monument
Beside Upper Canada Village in the park. This monument commemorates the **Battle of Crysler Farm** in 1813, when a small force of British and Canadian troops routed a much larger American force. It stands beside the St. Lawrence River with a fine **view** over the site of the farm now flooded by the Seaway. (*Visitor Centre* ◎$3).

Long Sault Parkway
5km/3mi east of Upper Canada Village, between Ingleside and Cornwall via Rte. 2.

This scenic drive departs from the mainland and traverses a chain of connected islands in the St. Lawrence River. Activities along the way include fishing, boating *(canoe rentals available)* and picnicking. Bicycle and walking trails abound within the wooded glens and along the coastal rims of these small islands. Fine sand beaches afford opportunities for swimming *(unsupervised)*, and birdwatching is popular within the expansive wetlands. There are three campgrounds administered by the St. Lawrence Parks Commission. *Information and reservations:* ☎613-543-3704.

Battlefield Monument

Merrickville ★

POPULATION 968 – MAP P 109

This former industrial village on the Rideau River, about 73km/45mi southwest of Ottawa, has become a popular weekend destination, visited both by road and by pleasure craft along the Rideau Canal. One of the many Ontario villages claiming to be Canada's prettiest, Merrickville has been dubbed "the Jewel of the Rideau." It got its start in 1791 when William Merrick, a Loyalist from New York state, noted the river's potential as a power source for mills. Arrival of the canal, completed in 1832, only increased the town's prosperity, but the rise of modern industrial methods and the canal's decline in the latter 19C meant an end to growth. Today some of the factory and commercial buildings house shops, restaurants and art galleries, while others lie in picturesque ruins carefully preserved by Parks Canada. The Rideau Canal locks, which operate now as in 1832, and the defensive blockhouse are National Historic Sites. Stone Victorian houses built by factory owners house pleasant inns, and lovely gardens are a major tourist attraction.

- **Information:** Merrickville and District Chamber of Commerce, 446 Main St. W. ☎613-269-2229. www.realmerrickville.ca.
- **Orient Yourself:** Most of the village, including the blockhouse, lies south of the canal locks, crossed by the St. Lawrence Street Bridge.
- **Don't Miss:** Merrickville is a true artists' colony, with many galleries selling handmade pottery, sculpture, paintings and crafts.
- **Organizing Your Time:** The Merrickville and District Historical Society has developed a concise walking tour. Visit www.merrickvillehistory.ca for details.
- **Especially for Kids:** The locks and Industrial Heritage Complex provide opportunities for hands-on exploration.
- **Also See:** KINGSTON AND THE THOUSAND ISLANDS

Sights

Rideau Canal Locks★

Open mid-Jun–Labour Day daily 8:30am–7:30pm. Mid-May–mid-Jun Mon–Thu 8:30am–4:30pm, Fri–Sun & Victoria Day 8:30am–7:30pm. Early Sept daily 8:30am–4:30pm. Mid-Sept–mid-Oct Tue–Thu 9:30am–3:30pm, Fri–Mon 8:30am–4:30pm. ⚬$3. ⚬ ⚬ ☎613-283-5170 or 888-773-8888. www.pc.gc.ca.

This National Historic Site in Merrickville comprises three **locks** *(at lower end of an artificial channel)*, a dam constructed in 1914 and 1915, with a roadway over the top and the Merrickville **blockhouse** *(adjacent to the locks)*, one of four blockhouses built along the Rideau Canal to defend it from American assault.

Never attacked, the blockhouse served as a home for the lockmaster and his family. The upper storey of the two-storey structure overhangs the lower, whose walls are constructed of stone. Built of wood, the walls of the upper storey are pierced by square portholes as firing positions. Inside is a museum operated by the Merrickville and District Historic Society; it contains furnishings, household goods and implements of the period (*open mid-Jun–Labour Day Thu–Mon 10am–5pm, Tue & Wed 11am–4pm, mid-May–mid-Jun weekends noon–4pm; ⚬contribution suggested; www.merrickvillehistory.ca*). Around the locks and on the island in the canal is the **Industrial Heritage Complex,** a parklike open-air museum constructed around the ruins of former industrial buildings.

Rideau Woodland Ramble

210 Burritt's Rapids Rd., County Rd. 23. Open Apr–Nov daily 9am–5pm. ⚬ ⚬ ☎613-258-3797. www.rideauwoodland ramble.com.

In a town renowned for its gardens, this 2.8ha/7-acre nursery, created 25

Merrickville's main street

R. Lissia /Ontario Tourism

years ago by two garden enthusiasts, comprises a series of "garden rooms" set within woodlands. Reached by winding trails, the gardens feature plants, bushes and trees, many of them rare, that are reliably hardy for this area. The hosta and conifer collections are particularly extensive. There are also ponds, fountains and a small waterfall. A garden centre sells plants and supplies.

Excursion

Prescott★

From Merrickville, take Rte. 15 south 40km/25mi, then take Hwy. 401 northeast 20km/12.5mi. Town of Prescott. ☏613-925-2812. www.prescott.ca.

This small industrial town, with a population of roughly 4,000, is situated on the edge of the St. Lawrence River, 80km/50mi south of Ottawa. It has the only deepwater port between Montreal and Kingston. Originally settled by Loyalists, the site was the chosen location for a fort to protect ships from American attack during the War of 1812. It was

also the site, in 1838, of the **Battle of the Windmill,** when rebel supporters of William Lyon Mackenzie and their American sympathizers were dislodged, with difficulty, from a windmill on the riverbank. Today an international bridge spans the river near the town, one of 13 bridges linking Ontario with the US.

Fort Wellington★

On Hwy. 2, just east of town. ◷Open mid-May–Sept daily 10am–5pm. ✆$4. ☏613-925-2896. www.pc.gc.ca.

Built by the British during the War of 1812, this small earthen fort includes officers' quarters and a three-storey stone **blockhouse,** restored to reflect its 1840s appearance. Among the costumed interpreters are those attired in British regimental uniforms of the period. A paved trail along the waterfront provides pretty views.

East of the fort *(1.5km/1mi)*, between Highway 2 and the river, stands the **windmill** of battle fame. It features displays on the battle and offers a pleasant **view** of the river *(picnic tables)*.

SOUTH CENTRAL ONTARIO

Ontarians usually think of cottage country as that southern section of the Canadian Shield lying between Georgian Bay and the Ottawa River, all the way north to Algonquin Park. Some 1,600 lakes litter this largely forested landscape with jagged corridors of stunning pink granite. The area's many lakes and rivers were gouged out of the Canadian Shield by retreating glaciers. Two distinct chains are apparent. The Kawartha Lakes lie to the north and west of Peterborough, with Rice Lake to the southeast. The three Muskoka Lakes (Rosseau, Joseph and Muskoka) lie farther northwest, just to the east of Georgian Bay and north of Lake Simcoe. During cottage season (traditionally Victoria Day to Thanksgiving), families and sports fishermen abandon their permanent residences for cabins, small houses and multi-roomed mansions—all called "cottages" by Canadians. Boating and fishing are prime pursuits. The Trent-Severn Waterway, another popular recreational boating venue, links Port Severn on Georgian Bay, with Trenton on Lake Ontario. Small towns like Orillia and Gravenhurst have developed largely because of summer visitors.

Early explorers, notably Samuel de Champlain in 1615, arriving by canoe, found Mississauga Indians, a branch of the Ojibwa tribe, fishing and hunting here. Their descendents live at the Curve Lake Indian Reserve and many participate in the tourism economy as guides and creators of high-quality crafts.

The earliest European inhabitants in the 19C exploited the forests for lumber, floating logs down the waterways. Immigrant farmers were largely defeated by the thin soil and short growing season north of Peterborough. The earliest Canadian literature, by sisters Catharine Parr Traill and Susanna Moodie, who immigrated from Britain in the early 19C, describes trying to farm in "the bush."

In 1875 the arrival of the railroad almost immediately brought in tourists, and by the end of the 19C wealthy Torontonians and Americans had built comfortable "cottages" on the Muskoka Lakes. Amenities range from just the bare essentials to grandiose furnishings, a float plane and a water-worthy craft. The Kawartha Lakes (the name "Kawartha" was coined from a Huron phrase meaning "shining waters) were slower to develop their

Sunset at Lake Rosseau

Wilson/Ontario Tourism

Practical Information

AREA CODES

The area code for this region is 705. For local calls, dial all 10 digits (area code plus the number, but without the 1-prefix). For more information: ☎1-800-668-6878 or www.bell.ca.

GETTING THERE AND GETTING AROUND

BY AIR

Toronto Pearson International Airport (www.gtaa.com) (👒 *see Toronto Practical Information*) lies 140km/90mi from Peterborough.

Coach Canada (👒 *see below*) provides scheduled bus service and shared van service between Peterborough and the airport. The Peterborough Municipal Airport serves business and general aviation only.

BY RAIL

VIA Rail provides passenger service to Oshawa, the closest station to Peterborough (915 Bloor St. W., Oshawa. ☎888-842-7245). Ontario Northland provides passenger service from Toronto to Bracebridge and Gravenhurst (☎800-461-8558; www.ontc.ca).

BY BUS

Coach Canada (*departs from City Bus Terminal, 190 Simcoe St.; purchase tickets online, from office at 491 Webber Ave. or from driver;* ☎705-748-6411 or 800-461-7661; www.coachcanada.com) provides service within Ontario and Quebec.

Greyhound (*Liftlock Coach Lines, 220 Simcoe St. Peterborough;* ☎705-743-7247; www.greyhound.ca) provides service with connections across Canada and the US. In the lakes area, Greyhound serves several towns.

PETERBOROUGH CITY TRANSPORT

Peterborough Transit (www.cityofpeterborough.on.ca) provides bus service within the city and an express service to Trent University. Fare is $2.

GENERAL INFORMATION

VISITOR INFORMATION

Peterborough and the Kawarthas Tourism, 1400 Crawford Dr., Peterborough. ☎705-742-2201or 800-461-6424. www.thekawarthas.net.

Muskoka Tourism, ☎800-276-9700. www.discovermuskoka.ca

Gravenhurst, Municipal Offices, 190 Harvie St., Gravenhurst ☎705-687-3412. www.gravenhurst.ca.

Bracebridge, 100 Taylor Court, Bracebridge ☎705-645-5264. www.town.bracebridge.on.ca

Huntsville, 37 Main St. E., Huntsville. ☎705-789-1751. www.town.huntsville.on.ca

Orillia, 50 Andrews St. S., Orillia. ☎705-325-1311. www.city.orillia.on.ca

Curve Lake Indian Reserve, Curve Lake. ☎705-657-3661. www.whetung.com or www.curvelakefn.com.

ACCOMMODATIONS

Bed and Breakfast accommodations: www.bbmuskoka.com. 👒*See also the Address Book.*

CRUISES

Cruises on the Kawartha and Muskoka lakes are part of the cottage experience. Unlike Stephen Leacock's fictional *Mariposa Belle,* the real cruise boats don't include a sinking as part of the fun.

Stony Lake Cruises – Lakefield. ☎705-654-5253. www.stonylakecruises.on.ca. ✕占. Cruise among the 1,128 islands of Stony and Clear lakes aboard the 140-passenger Chippewa II, a replica of old lake steamships like the Mariposa Belle. Commentary. Jul–Aug Tue–Sun 1pm, Jun & Sept–mid-Oct weekends 1pm. ☞$15.

LiftLock & the River Boat Cruises – Peterborough. ☎705-742-7792 or 888-535-4670. www.liftlockcruises.com. ✕. Cruises down the Trent-Severn Waterway leave from Del Crary park in central Peterborough Ju–Aug 3 times daily. Mid-May–Jun & Sept–mid-Oct twice daily. ☞$16.50.

Muskoka Lakes Navigation Company – 185 Cherokee Lane, Gravenhurst. ☎705-687-6667 or 866-687-6667. www.realmuskoka.com. 占✕. The 99-passenger, refurbished coal-fired steamship *Segwun* sails around all three

Muskoka lakes, leaving from Sagamo Park dock *Jun–Labour Day.* Its sister ship, the 200-passenger *Wenonah II,* looks like a 1906 steamship but is modern (2002). Call for departure times. Round trip 1hr–4hrs. Reservations required. Sightseeing ⊚$16–$47.

Lady Muskoka Cruises – 330 Ecclestone Dr., Bracebridge. ☎705-646-2628 or 800-263-5239. *www.ladymuskoka. com.* ⚓✂. The 300-passenger double-decker cruise boat offers three-hour cruises leaving at noon daily Jul– Aug and on weekends and Wed Jun &Sept– mid-Oct; weekends only last 2 wks May. ⊚$26. Optional lunch on some cruises. Call or check website for schedule. Cruise leaves from the Riverside Inn on the Muskoka River, then enters the lake.

Waterway Tours – *20 Arbor Lane, Tilsonburg.* ☎705-687-3805. *www.water waystours.com.* For a distinctly low-key tour, hop on a pontoon boat with a striped awning. Tour leaves the public docks at the swing bridge at Lake Rosseau in Port Carling daily Jul–Aug and weekends mid-May-Jun and Sept– mid-Oct. ⊚$15. Call for schedule.

Lake of Bays Tours – *Riverfront Dock, Baysville.* ☎705-645-6954 or 866-408-7495. *www.discovermuskoka.ca/lakeof baysboattours.* Aboard a pontoon boat, see this pretty lake on 2½ hour tours Jul-Labour Day at 10:30am and 1:30pm. For May– Jun and Sept–Oct, call for times. Boat leaves from the Riverfront Dock in Baysville. ⊚$30.

RECREATION

GUIDES AND OUTFITTERS

Al's Adventures (*469 King St. W., Second Floor, Toronto;* ☎416-220-7451; *www.alsadventures.ca*). Professionally guided fishing tours organized by Alan Slocombe. You must provide your own Ontario fishing licence (⚓ *see below*), appropriate clothing, sunglasses, and a lunch but all fishing gear is provided. ⊚Rates vary according to Ontario area and type of expedition. $100 deposit and reservations requested.

Williams Outfitters (*25 Cedar Bay Rd., Curve Lake;* ☎705-657-7831 or 877-266-9351; www.williamsoutfitters.com). Trips on the Kawarthas are organised by Michael Williams, an Ojibwa Indian who includes talks on aboriginal culture

in his outings. Bring all personal kit and Ontario licence; gear is provided.
⊚Full day (8 hours) $250 per person, or $300 for up to three people. Shore lunch $50 for one person, $75 for up to three people. Overnight camping on Fox Lake, Curve Lake First Nations Reserve also possible.

Purks Place (*1038 Bala Farm Rd., Bala;* ☎705-762-5311 or 877-903-2252; *www. purksplace.com*). Boat rentals (fishing boats, canoes, kayaks, pedal boats, waterskis), bait, tackle, ice—and lots of opinions. Licenses for boat operators, fishing and hunting. Rates vary according to expedition.

Baysville Marina (*10 East Rd., off Hwy 117, Baysville;* ☎705-767-3323; *www. purksplace.com*). Boat sales and rentals of all kinds, waterskis, parts and accessories. In winter snowmobile sales and rentals. Boat rentals $250-$350 per day.

Muskoka Outfitters (*271 Ecclestone Dr., Bracebridge;* ☎705-646-0492; *www. muskokaoutfitters.com*). Rentals and sales of boats, canoes and kayaks as well as camping equipment such as tents and packs, supplies for hiking, climbing, skiing and snowshoeing. Also courses and tours for skiing, ice-climbing, kayaking, climbing, white-water kayaking, and other sports. A recent service lets you order on the web and have things delivered to the cottage. ⊚ Prices vary according to expedition. ⓒStore hours open year-round *Mon–Fri 10am–6pm (Sat 5pm), Sun 11am–4pm.*

FISHING

The fishing in area lakes is abundant; species include yellow perch, walleye pike, largemouth bass, rock bass, muskie, carp and many smaller fish. Canadians ages 18-65 need an Outdoors Card (a laminated card to which the licence tag is affixed, valid for three years) plus a valid fishing licence. Outdoor Cards and licences are available from more than 2000 sports stores and other outlets in the province or you can call ☎800-387-7011(from Canada only). There are two kinds of licences: a sports fishing licence has a high catch limit for an angler who wants to keep his catch; a conservation licence has a lower catch limit. Limits vary according to the species, zone and season. Non-residents of Canada between ages 18-65 must purchase a licence. Licences can be purchased for a year, for eight days or for only one day and are available at many sporting goods stores.

BOATING

The Trent-Severn Waterway, a 386km/240mi watercourse of natural waterways and canals pieced together between 1833 to 1920 is maintained by Parks Canada. No longer used for commercial transport, the waterway is now a popular boating route. Permits are required for transiting the locks, based on number of locks to be crossed and length of time you will be navigating the system. You also need permits to moor and to camp at the locks (camping sites are provided for boaters only). These permits can be purchased at the locks or at the main office in Peterborough (*705-750-4900 or 888-773-8888; www.pc.gc.ca/ihn-hns/on/trentsevern*). To operate a motorboat under 4m in length (even if the motor is turned off), you need a proof of competency. You can complete a Canadian Coast Guard approved test, or a rental operator can provide a safety check-list to be completed. Non-residents can use operator cards from their own state or country. Check with *www.tc.gc.ca/BoatingSafety* for more details.

SHOPPING

SPECIALTY STORES

Johnson's Cranberry Marsh – *1074 Cranberry Rd., Bala.* ⏱*Store hours Jul–mid-Sept Mon-Sat 9am–6pm, Sun 11am–5pm, late Sept–Oct (harvest time) daily 9am–6pm, rest of year Mon–Sat 9am–5pm, Sun 11am–4pm.* ⏱*Closed major holidays.* ☎*705-762-3203. www. cranberry.ca.*

This 50-year-old family-owned cranberry farm offers its products (cranberry preserves, beverages, dried fruit, gift baskets) for sale, and also lets visitors tour the farm on five all-season trails to observe the meticulous care required of a cranberry bog all year round. The most interesting period is the harvest in October, when the bog is flooded and berries combed off the vines. Since 2002 the family has operated the Muskoka Lakes Winery, which produces wine from blueberries and cranberries.

Muskoka Store –*Hwy. 11, North Gravenhurst.* ⏱*Store hours Sun–Wed 9am–9pm, (Thu 10pm, Fri midnight), Sat 8am–9pm.* ☎*705-687-7751 or 800-687-5652. www.muskokastore.com.* This huge purveyor of home accessories and recreational equipment stocks wooden furniture (including the ubiquitous Muskoka chair), casual clothing and sportswear, canoes and kayaks, snowmobiles, snowshoes, kitchen utensils, gardening tools, and just about anything else cottagers need to enjoy their vacations. Note the very expansive hours for those arriving late at night from afar.

Whetung Ojibwa Crafts and Art Gallery – *Curve Lake Indian Reserve.* ☎*705-657-3661. www.whetung.com.* Store hours daily 9am–5pm. A large selection of crafts (basketry, beadwork, etc), clothing, ornaments and household items as well as original and reproduction artwork is for sale. Throughout the summer months, special events and festivals are held, culminating in the annual pow-wow held in mid-Sept, to which visitors are invited.

FARMERS' MARKETS

Peterborough Farmers' Market is held Sat and Sun morning year-round 7am–1pm in Morrow Park at the foot of George St. The **Downtown Country Fare Market** is held late May–mid-Oct on Wed 9am–2pm on Charlotte St. between George and Water streets; in the fall, until Christmas, it transfers inside to the upper level of the modern Peterborough Square.

Orillia Farmers' Market, held since 1872, offers produce, crafts and entertainment by the Orillia Folk Society year-round every Sat 7:30am–12:30pm. It sets up on the plaza next to the Opera House. ☎*705-326-1789. www. orilliafarmersmarket.on.ca.*

Gravenhurst Farmers' Market Co-op is open from late May–early Oct Wed 9am–2pm in the special events field at Muskoka Wharf. Products include local produce and crafts. ☎*705-684-8731. www.vendors.gravenhurstfarmers market.com.*

Bracebridge Farmers' Market is held late May–early Oct Sat 8:30am–1pm in Memorial Park between Manitoba and Kimberly streets in downtown Bracebridge. Besides produce and crafts, there is often entertainment on the bandstand. ☎705-644-7132. www.thebracebridgefarmersmarket.com

Two **Huntsville Markets** are held. A market is held mid-May–late-Oct Thu 9am–2 pm in the Canadian Tire parking lot at 77 King William St, while another is held early Jun–early Sept Fri 9am–2pm on the property of Robinson's Independent Grocer, 131 Howland Drive. ☎705-789-4771 (Huntsville Tourism). **Rosseau Market** is held Jul–Sept Fri 9am–2pm on the Rosseau waterfront at the end of Short St. Signs will direct you. Products, besides garden produce, include honey, bakery goods, berries, baskets and more. ☎705-789-8381. www.rosseaumarket.com.

THEATRE

Algonquin Theatre – 35 Main St. E., Huntsville. ☞Ticket prices vary according to performance. ✕🕐Summer box office opens Mon 11am–3pm,Tue–Fri 5pm, Sat 11am–3pm. Rest of the year Tue–Fri noon–4:30pm, Sat 11am–2pm. ☎705-789-4975 or 888-696-4255. www.algonquintheatre.ca. This 408-seat theatre, part of the new Huntsville Civic Centre, offers concerts, films, cabaret, plays, musicals, dance, comedy and even the occasional politician during a very full summer season.

Gravenhurst Opera House – 295 Muskoka Rd. S., Gravenhurst. 🕐Box office open Mon–Fri 10am–4pm (longer on show days). ☎705-687-5550 or 888-495-8888. www.gravenhurst.ca. This century-old, 338-seat theatre has been modernized for presentation of variety shows, concerts, plays, dance, comedy acts, but no opera.

Market Hall Performing Arts Centre – 336 George St. N., Peterborough. ☞Ticket prices vary according to performance. 🕐Call ahead for schedule. ☎705-749-1146. www.markethall.org. Under the clock tower in Peterborough's old downtown, this centre has adjustable seating for from 50 to 350 spectators. Programs range from concerts and plays to discussions with notable artists.

Orillia Opera House – 20 Mississauga St. W., Orillia. ☞Ticket prices vary according to performance. 🕐Call ahead for schedule. ☎705-326-8011. www.operahouse.orillia.on.ca. Twin turrets front this splendid 1917 redbrick building, which was actually built as an opera house, but with the first floor devoted to city business. Productions include Broadway musicals, plays, concerts and touring shows. Some plays are by local talent.

Rene M. Caisse Theatre – 100 Clearbrook Trail, Bracebridge. ☞Ticket prices vary according to performance. 🕐Call ahead for schedule. ☎705-645-8400. www.renemcaissetheatre.ca. This modern, 300-seat theatre presents concerts, plays, cabaret acts, dance and much more. There are also theatre camps and workshops for children and adults.

Showplace Performance Centre – 290 George St. N. Peterborough. ☞$15–$59. 🕐Box office hours Mon–Fri 11am–5pm (Sat 4pm) and 1hr prior to show time. ☎705-742-7469 or 866-444-2154. www.showplace.org. This modern 647-seat space, located in the old Odeon movie palace, hosts the Peterborough Symphony Orchestra, jazz groups, bands, drama, children's festivals, etc.

FESTIVALS

Bala Cranberry Festival – Bala. ☞$5. ☎705-762-1564. www.balacranberryfestival.on.ca. On the weekend after Thanksgiving (mid-Oct), the town of Bala is given over to the cranberry. Cranberry products are sold at the community centre, cranberry arts and crafts are judged and sold at the Bala Arena, and outdoor markets are held at specified venues, normally Maple Avenue and the public market in the Shield Parking lot.

Muskoka Lakes Music Festival – Port Carling. ☞$25. ☎705-765-1048 or 888-311-2787. www.artsinmuskoka.com. Since 1996, concerts have been held in a variety of venues in towns around the lakes late June–Aug. Artists range from classical to folk, and the festival include programs by children.

Peterborough Festival of Lights – Peterborough. ☎705-755-1111. www.festivaloflights.ca. Each year the city celebrates summer with music and entertainment from late June to late August. Free concerts and fireworks in Del Crary Park, overlooking Little Lake, are attended by hundreds who bring their own or rent lawn chairs ($2). Music ranges from classic rock, country and bluegrass to jazz, big band and Irish dances.

Address Book

For dollar sign categories, ⚭ see the Legend on the cover flap.
Note that four-season resorts offer substantially different rates depending on the season, with Jul–Aug and holidays being the most expensive. As well, many resorts book only for a minimum of two or three nights. Reserve early as accommodation is often booked months in advance.

WHERE TO STAY

$ Beacon by the Bay Guest House – *199 Crescent St., Peterborough.* ☎*705-745-9165 or 866-745-9165. www. nexicom.net/~beaconbythebay. 3 rooms.* ⊞⊡. This lovely 1910 brick house lies on Little Lake near Del Crary park in downtown Peterborough; if you like, you can arrive by boat on the Trent-Severn Waterway. The beacon refers to a little lighthouse in the garden. Rooms are small (the top-floor suite is more spacious), but air conditioned and nicely decorated in shades of plum. Facilities include a kitchenette and ensuite bathroom in the Cloud Nine suite, or shared kitchen and bathroom for the two other rooms. Breakfast fixings are provided in the kitchen for guests to assemble at their leisure.

$$ Bellhaven Bed & Breakfast – *1022 Guy's Rd., Bala.* ☎*705-762-0938. www. bellhaven.ca. 2 rooms. No children, no pets.* ⊞⊡. Staying at this lovely house on Lake Muskoka is like having your own cottage, minus the responsibilities. Both rooms overlook a terraced lawn that descends to the lake and a wide dock with chairs. Interiors are Muskoka-style, with polished wooden furniture, chintz fabrics, a fireplace in the sitting room, and splendid views out of large windows. Nearby are sports facilities, art galleries, theatres and village shopping.

$$ Shamrock Lodge – *Shamrock Rd., Port Carling.* ☎*705-765-3177 or 888-742-6742. www.shamrocklodge.com. 24 cottages or suites. Minimum 3-night stay in summer. Rates include all meals.* ⊞✕⊡ Set on Lake Rosseau, this lodge is the sort of traditional (since 1934) Muskoka resort where children participate in organized activities *(included in room rates)* such as boat rides, hikes, swimming and picnics, while parents follow their own preferences.
The old-fashioned American Plan applies: all meals are taken in the dining room, with barbecues and outdoor lunches in the summer. The fare is varied and home-cooked, wine is served, and picky children will find something familiar on the menu. There is an adult-only dining room, a family room and a kids' dining room.

$$ The Village Inn – *39 Queen St. Lakefield.* ☎*705-652-1910 or 800-827-5678 . www.thevillage inn.ca. 26 rooms, 2 suites.* ⊞✕⚭. Located on Lock 26 of the Trent-Severn Waterway, near the marina of the town of Lakeview and near the shores of Lake Katchewanooka ("water of many rapids"), this new hotel is furnished with spiffy country-style furniture and bright chintz fabrics. As befits a conference centre, each room has a desk with a lamp, as well as all the high-speed data amenities. In the hotel **The Thirsty Loon ($)** offers pub fare and a kid's menu, but several restaurants are within walking distance.

$$$ Cranberry Cove Wellness Resort – *3571 Muskoka Rd., Bala.* ☎*705-762-4223 or 877-762-5501. www.cranberry cove.net. 13 guestrooms, 11 suites, 1 cottage, 1 townhouse.* ⊞✕⚭ spa ⊒ For total de-stressing, check into this full-service, four-season spa set on 17.5ha/43 forested acres on a bay of Lake Muskoka. Accommodations, all decorated in the traditional Muskoka cottage style with lots of pine surfaces, range from simple rooms to luxurious suites with fireplaces (even summer evenings here can be nippy), as well as a townhouse and a cottage. Spa services include massages, aesthetic treatments and yoga instruction. A fitness centre with an indoor saltwater pool and an outdoor pool, tennis and basketball courts and hiking trails round out the amenities. Open to the public, the **restaurant ($$)** offers a range of healthy menus, including vegan, vegetarian and raw options, but also plenty of high-quality beef and seafood. In fine weather, dine on the patio or in the airy, cottage-style Muskoka room. In colder weather, sit near the fireplace indoors.

$$$$ The Irwin Inn – *Stony Lake, RR#2, Lakefield.* ☎705-877-2240 or 800-461-6490. *www.irwininn.com. 7 rooms in main lodge, 10 cottages, 21 suites in 2 bldgs, 4 lakeside cottages. Minimum 2 nights.* ⊡✕⊠. Located 55km/34mi north of Peterborough, in Crowe's Landing on Stony Lake, this expansive resort, owned by the Irwin family since 1947, has its own par-3 golf course and riding stables with lessons *(www.stoneylakeequestrian.ca)*, as well as a children's program to keep the wee ones busy. Accommodations range from simple but comfortable rooms to luxurious suites and lakeside cottages with fireplaces and whirlpool baths. Bed & breakfast rates are available for the main lodge rooms. Otherwise, the modified American Plan includes breakfast and dinner.

$$$$$ Delta Sherwood Inn – *1090 Sherwood Rd., Port Carling.* ☎705-765-3131 or 866-844-2228. *www.deltahotels. com. 50 guestrooms, including main lodge and cottages.* ⊡✕⊛⊠⊡⊞
Rates include breakfast and dinner. Set on Lake Joseph, this modern, luxurious four-season complex is entirely within the cottage country spirit, where wilderness emphatically does not mean roughing it. Rooms are decorated in country fabrics and touches of wood, some with gas fireplaces or screened porches. Activities include a swimming on the inn's beach, boating, canoeing, lake cruises, tennis, badminton and in winter, snow-shoeing, tobogganing. The on-site spa (www.angelsspa.ca) offers a full relaxing and beautifying regime. The **dining room ($$$,** *moderately formal dress-code)* serves Canadian dishes such as the Québécois plate of roast pork, tourtière and smoked bacon.

$$$$$ Egan Houseboat Rentals – *23 Lila Court, RR#2, Omemee.* ☎705-799-5745 or 800-720-3426 . *www.houseboat. on.ca. 27 houseboats.* Cruise the Trent-Severn Waterway in your own floating house, equipped with a kitchen, deck-top barbecue and hot-water shower stall. Boats, 40ft or 32ft, accommodate up to three couples or a family. For chilly weather, living quarters can be heated. Rates depend on the specific week. The company, in business for 35 years, gives lessons in houseboat steering; max speed is 16kph/10mph. In July-Aug the 32-footer rents for $869 to $970 for a three-day weekend (four adults maximum). May, June and Sept rates are considerably cheaper.

WHERE TO EAT

$ Only Café and Gordon Best Theatre – *216 Hunter St. W., Peterborough.* ☎705-876-8884. **Canadian.** Certainly one of the livelier local venues, this pub and cafe is open daily from 9am to 3am. Interior walls are lined with literally hundreds of framed reproductions of famous paintings. Patio dining overlooking Jackson's Creek is an option. The pub offers a huge selection of beer, including local micro-brewery products. The food is casual: mostly salads, omelettes and sandwiches. The Ginger Mick salad contains turkey, greens and a secret dressing, while the Marakesh Club sandwich is made with Gouda cheese and turkey, flavoured with cumin. Upstairs, the Gordon Best Theatre (☎705-876-8884) presents live performances, movies and dances; posters around town list the program, or call the theatre for what's playing.

$$ Aroma Dining & Drinks – *50 Main St. E., Huntsville.* ☎705-788-5150. *www. aromadining.ca.* **Fusion.** The atmosphere is relaxed, as it should be around Muskoka, but standards are high here, with crisp white tablecloths and soft lighting. The vodka martinis are justifiably popular, but chef-owner Jennifer McCague's inventive menus, based on French cuisine but accented with an international fusion, draw in visitors, especially on theatre nights *(reservations essential)*. Dishes stress Canadian beef, grilled to perfection, and seafood such as salmon.

$$ Blue Willow Tea Shop – *900 Bay St., Unit 2, Gravenhurst.* ☎*705-687-2957. www.bluewillowteashop.ca.* **British.** For a full cream tea, a light lunch, or even coffee and dessert, find it at this pleasant stop on the new Muskoka Wharf. Wide windows let you follow the action on the boardwalk. The classic blue-willow pattern decorates the china, although the decor is clean-lined modern with blond wood. In the evening there's roast beef and Yorkshire pudding, or steak and mushroom pie, with a choice of dessert.

$$ St. Veronus Café and Tap Room – *129 Hunter St. W., Peterborough.* ☎*705-743-5714.* **Belgian.** For those who like their beer Belgian, this friendly watering hole, with its polished wooden bar, offers an assortment of imported and domestic beers on tap as well as in bottles. The food is delicious, filling and indubitably Belgian: mussels prepared in a variety of ways (steamed in beer with garlic and coriander, in beer with green curry) always served with pommes frites and mayonnaise. Other main courses include Flemish pork tenderloin with leeks, or roast tarragon-flavoured chicken with mushrooms and cabbage. The King Baudouin soup, rich with seafood and potatoes in a cream broth, does the monarchy proud.

$$$ Burnham Mansion Restaurant – *2235 Keene Rd., RR#8, Peterborough.* ☎*705-740-2553 or 866-949-5514. www. burnhammansion.com.* **International.** The dramatic history of this 1873 Italianate farmhouse (its original owner survived the California gold rush and 5 children, but was gored by his prize bull) and its well-restored interior make it worth a visit, and the dining experience is certainly pleasant. The menu is extensive, with a range of steaks, chicken and pasta, and a few surprises such as Jambalaya (chicken, shrimp and sausage in a spicy sauce over rice) or chicken Normandie, stuffed with apples and brie in a cream sauce. The dessert cart includes apple strudel, cakes and pies. The dining room is modern, with comfortable Windsor chairs.

$$$ Victoria Inn –*Gore's Landing (on Rice Lake).* ☎*905-342-3261. www.eagle. ca/victoriainn.ca.* **French.** Located south of Peterborough, this charming 1902 inn overlooks Rice Lake from a promontory. The dining room, open to the public for three meals a day *(call ahead to reserve)*, serves haute cuisine such as wild boar cooked on kebabs on a bed of summer vegetable risotto, or lake trout served with a blueberry-mint marmalade. Appetizers include smoked trout terrine. The light-filled, vaguely Victorian dining room is decorated in soft mint tones. Upstairs are 9 **guest rooms ($$)**.

$$$ Winston's Inn – *475 Lindsay Rd., Peterborough.* ☎*705-743-0968. www. winstonsinn.com. Dinner only.* **Canadian.** This unpretentious restaurant is located in a fine old-brick farmhouse about 5km/3mi north of Peterborough centre. The sunny dining room is simple, with uncluttered Victorian touches such as lace curtains and flowered wallpaper. The food is familiar but well-presented: sirloin steak with tomato and mushrooms, lemon sole topped with a basil cream sauce, filet of pork wrapped in bacon with an apple cider sauce. Upstairs are six guestrooms **($)**.

---

tourist potential but now are a prime recreational area.

Water also spawned industrial development. Hydroelectric dams set up even before those of Niagara Falls launched Peterborough's industrial development in the late 19C. Boat-building was the first venture: canoe manufacturing started in the 1850s and thrived for a century. Although these companies are no more, they launched Peterborough's still thriving economy, today based on manufacturing, the health care sector, and Trent University; still, the most important industry is all-season tourism.

North of the palatial cottages and postcard-pretty small towns lies the rough-and-tumble mining region of northern Ontario. Orillia summer resident Stephen Leacock, in his humorous *Sunshine Sketches of a Small Town,* mined the rich seam of contradictions that this juxtaposition has produced.

Peterborough★

POPULATION 81,084 – MAP P 109

This pleasant city is set on the Trent Canal, part of the Trent-Severn Waterway, which links Lake Ontario with Georgian Bay. At this point there are three locks on the canal, including a famous lift lock. Boating is popular in the region, particularly on the 134 Kawartha Lakes to the north. From the days of the early aboriginal canoe makers to the late Peterborough Canoe Company, the city has long been associated with canoe building. Peterborough offers boating on the Otanabee River, which flows through town. In summer, some 30,000 cottagers flood into the area, the gateway to cottage country. Despite its bucolic backcountry, Peterborough lies within Ontario's industrial heartland: some 6 million people live within 320km/200mi of the city. The city itself is a manufacturing centre, notably for electrical and high-tech industries and food processing, and is part of the Oshawa General Motors auto-making hub. Founded in 1964, Trent University, with 4,000 full-time students, occupies a campus on the Otanabee River. The area is also known for its petroglyphic Indian relics and serpent mounds.

🛈 **Information:** Peterborough and the Kawarthas Tourism, 1400 Crawford Dr. ☎705-742-2201 or 800-461-6424. www.thekawarthas.net.

▶ **Orient Yourself:** The old downtown sector centres on Market Hall, built in 1889 and now a theatre. Little Lake, located a few blocks south, is bordered by Del Crary Park, with trails, an art gallery, free summer concerts and a fountain that shoots water 76m/250ft into the air. The downtown area around the Trent-Severn lift lock park has undergone considerable renewal, notably construction of Peterborough Square, a commercial and entertainment complex in the old market area. There remain several heritage buildings and old residences, as well as lovely downtown parks. Little Lake, a widening of the Otanabee River, lies at the city centre, flanked by green spaces. The best downtown shopping lies along Water and George streets, and into "East City," on the east bank of the Otonobee along the Trent Canal and lift lock.

🚢 **Don't Miss:** Take a cruise to observe the locks in action.

🕐 **Organizing Your Time:** Plan to spend a leisurely 3 days: one for the lift lock and museums, one for a cruise and shopping and one for excursions. You may want to time your visit to enjoy one of the many festivals and events here.

Especially for Kids: Lang Pioneer Village for make-believe.

Butterill/Ontario Tourism

Peterborough Lift Lock on Trent-Severn Waterway

A Bit of History

The city was founded in 1825 by poor Irish immigrants from Cork, whose passage and resettlement were promoted by a Toronto politician named Peter Robinson, in whose honour the city was named. Other settlers arrived from Scotland and one of them, **David Alexander Fife** (1805-1877), stumbled upon a new wheat variety that he had the genius to recognize as not only early-germinating, but remarkably immune to rust, smut and frost damage. He carefully nurtured his few seeds into the Red Fife variety that, after 1850, transformed the Prairies into Canada's granary.

Lumber was a major industry well into the 20C, but early exploitation of area waters for hydroelectricity in the late 19C attracted manufacturers. The earliest industry, starting in the 1850s, was canoe-making, an outgrowth of the sawmills that produced basswood, butternut and cedar planks. The Peterborough Canoe Company, founded in 1893, branched into distributing boat motors and in 1928, the Johnson Motor Company, a Chicago-based company, set up manufacturing here. Peterborough's reign as Canadian boat-building capital came to an end in the 1960s, but the manufacturing know-how from this industry lives on in other local businesses.

The city's chief literary light is **Robertson Davies** (1913-1995), the grand old man of Canadian literature and author of 18 books, who edited the *Peterborough Examiner* from 1942-1965.

Sights

Lift Lock★
Hunter St. E. ○*In operation mid-May–mid-Oct.*
Along its 386km/24mi length from Port Severn on Georgian Bay to Lake Ontario, the **Trent-Severn Waterway** passes through 44 locks, 75 control dams, 15 swing bridges and two marine railways (at Big Chute on the Severn River). Built in 1904 the Peterborough lock (Lock 21), and its sister at Kirkfield, are the only two of this kind in North America and

eight in the world. This hydraulic lift lock, at 20m/65ft, is the world's highest. The massive lock system is needed to overcome the waterway's geological difficulties: a rise of 182m/590ft to Balsam Lake, followed by a drop of 80m/272ft to Georgian Bay. Begun in 1833 the waterway took 87 years to complete; within a decade of completion, rail and road had rendered it largely obsolete. The system was modernized in the 1960s, and today serves recreational boaters, as well as providing municipal water for some communities, hydroelectric power and flood control.

In two chambers mounted on large hydraulic rams, recreational vessels are lowered and raised 20m/65ft. Visitors can watch the lock in action from the park beside it.

Trent-Severn National Historic Site Visitor Centre
At the Lift Lock site (Hunter St. E.). ○*Open mid-May–mid-Jun Mon–Thu 9am–4pm, Fri–Sun 9am–7pm. Late Jun–Labour Day daily 8:30am–7pm. Rest of Sept–late Oct Mon–Fri 9am–3:30pm, weekends 9am–5:30pm.* ○*Closed Good Friday.* ♿ 🅿 ($2) ☎705-750-4950 or 888-773-8888. www.pc.gc.ca.
The lock's construction and operation and the history of the Trent-Severn Waterway are explained by exhibits at the visitor centre.

Boat Cruise★
Departs from Peterborough Marina (92 George St.; www.peterboroughmarina.ca) at Del Crary Park. ○*Jul–Aug 3 times daily. Mid-May–Jun & Sept–mid-Oct twice daily.* ☞*$16.50. Reservations suggested. Liftlock Cruises: 150 George St.* ✕♿ ☎705-742-9912 or 888-535-4670. www.liftlock cruises.com.
Visitors can experience the lift lock by taking a leisurely boat cruise *(2hr)* along the Trent-Severn Waterway. Departing from the busy marina at Del Crary Park, where a bandshell marks the site of concerts and city festivals, the boat crosses Little Lake with its fountain that shoots water 76m/250ft into the air. The cruise proceeds into the main channel of the waterway, heading upstream to Lock 21, the famous Peterborough hydraulic

lift lock, the highest in the world. Here, the canal is surrounded on both sides by a lovely park, which holds the visitor centre for the lift lock.

Peterborough Centennial Museum and Archives

Museum Dr. at Hunter St. E. ○*Open year-round Mon–Fri 9am–5pm, weekends & holidays noon–5pm.* ☜*Contribution requested.* 🅿&☎*705-743-2614. www. pcma.ca.*

Located in a modern facility near the Peterborough Lift Lock, this pleasant museum, which also serves as a training centre for budding museologists at Trent University, was originally founded in 1897. Its collection is the second-oldest in Canada and includes a fine textile exhibit, archaeological artifacts, examples of old technology and furniture that belonged to **Catharine Parr Traill** (1802-1899) who, along with her sister **Susanna Moodie** (1803-1885), wrote accounts of pioneer life in this area. She lived for many years in Belleville, as did Susanna, and died in Lakeview.

Canadian Canoe Museum★★

910 Monaghan Rd. ○*Open year-round Mon–Sat 10am–5pm, Sun noon–5pm.* ○*Closed Dec 24–27, Dec 31–Jan 1 & major holidays.* ☜*$7.50* 🅿&☎*705-748-9153 or 866-342-2663. www.canoemuseum.net.*

The canoe-making industry thrived in Peterborough from the 1850s through the 1960s, when labour costs and the advent of fibreglass and aluminium doomed this labour-intensive craft. The city's gift to Princess Elizabeth on her 1948 marriage was a Peterborough Cedar Rib canoe. Opened in 1997 in a former motorboat factory, this modern museum houses a fascinating array of more than 600 canoes, kayaks and rowing craft of all types and construction—reputedly the largest and most comprehensive collection of paddled watercraft in the world. Exhibits employ the latest museum technology, including interactive and sensory exhibits.

Displays are organized according to themes, such as Indian canoe building and trade routes, or watercraft from around the world including New Guinea, Oceania and Africa. The museum incorporates the Kanawa International Collection of watercraft assembled by Professor Kirk Wipper from 1957 until 1990. Boats of various aboriginal cultures featured are West Coast dugouts, Inuit kayaks, a Kutenai canoe from central British Columbia, a Mandan Bull boat used by the Prairie Indians used to cross rivers and other examples. One exhibit is devoted to the paddling accoutrements of the late prime minister **Pierre Elliott Trudeau** (1919-2000). Paddles, models and related artifacts are also on view. A Visiting Artisans program brings canoe-builders into the museum, where visitors can watch them at work and discuss their craft. In summer canoe-building courses are available to the public.

The Origins Gallery, Canadian Canoe Museum

Don Rankin/The Canadian Canoe Museum

Hutchison House Museum

270 Brock St. ○Open mid-Jun–Sept Tue–Sun 1pm–5pm. Rest of the year Tue–Fri 1pm–5pm. ⊚$3. Scottish tea and tour Jul-Aug Tue–Sun 1pm–4pm, Jun & Sept weekends 1pm–4pm; ⊚$6. ☎705-743-9710 or 866-743-9710.www.nexicom.net/~history.

This 1836 Victorian stone cottage with white gingerbread trim was built by Dr. John Hutchison, who lived here with his wife and five children. In those days the area had been settled only for a decade. The two lower floors have been restored to reflect the family's life in the 1840s, while the upper floor, added by later owners, has been restored to reflect the 1860s. The lowest level, containing the kitchen and scullery, demonstrates the effort needed to produce even simple meals. Light-filled and well furnished, the parlour and doctor's office upstairs show the family's public face. Dr. Hutchison's Scottish-born cousin, **Sir Sandford Fleming** (1827-1915), a great Canadian railroad magnate and founder of standard time, stayed here when he first arrived in Canada.

Excursions

Lang Pioneer Village

104 Lang Rd., in Keene. 16km/10mi southeast of Peterborough by Rte. 7 and Country Rd. 34. ○Open mid-Jun–Labour Day daily 10am–4pm (last admission 3pm). Late May–early Jun Mon–Fri 10am–3pm. Early–mid-Sept Mon–Fri 10am–4pm for hourly ✎ guided tours only. ⊚$6. ☎705-295-6694 or 888-289-5264. www.langpioneervillage.ca.

[kids] This 19C village is situated on 10ha/25acres in a delightful rural setting on the banks of the Indian River. Some 20 reconstructed buildings were moved here from all over the county; an original gristmill (1846) is still in working order. The log cabin of David Fife, famed for his hardy strain of wheat, has been moved here from its nearby place of construction.

Farm animals and small vegetable plots are on hand, as evidence of how food

Petroglyphs in Petroglyphs Provincial Park

R. Simpson/Ontario Tourism

was provided. Costumed staff demonstrate daily chores such as baking, weaving and trades—and answer questions as well.

For technology buffs, the collection of farm, household and trade machinery is fascinating. A 19C Jacquard loom creates patterned fabric using punch-cards and is the direct ancestor of the computer.

Petroglyphs Provincial Park

55km/34mi northeast of Peterborough via Hwy. 28, near Woodview. ○Open mid-May–mid-Oct daily 10am–5pm. ⊚$11.85/vehicle. ☎705-877-2552. www.ontarioparks.com.⊘Photographing the carvings is not permitted.

The largest concentration of petroglyphs anywhere in Canada is protected in this park, located near Stony Lake. About 900 carvings showing animals and people range in age from 500 and 1,100 years.

A modern **interpretive centre** offers exhibits and a movie *(20min)* that explain the site. The glyphs themselves are protected from the elements by a glass enclosure, with explanatory plaques; guides are on hand to answer questions.

Four marked trails, of easy to moderate difficulty, meander through the forest and wetlands of the park.

Gravenhurst ★

POPULATION 10,899 – MAP P 108

This attractive town with its tree-lined streets, elegant houses, and opera house (now a performing-arts centre) lies at the southern end of picturesque Lake Muskoka, with its indented shoreline and numerous islands. A former logging settlement, with 14 mills operating in its heyday, Gravenhurst is known as the "first town in Muskoka"; in 1887 it was the initial community to acquire official town status. Today, given its southern location, Gravenhurst serves as the geographic gateway to the Muskoka Lakes area. It is particularly noted for spectacular sunset views over the lake. A new $170-million 89-acre development on the lakeshore, Muskoka Wharf, includes parklands, playgrounds, hiking trails, shops, restaurants and condominiums. A boardwalk runs the length of the development. The town is also the birthplace of Dr. **Norman Bethune** (1890-1939), surgeon, inventor, advocate of socialized medicine and a national hero in China.

- **Information:** Municipal Offices, 190 Harvie St. ☎705-687-3412. www.gravenhurst.ca.
- **Orient Yourself:** Gravenhurst lies between a bay of Lake Muskoka (west) and Gull Lake (east). The wharves and city centre lie on Muskoka Bay, while Gull Lake Park stretches along the town's east side. The distance between them is only a few blocks.
- **Don't Miss:** A lake cruise will help you appreciate the Muskoka area's popularity as a vacation region. A visit to the Muskoka Store (🛍 see Shopping in Practical Information).
- **Organizing Your Time:** Gravenhurst and the Muskoka Lakes can be fit into a leisurely tour of the Georgian Bay. Allow 2 days here to see all the sights and enjoy a leisurely cruise.

Sights

Bethune Memorial House National Historic Site★

235 John St. N. 🚶*Visit by guided tour (1hr) only, Jun–Aug daily 10am–4pm. Sept–Oct Sat–Wed 10am–4pm.* 🎟*$4.* ☎*705-687-4261. www.pc.gc.ca.*

The son of a Gravenhurst Presbyterian minister, Norman Bethune (1890-1939) studied medicine in Toronto, then practised in Detroit, where he contracted tuberculosis. Confined to a sanitorium, he learned of a little-known method of treatment by collapsing a lung and insisted that this operation be performed on him. The operation was successful. Between 1928 and 1936, he worked as a chest surgeon in Montreal but, disillusioned with the lack of interest in socialized medicine in Canada, he departed for Spain to fight on the Republican side in the civil war. There Bethune set up the first mobile blood-transfusion unit. In 1938 he went to China and worked as a surgeon alongside the Chinese Communists fighting the Japanese. The surgeon organized a medical service for the Chinese army, but died of blood poisoning late in 1939. Fame in his own country stemmed from Bethune's status as a hero to the Chinese.

The doctor's birthplace contains several rooms restored to their 1890s appearance, and an excellent **interpretive display** in three languages (English, French and Chinese) on his life and importance. A visitor centre offers an orientation video *(15min)*.

Muskoka Boat and Heritage Centre

275 Steamship Bay Rd. 🕐*Open mid-Jun– mid-Oct daily 10am–6pm. Rest of the year Tue-Sat 10am-4pm.* 🎟*$6.75.* ☎*705-687-2115. www.mbhc.ca.*

This colourful new (2006), $6-million complex is devoted to the boats of Muskoka: the steamships that hauled freight and passengers and the wooden

Cruising on the RMS Segwun in Lake Muskoka

Ontario Tourism

runabouts that required hours of loving maintenance and layers of varnish. The Grace & Speed boathouse displays 20 vintage, highly varnished wooden motorboats sitting in the water; the display rotates often, so the same boats are not there for long. The exhibit shows how the boats were made by local people during the 1930s, the heyday of the Muskoka boat. Visitors can tour the stateroom, dining room, freight deck and wheelhouse of a steamship and even blow the whistle. Part of the display area is devoted to the old resorts that drew a wealthy international clientele.

Steamship Cruises

Departs from Sagamo Park dock Jun–Labour Day. Call for departure times. Round trip 1hr–4hrs. Reservations required. Sightseeing cruises $16–$47. Muskoka Lakes Navigation Co. ☎705-687-6667 or 866-687-6667. www.real muskoka.com.

Visitors can board the **RMS Segwun,** the last coal-fired steamship in North America, at Gravenhurst's wharf to appreciate the beauty of the lakes and see some of the summer houses along their shores. The tour takes in "Millionaires Row" on Tondern Island in Lake Muskoka, which is lined with palatial mansions built by wealthy industrialists. Built in 1887 the former Royal Mail Ship transported mail, passengers and cargo in the area until 1958. A range of sightseeing tours as well as lunch and dinner cruises are offered.

Excursion

Orillia★

About 37km/23mi south of Gravenhurst via Hwy. 11.

Set on the Narrows where Lake Simcoe meets Lake Couchiching, this small industrial centre and resort town has a reputation out of all proportion to its size (pop. 30,259). Orillia served as the model for the imaginary town of "Mariposa" in *Sunshine Sketches of a Little Town* by famed humourist and author **Stephen Leacock** (1869-1944). Possibly the best known of Canada's literati, this political science professor at McGill University spent his summers here.

The port of Orillia is set in lovely Centennial Park; other parks dot the town as well. A 9.5km/6mi paved trail crosses from the Narrows at one end of the town to Wilson's Point at the other.

Stephen Leacock Museum★

50 Museum Dr., near Old Brewery Bay off Hwy. 12 Bypass. Turn left onto Forest Ave., then right on Museum Dr. ✕ Open May–Sept daily 9am–5pm. Rest of the year Mon–Fri 9am–5pm. $5. ☎705-329-1908. www.leacockmuseum.com.

Set amid pleasant grounds overlooking Brewery Bay, this white-frame house, designed by Wright & Noxon of Toronto, was built by **Stephen Leacock** (1869-1944) in 1928. Unusually for a Canadian author of his time, Leacock realized substantial income from his 35 books. His textbook, *Elements of Political Science* (1906), was in use for decades, while *Literary Lapses* (1910), *Sunshine Sketches of a Little Town* (1912), and *Arcadian Adventures of the Idle Rich* (1914), were international best-sellers. It was *Sunshine Sketches* that created Leacock's reputation. It is a funny account of a small town on the edge of the wild mining country.

Born in England, Leacock immigrated as a small boy to a farm near Lake Simcoe with his family. His childhood was marked by poverty and his alcoholic father abandoned the family. Extremely bright, Leacock pursued his studies at the University of Toronto and the University of Chicago. At this house, he wrote intensely.

While the rooms recall Leacock's life, exhibits are devoted to the work of other Canadian literary notables. But the uproarious humour of this man, who stated he would rather have written *Alice in Wonderland* than the whole of the *Encyclopaedia Britannica*, pervades the house.

Muskoka Lakes/ Cottage Country

MAP P 108

The District of Muskoka covers some 6,475sq km/2,500sq mi, reaching from Georgian Bay northeast to Algonquin Park. Besides the three major lakes—Muskoka, Rosseau and Joseph—some 1,600 lakes litter this rugged, forested landscape that lies on the pink granite of the Canadian Shield. During cottage season, whole families move from their homes to spend the summer in cabins, small houses and mansions (all referred to as "cottages" no matter the size) built at water's edge. "Millionaires Row" on Tondern Island in Lake Muskoka, a favourite route for cruise boats, is lined with palatial mansions built by Pittsburgh industrialists. The many resorts and inns dotting the lakes cater to all categories of guests, from adults only to family-oriented villages with programs for children; the common theme is water and forest. This annual migration began in 1875, when the railway reached the region; today, four-lane highways have brought the lakes within two hours of Toronto. The major towns in the area with substantial permanent populations are Gravenhurst, Bracebridge and Huntsville, while Bala and Port Carling are lively in summer months. The name "Muskoka" is very likely derived from "Misquuckkey," the name of an Algonquin chief, whose name appears on treaties ceding this area to Britain in 1815.

- **Information:** Muskoka Tourism. ☎800-267-9700. www.discovermuskoka.ca.
- ▶ **Orient Yourself:** It is possible to boat from one Muskoka lake to another, thanks to a lock at Port Carling (Rosseau/Muskoka) and a canal at Port Sandfield (Joseph/Rosseau); the Moon River drains Lake Muskoka into Georgian Bay. Gravenhurst, Bracebridge, Huntsville all lie along Highway 11 (south to north), within no more than 30km/18mi of each other; Port Carling sits at the northern end of Lake Muskoka, and Bala on the lake's mid-western side. All of these towns are worth visiting.
- **Don't Miss:** A lake cruise will help you appreciate why the Muskoka area is Ontario's most popular vacation region. *See Cruises in the Practical Information section.*
- **Organizing Your Time:** Many resorts and B&Bs book minimum stays of two or three days in high summer season. Book well in advance as accommodations fill up in high season. Plan to spend at least a week in the area, during "cottage season," of course (late May to mid-Oct).
- **Especially for Kids:** Muskoka Heritage Place.

Ontario Tourism

Muskoka Lake

Sights

Muskoka Heritage Place★

88 Brunel Rd., Huntsville. ⏰*Open mid-May–mid-Oct daily 10am–4pm. Train rides Jul–Aug Tue–Fri 1pm & Sat noon, 1pm, 2pm, & 3pm. Muskoka Museum open year-round 10am–4pm.* ∽*Village $10, Museum $2, Train $5.* ♿✕*(Jul-Aug only)* ☎*705-789-7576. www.muskoka heritageplace.org.*

🅺🅸🅳🆂 Life in the late 19C is recalled in the **Muskoka Pioneer Village,** a collection of community structures, many of which were moved here from area towns. A 1948 diesel-electric narrow gauge engine pulling open-air coaches and an old **steam train**, the *Portage Flyer,* offer rides around the village. Building highlights include an 1875 Methodist church (still in use), a reproduction trapper's log cabin, a small 1872 log farmhouse where 14 children grew up, a diminutive 1878 municipal building where dances were somehow accommodated, the 1874 white frame house of a prosperous Methodist minister and farmer, an 1878 general store, a stable, blacksmith shop, Temperance boarding house and a summer aboriginal settlement. The museum showcases aboriginal artifacts, vintage photographs, 19C household goods and furnishings as well as parlour handiwork like needlework and other crafts. Costumed interpreters demonstrate 19C domestic skills and trades such as candle-making, spinning, blacksmithing, and sawmilling operations. There are tractor-pulled wagon rides around the 36ha/90-acre site, which features a lake and nature trails.

Woodchester Villa

15 King St., Bracebridge. ↝*Visit by guided tour only, Jul–Labour Day Tue–Sat 10am–5pm.* ∽*$2.* ☎*705-645-5501. www. octagonalhouse.com.*

This odd, three-storey octagonal house was built according to the latest scientific principles in 1882 by British immigrant Henry J. Bird, a successful woollen mill owner. Constructed of poured concrete, it had electric lighting, forced-air heating and indoor plumbing and other conveniences, when the surrounding area was a logging wilderness. After restoration by the Bracebridge Rotary Club, the house became the town museum in 1980. The exhibits are mostly of local interest, but captivating. Especially intriguing is the story of Rene M. Caisse (1888-1978), a local nurse who discovered an herbal "cure for cancer" and spent her life quite lucratively promoting it; the Bracebridge theatre is named for her.

GEORGIAN BAY AND LAKE HURON

Lake Huron, 332km/208mi long and 295km/183mi wide, is the second-largest Great Lake and the fifth largest freshwater lake in the world, with a maximum depth of 229m/750ft. Like the other Great Lakes, it was formed during and subsequent to the last Ice Age, as glaciers gouged out the land, and great surges of water from melting ice created massive waterfalls and mighty rivers, all now gone. Named for George IV of England, Georgian Bay is almost a lake in itself, cut off from the rest of Lake Huron by the Bruce Peninsula and Manitoulin Island. Immortalized by the Group of Seven painters, the bay's eastern and northern shorelines, set on the Canadian Shield, are wild and rocky, with numerous indentations and thousands of islands. In 2004 the Georgian Bay Littoral—the islands and freshwater coastline of Georgian Bay—were designated a UNESCO Biosphere Reserve. In contrast, the Nottawasaga Bay, at the southern end of Georgian Bay, has long sandy stretches, especially in the region of Wasaga Beach. Georgian Bay Islands National Park, established in 1929, comprises some 40 islands stretching from Honey Harbour in the southeastern corner of the bay. A popular vacation spot, Georgian Bay's shores and thousands of islands are lined with summer cottages, parks and resorts. Watercraft of all sorts—cargo freighters and cruise ships as well as sailboats, canoes and kayaks—ply the clear, blue waters of the bay. The region also supports considerable light industry, and Owen Sound, Collingwood, Midland, Port McNicoll and Parry Sound are busy commercial ports.

About 400 million years ago, this area resembled Australia's Great Barrier Reef: a shallow tropical sea with coral reefs and thousands of primitive plant and animal species. In fact, this sea lay near the equator; plate tectonics over the eons have moved the land to its present position halfway between the equator and the pole. As the sea dried up, layers of limestone formed by calcium from dead sea animals was suffused with magnesium from the water, forming harder dolomite. In the eons since, especially during ice ages, the soft limestone

Georgian Bay as seen from Bruce Peninsula

Practical Information

AREA CODES

The area codes for this region are 705 and. 519. For local calls, dial all 10 digits (area code plus the number, but without the 1-prefix). For more information: ☎1-800-668-6878 or www.bell.ca.

GETTING THERE AND AROUND

BY AIR

The closest major airport, about 2hrs away, is **Lester B. Pearson International Airport in Toronto** (&See Toronto Area Practical Information). Regional airports serving private and corporate aircraft are Lake Simcoe Regional Airport (☎705-487-0999. www.lakesimcoeairport.com) at Barrie and Huronia Airport (☎705-526-8086. www.huroniaairport.com) near Midland and Penetanguishene.

BY BUS

Greyhound (www.greyhound.ca) provides service to this area.

BY FERRY

The Chi-Cheemaun Ferry links Little Tub Harbour in Tobermory on the Bruce Peninsula with South Baymouth on Manitoulin Island. The ferry operates mid-May–mid-Oct, four sailings each direction daily of 1hr 45min each; check website for times. The ship accommodates 143 vehicles and 638 passengers and offers full meal service in its cafeteria. Reservations are highly recommended. ⊷$14.50/passenger one-way, $33/vehicle one-way (✕⅂P⊡☎800-265-265-3163; www.ontarioferries.com). Chi-Cheemaun means "big canoe" in Ojibwa.

GENERAL INFORMATION

VISITOR INFORMATION

Southern Ontario Tourism Office. www.soto.on.ca.
Georgian Bay Tourism (Midland, Penetanguishene and Honey Harbour) 980 King St., Midland. ☎800-263-7745. www.georgianbaytourism.on ca.
Manitoulin Tourism Assn., Little Current. ☎705-368-3021. www.manitoulintourism.com or www.manitoulin-island.com.

Tobermory Chamber of Commerce, Tobermory. ☎519-596-2452. www.tobermory.org.
Bruce Peninsula Tourism ☎519-793-4734 or 800-268-3838. www.bruce peninsula.org
South Bruce Peninsula Chamber of Commerce, Wiarton. www.wiarton chamber.ca.

ACCOMMODATIONS

&For a selection of area lodgings, see the Address Book.

CRUISES AND CHARTERS

Blue Heron Cruises – Trips to Flowerpot Island on the Heron V, a glass-bottomed boat holding 96 people, departing from Little Tug Harbour in Tobermory. Tour crosses over two shipwrecks and docks at the island. Cruise lasts 1hr20min, plus time spent on the island. Six sailings daily late Jun–Aug, 4 sailings early May–Jun & first 3 weeks Sept, 3 sailings (4 on weekends) late Sept–mid-Oct. ⊷$37.50 (including drop-off on island) (Blue Heron Company ☎519-596-2999; www.blueheronco.com).
Fathom Five National Marine Park Cruise (2hr) on 125-passenger Great Blue Heron glass-bottomed boat. View shipwrecks, Russel Island, Cove Island Harbour, Otter Islands, Flowerpot Island. Four sailings daily in Aug, 3 in Jul, call for May–Jun & Sept–Oct (Blue Heron Company ☎519-596-2999; www.blueheronco.com).Call to confirm. ⊷$37.50.
Cruises of 30,000 Islands. From **Midland** town dock, the 300-passenger Miss Midland departs May–Oct daily 1:45pm, additional cruises (up to 4 daily) mid-Jun–Sept. Round-trip 2hrs 30min. ⊷$23. Reservations suggested. (10 Robert St. E.,Penetanguishene; ✕⅂&P☎705-549-3388 or 888-833-2628; www.midlandtours.com).
From **Penetanguishene** town dock, the 200-passenger MS Georgian Queen departs Jul-Aug Mon-Tue and Fri-Sun 2pm, also 6:30pm dinner cruises Wed, Thu, Sat May–Jun & Sep–Oct less

frequently. Round-trip 3hrs 30min. Reservations suggested; call ahead to verify times. ⏚$25. *(Argee Boat Cruises, Ltd.* ✖❎🅿 ☎*705-549-7795 or 800-363-7447; www.georgianbaycruises.com).* From **Parry Sound** town dock, the 550-passenger *Island Queen* departs on 2hr morning cruises Jul–Aug daily 10am ⏚$24 and 3hr afternoon cruises Jun–mid-Oct daily 1pm ⏚$32. Reservations required. *(30,000 Island Cruise Lines Inc. 9 Bay St. Parry Sound;* ✖&🅿☎*705-746-2311 or 800-506-2628; www.island-queen.com).*

Great Lakes Cruise Company – One week to 12-day luxury (May–Oct) cruises from Toronto to Duluth, Minn., taking in all the Great Lakes and stopping at Little Current on Manitoulin Island. Also cruises of four Great Lakes and Georgian Bay, taking in Parry Sound, Midland and Little Current. ⏚Cruise prices vary according to excursion and room. Call ahead for reservations *(3270 Washtenaw Ave., Ann Arbor MI;* ☎*888-891-0203; www.greatlakescruising.com).*

Canadian Yacht Charters – *May–Oct.* Charter a sail or power boat, with or without a skipper, or enjoy a day's sail around the North Channel. Jul–mid-Aug rates from ⏚$2100/wk for a boat berthing 4 people; the largest can berth 8 people. Cruise prices vary according to excursion, date and vessel *(30 Water St., Gore Bay;* ☎*705-282-0185 or 800-565-0022; www.cycnorth.com). Call ahead for reservations.*⏚

Discovery Yacht Charters – *Little Current. May–Oct.* Rent a luxury yacht for a cruise among the islands of the North Channel. Catamarans or monohull vessels with 2 or 3 cabins berth up to 8 people. High season (mid-Jul–mid-Aug) rates range from ⏚$2,400 to $6,100. Skipper services available. Call ahead for reservations.⏚Cruise prices vary according to excursion, date and vessel. *(*☎*705-368-3744 or 800-268-8222; www.discoveryyachtcharters.com)* .

Mega-Yacht Vacation Company – *Little Current. May–Oct.* Cruise the Georgian Bay in a rented yacht (30m/98ft or larger, sail or power) complete with 5-person crew. One-week charter $50,000 up; can be divided among 4 to 12 passengers. *Call ahead for reservations.*⏚Cruise prices vary according to excursion,

date and vessel. ☎*866-389-1367.www. megayachtvac.com).*

Ojibway Canoe Wilderness Adventures – Canoe trips with a guide, including fishing tackle, camping gear and meals. One day excursion to 6-night camping trips. May–Oct. ⏚$145. *(Whitefish River First Nation, 6791 Hwy 6, Birch Island,* ☎*705-285-7668; www. ojibwaycanoe.com). Call ahead for reservations.*

RENTALS AND OUTFITTERS

Divers Den – *Tobermory. May–Oct.* Rent a power boat to tour islands of Fathom Five National Marine Park or along the shores of the Bruce Peninsula. Also scuba charters and instruction and gear rental. *Call ahead for reservations.*⏚*$160/day.* ☎*519-596-2868. www. diversden.ca.*

Killarney Mountain Lodge and Outfitters – *Killarney. May–Oct* This resort near Killarney Provincial Park opposite Manitoulin Island rents canoes and kayaks, including sea kayaks that can navigate Georgian Bay. Also guided canoe and kayak day trips and camping trips, and kayaking lessons. The **lodge ($$)** offers comfortable wilderness accommodations, with a restaurant and recreational facilities. ⏚$45 for afternoon and evening sailing. Other prices vary per excursion and equipment rental *(*☎*705-287-2691 or 800-461-1117. www.killarney.com). Call ahead for reservations.*

Thorncrest Outfitters –*Tobermory. Apr–Oct.* Complete outfitting for paddlers. Rent a kayak or canoe, join a guided trip or take a course on paddling; also courses for children. ⏚$30/day for a canoe. Other equipment rentals vary. *(7441 Hwy 6;* ☎*519-596-8908; www. thorncrestoutfitters.com).*

FISHING LICENCES

To fish in Ontario, you must have a fishing licence. *For details, see Practical Information for South Central Ontario chapter in this book.* Ontario Ministry of Natural Resources ☎800-667-1940. www.mnr.on.ca.

SUMMER THEATRE

Gore Bay Theatre – *Gore Bay Community Hall, 52 Meredith St., Gore Bay.* 🕐Box office open Jun–Aug Mon–Fri

8:30am–4:30pm and at showtime. ☎705-282-0538 or 800-529-5518. *www. gorebaysummertheatre.ca.* A program of Canadian plays in Jul 7:30pm, with Sun matinees 2pm. ☎$15.

Charles W. Stockey Centre *–2 Bay St., Parry Sound.* ⏱Box office open Jul–Labour Day daily 10am–6pm. Mid-May–Jun Tue–Sat 9am–5pm. Rest of the year Wed–Sat 10am–6pm and at showtime. *☎Ticket prices vary according to performance. Call ahead for reservations.* ☎705-746-4466 or 877-746-4466. *www.stockeycentre.com.* Musical performances by popular artists and bands, as well as story readings. **Festival of the Sound** at the Stockey Centre mid-Jul-mid-Aug. *(Festival of the Sound, 42 James St., Parry Sound)* ⏱Box office

open Apr–Jun Mon–Fri 9am–5pm, Jul–Aug Mon–Sat 9am–5pm and 1 hr prior to show. ☎Ticket prices vary according to performance. Call ahead for reservations. 705-746-2410 or 866-364-0061. www.festivalofthesound.ca.

King's Wharf Theatre – Discovery Harbour, **Penetanquishene**. ⏱*Box office open Mon 10am–5pm, Tue–Sat 10am–9pm and 2 hours prior to show.* ☎*Ticket prices vary according to performance. Call ahead for reservations.* ♿☎888-449-4463 and 705-549-5555. *www.drayentertainmentcom.* Barnlike 385-seat theatre in reconstructed 19C British naval harbour. Productions include plays, concerts and variety shows, year-round.

Address Book

♿ *For dollar sign categories, see the Legend on the cover flap.*

WHERE TO STAY

$ Thurso House B&B – *167 Pine St., Collingwood.* ☎705-445-7117.*www. thursohouse.com. 3 rooms.* 🖵🅿
This 1902 pink stone Romanesque Revival style house sports a turret and large, ballustraded veranda. The guest rooms feature hardwood floors and high windows, and come with ensuite bathrooms. The master suite has a fireplace. Clawfoot tubs equip two of the guest bathrooms. Interior decoration is restrained Edwardian, with many antiques, as befits the home a doctor built for his wealthy bride. Local artwork is on display.

$$ Baker's Birch Island Lodge – *Little Current, on Manitoulin Island.* ☎705-285-5000 (Apr–Oct) or 705-665-5143 (Nov–Mar). www.birchislandlodge.com. 10 cottages.* 🅿✕. Located just off Manitoulin Island—guests are ferried in from the parking lot—this tranquil resort offers accommodation and a restaurant (American plan or bed & breakfast plans available). Cabins have refrigerators, but no cooking facilities. Swimming, fishing, two golf courses are nearby and it's only a short drive to Little Current on the northeastern part of the island.

The rustic **restaurant ($)** offers a set meal and you can bring your own wine. Boat rentals are also available.

$$ Blue Bay Motel – *32 Bay St., Tobermory.* ☎519-596-2392.www.bluebay-motel.com. 16 rooms. 2-day minumum weekend stay Jul-Sept.* 🅿. Clean, simply furnished rooms overlook Little Tub Harbour at this well-located, two-storey motel, which is close to the ferry dock—a plus for visitors taking an early departure to Manitoulin Island on the Chi-Cheemaun ferry. Wireless Internet connection available.

$$ Grandview Motel – *Bay St., Tobermory.* ☎519-596-2220.www.grandview-tobermory.com. 18 units.* ✕🅿. Located on the east side of Little Tug Harbour, near its entrance, this motel offers grand views of the channel waters from its popular patio dining area, especially at sunset. The **restaurant ($$)**serves, among other dishes, Georgian Bay whitefish, pork tenderloin, roast duck and seafood platters. Rooms are simply but comfortably fur-nished.

$$ Harborside Motel – *24 Carlton St. E., Tobermory.* ☎519-596-2422. www. blueheronco.com. 37 units.* 🅿. From your patio of this motel, you can watch fishing boats dock in Little Tub Harbour. Some rooms have kitchenettes. Off Bay Street there are also seven waterfront cottages (one two-storey) with a kitchen, shower, private dock, beach and fire pit *(Wireless Bay Cottages, 109 Bay St., ☎519-596-2504).*

$$ Lioness Lake B&B – *64 Lioness Rd., Parry Sound. ☎705-378-0499.www. lionesslake.com. 3 rooms.* ⌨ 🅿
A good alternative to a resort, which often book for longer stays, this B&B near Parry Sound offers a tranquil lakeside setting, with a dock (stairway down), a lake to canoe and swim in and forested surroundings. Decorated with flower patterns and comfortable furniture, sunny rooms are candy-box pretty, with private bathrooms.

$$ The Queen's Inn – *19 Water St., Gore Bay, on Manitoulin Island. ☎705-282-0665. www.thequeensinn.ca. 8 rooms. Closed Jan–Apr.* ⌨ 🅿. Built in 1880 this three-storey inn offers light-filled rooms furnished with antiques and colourful chintz fabrics. Five of the rooms have private bathrooms. The verandas surrounding the lower and upper storeys provide a pleasant point from which to watch boat traffic on the tranquil bay. The parlour, with a piano, gas fireplace and long windows, is a comfortable refuge on rainy days. Homemade breakfasts are served in the spacious dining room. Cable TV and internet. Gore Bay is a charming town with pretty sights, golf courses and tennis courts.

$$ Saga Beach Resort – *88 Main St., Wasaga Beach. ☎705-429-2543 or 800-263-7053.www.sagaresort.com. 16 motel rooms, 4 chalets, 13 cottages.* 🛏🅿. Open year round, this sprawling compound close to Beach Area One (the main Wasaga beach) includes a variety of accommodations, in sizes to fit every need, from 1 to 4 bedrooms, as well as an outdoor heated swimming pool, hot tubs, recreation area and a children's program to keep the little ones occupied. All accommodations have kitchens, although some have no telephone. Bikes can be rented.

$$ Waterview on the Bay – *501205 Island View Dr., Wiarton. ☎519-534-0921 or 877-534-0921.www.waterview.ca. 19 rooms.* 🛏🅿. Located on Colboy's Bay on the southern reach of the Bruce Peninsula, this motel offers three levels of comfort: Simply furnished ground level rooms open onto a lawn and a

heated swimming pool; the waterview and Colpoys level rooms have finer furnishings, Jacuzzis or hot-tubs, fireplaces and a private deck. The four-acre resort offers boats, a swimming beach and walking trails. Breakfast is served in a separate dining hall (bed and breakfast rates available).

$$ A Wymbolwood Beach House B&B – *533 Tiny Beaches Rd. S., Wymbolwood Beach. ☎705-361-3649 or 866-361-3649. www.wymbolwood.com. 3 rooms.* ⌨ 🅿
Open for both winter and summer guests, this large, modern house with a well-maintained garden on Nottawasaga Bay sits near the beach and many other area attractions. The well-appointed guest rooms, decorated in soft colours, include a two-bedroom suite, a king bed suite with fireplace and a self-catering suite with its own sitting area and fireplace, sauna and little kitchen. Both the two-bedroom and the self-catering suites can accommodate a family of four. A copious cooked breakfast is served in the dining room.

$$$ Westin Trillium House – *220 Mountain Dr., Collingwood. ☎705-443-8080 or 866-716-8101. www.starwood hotels.com. 222 rooms.* ✕🛏♿🅿
This resort in the Village at Blue on Blue Mountain caters to skiers in the winter, while summer guests can enjoy the area's many attractions nearby. The sprawling, multi-gabled chalet-style hotel has balconies for seemingly every window. Inside, the decor is modern, dominated by beige and taupe accents. Sleek, well-furnished rooms have all the desired amenities, including gas fireplaces and kitchens or kitchenettes. The on-site restaurant, **Oliver & Bonachini Café-Grill ($$)** offers a fusion menu with specialities like yellowfin tuna seared in sesame oil on a green mango and crispy noodle salad, or classic dishes such as beef or rack of lamb as well as hamburgers, pizza and pastas. A gym and outdoor pool are on the premises.

$$$$ The Inn at Christie's Mill – *263 Port Severn Rd. N., Port Severn. ☎705-538-2354 or 800-465-9966.www. christiesmill.com. 43 rooms.* ✕🛏🆂🅿
Situated near the waters and forests of Georgian Bay Islands National Park, this luxury spa also sits near the attractions

of Severn Sound, including several golf courses. Offering lovely views, rooms feature French provincial furniture and soft colours. **Twigs Restaurant ($$)** serves a menu with a multicultural cast: grilled venison loin, five-spice grilled chicken, tamarind salmon. The on-site spa makes several packages available, including a beautification session, and a couple's relaxation session. Off-season packages are bargains, especially in winter when cross-country and alpine skiing are not far away.

$$$$ The Inn at Manitou – *81 Inn Rd., McKellar, 30km/19mi northeast of Parry Sound. ☎705-389-2171 or 800-571-8818. www.manitou-online.com. 35 rooms. 2-night minimum. Closed mid-Oct–mid-May.* ✕ ⬛ Spa P . This luxury estate, a Relais & Châteaux property, overlooks Manitouwabing Lake from within a 200ha/495-acre forested setting. Accommodations range from large hotel rooms to a 4-bedroom house. Standard rooms are simply furnished; luxury rooms come with a log-burning fireplace and a balcony. Included in the rate are all meals, as well as afternoon tea. The dining room (for guests only) specializes in fine French cuisine and offers splendid views; lunch is served on the terrace in warm weather. Activities include golf, tennis, yoga, bicycling, swimming in the inn's pool, boating, artists' workshops and cooking classes. An on-site spa and fitness centre and a 5km/3mi walking trail round out the amenities. Limo service from the airport and floatplane docking are available.

WHERE TO EAT

$ Anchor Bar & Grill – *1 Water St., Little Current, on Manitou Island. ☎705-368-2023. www.anchorgrill.com. Open 7am–11pm in summer high season.* **Canadian.** Open since 1888 on the port of Little Current, this impressive redbrick hostelry remains a hub of town activity. Enjoy fresh lake fish such as whitefish, trout and pickerel, as well as steak, chicken or even the Quebec favourite, poutine, while sitting on the patio and observing North Channel activity. On weekends the bar rocks with recorded music. Upstairs are 6 recently remodelled guestrooms **($)** and 8 apartments **($)**, without air conditioning or phones, but with wireless internet (weekends are not restful, however).

$ Leeside Restaurant – *3 Eliza St., Tobermory. ☎519-596-8375. www.leesiderestaurant.com.* **Canadian.** Located near the ferry terminal, this restaurant serves a complete whitefish dinner at a wallet-pleasing price, as well as other seafood plates, hamburgers and sandwiches. The apple dumpling, topped with ice-cream, is a treat. Enjoy a beer or a glass of wine on the patio, watching traffic in Little Tub Harbour. Leeside opens well before morning ferry departure so early risers can enjoy a cup of coffee or full breakfast.

$$ First Street Bistro – *188 First St., Collingwood. ☎705-446-3337. www.firststreetbistro.com. Dinner only. Closed Sun.* **French.** Located in a century-old brick building in Collingwood's old downtown, this restaurant serves fine bistro fare accompanied by fresh local vegetables. The sliced veal with mushrooms and rösti or the duck leg confit with baked Brussels sprouts reveal Chef Andi Furrer's Swiss roots, while the steak-frites is familiar and perfect. The fruit pies, baked with custard in a crumbly crust, provide a great finish.

$$ Garden's Gate Family Restaurant – *Hwy. 542, Tehkummah, on Manitoulin Island. ☎ 705-859-2088. www.manitoulin-island.com/gardensgate.* **Canadian.** This unprepossessing little white cottage, fronted with an English flower garden, offers inventive interpreta-tions of traditional Manitoulin Island cuisine: fried whitefish or perch, chicken supreme improved with a strawberry sauce, grilled lamb chops with local herbs. Owner Rose Diebolt finds the best fresh produce in the area—no small task on the edge of the Canadian Shield. She is justifiably proud of her desserts, such as apple pie or raspberry torte. The dining room is panelled in pine and decorated in tones of apple green and pink.

$$ Lion's Head Inn Restaurant – *8 Helen St., Lion's Head. ☎519-793-4601. www.lionsheadinn.ca. Closed Sun–Tues in winter.* **Canadian.** Located on the Georgian Bay side of the peninsula, this venerable establishment was built in 1879 and served as a boarding house and a church before being converted to a country inn in 1996. The two patios are comfortable, the pub friendly and well-stocked, and the restaurant offers lake whitefish and trout, as well as sturdy fare such as sirloin steak, pork chops and prime rib. Upstairs are three cheerfully appointed guest rooms **($)**, one with private bath.

$$ MeRitz Bistro – *102 Main St., Penetanguishene.* ☎*705-549-0444. www.meritzbistro.com. Closed Tues.* **French.** Run by three siblings (two brothers and a sister), this friendly, upscale bistro in downtown Penetanguishene serves lunch and dinner. Specials based on market fare are offered daily. From the menu, you can choose chicken (stuffed with peaches, or with Boursin cheese), grilled sesame salmon, steak or pasta. Among the delicious choices, try the key lime cheesecake for dessert.

$$ The Mill Café – *12 Bridge St. E., Thornbury (about 25km/16mi west of Collingwood on Hwy. 26).* ☎*519-599-7866. www.themillcafe.com.* **French.** Rising above the Beaver River, this fine-dining restaurant overlooks a rushing millrace; dining on the terrace, you feel the splash. The unpretentious interior features oak floors and Windsor chairs. Incorporating local seasonal produce, the cuisine is French, but with an Italian component in dishes such as potato gnocchi with shredded duck confit and mushrooms or squash risotto. Main courses include roast striped bass Sicilian style, in a fennel and artichoke sauce with chick peas, or a grilled lamb chop accompanied by lamb sausage, with truffle whipped parsnips. The bar is most convivial.

$$ SiSi on Main – *27 Bruce St., Thornbury.* ☎*519-599-7769. http://sisionmain. com.* **Italian.** Lunch, tea and dinner are served in this brick storefront downtown; you can dine outside on the sidewalk, or enjoy the intimate atmosphere inside, where soft lighting and exposed brick walls (as well as excellent martinis) induce relaxation. The menu is seasonal, but the Steak Diane, a signature dish sauced with mushrooms, leeks and green peppercorns, is delicious any time of year. Try also the Italian specialties based on polenta or gnocchi.

has worn away, creating the spectacular overhanging rocks, caves, sculpted rocks and intriguing pitted surfaces of some rocks, particularly on the Bruce Peninsula. The western and southern shores form a section of the **Niagara Escarpment**, with one gently rolling slope and one steep escarpment. This ridge of limestone crosses Ontario from Niagara Falls, mounts the Bruce Peninsula, submerges and then resurfaces to form Manitoulin and other islands and ends in Wisconsin. A complete contrast to these rocky shores, the coast along the western side of the Midland Peninsula has long sandy stretches, especially in the region of Wasaga Beach.

Weather systems from the Arctic, Pacific, Atlantic and the Gulf of Mexico converge here, creating wide seasonal temperature variations and the treacherous storms that have taken many ships to the bottom. Scuba diving among the shipwrecks is a popular attraction in the waters of Georgian Bay.

Étienne Brûlé, one of Samuel de Champlain's men, visited Georgian Bay in 1610 to learn the Huron language; Champlain passed through in 1615. Fur traders and Jesuits soon followed, arriving via the 1,300km/800mi canoe route from Quebec. Eager to convert Huron Indians to Christianity, the Jesuits built a mission post called Sainte-Marie near the present site of Midland in 1639. Weakened from European disease, the Huron were frequently under attack from Iroquois tribes to the south. Caught in the middle, several Jesuits were killed after being tortured. Sainte-Marie was abandoned in 1649. In the 19C Ojibwa tribes, related to the Algonquin, moved into the area. Gradually pushed out by settlers, they moved to reserves on the mainland and on Manitoulin Island. In the early 19C warfare erupted between the British and Americans over control of the Great Lakes; the Treaty of Ghent (Dec. 24, 1814) ended the war with neither side gaining or losing territory. With peace, the present borders were established.

Parry Sound

POPULATION 5,818– MAP P 108

The deepest freshwater port in the world, Parry Sound is a commercial and shipping hub for the surrounding region, which depends largely on timber and mining. Canada's two transcontinental railroads (Canadian Pacific and Canadian National railways) and the Trans-Canada Highway pass through the town. It is set at the mouth of the Seguin River, on the largest natural harbour of the Great Lakes, and protected by an island—Parry Island—at its entrance. At its door front lie more islands, the **Thirty Thousand Islands**, a major tourist attraction, especially in warm weather. This profusion of large and small islands extends out from Parry Sound into Georgian Bay. Many islands are occupied by vacation houses and resorts, and cruise ships and pleasure craft ply among them. In summer Parry Sound hosts sailing races and regattas, and in winter there is ice-boating. Resorts abound in the area, so much so that during vacation season, the town's 5,000-plus population swells to some 35,000. The town hosts the annual **Festival of the Sound,** a series of 50 classical and jazz concerts in summer *(Jul–Aug)*. Recently, the event's venue has been the 480-seat Festival Performance Hall within the new Charles W. Stockey Centre for the Performing Arts, situated on the waterfront. The impressive building, opened in 2003, rises three storeys and incorporates area pine, granite and stone into its design.

- 🛈 **Information:** Parry Sound Information Area on Hwy. 400 *(Trans-Can Hwy.)* south of town, open daily. ☎705-378-5105 or 800-461-4261. www.townofparrysound.com or www.tourparrysound.com.
- ▶ **Orient Yourself:** Accessible from Highway 400/69, the town lies at the far eastern end of the sound, opposite Parry Island. From Mill Lake, the Seguin River flows west into the bay, bisecting the town. The downtown occupies a point overlooking the river and the bay, on the north bank of the river. Bay Street (a continuation of James St.) runs down to the town docks.
- 🚢 **Don't Miss:** A cruise of the 30,000 Islands. An excellent way to see the natural beauty of Georgian Bay and its many islands is one of three boat cruises from Parry Sound, Midland or Penetanguishene. (*See below and see Cruises in Practical Information*).
- 🕐 **Organizing Your Time:** Many resorts book only week-long stays during Jul-Aug, a sufficient time to enjoy the area.

View of Parry Sound from Tower Hill

Zeuter Development Corporation/www.tourparrysound.com

A Bit of History

In the mid-19C the sound was surveyed by Captain **Henry Wolsey Bayfield** (1795-1885), a British-born naval officer who, as surveyor for the Admiralty, was responsible for surveying the Great Lakes. While surveying Lake Huron and the lower Great Lakes, he set up headquarters in Penetanguishene in 1819. It was Bayfield who gave the sound and the town its name, in memory of the great Arctic explorer Sir **William Edward Parry** (1790-1855). Originally founded around a sawmill about 1865, Parry Sound boomed when the first railway came to town in 1897. The arrival of the Canadian Northern in 1906, followed by the Canadian Pacific Railway (CPR) the next year increased the number of visitors to the area and the number of resort hotels. The CPR railway trestle over the Seguin River still stands today, the longest trestle bridge in the province, at 595m/1,950ft.

During both world wars, the population grew again when labourers moved to the area to work at two munitions and explosives factories (now closed) in the nearby town of Nobel, named for the inventor of dynamite, Alfred Nobel. Explosives made at the plants were used initially in the north's mining industry, but manufacturing was converted in wartime to military explosives for Allied forces' use. The plants were later acquired by Orenda Aerospace Corp., an aircraft engine manufacturer, which tested its turbojet engines near Nobel in the late 1940s. At the time, these engines were the most powerful in the world, until replaced by supersonic designs.

Painter Tom Thomson, who inspired the Group of Seven, grew up in Owen Sound in Georgian Bay, and found inspiration for his works in the stark and rugged landscape of the area, especially Algonquin Park to the east. Hockey great Bobby Orr, of the Boston Bruins, was born in Parry Sound; the town named its community centre and dedicated a hall of fame in his honour.

Sight

Cruise★★

◷*Departs Jul–Aug daily 10am for 2hr morning cruise ⬤$24; and Jun–mid-Oct daily 1pm for 3hr afternoon cruise ⬤$32. Reservations required. 30,000 Island Cruise Lines Inc. 9 Bay St.* ✕🚻🅿︎ ☎705-746-2311 or 800-506-2628. www.island-queen.com.

The following describes the 2hr route within the inner islands just offshore. From **Parry Sound** town dock, the 550-passenger *Island Queen* begins a leisurely voyage through some of the **Thirty Thousand Islands**★ within Parry Sound. As the vessel exits the harbour,

Cruise on the Island Queen through Thirty Thousand Islands

Ehricht/Ontario Tourism

good views are provided of the **Stockey Centre,** home of the Bobby Orr Hall of Fame; the Coast Guard base, where icebreaker ships are moored; and the salt dock, where some 100,000 tons of salt are unloaded for winter highway use. As the boat curves around the northern end of Huckleberry Island, on which wild huckleberries actually grow, mansions and summer homes on the mainland come into view. Surprisingly, many cottages built on the islands themselves have running water and electricity. Grave and then Goat Island are passed before the boat threads the islands of Loon Bay. Loons, herons and Canadian geese favour these waters, and sometimes raccoons, deer and even a fox can be spotted on the shore. A passage between Huckleberry and Wall islands—a **channel**★★ so narrow that passengers can almost touch the 24m/80ft-tall granite cliffs flanking it is a highlight. As the boat heads for the harbour, Three Mile lighthouse is seen on a promontory of Parry Island.

Additional Sights

Killbear Provincial Park★

23km/14mi southwest of Nobel by Rte. 559. ◷*Open early May–mid-Oct daily. Visitor centre open Jul–Aug daily 10am–5pm.* ✆*$11.85/vehicle.* ☎*705-342-5492. www.ontarioparks.com.* ⊘*Campsites are much in demand: reserve ahead.*

Just west of the town of Parry Sound, as the crow flies, this 1,756ha/4,449acre park stretches inland from a promontory named Killbear Point at the entrance to Parry Sound. Parry Island and smaller Rose Island sit offshore. A road threads the park, which offers swimming beaches, picnic areas, a boat launch and campsites at water's edge. The rugged scenery of the Canadian Shield provides the setting for fishing, hiking, and cycling the new bike trail that crosses the park, as part of a projected trail to extend to Algonquin Provincial Park farther east. The new visitor centre offers guided hikes, children's activities, and evening programs in the amphitheatre.

Killbear Provincial Park

Bierwagen/Ontario Tourism

Massasauga Provincial Park★

40km/25mi southwest of Parry Sound. ◷*Open last Fri in Apr–last Sat in Oct daily 7am-7pm; visitor centre open same hours.* ✆*$9.90. Canoe rentals $42 per day.* ♿⊘☎*705-378-0685. www.ontario parks.com.*

Accessible only by boat, this provincial park extends from the shoreline opposite Parry and McLaren islands south to the mouth of the Moon River. Although much of its 131sq km/50sq mi covers the mainland, the park also encompasses an archipelago of hundreds of islands. Many of these islands have colourful names such as Fryingpan, Wreck, Copperhead, Sharp and Moon. A paradise for boaters and anglers (muskie, bass, pike, panfish) as well as hikers (40km/25mi of trails), the park features small, sandy beaches and 135 campsites. **Calhoun Lodge,** a 1930s summer cottage, houses the park visitor centre. Visitors can rent canoes at Pete's Place on Black Stone Harbour, the park's entry point and the launching site for boats and canoes. The Massasauga rattlesnake, Ontario's only venomous snake, hides out here.

Midland ★

POPULATION 16,700 – MAP P 108

Once a centre of shipbuilding, lumbering and shipping (especially grain), Midland now thrives on tourism, light industry and the service sector. This busy town on Georgian Bay is known for its numerous historical and natural attractions—and its many summer cottages and resorts. In the warmer months, the population swells to some 100,000 people. Located on Midland Bay, on the west side of Severn Sound, the town is well-served by its deep harbour. It also benefits from the tourist attractions of the Thirty Thousand Islands of Georgian Bay to the north and the sandy beaches of Nottawasaga Bay, only a short distance west, on the other side of the Midland Peninsula. Within the town, Little Lake has a park and swimming beach, and is the site of the Huronia Museum and a reconstructed Huron village. Following the waterfront, the Rotary Waterfront Trail is bordered by several public parks as well as the town dock, from which lake cruises depart.

On the eastern edge of the community are the historical complex recalling the 17C Jesuit mission to the Hurons and the Wye Marsh, a birding and nature reserve. The considerable French-speaking population in Midland and neighbouring Penetanguishene dates back to the 1840s, when families from Quebec settled present-day Lafontaine and Perkinsfield. The town was named for the Midland Railway, which arrived here in 1879.

- **Information:** Town of Midland, 575 Dominion Ave. ☎705-526-4275. www.town.midland.on.ca.
- ▶ **Orient Yourself:** Midland and Penetanguishene are only 5km/3mi apart. The town faces Midland Bay on the east and Highway 93 runs along the western edge of the town centre.
- ⊚ **Don't Miss:** The site of Sainte-Marie-among-the-Hurons, with its reconstructions of the mission and dramatic history.
- ⛄ **Also See:** SOUTH CENTRAL ONTARIO

Sainte-Marie among the Hurons

Speed/Ontario Tourism

Sights

Huron Ouendat Village★

549 Little Lake Park, on King St. &♿ 🕐*Open May–Oct daily 9am–5pm. Rest of the year Mon–Fri 9am–5pm.* 🕐 *Closed Good Friday & Dec 25–26.* 📷 *$8 (includes museum).* ☎*705-526-2844. www.huronia museum.com.*

🐾In May 2007, the village caught fire and restoration is underway; the palisade is in place, and the village in full operation.

This village is a replica of a 16C Huron community, prior to European arrival (Ouendat is the name the Huron called themselves). A wooden palisade surrounds the village, with a clever entrance to foil attackers. Within are examples of the long, rectangular, bark-covered frame houses in which the Huron lived communally. Animal skins, plants and herbs hang to dry.

The medicine man's house, a sweat bath, storage pits and a canoe-making site can also be seen.

Located beside the village, the **Huronia Museum** *(same hours)* possesses a collection of one million objects and has an extensive number of artworks; the exhibits focus on early settler life in the area.

Sainte-Marie among the Hurons★★

5km/3mi east on Hwy. 12. 🕐*Open mid-May–mid-Oct daily 10am–5pm. Early May and late Oct Mon–Fri 10am–5pm.* 📷 *$11.25.* ✕🅿 ☎*705-526-7838. www. saintemarieamongthehurons.on.ca.*

Located on the edge of town, the mission on the banks of the Wye River, the first European community in Ontario, was established by the Jesuits in 1639. It flourished for a decade, before the Huron, weakened by diseases, succumbed to their enemies, the Iroquois, who sought to dominate the fur trade. When Jesuit priests Jean de Brébeuf and Gabriel Lalement, captured by the Iroquois, were martyred after incredible torture, the remaining Jesuits and Hurons destroyed the site in 1649 and fled to Quebec City.

Archaeological research has permitted reconstruction of the site much as it was in the 17C, when some 66 Europeans (but no European women), one-fifth of the population of New France, lived here.

An audiovisual presentation *(20min)* explains the mission's history and should be viewed before the rest of the visit. The complex consists of several re-created structures within a wooden palisade. The chapel, forge, saw pit, carpentry shop, residences and Huron area are peopled by guides in 17C costume, demonstrating skills of the period. A rectangular, bark-covered longhouse and a hospital where the Jesuits tended the sick have been constructed in the Indian section. Buildings destroyed in a fire in 2006 (Chapel of Ste-Marie and the blacksmith and carpenter shops) have been replaced. In the interactive museum excellent exhibits explain the lives of the Jesuits and Hurons in the historical and social context; topics include 17C Europe and New France.

Wye Marsh Wildlife Centre

16160 Hwy. 12 East, beside Sainte-Marie. 🕐*Open year-round daily 9am–5pm.* 📷*$10.* &✕ ☎*705-526-7809. www.wye marsh.com.*

Situated beside Sainte-Marie among the Hurons, the centre is devoted to the surrounding marshland, which acts as a refuge for many birds, including the rare least bittern and black tern. Numerous sorts of small wildlife also live here. Walking paths, a boardwalk and an observation tower allow nature lovers to appreciate the life of a marsh. The unmistakable hornlike sound of a growing number of Trumpeter swans draw visitors to the swan pond. The centre features films and a display area. In summer paddlers can canoe through the marsh, and in winter skiing and snowshoeing are popular here.

Martyrs' Shrine★

5km/3mi east on Hwy. 12, near Wye Marsh Wildlife Centre. 🕐*Open mid-May–early-Oct daily 9am–dusk.* 📷 *$3.* ✕& ☎*705-526-3788. www.martyrsshrine.com.*

This large, twin-spired stone church above the Wye River was built in 1926 as a memorial to the eight Jesuit martyrs of New France killed by the Iroquois

Bierwagen/Ontario Tourism

Wye Marsh Wildlife Centre

between 1642 and 1649 and declared saints in 1930. The first five were killed while they were missionaries at Sainte-Marie. On the front portico stand **statues** of Jean de Brébeuf and Gabriel Lalemant, the two Jesuits who were tortured before death. The church has a striking **interior** with wood panelling.

Excursion

Beausoleil Island
Part of the **Georgian Bay Islands National Park.** *Access by private boat or water taxi only from Honey Harbour (about 40km/25mi northeast of Midland via Hwy. 12, Hwy. 400 and Rte. 5). Parks Canada operates a Daytripper taxi from Honey Harbour, a 15mn ride to the island, Jul-Aug Thu-Mon, leaving at 11am, noon and 1pm, returning 4hrs later. ⊚$16 For*

details: ☎705-526-8907. ♿🕐*Open daily year-round, services available mid-May to mid-Oct.* 🅿*Parking in Honey Harbour (no vehicles on island). ⊚$6 adult day-use fee (mid-May–early Oct). Park office in 901 Wye Valley Rd., in Midland. ☎705-526-9804. www.pc.gc.ca.*

This 8km/5mi long island offers walking trails, a picnic area, campsites and a visitor kiosk. The island is a microcosm of area scenery, with its pink Canadian Shield granite, pines and great stretches of boat-dotted water. Stone projectiles, tools and pottery attest to human habitation at least 7,000 years ago. The last aboriginal inhabitants, the Ojibwa, left in 1856 for Christian Island at the tip of the Midland Peninsula, although they are still called the Beausoleil First Nation. Beausoleil Island has been uninhabited since 1929, when the park was founded.

Trumpeter Swans

Distinguished by their loud call, which resembles the sound of a trumpet, Trumpeter swans are native to North America. Pure white in appearance, adults can weigh from 21 to 35 pounds; their wings span up to 2.5m/8ft. Swans mate for life. Offspring under a year old are called cygnets and are grey in colour. If brown spots are seen on the heads and necks of swans, this discoloration is due to high iron content in the water. Along the edges, their broad, flat bills possess toothlike serrations that enable the birds to strain out aquatic plants from the water. Strong feet and long necks help them loosen plants rooted as deep as four feet in water. Strictly vegetarians, the swans live on plants that grow underwater and sometimes on leaves of above-water plants like wild rice. To help digest their food, swans swallow pebbles. Before being banned, lead shotgun pellets were the leading cause of death for trumpeter swans.

Penetanguishene ★

POPULATION 9,354 – MAP 108

Once an important naval base established in 1817, Penetanguishene was settled by military personnel withdrawn from territory ceded to the Americans after the War of 1812 and by *voyageurs,* fur-traders and adventurers of mixed French and aboriginal blood who had remained loyal to Britain. This French heritage was reinforced by settlers from Quebec arriving in the 1840s. Today, the southern entrance to this town, which has a large French-speaking community, is guarded by two angels symbolizing the harmony between the English and French cultures. The famed Canadian Group of Seven painter A.Y. Jackson sojourned briefly in Penetanguishene and collected material for later works, including *March Storm, Georgian Bay* (1920). Today, Penetang, as it is often called, is a tourism centre, a gateway to the **Thirty Thousand islands** and a short drive to the beaches of Nottawasaga Bay. The name Penetanguishene is derived from an Ojibwa word meaning "white sand dunes."

- **Information:** Tourism Centre on Town Dock, 1 Main St. Georgian Bay Tourism, 980 King St., Midland. ☎800-263-7745 www.georgianbaytourism.ca
- **Orient Yourself:** The town stretches along the east side of the long, narrow bay, only 5km/3mi west of Midland by Rte. 93 (Penetanguishene Rd.). It centres on Penetanguishene Harbour.
- **Don't Miss:** Discovery Harbour, a re-created 19C British naval base.
- **Organizing Your Time:** You can cruise the 30,000 Islands from the Penetanguishene town docks (🎧 *See Practical Information for cruise companies*).
- **Also See:** SOUTH CENTRAL ONTARIO

A Bit of History

The first European to visit the Penetanguishene area, probably between 1610-1611, was the 18-year-old Frenchman, Étienne Brûlé. He had been sent by Samuel de Champlain to learn the language and customs of the Hurons, whom the French had befriended. Champlain himself visited the area during 1615. Brûlé lived here for about a year, learning enough to become Champlain's interpreter and lieutenant. After many adventures, he came to a mysterious end in 1633, when he was killed and possibly eaten by the Huron, although the

Discovery Harbour as seen from aboard ship HMS Bee.

Ontario Tourism

reasons are unclear. The Hurons attributed later misfortunes, including terrible epidemics and defeat by the Iroquois, to a curse laid at Brûlé's death.

Sight

Discovery Harbour★

93 Jury Dr. ⏱*Open Jul–Labour Day daily 10am–5pm. Late May–Jun Mon–Fri 10am–5pm.* ⏱*Closed Victoria Day.* ✆*$6.* ✕🅿☎*705-549-8064. www.discovery harbour.on.ca.*

On a pleasant site above Penetanguishene Harbour stands this reconstruction of a British Naval dockyard and military garrison established here after the War of 1812.

An audiovisual presentation (15min) in the visitor centre presents the site's history. In the naval complex, which existed from 1817 to 1834, boardwalks line the waterfront, 15 buildings have been reconstructed and costumed interpreters explain the site in both French and English. At the wharf two replica British ships are moored: the HMS *Bee*, a transport schooner, and the HMS *Tecumseth*, a warship. The military garrison was located here from 1828 to 1856; the original officers' quarters can be visited.

The Kings's Wharf Theatre (⏱*See Practical Information*) presents plays, concerts and variety shows.

Wasaga Beach★

POP 12,419 – MAP P 108

This popular resort on Nottawasaga Bay rejoices in a 14km/9mi stretch of white sand, the longest freshwater beach in the world. The central town beach, called Beach Area One, is the liveliest, with attractions as well as restaurants and shops. Beach Areas One through Six, stretching towards the southwest, can be reached off Mosely Street the town's main thoroughfare, while Allenwood and New Wasaga beaches are located north of the Nottawasaga River mouth, off River Road East. Wasaga Beach Provincial Park, which includes all the beach area, provides picnic facilities and washrooms. The bay is quite shallow and sandy, so much appreciated by parents of small children. Starting in the late 19C, Wasaga Beach attracted the wealthy who could afford to travel here; palatial hotels lined the shore. The area changed after World War II, when residents of Barrie began flocking in; today the atmosphere is quite egalitarian.

- 🛈 **Information:** Wasaga Beach Chamber of Commerce, 550 River Rd W. ☎705-429-2247 or 866-292-7242. www.wasagabeach.com/visitors.
- ▶ **Orient Yourself:** The quieter beaches are towards the west.
- 👁 **Don't Miss:** Take a drive westwards towards the Blue Mountains and Collingwood; walk in the dunes nature park behind the beach.
- 🕐 **Organizing Your Time:** Much of the accommodation is open only in summer months. Be sure to reserve ahead.
- 🚸 **Especially for Kids:** The Wasaga Waterworld and Collingwood's Plunge Aquatic Centre will keep them busy.
- 👁 **Also See:** SOUTH CENTRAL ONTARIO

Sights

Wasaga Beach Provincial Park

11–22nd St. N. ⏱*Open Apr–mid-Oct daily 8am–10pm. Early Dec–Mar limited hours for cross-country skiing. Admin-* *istration office mid-May–Labour Day daily 8:30am–4:30pm; rest of the year Mon–Fri 8:30am–4:30pm.* ⏱*Closed to vehicles rest of the year.* ✆*Day entry fee mid-May–Labour Day $13.85/vehicle Mon–Fri, $16.80/vehicle on weekends.*

Aerial view of Wasaga Beach

T. Campbell/Ontario Tourism

Prices vary rest of the year. ♿☎*705-429-2516. www.ontarioparks.com.* ☺Wasaga Beach does not have lifeguards. Watch children carefully.

This provincial park incorporates not only the beach, but a vast area of dunes as well as wetlands, crisscrossed by hiking and cross-country ski trails. Behind the beaches, in a wide curve of the river, stretch 800ha/1,977 acres of dunes that can be visited on foot (☺*watch for poison ivy*); delicate grasses and plants hold the dunes in place. As well, some 230 species of birds have been sighted in the park. The park maintains a visitor centre and rents cross-country skis and personal flotation devises. Wasaga is a blue-flag beach, meaning it has exceptionally clean water.

Nancy Island Historic Site★

In Wasaga Beach Provincial Park, Mosley St., across from 3rd St. ◷*Open mid-Jun–Labour Day daily 10am–6pm, late May–mid-Jun weekends 10am-6pm, Labour Day–mid-Oct weekends 11am-5pm.* ◷*Closed rest of year.* ☎*705-429-2728. www.wasagabeachpark.com.*

This dramatic edifice, designed to resemble a ship under sail, stands on an island in the Nottawasaga River. The island was created by silt collecting around the hull of a sunken schooner, the **Nancy.**
After the American victory at the Battle of Lake Erie, this schooner was the last British ship sailing the Great Lakes. On August 14, 1814, it was discovered hiding in the estuary by three American warships, which pounded it with heavy shot. The *Nancy* caught fire and sank, but the crew of 22 British seamen, 23 Indians and 9 French Canadian *voyageurs,* under Lt. Miller Worsley, escaped and made their way 360 miles to Fort Michilimackinac, now Makinaw City, Michigan. In September they were back, and captured two of the American ships. The hull of the *Nancy* was discovered in 1911 and raised in 1928. It is now displayed in the museum building with explanations of her history and that of the War of 1812. The site also includes a lighthouse and a theatre.

Wasaga Waterworld

Hwy. 92 E. Wasaga Beach. ◷*Open Jul–Labour Day daily 10am–6pm (weather permitting).* ☜*$24 day pass.* ✕🅿☎*705-429-4400. www.wasagawaterworld.com.*
🅺🅸🅳🅸 Everything here at this water park will delight children, and their parents as well: a giant wave pool, speed slides, serpent slides, bumper boats and a little pool for small children. On dry land, there are opportunities to play miniature golf, basketball, volleyball and horseshoes, and there's a picnic area and a restaurant. A kids' day camp, supervised by qualified staff, permits parents to pursue their own interests.

Additional Sight

Collingwood★

9km/5.5km west of Wasaga Beach via Hwy. 26.

Now largely known as a resort town, Collingwood (pop. 17,290) developed around its excellent harbour, at the southern end of Nottawasaga Bay. When the Canadian National Railway arrived in 1855, the town's importance as a Great Lakes shipping port boomed. For a century until 1986, it was the principal shipbuilding centre on the Great Lakes. This prosperity left a large number of 19C heritage buildings in the downtown area, many of which have been restored, particularly along 3rd Street. The harbour has been reclaimed as **Harbourland Park,** with gardens and a boardwalk, from which sailboats can be viewed.

Recreational facilities include hiking trails, horseback riding, tennis and the **Plunge! Aquatic Centre** *(220 Mountain Dr.; ⏱open daily late Jun–Aug 9am–9pm; rest of year, call for hours;* ✇*$17;* ☎*705-444-8705; www.plunge-bluemountain.ca),* a water park with outdoor and indoor pools, slides, rope swings and hot tubs, situated at the base of Blue Mountain Ski Resort.

The **Scenic Caves Nature Preserve,** a series of limestone caves near the summit of Blue Mountain, can be visited on self-guided tours. (⏱*open daily Jul–Aug 9am–7pm, May–Jun & Sept–late-Oct daily 10am–5pm;* ✇*$18.50;* ☎*705-446-0256; www.sceniccaves.com).* The view over Georgian Bay, some 100m/305ft below, is spectacular, and the new suspension bridge over a 25m/76ft gorge is an added thrill.

Just outside Collingwood lies the **Blue Mountain Ski Resort,** Ontario's premier ski area, with a vertical drop of 219m/720ft, and home mountain to several World Cup ski racers.

On the 35km/22mi drive west to Meaford from Collingwood along Highway 26, the waters of Georgian Bay lie on one side of the road and the **Blue Mountains,** the highest part of the Niagara Escarpment, on the other.

Bruce Peninsula

MAP P 108

The Bruce Peninsula juts into Lake Huron and forms the western shore of Georgian Bay. With no agricultural or industrial potential, the area attracts tourists with golf courses, boating, sandy swimming beaches, lake cruises, festivals, fairs and a range of pleasant accommodations. Winter draws cross-country skiers, snowshoers and snowmobilers. The principal towns are Tobermory, Wiarton and Owen Sound. Wiarton has nearly universal recognition in Canada as the home of Wiarton Willie, an albino groundhog whose behaviour every February 2 (Groundhog Day) leads the Canadian news for 24 hours. Tobermory, at the tip of the peninsula, is connected to Manitoulin Island by the Chi-Cheemaun Ferry. At the tip of the peninsula are two national parks: Bruce Peninsula National Park and the Fathom Five National Marine Park, mostly underwater, as well as provincial parks and nature reserves.

▪ **Information:** Bruce Peninsula Tourism ☎519-793-4734 or 800-268-3838. www.brucepeninsula.org. Walk-in information centres located: Hwy 6 at **Ferndale** 519-793-3178.; at the train station in Blue Water Park, **Wiarton** (☎ 519-534-2592.www.wiartonchamber.ca); at the **Tobermory** Community Centre (☎519-596-2452. www.tobermory.org; and at **Sauble Beach** on Main St across from Sauble Beach Amusements. (☎519-422-1262. www.southbrucepeninsula.com)

▸ **Orient Yourself:** The beaches are on the east side of the peninsula, the cliffs on the west side. The driving distance between is generally under 30 minutes.

☺ **Don't Miss:** A cruise out to Flowerpot Island; if you have time, hop off to explore the extensive trail system. (🜚 *See Green Address Book)*

Chi-Cheemaun Ferry in Tobermory

Ontario Tourism

🕐 **Organizing Your Time:** Once at Tobermory, you can take the ferry to Manitoulin Island, and take Hwy 6 back to the mainland through Little Current.

📷 **Especially for Kids:** The beaches along the western side of the peninsula are lovely, with warm, shallow water and renowned sunsets. Sauble Beach offers boat rentals and attractions.

🖐 **Also See:** NORTH BAY REGION, SAULT ST. MARIE

A Bit of Geography

Bruce Peninsula is an extension of the **Niagara Escarpment,** which starts in New York state, crosses Niagara Falls and loops across the peninsula to Manitoulin Island and into Michigan and Wisconsin. Rugged dolomite escarpments line the Georgian Bay side of the peninsula, along which winds the Bruce Trail, while wide, sandy swimming beaches beckon on the Lake Huron side. Sauble Beach, notably, has 11km/7mi of clean, sandy beach and celebrated sunsets. The peninsula's shoreline stretches some 800km/500mi, with many coves and harbours and on the bay side, two large fjords, Colpoy's Bay and Owen Sound. The geographical location, at the conjunction of southern, transition and northern growing climates, results in a particularly rich range of botanical species. Bruce Peninsula is part of UNESCO's Niagara Escarpment World Biosphere Reserve.

Sights

Tobermory★

📱☎519-596-2452.*www.tobermory.com.* Named for a town in Scotland, this small port lies at the end of the Bruce Peninsula, and is the terminus of the Bruce Trail. Tobermory provides hundreds of protected moorings around its double harbour known as Big Tub and Little Tub, which are dotted with sailboats and other pleasure craft in summer (boats can be rented locally: 🖐*see Practical Information).* The ferry for Manitoulin Island, the Chi-Cheemaun, and cruise ships for Fathom Five National Marine Park leave Little Tug Harbour daily during summer months. Visitors can stroll the paved path around the marina for a closer view of the yachts, many quite splendid, moored here, and follow the lakeside boardwalk for views of the harbour, the ferry terminal and nearby islands. Just outside the protective harbour lie wrecks of ships caught in Lake Huron's notorious storms. These old shipwrecks and a number of underwater rock formations, as well as the clear blue-green waters, attract scuba divers.

For a look at the past, visit the **St. Edmund's Township Museum,** located in an 1898 stone building, formerly a school for Indians. *(Hwy. 6;* ⏰*open Jul–Labour Day daily 11am–4pm, mid-May–Jun & Sept–mid-Oct weekends only;* 💰*contribution requested;* ☎*519-596-2452; www.tobermory.org/museum).* On the grounds is an 1875 log cabin, authentically furnished.

Bruce Peninsula National Park★

Visitor centre: 77 Chi-Sintubdik Rd., Tobermory (turn east from Hwy 6 onto Codrington St., go about 1km/.5mi). ⏰*Park open daily year-round.* ⏰*Visitor centre mid-May–Labour Day daily 8am–8pm (Fri and Sat 9pm), Sept–early-May Tues–Sat 10am–4:30pm;* 💰*$10.40/vehicle;* ♿🅿⚠☎*519-596-2233; www.pc.gc.ca.* To help visitors understand the complex ecology of this area, Parks Canada offers interpretive programs in Jul and Aug; check at the visitor centre.

Established in 1987, this national park on the northern tip of the Bruce Peninsula is known for its trails along the spectacular Niagara Escarpment, extraordinary cliff-side ecosystem and ancient cedar trees. It is worthwhile to stop at the new **visitor centre** to study the intriguing geological history of the area, which once lay under a shallow tropical sea, and the many ecosystems represented in the park. In the park can be found 43 varieties of orchid, 20 kinds of fern, about half the world's dwarf lake iris and most of Canada's Indian plantain. Many of the cedar trees here are more than 500 years old; the oldest live cedar clocks in at about 850 years, while one found on Flowerpot Island lived for 1,845 years, and has been dead for another 1,500 years. Among the larger animals living in the park are white-tailed deer and black bears (⚠*store garbage carefully).* A portion of the Bruce Trail runs through the park, and is clearly marked for visitors. There is a 242-site campground at Cyprus Lake, 15km/9mi south of Tobermory. *For reservations:* ☎*877-737-3783 or www.pccamping.ca.*

Fathom Five National Marine Park★

Visitor centre: 77 Chi-Sintubdik Rd., Tobermory (turn east from Hwy 6 onto Codrington St., go about 1km/.5mi). ⏰*Same hours and contacts as Bruce Peninsula National Park.*

Canada's first national marine park, this "underwater" preserve encompasses 20 islands and the treacherous waters off Tobermory, where lie 22 known wrecks of sail and steam vessels from the mid-19C to 20C. Some of the islands and two of the wrecks can be seen on a **glass-bottomed boat** (👓 *see Cruises in Practical Information).*

The best known of the park's islands, tiny **Flowerpot Island,** at 200ha/495acres, was at one time completely covered by

Viewing a shipwreck in Fathom Five National Marine Park

Ontario Tourism

the waters of Lake Huron. Caves high up on the cliffs and two rock pillars, known as the **flowerpots**, are evidence of the ancient water levels. These grey pillars have a dolomite base that has been eroded. They stand 7m/23ft and 11m/35ft high, and can be closely approached by boat or on foot *(⌾$2 day-use fee)* from the island. The tour boats afford good views of the flowerpots. Today, the park hosts a unique ecosystem that includes the rare calypso orchid, lots of garter snakes (no predators) and red squirrels that scurry back and forth to the mainland on the winter ice bridge *(⌾wandering off the trails damages the delicate plant life).*

The Bruce Trail

This footpath, marked by white blazes on trees and fence posts, extends some 780km/488mi along the Niagara Escarpment, from Queenston Heights in the Niagara Peninsula and along the spectacular cliffs of Georgian Bay on the Bruce Peninsula to Tobermory at the peninsula's tip. The trail is maintained by the Bruce Trail Assn., a voluntary group that publishes a brochure and map *(Bruce Trail Conservancy, PO Box 857, Hamilton ON, L8N 3N9. ☎905-529-6821 or 800-665-4453. www.brucetrail. org).* Although serious hikers backpack the trail on expeditions, portions of the trail and many side trails provide shorter hikes of a few hours or a day in duration. In towns along the route such as Wiarton, Cape Croker or Lion's Head, access is clearly marked. The trail crosses the Bruce Peninsula National Park, where day hikes are signposted.

Manitoulin Island ★

MAP P 108

Separated from the Ontario mainland by the North Channel of Lake Huron, Manitoulin is the largest island in the world located in a lake: 160km/100mi long and a surface area of 2,765km2/1,068mi2. It is part of an archipelago of limestone and dolomite islands that form the northwestern tail of the Niagara Escarpment, stretching up from the Bruce Peninsula and extending into Wisconsin. Its topography, scoured by glaciers, is rocky, with towering escarpments and 106 lakes, of which Lake Manitou (48km/30mi long) is the largest. Pockets of soil deposited by glaciers permit mixed agriculture. With the decline of logging and fisheries, the island's major economic activities are farming (despite marginal conditions), dairy farming and tourism. Tourist activities include hiking along beautiful trails, water sports, fishing, golf. Additionally, the still thriving Ojibwa culture can be appreciated by visits to reserves and annual ceremonies. About half of the island's 12,000 permanent residents are aboriginal. The North Channel, protected from lake swells and packed with some 30,000 little islands as well as coves and inlets, is a popular boating and yachting venue. Little Current, the principal town (pop. 1575), is a popular stop-off for lake cruise ships. The name Manitoulin is derived from the Algonquin word for a great spirit, Manitou, believed to inhabit the island. The people born on the island are called Haweaters, from the local wild fruit, the hawberry.

- **Information:** Manitoulin Tourism Association, Little Current ON. ☎705-368-3021 www.manitoulintourism.com. The Manitoulin Welcome Centre is located just off the swing bridge in Little Current.
- ▶ **Orient Yourself:** Little Current and South Baymouth are the entry points for the island, with accommodation and restaurants. Gore Bay, west of Little Current, is a pretty village with pleasant inns and restaurants popular with visitors.
- ⌾ **Don't Miss:** The island has scenic hiking trails of varying difficulty. The 12km/7.5mi Cub and Saucer trail network *(on Hwy. 540, about 15km/9mi southwest of Little Current)* offers a celebrated view from the top of the 70m/230ft escarpment.

Craft workshop on the Great Spirit Circle Trail

🕐 **Organizing Your Time:** The only land link with the mainland is over the North Channel on Highway 6, which passes over the 1913 swing bridge at Little Current; at the top of every hour during navigation season, the bridge opens for 15min to let boat traffic pass. In the summer the Chi-Cheemaun ferry operates between Tobermory on the Bruce Peninsula and South Baymouth (🕐 *See Practical Information for details*).

🚶 **Also See:** NORTH BAY REGION, SAULT ST. MARIE

A Bit of History

Until some 5,000 years ago, Manitoulin was connected to the Bruce Peninsula by a land bridge, over which passed animals and people. Archaeological exploration has shown ancient traces of human habitation on the island, going back some 10,000 years, among the oldest on the continent. When Jesuits visited around 1650, the island was inhabited by the Ottawa Indians, speaking a language related to Ojibwa, part of the Algonquin group. Diseases introduced by Europeans devastated the population, and the island remained largely unoccupied until the early 19C, when aboriginal inhabitants of the mainland were moved here to make way for British settlers. Although the island was reserved for Indians, settlers steadily made inroads. In 1862 the provincial government purchased most of the land and distributed it to settlers, who cleared the forest and laid out farms. The aboriginal inhabitants moved onto small reserves. Today's inhabitants, the Ojibwa, the Odawa and the Pottawatomi, are related by customs and the Anishnaabek language, although their dialects are distinct.

Sights

Manitowaning and the Assignack Museum Complex

Arthur St., Manitowaning. 🕐 *Open Jun–Oct daily 10am-5pm.* 🔄 *Contribution requested.* ☎ *705-859-3905. www.manitoulin-island.com/museums/assiginack_complex.htm.*

The small town of Manitowaning was founded in 1837 as an administrative centre for Manitoulin island. Settlers moved into the area, and it was in St. Paul's Anglican Church (1845), a pretty white-frame structure, that in 1862 the Indians agreed to cede the island to settlement.

The museum complex of old settler buildings includes a tiny, dimly-lit school house, a smithy and a pioneer's log home. A handsome two-storey stone building, built in 1878 as a jail, then used successively as a municipal building and library, has served since 1955 as a museum. Inside are a collection of island artifacts, notably glassware, and exhibits on local First Nations and on the bird population. The SS *Norisle*, a 61m/200ft steamship that carried passengers and cargo until 1974, is permanently berthed at the wharf and can be visited.

Great Spirit Circle Trail

Ojibwe Cultural Foundation, #15 Hwy 551 (junction Hwys. 551 and 540), M'Chicheeng. ☎705-377-4404 or 877-710-3211. www.circletrail.com.

This trail, set up by island aboriginal people to encourage cultural tourism, is signposted along the roads. It encompasses seven First Nations communities on the island as well as the Sagamok Anishnawbek community on the mainland, over the North Channel just west of LaCloche Provincial Park. The seven island communities are Aundeck Omni Kaning, M'Chicheeng, Sheguiandah, Sheshegwaning, Whitefish River, Wikwemikong, and Zhiibaahaasing.

Held on the reserves, **pow-wows,** open to the public, *(Jun–Aug),* serve a spiritual purpose and help educate the general public about First Nations traditions (✪ schedule on website).

Among the Circle programs are a hike, escorted by a guide, along the **M'Chicheeng Nature Trail** weekday mornings *(May–Oct ⊜$25)* explaining the use of plants in medicine and cooking. Craft workshops introduce visitors to beading and leatherworking *(Jun–Oct Mon–Fri afternoons ⊜$25 including museum tour).* The **Mnidoo Mnising Art Tour** takes visitors around to private studios to meet artists and view their work *(⊜$25; call to reserve).*

The **Ojibwe Cultural Foundation** housed in an attractive modern (2000) glass and wood building, informs visitors about aboriginal culture via a museum, archives and daily dance performances during the summer (✪ *open Jun–Oct daily 10am–5pm, rest of the year Mon–Fri 9am–4pm; ⊜$7; ☎705-377-4902; www. theocf.ca).* The nearby **Lillian's Indian Crafts** (✪*Jul–Aug Mon–Fri 9am–8pm, weekends 6pm; rest of the year Mon–Fri*

The detail of a locally crafted boxs

Kellner/Ontario Tourism

9am–6pm, weekends 10am–5pm; 5950 Hwy. 540, M'Chicheeng; ☎705-377-4987; www.lillianscrafts.com) offers for sale local crafts, notably boxes decorated with coloured porcupine quills and sweetgrass. During three weeks in July-Aug, the **De-Ba-Je-Mu-Jig Theatre Group** *(8 Debajemujig Lane, Wikwemikong; ☎705-859-2317; www. debaj.ca)* performs at the old Holy Cross mission ruins at Wikwemikong. Its new centre in Manitowaning is due to open in fall 2008.

Centennial Museum of Sheguiandah

10862 Hwy. 6, Sheguiandah. ✪*Open mid-May–mid-Oct daily 10:30am–4:30pm, early April–early May & mid-Sept–mid-Oct Tue–Sun 12:30pm–4:30pm. ⊜$4 during mid-May–early Sept; other times entry fee by donation. ☎705-368-2367. www.townofnemi.on.ca.*

This museum, opened during the centennial of Canadian Confederation in 1967, is a collection of buildings that include reconstructed log settler houses. Inside are local memorabilia and notable artifacts from the Sheguiandah dig in the 1950s, which uncovered evidence of human habitation of the island going back 10,000 years; information about the island's tumultuous geological past, particularly during the last ice age, is also a topic.

NORTH BAY REGION

This sprawling expanse of land north of Parry Sound centres on vast, 80km/50mi-long Lake Nipissing and is flanked by the cities of North Bay, bordering the lake's east shore, and Sudbury, 160km/99mi to the west. The region straddles the frontier between north and south Ontario, at the point where the Canadian Shield asserts itself in earnest, with great stretches of boreal forests, a profusion of lakes and granite outcroppings. Mattawa, a small community east of North Bay, sits at the convergence of the Ottawa and Mattawa rivers, making it a hub of water sports. South of Mattawa lies mammoth Algonquin Provincial Park, Ontario's third largest park, founded in 1893. Here tourists and artists discovered a northern paradise that is today Ontario's most prized expanse of wilderness. The North Bay region in general is a vacation mecca, with resorts, parks, campgrounds and recreational facilities in abundance. In Sudbury, railroad workers discovered the world's richest nickel-copper deposit, launching a mining boom. Today, this area still thrives on natural resources and tourism, but Sudbury's economy in particular has shifted to modern tech industries, the service sector and educational institutions. In fact Sudbury's successful emergence from the blight of industrial pollution by smelters and over-logging is studied around the world.

When Europeans arrived, starting with Étienne Brûlé in 1610, this region was occupied by tribes belonging to the Algonquin group: the Ojibwa and around Mattawa, the Montagnais. Today First Nations reserves are located throughout the region. Unsuitable for agriculture, the area was initially explored by *voyageurs* transporting furs between Fort William (now Thunder Bay) and Lachine, near Montreal. In the mid-19C loggers moved in, cutting white pine in such quantity that logs filled the Mattawa and Ottawa rivers bank to bank, obscuring the water. Settlement did not begin until the late 19C, when the railroads arrived.

The Mattawa River, flowing 72km/45mi east from North Bay to join the Ottawa River, runs along a 600 million year old fault line, the Mattawa Fault, in the Algoma Highlands; small earthquakes are not uncommon in the area. During the last Ice Age, the Mattawa drained

Snowshoeing in North Bay's forests

Sander/Ontario Tourism

Practical Information

AREA CODES

The area code for this region is 705. For local calls, dial all 10 digits (area code plus the number, but without the 1-prefix). For more information: ☎1-800-668-6878 or www.bell.ca.

GETTING THERE AND GETTING AROUND

BY AIR

North Bay – Jack Garland Airport (CYYB) *(50 Terminal St. ☎705-474-3020. www.northbayairport.com)* is served by Air Canada Jazz with flights daily to Toronto and by **Bearskin Airlines** with direct flights to Ottawa and Sudbury. Avis (☎705-476-9730. www.avis.com), National Car Rental (☎705-474-3030. www.nationalcar.com) and Enterprise (☎705-840-777. www.enterprise.com) have counters at the airport.

Sudbury – Greater Sudbury Airport (YSB) *(2621 Skead Rd, Garson ON. ☎705-693-2514. www.city.greatersudbury. on.ca)*. Air Canada Jazz provides flights daily to Toronto, while Bearskin Airlines offers direct flights to Ottawa, North Bay, Timmins, Thunder Bay and Sault Ste-Marie. The **Sudbury Airport shuttle** (☎705-566-0375 or 866-230-3332) provides regular service between town and airport. **Rental cars:** Avis (☎705-693-4022 or 800-879-2847. www.avis.com), Enterprise (☎705-693-9993 or 800-736-8222. www.enterprise.com) and National Car Rental (☎705-693-5833 or 800-227-7368. www.nationalcar.ca) have counters at the airport.

BY TRAIN

Ontario Northland (555 Oak St. E., North Bay. ☎800-561-8558. www.ontc.on.ca) provides train service to North Bay from Toronto and to points north along the Highway 11 corridor, including Temagami and Temiskaming Shores.

BY BUS

Greyhound *(www.greyhound.ca; ☎800-661-8747)* provides service to this area. **Ontario Northland** (555 Oak St. E., North Bay. ☎800-461-8558.

www.onatrionorthland.ca) provides service from Toronto along Hwy 11, passing through Huntsville on the west side of Algonquin Park. From Huntsville, **Hammond Transport** (Ecclestone Dr., Bracebridge. 705-645-5431. www.hammondtransportation.com). provides transport Jul-Aug Mon, Wed and Fri to Canoe Lake or Lake of Two Rivers in Algonquin Park, with other drop-offs as requested.

Northland also provides service from Toronto to North Bay via Hwy 11 and to Sudbury via Hwy 69.

BY RAIL

Via Rail (www.viarail.ca; ☎888-842-7245) runs two trains through Sudbury. The Canadian connects Sudbury Junction and Capreol with Toronto and Winnipeg. The Lake Superior connects Sudbury to Chapleau and White River. Sudbury downtown station, 233 Elgin St., Sudbury, and Sudbury Junction at 2750 Lasalle Blvd. E. in Sudbury Juction.

GENERAL INFORMATION

VISITOR INFORMATION

Algonquin Park – Superintendent, PO Box 209, Whitney ON, K0J 2M0. ☎705-633-5572. www.algonquinpark.on.ca.

Almaguin-Nipissing Travel Assn. – 7626 Whippoorwill Ave., North Bay. ☎705-474-6634 or 800-387-0516. www.ontariosnearnorth.com.

Rainbow Country Travel Assn. – Ontario's Near North, 1375 Seymour St. Sudbury. ☎705-522-0104 or 800-465-6655. www.rainbowcountry.com.

North Ontario Tourist Outfitters Assn. – 386 Algonquin Ave., North Bay. ☎705-472-5552. www.noto.net.

ACCOMMODATIONS

For a selection of lodgings, ⟳see the Address Book.

RECREATION

RENTALS AND OUTFITTERS

⟳*Many resorts supply or rent watercraft and other equipment to their guests.*
Algonquin Outfitters – (Four locations: *in Huntsville and three locations in*

and around the park, see map on website; ☎705-635-2243; www.algonquinoutfitters.com). Rent a canoe, kayak or mountain bike for a summer adventure in Algonquin Park, or rent skis, snowshoes or skates for the winter, as well as camping gear or any outdoor equipment you may find you need. Gear also available for sale. One-day, overnight or longer guided trips also available.

Opeango Outfitters – *(in Whitney. ☎613-637-5470 or 800-790-1864; www.opeongooutfitters.com).* Kayaks, canoes, rowboats as well as associated gear, maps, camp food and fishing tackle. Well-located for those arriving from the eastern side of Algonquin park.

The Portage Store – (Two locations: on Canoe Lake and on Hwy.60 at km 31, opposite Lake of Two Rivers Campground; *☎705-633-5622 in summer, 705-789-3645 in winter. www.portagestore.com).* This large emporium rents boating, fishing and camping equipment and operates a grocery store for camping foods (no bottles or cans allowed in the park). Guided trips available. Enjoy an informal a meal at the store's **restaurant** (☝*see Address Book*) overlooking Canoe Lake.

FISHING LICENCES

To fish in Ontario, you must have a fishing licence. *For details, ☝see Practical Information in the South Central Ontario chapter.* Ministry of Natural Resources: ☎800-667-1940. www.mnr.on.ca.

WINTER SPORTS

Snowshoes can be rented and can be used with hiking or even running shoes (for racing). Parks, resorts and ski centres sometimes offer snowshoeing trails. For steep terrain, ski poles or trekking poles are a great help.

All **snowmobiles** must have an Ontario permit; expect to pay $90 for a 3-day permit. Operators over 16 must have a driver's licence or a Snow Vehicle Operator's Licence, proof of machine ownership, registration, insurance and helmets. For trails and regulations, access the Ontario Federation of Snowmobile Clubs at www.ofsc.on.ca. Dog sledding is a popular tourist excursion. For a list of **dog sledding** excursions, go to www.ontariooutdoor.com/en/getaways/snow/sledding.

SHOPPING

Maxwell Pottery – *RR#2, Mattawa. ☎705-744-0543 or 877-421-9674. www.maxwellpottery.com.* Two young potters, Daniel and Jodi Maxwell, have set up this workshop on the access road to the Kiosk Peripheral Campground, at Eau Claire. The bright, original pieces are completely microwaveable, dishwasher and oven safe. Designs come in three varieties: Canadiana, with maple leaves on a green background; Provence, with the typical vivid blue/yellow design; and the Maxwell signature design, an original variation on classic folk pottery.

Sudbury Farmers' Market – *Market Square, corner of Elm and Elgin Sts. downtown Sudbury. ☎705-671-2489. Open Jun-late-Oct, Sat 8am-3:30pm, Sun 10am-3pm.* Local produce, baked goods, cured meat, crafts, and more.

North Bay Farmers' Market – *Oak St., North Bay. ☎705-7729-2939 . Open late May-mid-Oct Sat9-11am.* A small market selling produce and crafts.

Ramakko's – *125 Loach's Rd, Sudbury. ☎705-522- 8889.www.ramakkos.com.* This popular sporting goods store sells fashionable outdoor duds, as well as gear such as fishing tackle, hunting supplies and guns, canoes and kayaks, souvenirs and gift items. The Rocks line of sports clothes, unique to the store, is attractive and practical.

THEATRE

Capitol Centre – *150 Main St., E., North Bay. ☎705-474-4747 or 888-834-4747. www.thecapitoltheatre.com. Box office open Mon-Fri 11am–5pm, Sat noon-4pm.* This renovated 1929 movie palace is the region's performing arts centre, presenting music, plays, comedy and the North Bay Symphony in concert.

Sudbury Theatre Centre – *170 Shaunessey St., Sudbury. ☎705-674-8381 ext. 21. www.sudburytheatre.on.ca.* A professional theatre company presenting drama and comedy Oct–May in a modern purpose-built theatre downtown.

Le Théâtre du Nouvel-Ontario – *21 Lasalle Blvd., Sudbury. ☎705-525-5606. www.letno.ca.* Locally produced plays in French, as well as touring productions Oct–May.

Address Book

For dollar sign categories, see the Legend on the cover flap.

WHERE TO STAY

$ Algonquin Park Cabins – *Algonquin Park Information Office.* ☎*705-633-5572. www.algonquinpark.on.ca. Available late Apr–mid-Oct.* *No pets.* Reservations essential. 13 cabins. Historic cabins built and formerly occupied by park rangers (some cabins date from the 1920s) have been renovated and made available to visitors. Some of them are accessible only by canoe or hiking trail, and furnishings are basic: wood stove, bunk beds, table and chairs, outside privy; no linens, mattresses or kitchen utensils are supplied. Three cabins have electricity and are comparatively luxurious, with propane stoves and refrigerators.

$ Algonquin Park Peripheral Campgrounds – *Algonquin Park Information Office.* ☎*705-633-5572. www.algonquin park.on.ca.* Reservations essential. 98 campsites. Most people head for shelter along Highway 60, the parkway corridor, but four of the park's campgrounds are relatively isolated, although accessible by car (*see map on website*): **Kiosk**, on Lake Kioshkokwi at the north end of the park, is accessible via Hwy. 630, which branches from Hwy. 17 west of Mattawa; **Brent** sits on Cedar Lake, accessible from Hwy. 17 near Deux Rivières via a 40km/25mi-long gravel road; **Achray** borders Grand Lake, accessible from Pembroke, on the east side of the park, via the Sand Lake Gate and some 25km/16mi of gravel road; **Algonquin South,** located in the southern tail of the park, offers three camping areas, one at Kingscote Lake, accessible by car and with a parking lot and facilities, and two others accessible by easy canoe routes.

$ Algonquin Park Yurts – *Algonquin Park Information Office. Reservations:* ☎*888-668-7275, outside Canada/US:* ☎*519-826-5290. www.algonquinpark. on.ca. 3-night minimum stay holiday weekends in peak season, 2-night minimum in peak season. Reservations essential. 8 yurts.* Of the eight yurts available for rent within the park, seven are located at the Mew Lake Campground along the park corridor, and one at the Achray Campground (*see above*). The Mew Lake yurts have electricity and an insulated floor platform, so they are comfortable in cold seasons. During the summer they are equipped with barbecues and kitchen utensils; a comfort station with flush toilets, showers and washers and dryers is located nearby. The Achray yurt offers only access to cold water and flush toilets. Each yurt measures 4.8m/16ft in diameter and is eight-sided. Furnished with a table and chairs, it stands on a wooden platform and sleeps up to six people in two bunk beds (double bed under, single bed above); there is an outdoor fire pit for cooking.

$ Parker House Inn – *259 Elm St., Sudbury.* ☎*705-674-2442 or 888-250-4453 . www.parkerhouseinns.com. 4 rooms, 4 suites.* . Housed within two former residences located across the street from each other, this gracious inn offers comfortable modern rooms with many amenities like Internet and ensuite bathrooms. Each room is individually decorated in warm colours, with Victorian architectural details and charmingly appropriate, if not always antique, furniture. Breakfast, lunch and dinner are served in the **restaurant ($$)**, which comprises the parlour, the den, the sunrooms and the umbrella-bedecked garden terrace.

$ Wolf Den Bunkhouse and Cabins – *4568 Hwy. 60, Oxtongue Lake.* ☎*705-635-9336 or 866-271-9336. www.wolfdenbunkhouse.com. 30 beds in winter, 60 in summer.* For an outdoors experience without actually braving the woods, a stay at this rustic hostel located just outside the West Gate of Algonquin Provincial Park offers private log cabins and individual rooms or a dormitory with bedding and towels included. In the main lodge are washrooms, a self-catering kitchen and a lounging area with a fireplace and library. A cedar-log sauna, fire pit, barbecue grills and volleyball court are on the premises. Guided nature hikes in the area are available.

$$ L'Auberge des Pionniers – *Hwy. 17. W., Mattawa.* ☎705-744-5020. *www.lauberge.ca. 14 cabins.* 🅿️. Set on a sandy beach on the Mattawa River, this resort offers a range of completely equipped housekeeping cabins, from one- room to a chalet-style cabin large enough for up to 12 people. Each cabin has a view of the river; several have wood-burning stoves, and the bigger cabins have kitchens. Canoes and kayaks are part of the rental, or you can rent motor boats for serious fishing. There are 56ha/140 acres on which to hike or bike, and in winter, there's cross-country and alpine skiing, snowshoeing and snowmobiling. The sunsets are spectacular.

$$ Hummingbird Hill Spa and Country Retreat – *254 Edmond Rd., Astorville.* ☎705-752-4547 *or 800-661-4976. www.hummingbirdhill.ca. 3 rooms. No children under 16.* 🛏️ Spa 🅿️ This bed and breakfast southeast of North Bay, near Lake Nosbonsing, offers spa services and a **restaurant ($$)** serving healthy choices, with decadent touches (especially desserts). The house comprises two cedar geodesic domes, providing interesting interior spaces. The lounge area is attractive, with a stone fireplace and curved iron staircase. Guest rooms are small but fancifully decorated in a romantic style. Two guest rooms have ensuite bathrooms, but the third shares a bathroom with the owners. Outside, a screened gazebo serves as a setting for some meals, the hot tub is useable in all seasons, and a garden brims with hardy perennials.

$$ Torbay Cottage Resort – *585 Banner Ave., North Bay.* ☎705-476-0076 *or 888-786-7229 . www.torbay.net. Jul & Aug one-week minimum. 9 units.* 🅿️♿. For the resort experience, but within a city environment, stay at this small resort, founded in 1939, which lies near downtown North Bay, on a beach in a residential neighbourhood. Cabins have full kitchens and baths, gas fireplaces and cable TV. You can enjoy city amenities such as restaurants and shops, and return to watch the sunset from a deck chair. Kayaks, pedal boat and canoes are on hand in summer for guest use, and the resort is open for winter sports. Services are available for corporate guests (fax, Internet access, transport to meetings and others).

$$ Waltonian Inn Resort – *550 Waltonian Dr., Callendar.* ☎705-752-2060 *or 800-268-9025 . www.waltonian-inn.com. 23 cottages.* 🅿️✖️. Set on a sandy beach on the south shore of Lake Nipissing, this resort, in business since 1925, offers everything you'd expect: either motor boats for fishing or canoes for exploring, comfortable housekeeping cottages with complete bathrooms and screened porches, propane barbecues and a lodge building with a stone fireplace and a large screen TV for those inevitable rainy evenings. You can opt for a full American plan: the **dining room ($$)** serves lake pickerel as well as steaks, chops, and other hearty fare.

$$$$ Arowhon Pines – *Little Joe Lake.* ☎705-633-5661 *(winter* ☎416-483-4393*) or 866-633-5661. www.arowhonpines. ca. 50 rooms. Closed mid-Oct–May. American plan.* 🅿️✖️. This 70-year-old resort, owned by the Kates family, sits deep in the woods within Algonquin Park, with tennis courts, hiking trails and a sauna. Three hearty meals a day are served in the large, teepee-shaped log **dining hall ($$)** *(bring your own wine)*, which is open to nonguests (advance reservations required); dishes at dinnertime feature Canadian fare. Accommodations are available in 13 very comfortable log cabins and lodges with between one and 12 bedrooms; all have a lounge and fireplace, but no TV, radio or telephone (communal phones available). The resort is located on Little Joe Lake 8km/5mi north of Highway 60, 16km/10mi from the West Gate entrance to Algonquin park. Canoes, kayaks and sailboats available for guests' use.

$$$$ Bartlett Lodge – *In Algonquin Park.* ☎705-633-5746 *or 866-614-5355. Winter* ☎905-388-3039. *www.bartlett-lodge.com. May. Modified American plan.* 🅿️✖️. Set on Cache Lake and reached by boat, this lodge, built in 1917, offers one- to three-bedroom cottages with knotty pine interiors, wide windows and screened-in porches. Each cabin comes with a canoe; and kayaks and paddleboats are available. For the real backwoods experience, there are also two comfortable platform tents.

No TV, radio or telephone in rooms. The **dining room ($$$)** is open to nonguests, but call ahead for reservations. The five-course dinner is worth a long hike: duck breast with star anise, rhubarb compote and black trumpet mushrooms, or perhaps tuna with black-bean cilantro puree and roast tomatoes. Cache Lake is on the south side of Highway 60, about 20 km/12mi from the West Gate entrance.

$$$$ Killarney Lodge – *Lake of Two Rivers, in Algonquin Park.* ☎705-653-5551 (May-Oct), 416-482-5254 (Nov-Apr) or 800-473-5551. www.killarneylodge. com. Closed Nov–Apr. P X

This 70-year-old lodge is a wonderful anachronism: one- ,two- or three-bedroom lakeside log cabins and the sort of comfort well-to-do travellers in the past expected. The cabin interiors, done in knotty pine and country fabrics, are shiny-bright, with modern bathrooms, and at the dock your private canoe is tethered. At the main lodge, the **dining room ($$$)** serves three delicious meals daily, as well as all-day refreshments. The dining room is open to nonguests, but call ahead for reservations. The road to the lodge branches off Highway 60 at Lake of Two Rivers, about equidistant from each main entrance.

WHERE TO EAT

$ Le Voyageur Inn – *351 Main St, Mattawa.* ☎705-744-2370 or 877-744-2370. www.levoyageurinn.ca. **East Indian.** The special charm of this restaurant is its history as the former Mattawa House Hotel, built in 1881, one of the town's first hotels. Both traditional Indian meals as well as Canadian dishes are served.

$ The Portage Store – *Off Hwy. 60 in Algonquin Park at Canoe Lake.* ☎705-633-5622 in summer, 705-789-3645 in winter. www.portagestore.com (see Outfitters in Practical Information). **Canadian.** A park outfitter since 1937, the Portage Store sits off Highway 60 within Algonquin Park, nearer the west side. Breakfast, lunch and dinner are served in its spacious restaurant, which overlooks Canoe Lake. Burgers, wraps, sandwiches, fajitas and salads are main stays of the menu. The haddock fillets are done in a batter made with Cana-

dian beer and served with french fries and coleslaw. Ice-cream sundaes start with handmade ice cream.

Iced cappuccino is a popular drink in summer, as is cold beer. There's also a children's menu.

$$ Apollo – *844 Kingsway, Sudbury.* ☎705-674-0574. **Greek.** Out on Kingsway, east of the downtown core, this elegant venue serves crowd-pleasing Greek dishes. Locals rave about this restaurant's moussaka and souvlaki. Pasta dishes, steak and seafood are also available.

$$ Alexandria's Restaurant and Lounge – *211 Shaughnessy St., Sudbury.* ☎705-688-1453. Closed Sun. **Mediterranean.** Quiet and well-bred, this dining spot serves meals indoors or outside on the patio. The menu features the foods of Greece, southern France, Italy, Spain, and a bit of the Arab Levant as well. Many dishes are an inventive fusion of influences. Local pickerel also figures prominently on the menu.

$$ Pasta è Vino – *118 Paris St., Sudbury.* ☎705-674-3050. Dinner only. Closed Sun. **Italian.** Occupying a century-old house in the downtown area, this ristorante serves up traditional pasta, seafood and other Italian dishes, prepared with a creative flair. Enjoy the baccio for dessert, with espresso granita. Dining offered indoors and on the outside patio.

$$$ Churchill's – *631 Lakeshore Dr., North Bay.* ☎705-476-7777. www. churchills.ca. Reservations advised. **Canadian.** For fine dining in the North Bay area, head to Churchill's. The wide-ranging menu includes pan-fried lake pickerel and beef tenderloin with Yorkshire pudding as well as dishes from farther afield like lobster tails or curried tiger shrimp, all accompanied by well-prepared seasonal produce. Upstairs is Chumbolly's bar, while Winnie's pub, a popular watering hole, is just at hand. After dinner stroll to nearby Sunset Park for a view of the lake.

$$$ 100 Georges – *246 First Ave. W., North Bay.* ☎705-476-2666. www.100georges.com. Dinner only. Closed Sun. **Canadian.** Come to 100 Georges for a good dinner with lively entertainment, for the complete night out. Inside an old redbrick house lies a modern, clean-lined interior with soft colours, a fireplace and a convivial bar. The cuisine is fastidious, with house-made pasta and main dishes such as pan-seared rainbow trout, duck confit with a wild-mushroom ragout and lovingly cut Angus steaks. Desserts are trendy: try the panna cotta with balsamic strawberries. Several nights a week musicians perform—check out the program ahead of time.

ancient Lake Algonquin, and great volumes of water carved the deep canyons through which the much-reduced river now passes. The dry traces of ancient water courses now serve as hiking trails. Lake Nipissing, like the Great Lakes a remnant of Lake Algonquin, is relatively shallow and a popular fishing site. This river and lake system is little changed from the days of the voyageurs. In winter, the mercury can dip to -40° but temperatures average about -10°C/13°F in January. Daytime summer temperatures average about 22.5°C/75°F, and nights are cool. The dreaded black fly, a tiny biting insect, thrives from late May to late June, followed by mosquitoes in July and deer flies in August. Outfitters sell net jackets that cover head and torso, and fishermen are advised to wear thick wool socks, into which they tuck their trouser legs. Products called Deep Woods Off and Muskol are universally applied.

Algonquin Provincial Park★★

MAP P 109 AND P 228

Covering 765,345ha/1,891,167acres, Algonquin is Ontario's third largest park. This popular recreation spot occupies a special place in the hearts of Ontarians as the site of memorable vacations at children's sleep-away camps, family camp-grounds and resorts. Encompassing 7,725sq km/2,983sq mi of forested wilder-ness in the eastern portion of the province, the park offers 2,000km/1,250mi of canoe routes on 2,400 pristine lakes and 1,200km/750mi of rivers and streams, extensive camping facilities, fishing (54 species in the park) and swimming holes, hiking trails and cross-country ski trails. Wildlife is abundant: moose, beavers, black bears and timber wolves roam here. Plants are too—some 1,000 species of them—since the park's topography transitions from coniferous forests in the northern reaches to deciduous forests in the southern parts. Amazingly, this vast protected wilderness is only about three hours from Toronto and Ottawa via good roads. Known as the Parkway Corridor, Highway 60, along which are principal access points, traverses the southern portion of the park for 56km/35mi.

🛈 **Information:** Algonquin Park Information Centre ☎705-633-5572. www.algonquinpark.on.ca.

▶ **Orient Yourself:** To enter the park, even on back roads, you need an entry permit: contact the park information service. Hwy. 60 runs through the south-ern portion of the park for 56km/35mi. Information centres are located at the East and West gates and the **visitor centre** is situated 13km/8mi from the **East Gate** and 43km/29mi from the **West Gate.** It contains a cafe, bookstore, theatre, exhibits and an outdoor viewing deck. Points along the Park Corridor are identified by kilometre **signposts,** starting at the West Gate: for example, "The Visitor Centre is at Km 43." Park offices are located in the town of Whitney on the east side, while Dwight and Huntsville are the principal towns to the west. Some 1,250 campsites are accessible from Hwy. 60. Visitors can also access remote campgrounds from Hwy. 17 on the north and east sides, and Hwy. 11 running along the western side. (🍁 *For additional suggestions*

Opiola/Ontario Tourism

Algonquin Provincial Park

for where to stay, see Address Book). Daytime summer temperatures average about 22.5°C/75°F, but nights are cool. Late May to late June is black fly season, mosquitoes arrive in July and deer flies in August: local outfitters sell net jackets and insect repellents containing DEET.

Don't Miss: The visitor centre offers many excellent nature programs. Particularly memorable are the wolf-howl forays, where participants are guided to spots where the howls can usually be heard *(late summer-early fall)*.

Organizing Your Time: For accommodations within the park, reservations are essential as far in advance as possible. To truly enjoy the park, allow one week. Outfitter stores within the park and near Dwight, Huntsville and Whitney *(see Practical Information)* have camping supplies and recreational equipment for sale or rent.

Also See: OTTAWA, TORONTO

A Bit of History

Canada's first provincial park was established in 1893 in order to protect a great natural site from the depredations of logging and agriculture. In the early days of the 1800s, great white and red pines were felled and squared during winter, then floated down rivers swollen with spring meltwaters to the Ottawa River and sawmills. Today, trucks loaded with timber rumble down dusty remote roads. A logging museum near the East Gate explains the history of the industry in the park. Besides the timber men, the early rangers, involved in forest and fire protection, led a harsh existence in primitive conditions amid the rugged wilderness, fraught with biting insects and wild animals. Among the historic

cabins available for lodging in the park, several were constructed in the 1920s to house the rangers—some of them built by the rangers themselves, at astoundingly low cost compared to today.

An enduring mystery surrounds the death of artist **Tom Thomson** (1887-1917), whose hugely influential landscapes, many of Algonquin Park, inspired the Group of Seven, the first truly Canadian school. (No longer standing, a pine tree once located near the mouth of Carcajou Bay reputedly inspired his 1917 painting *The Jack Pine*, which hangs in the National Gallery.) Thomson was living on Canoe Lake when, on July 8, 1917, he drowned while paddling. Thomson was a fit young man and an experienced wilderness guide. So, did he jump, was he pushed, or did he just fall out of his

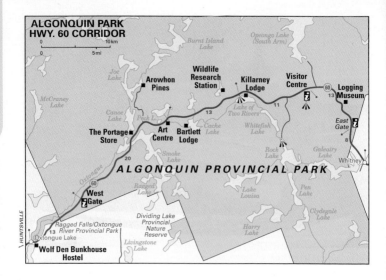

canoe? Was the culprit a broken heart, a poacher, a lethal submerged log or a German spy? The Department of Canadian Heritage maintains a website (www.canadianmysteries.ca) devoted to this and other unsolved mysteries. A commemorative cairn in Thomson's memory erected by fellow artists and friends stands at Hayhurst Point, at the north end of Canoe Lake.

From the early anglers who discovered the area's peaceful lakes, the wealthy tourists who arrived by train for lengthy stays at resorts and the artists who painted its scenic beauty to today's wilderness adventurers, summer-camp children and vacationing families, the park continues to serve many needs. The park has been, and continues to be, the focus of intense environmental research among ecologists and biologists, in particular at the Wildlife Research Station, situated along Highway 60.

Visit

🕑 *Park open daily year-round. Vehicle permit required (via East or West gates): ☜$14/day.* ✕ ☎ *705-633-5572. www. algonquinpark.on.ca. Visitor centre* 🕑 *open late-Apr–late-Oct daily 10am–5pm (extended hours May–Oct);rest of the year check website for hours.*

Algonquin Park Visitor Centre★
Km 43 on Hwy. 60, 13km/8mi from the East Gate and 43km/29mi from West Gate.
🕑 *Open late-Apr–late-Oct daily 10am– 5pm (extended hours mid-May–mid-Oct). Rest of the year, check website for hours.* ☎ *705-633-5572. www.algonquin park.on.ca.*

A stop at this centre should really be obligatory if you want to learn about the park. Here excellent **exhibits**★★ on the park's human and natural history provide a comprehensive overview. For further inquiry there's an on-site bookstore with maps, trail guides, and tomes on a broad range of topics about the park as well as related subjects. A film *(12min)* in the theatre serves to orient visitors to the diverse landscapes and recreational opportunities in the park. Landscape paintings and nature photography are among the rotating works of art on view in the Algonquin Room. A cafe serves light refreshments, and a deck off the theatre affords a view of the park's spectacular scenery.

Logging Museum★
Km 54.5 on Hwy. 60, just inside the East Gate entrance 🕑 *Open mid-May–mid-Oct daily 9am–5pm.* ☎ *705-633-5572. www. algonquinpark.on.ca.*

This modern museum, appropriately constructed of timber, gives a fascinating look at the logging industry, which defined the character of this area. A video presentation *(10min)* introduces the subject, and a short (1.3km/.8mi), easy outdoor trail offers a look at logging life in a re-created "camboose camp." The "camboose," a wood-burning stove, warmed the primitive living quarters. Among the display of equipment used in the heyday of logging is a steam-powered amphibious tug.

Algonquin Art Centre

Km 20 on Hwy. 60, near Found Lake.
Open late Jun–mid-Oct daily 10am–5:30pm. ☎705-789-3205.www.algonquin artcentre.com. Contribution requested. Recently opened (2005), this museum displays paintings and sculpture that connect nature with art; many of the works are by area artists. As the park has always been a magnet for artists, the project has considerable support. The Creation Station invites visitors to express their inner artist.

Hiking and Biking Trails

Along Hwy 60.
Information ☎705-633-5572.
Easily accessible along the Park Corridor, 14 short loop **hiking trails** allow visitors to appreciate the beauties of the forest and water without special preparations or equipment. Difficulty ranges from easy to quite strenuous. Length ranges from under a kilometre (**Hardwood Lookout** at Km 13.8) to 10-11km/6-7mi hikes taking the whole day (**Centennial Ridges** starting 2km/1.25mi south from Km 37.6 and **Mizzy Lake** starting at Km 15.4). Trails wend around lakes and afford views from ridgetops. Maps and guidebooks are available at the East and West gates, at park bookshops and at trailheads *(May–Oct)*, or can be downloaded from the Friends of the Park website (www.algonquinpark.on.ca). Parking is available at trailheads.

Two **mountain bike trails** (*open Jun–mid-Oct)* loop out from the Park Corridor: the **Minnesing Bike Trail,** which has four loops of varying difficulty, and the **Old Railway Bike Trail,** a new 10km/6mi trail appropriate for families; it can be accessed from the campgrounds at Mew Lake, Lake of Two Rivers in the west, and Rock Lake and Cook Lake in the east. The **Byers Lake Trail** *(13km/8mi round trip)* is accessible from the High Falls parking lot in Algonquin South.

In addition, the park has three cross-country ski trails and three backpacking trails where visitors can camp overnight.

Fishing and Swimming Holes

The park is famous for its trout, specifically brook trout and lake trout. **Amable du Fond River** is a good spot for finding brook trout. **Kioshkokwi Lake** and **Cedar Lake** have healthy populations of lake trout; walleye can be found in Cedar Lake as well as splake, similar in taste to speckled brook or lake trout.

Three of the best places off Highway 60 for swimming are **East Beach** picnic area and **Lake of Two Rivers** picnic area, both with sandy beaches, and **Peck Lake** *(accessible from Peck Lake Trail parking lot at Km 19)*, whose waters are cold and refreshing on a hot day.

Winter Recreation

Cross-country skiing, also known as Nordic or xc skiing, through the woods and across the fields of the park is a great attraction. Traditional skiing, or tour skiing, can be practiced over a snow-covered path, frozen lake or field. Waxless skis make preparation less tedious. Dress in layers, take extra clothing and a high-calorie lunch along in a backpack and always make certain someone knows where you've gone.

Snowshoes, an ancient aboriginal invention first noted by Samuel de Champlain, have enjoyed a resurgence as narrow, lightweight metal and plastic equipment has made the sport more accessible to the reasonably fit. They can rented at the outfitters listed in the Practical Information.

Snowmobiling is permitted in Algonquin Park. There are groomed trails, and tours and rentals are available from local outfitters

Mattawa

POPULATION 2,003 – MAP P 109

Located at the junction of the Ottawa and Mattawa rivers, north of Algonquin Provincial Park, the small community of Mattawa is a popular centre for canoeing and white-water rafting. Almost the entire 72km/45mi length of the Mattawa River is protected by two provincial parks: the Mattawa River Waterway Provincial Park stretches from Trout Lake, near North Bay on Lake Nipissing, to the edge of Samuel de Champlain Provincial Park, which continues almost to the junction with the Ottawa River. The Mattawa River, which flows through a canyon formed during the last Ice Age, challenges canoeists and rafters with several rapids, an 8m/26ft waterfall and 14 portages. Hiking trails follow river beds formed when the Mattawa, then a mighty torrent, drained the Great Lakes area during the last Ice Age. Like much of this area of Ontario along the Quebec border, Mattawa has a large Francophone population, estimated at some 40 percent. Mattawa means "meeting of the waters" in Ojibwa. On the last week in July, the town holds a popular **Voyageur Days Festival,** *(www.voyageurdays.com)* involving lumberjack competitions, a canoe race on the Mattawa River (downstream; the voyageurs also had to paddle upstream) and entertainment.

- **Information:** Information Centre, 401 Pine St. ☎705-744-0222 or 800-267-4222. www.mattawavoyageurcountry.ca.
- ▶ **Orient Yourself:** Mattawa lies about 3hrs west of Ottawa, on the Trans-Canada Highway (Hwy.17). It is approximately 60km/37mi east of North Bay.
- **Don't Miss:** A hike and a swim in Moore Lake in Samuel de Champlain Provincial Park.
- **Organizing Your Time:** An access road leads to the Kiosk Campground in Algonquin Provincial Park at Eau Claire near Mattawa, but to access the park's principal recreation facilities, you have to enter from Hwy 60, at the south end.
- **See Also:** OTTAWA REGION

A Bit of History

For thousands of years, aboriginals used the Ottawa-Mattawa river route to cross between the St. Lawrence valley and the upper Great Lakes; it is possibly the oldest trade route on the continent. Starting in the 17C, the river junction at Mattawa was a stop on the 2,000km/1,250mi fur-trading voyageur canoe route between Lachine, near Montreal, and Fort William (now Thunder Bay) on Lake Superior. A visitors' book would have recorded Canada's most famous explorers, from Étienne Brûlé and Samuel de Champlain to Alexander Mackenzie and David Thompson. The Hudson's Bay Company set up a trading post here in 1830, closed only in 1908. In the mid-19C, timber replaced beaver fur as the economic engine, and logs were sent down the rushing Ottawa River until the railroad arrived in 1881. At Explorer's Point, where the rivers

meet, sits the **Mattawa and District Museum,** a log building with exhibits about the early settlement (*open daily Jun-Aug;* ☎705-744-5495).

Sight

Samuel de Champlain Provincial Park

Off Hwy 17, 15km/9mi west of Mattawa. Open mid-May–mid-Oct 8am–10pm. $12/vehicle. ☎705-744-2276. *www. ontarioparks.ca.*

Named for the famous 17C French explorer, this park covers 2,550ha/6,300 acres, marking the river junction where *voyageurs*—intrepid Frenchmen, who were often Métis—turned west up the Mattawa River for the most difficult series of portages on the trip to Lake Superior; on the return trip, down the Ottawa, overladen canoes and ambushes were

Highway in Mattawa

the principal dangers. *Voyageurs* could paddle all day, carry 90-pound packs over portages and sleep under their canoes. Since many *voyageurs* couldn't swim, drowning was common.

Close to the park entrance, **Lake Moore** is the principal recreational lake in the park. The park road loops *(turn right)* around the lake, passing the *voyageur* centre and then the ecology centre. Canoes and bicycles can be rented. Three hiking trails, moderately easy to strenuous, allow a close look at nature, aided by interpretive plaques. The **Voyageur Heritage Centre** (*open Jul–Aug daily 8:30am–6pm, mid-May–mid-Oct call for hrs*) describes the life of the *voyageurs*, and the fur-trade in general. The **Canadian Ecology Centre** (*www.canadianecology.ca*) offers courses on sustainable forestry. Some 200 species of birds have been spotted in the park and one plant, the bottle brush grass-wild rye hybrid, grows nowhere else.

North Bay★
POPULATION 53,966 – MAP P 108

This resort centre on the shores of **Lake Nipissing** lies on the ancient canoe route linking the St. Lawrence valley to the upper Great Lakes. The La Vase portage connected the waters of Trout Lake and the Ottawa and Mattawa rivers with Lake Nipissing, the French River and Georgian Bay. Today these waters are used solely for recreational purposes. The area was largely wilderness until the arrival of the Canadian Pacific Railway in 1882, when it developed into a railway transport hub, supported by lumber and mining industries. On May 28, 1934 the town became world famous when the **Dionne Quintuplets,** the first identical quintuplets known to have survived, were born in a farmhouse near the town. Still a transport hub, at the junction of Trans-Canada Highways 11 and 17, North Bay enjoys a diversified economy, with a growing high technology and light industry sector, as well as wood processing industries.

The city is also the home of Nipissing University, and a Canadian Air Force base. After four centuries, the fur-trapping industry remains strong. Four times a year *(Jan, Feb, May & Sept)* beaver, mink, muskrat and other furs are auctioned at Fur Harvesters Auction, Inc., which ranks among the largest in the world *(1867 Bond St.;* open Oct–Jun Mon–Fri 8am–4pm; rest of the year call ahead; ☎705-495-4688; www.furharvesters.com)*. Held on Labour Day each year, the **Nipissing First Nation Traditional Pow Wow** attracts visitors from far and wide *(Pow Wow Committee, 36 Semo Rd., Garden Village; ☎705-753-2050; www.nipissingfirstnationpowwow.ca)*.

A ride on North Bay's waterfront carousel

▸ **Information:** Tourist Information Centre, 1375 Seymour St. ☎705-472-8480 or 888-249-8998. www.city.north-bay.on.ca

▸ **Orient Yourself:** Central North Bay lies between Nipissing Lake and Hwys. 11 and 17. Memorial Drive, along which lies the waterfront park, branches off from Main St., which runs parallel to the lakeshore. The park offers swimming, boating, a boardwalk, botanical gardens and a bike path, with more park development underway. A 50km/31mi network of walking and bike trails crosses the city. Laurier Woods, in the city centre, provides 200 acres of marsh and forest with walking trails. Trout Lake lies on the east side of the city.

▸ **Don't Miss:** In late September, the Dreamcatcher Express train heads to Temagami for the fall colours *(555 Oak St. E. ☎800-268-9281;www.northlander.ca).*

▸ **Especially for Kids:** The waterfront's carousels and miniature train. The Sturgeon River fur museum has programs for children.

▸ **Organizing Your Time:** Guided tours of principal sights are offered mid-June through Labour Day. www.ontariosnearnorth.com or ☎866-325-8759. Allow at least a day to enjoy North Bay.

▸ **Also See:** TIMISCAMING REGION.

Sights

Quints' Museum

Hwy. 11/17 at Seymour St., beside the tourist centre. ◷*Open Jul–Aug daily 9am–7pm, mid-May–Jun & Sept–mid-Oct daily 10am–4pm.* ⬅*$3.50.* ⬅☎*705-472-8480. www.city.north-bay.on.ca.*
On May 28, 1934, the **Dionne quintuplets** were born in this farmhouse, which was moved here from outside the town of Corbeil. The parents were Elzire and Oliva Dionne, poor French-speaking Catholic farmers. These five little girls quickly became the world's sweethearts, attracting millions of visitors to North Bay at the height of the Depression. Their childhood remains a controversial issue: the Quints wrote two books about themselves, the most recent suggesting that their time in government care and in the public eye was relatively happy. The museum displays Quint memorabilia, such as toys, photographs with royalty and several sets of identical dresses.

The Waterfront★

Memorial Dr., below Main St.
Kate Pace Way, named after a local World Cup ski champion, bordering Memorial Drive, bustles with joggers, walkers, cyclists, pet owners and tourists. Two remarkable **carousels**★ operate in summer months (◷*open Jun–Labour Day daily 10am–dusk, mid-May & Sept–*

mid-Oct weekends 10am–dusk; ✆$1/ ride, $5/6 rides; ☎705-476-2323; www. northbaycarousel.com). They were created locally with hand-carved wooden animals (horses on one, northern animals on the other). A  **miniature train** chugs along a 886m/2,500ft, 38cm/15inch-gauge railway (🕐 same hrs & price as carousels; ☎705-476-2323; www.heritagenorthbay.com).

The **Discovery Centre** (100 Ferguson St.; 🕐 open year round Tue-Fri 9:30am-4:30pm, Sat 10am-4:30pm, Sun noon-4pm; ✆$6; ♿☎705-476-2323; www. heritagenorthbay.com) located in the old Canadian Pacific train station, across the tracks from the waterfront, displays interactive exhibits on railroad history and local life generations ago.

From the government dock, there are scenic **cruises** aboard the 300-passenger, twin-hulled Chief Commanda II on Lake Nipissing around the Manitou Islands in the middle of the lake. (🕐 Depart daily mid-Jun–Labour Day, mid-May–early Jun weekends only, Sept Sat only. Round trip 1hr 30min. Reservations required. ✆$20. Georgian Bay Cruise Co. ✕♿☎705-494-8167 or 866-660-6686. www.chiefcommanda.com.

Excursion

Sturgeon Falls
37km/23mi west by Hwy. 17.
Located halfway between North Bay and Sudbury, on the shores of Lake Nipissing, Sturgeon Falls is a former *voyageur* camp, and now a popular spot for fishing in the lake and in the Sturgeon River. Originally the town developed around sturgeon fishing and caviar. In mid-August, a week-long **Step Dance and Fiddle Festival** (☎705-753-5737; www. westnipissingouest.ca), with concerts and competitions, is held annually.

Southwest of this community, the **Sturgeon River House Museum,** a reconstructed Hudson's Bay Company post, built on the site of a former post, tells the story of the fur-trapping industry in Northern Ontario (250 Fort Rd.; 🕐 open Jul–Labour Day daily 9am-5pm; Rest of the year Mon–Fri 9am–4pm; 🕐 closed major holidays; ✆$3; ♿☎705-753-4716; www.sturgeonriverhouse.com). Other buildings on the site include an 1898 pioneer home of squared timber and a blacksmith's shop. Nature trails (4 km/2.5mi) thread the riverside property.

Sudbury ★★

POPULATION 157,857 – MAP P 108

Located on the largest single source of nickel in the world, Sudbury is the biggest and most important mining centre in Canada. Some 5,000km/3,107mi of mining tunnels lie under the Sudbury area. A transportation hub, the city lies at the intersection of two transcontinental railroads and two Trans-Canada highways, 69 and 17, and is the regional services centre. The city is also a principal centre of Francophone culture in Ontario; a third of the population of the region is Franco-Ontarian. Laurentian University, which serves the northeastern part of the province, is bilingual. Once derided for its blighted landscape caused by environmental damage from logging and smelting, Sudbury over the past 35 years has reinvented itself as an exceptionally attractive and ecologically conscious area, and has attracted scientists studying environmental regeneration.

The Sudbury region is typical Canadian Shield country, surrounded by boreal forests, beautiful lakes, and craggy stone outcrops; nine provincial parks are within 90km/56mi of the city. Within city limits are 219 lakes, including **Lake Ramsey,** which has enough yellow pickerel (walleye) to supply local fishermen; in Bell Park and along a 1km/.6mi boardwalk on the downtown waterfront are swimming beaches, while Moonlight Beach, on the east side of the lake, is the most popular.

Ontario Tourism

Science North and Lake Ramsay

- **ℹ Information:** Sudbury Tourism, City Hall, 200 Brady St. ☎705-688-7570 or 877-304-8222. www.mysudbury.ca.
- **▶ Orient Yourself:** Downtown Sudbury lies on the northwest side of Lake Ramsey and north of Lake Nepahwin. The downtown core is a tangle of twisting streets bounded by Paris St. on the Lake Ramsey side and Regent St. parallel to the west. Elm St., which becomes Kingsway, bisects the downtown east-west. The corner of Elm and Elgin is the city's central point.
- **⊘ Don't Miss:** Science North and Dynamic Earth.
- **Kids Especially for Kids:** Science North, a large science museum particularly aimed at children.
- **♨ Also See:** SAULT STE-MARIE

A Bit of Geology

The nickel-copper ore deposits were extruded when a meteorite about the size of Mount Everest slammed into the ground some 1.85 billion years ago, forming the Sudbury Igneous Complex, which is about 60km/37mi long and 28km/17mi wide. Although the Sudbury Basin crater is no longer visible, its presence accounts for many interesting geological anomalies in the area. The basin is a rare ring crater, and the deposits within it are unique, with underlying or basement rocks thrust to the surface and magma (molten rock)

created by the terrific heat of the impact surging upwards in a ring-shaped formation containing nickel, copper, cobalt, gold and platinum. Exhibits at Science North, a large science museum particularly aimed at children, explain this event.

The area's wealth was discovered in 1883 during the construction of the Canadian Pacific Railway. A blacksmith named Thomas Flanagan noticed a rust-coloured patch of rock while working with a crew in a recently blasted area just west of the present city. Today the discovery is commemorated by a plaque (on Hwy. 144 near the Murray Mine). Sudbury claims the world's largest integrated nickel mining, smelting and refining complex. The **Super Stack,** an enormous smokestack rising 380m/1,250ft above the surrounding countryside, tops the complex. Super Stack was built in 1970 to reduce the local impact of emissions of sulfur dioxide. Today some 90 percent of the sulphur in the ore is successfully contained.

Some 2.2km/6,800ft underground in a former mine shaft lies the **Sudbury Neutrino Observatory** (www.sno.phy. queensu.ca), designed to detect subatomic particles emitted by the sun; the rock above shields the detector from cosmic rays. The lab is currently being refitted.

Sights

Science North★★★

100 Ramsey Lake Rd., about 1.5km/1mi south of Trans-Canada Hwy. From Hwy. 69 bypass, take Paris St. to Ramsey Lake Rd. ◷Open late Jun–Labour Day daily 9am–6pm. Rest of Sept–early May daily 10am–4pm. Rest of the year daily 9am– 5pm. ◷Closed Jan 1 & Dec 24–26 & 1 week in Jan. ☞$19. ✕℔☎705-535-4629 or 800- 461-4898. www.sciencenorth.on.ca.

🄺Perched on a rock outcropping on the shores of Lake Ramsey, this dramatic science centre was designed by Raymond Moriyama in association with local architects. A hexagonal exhibit building resembling a snowflake (to represent the glacial action that shaped Northern Ontario) is set over a cavern blasted out of the rock (to represent the creation of Sudbury Basin by a meteor).

Visitors enter a large admissions area and proceed to the centre proper via a **rock tunnel.** Raw rock is exposed as it is in the impressive **rock cavern** (9m/30ft high by 30m/100ft in diameter), where a 3-D film and laser shows highlight geological history on a giant screen. Exhibit floors are reached via an ascending spiral ramp that zigzags over the **Creighton Fault.** This fault, a geological fracture within the Canadian Shield active more than 2 billion years ago, left a groove 4m/13ft deep at this point. Hanging over the fault is a 23m/72ft fin whale skeleton, weighing 1,800kg/4,000 pounds, recovered from Anticosti Island. The glass walls of the ramp permit views of Lake Ramsey outside. Nature Exchange allows kids to swap their finds for items from the centre's nature collection. The Butterfly Gallery lets visitors watch butterflies emerge from pupae. The third floor is devoted to the northern ecosystem and animals, with wounded wildlife in permanent residence. There are exhibits about the weather and fossils, among others, and in the Discovery Theatre, science shows are presented regularly.

From the dock, **boat tours** of Lake Ramsey can be taken in summer. *◷Depart late May–Sept daily. Round trip 1hr. ☞$11.75. Cortina Cruise. ℔☎705-523-4629 or 800-461-4898.*

Dynamic Earth★★

122 Big Nickel Rd., 5km/3mi west of Science North by Regent and Lorne Sts. ◷Open Jul–Aug daily 9am-6pm, May- Jun daily 9am-5pm, mid-Mar–Apr daily 10am-4pm. ☞$18 (combination pass with Science North $40). ☎705-522-3701 or 800-461-4898. www.dynamicearth.ca.

Operated in conjunction with nearby Science North, this attraction enables visitors to descend deep into the old Big Nickel Mine to learn about geology and, in particular, how mining shaped this part of Northern Ontario.

The Phase 2 of the museum opened in 2007, continuing the theme of the link between mining and science. Notably, new exhibits explain how gold is found and mined, and a film about gold is shown in the new 130-seat Atlas Copco Theatre.

Long a Sudbury landmark, the **Big Nickel,** a replica of the 1951 Canadian commemorative five-cent piece, has stood near the mine for more than 40 years.

SAULT STE. MARIE
AND LAKE SUPERIOR

The largest freshwater lake in the world, Lake Superior is the largest, deepest and coldest of the Great Lakes. At 563km/350mi long and 257km/160mi wide, it is bigger than the four other Great Lakes combined, with plenty of room left over. The northernmost and westernmost of the Great Lakes, it lies on the edge of the Canadian Shield, where rocks laid down in the early Precambrian era are up to 2 billion years old, and among the oldest exposed rock on the planet. This ancient landscape has been shaped by glaciers, volcanoes and earthquakes as well as the slow work of erosion. In the interior, lakes and waterways offer places to canoe, kayak, fish and swim (for the very stoic); hiking paths and cross-country skiing trails are plentiful. The Ontario government maintains several parks with excellent facilities, and wilderness resorts are a popular way to enjoy nature. The shore, viewed from the Trans-Canada Highway (Highway 17), which hugs the coast from Sault Ste. Marie northwest to Wawa, is particularly dramatic, with great headlands looming some 130m/400ft above wide sandy beaches. The climate on Superior's north and eastern shore is bracing: average temperature in January is -11°C/-11°F, and in July is 24°C/°75F. Snowfall can be heavy, the winter of 1989-1990 holding the record at 782cm/308in. Known for its locks, the city of Sault Ste. Marie is set on the rapids ("sault" in French) of the St. Mary's River, where Superior flows into Lake Huron. Set by an international commission, Lake Superior's water level is controlled by gates on the river at Sault Ste. Marie.

For some 4,000 years, Anishinaabe, or **Ojibwa,** came here to catch the white-fish that teemed in the rapids. French explorers arrived in the 17C, and the famed *voyageurs* ran terrible risks crossing Lake Superior in birchbark canoes, carrying furs to market in Montreal. In 1784 a trading post was established at the portage and the first canal was built in 1798. A shipping canal was completed on the American side in 1855 and the Canadian lock, then the longest in the

Sault Ste. Marie Canal

©Michael S. Yamashta/CORBIS

Practical Information

AREA CODES

The area code for this region is 705. For local calls, dial all 10 digits (area code plus the number, but without the 1-prefix). For more information: ☎1-800-668-6878 or www.bell.ca.

GETTING THERE AND GETTING AROUND

BY AIR

Sault Ste. Marie Airport (YAM) – (475 Airport Rd. ☎705-779-3031. www.saultairport.com) **Air Canada** Jazz operates service to Toronto, and **Bearskin Airlines** has direct flights to Sudbury and Thunder Bay, with connections onwards. Enterprise Car Rental (☎800-261-7331.www.enterprise.com), Budget Rent-a-Car (☎800-472-3325. www.budget.com) and Elite Limousines (☎705-759-5757. www.elitelimossm.com) all have counters at the airport.

BY BUS

Greyhound (☎705-949-4722 or 800-661-8747. www.greyhound.ca) provides service to this area.

GENERAL INFORMATION

See also local tourism contacts in each section.
Tourism Sault Ste. Marie, 99 Foster Dr., Sault Ste. Marie. ☎705-759-5432 or 800-461-6020. www.saulttourism.com, www.northernontario.com.

Algoma Kinniwabi Travel Assn., 485 Queen St. E., Suite 204, Sault Ste. Marie. ☎705-254-4293 or 800-263-2546. www.algomacountry.com.
North Ontario Tourist Outfitters Assn., 386 Algonquin Ave., North Bay. ☎705-472-5552. www.noto.net.

FISHING LICENCES

To fish in Ontario, you must have a fishing licence. *details, see Practical Information in the South Central Ontario chapter*. The Ministry of Natural Resources contact is ☎800-667-1940. www.mnr.on.ca.

SHOPPING

Agawa Indian Crafts and Canadian Carver – Hwy. 17, Pancake Bay. Open Jul-Sept daily 8am-9pm, May-Jun & Oct daily 8am-7pm. ☎705-882-2311 or 800-656-9676. www.pancakebay.com. This little cluster of three shops sells everything from fishing and hunting licences and gasoline to beautiful Indian crafts and wood carvings. At Agawa Indian Crafts, you will find embroidered items, leather goods, clothing and other crafted items. The Canadian Carver stocks carved items such as duck decoys as well as paintings and prints. The Campers Store is an outfitter offering camping and sports supplies; there's a grocery store, a gas station and 36 varieties of ice cream from which to choose.

Address Book

For dollar sign categories, see the Legend on the cover flap.

WHERE TO STAY

$ Algonquin Hotel – 864 Queen St. E., Sault Ste. Marie. ☎705-253-2311. www.hihostels.ca. 16 beds. ✕ 🅿. This hostel, part of the Hostelling International group, offers private, shared and family rooms, some with bathrooms. Internet access, self-catering kitchen. The 19C building is conveniently located in the city centre near the riverfront. The Alibi Pub shares the premises.

$ Bellevue Valley Lodge – 326 Kirby Rd., Goulais River, off Hwy. 552. ☎705-649-2880. www.bellvuevalleylodge.ca. 2 rooms and chalet. ⌷🍽🅿. Located north of Sault Ste. Marie, this comfortable lodge, built inside and out of handsome local wood, offers guided ski tours and ski rentals and a package with the nearby Searchmont alpine ski area. In summer, the lodge will direct visitors to canoeing, kayaking and hiking areas. The new Metsa Maja chalet sleeps up to 9 people in considerable comfort within a lovely woodland setting. Sauna on-site. Dinner for guests only is available upon request.

$ Eastbourne Manor – *1048 Queen St. E., Sault Ste. Marie.* ☎705-942-3648. *www3.sympatico.ca/eastbourne. 3 rooms.* ⌸ P

This vast 1903 home was built by Sir William Hearst, a local lawyer who became the provincial premier. From the front veranda, visitors command a view of St. Mary's River, while the lovely garden offers a terrace for enjoying good weather. Seasonally themed guestrooms, all with ensuite bathrooms, are well-appointed with period furnishings and colourful fabrics, while the public rooms have comfortable modern furniture and period touches.

$ Rock Island Lodge – *Off Hwy. 17, south of Wawa 5km/3mi.* ☎705-856-2939 *or 800-203-9020. www.rockislandlodge. ca. 4 rooms. Closed Dec–Apr.* ⌸ P

Set on the shore of Lake Superior, at the mouth of the Michipicoten River, this lodge is a bit hard to find (best come in daylight), but well worth it. The modern rooms, decorated with Ikea-style pine furniture, have very big windows to take in the natural splendour, and small ensuite bathrooms. The lounge boasts a fireplace and more giant windows. Extras include a sandy beach, kayak and canoe rentals, guided sea-kayaking adventures, and access to hiking trails. On request, the proprietors cook up simple meals, often with lake fish, but breakfast comes with the rate. A good stop on the scenic route north from Sault Ste. Marie.

$$ Algoma's Water Tower Inn – *360 Great Northern Rd., Sault Ste. Marie.* ☎705-949-8111 or 800-461-0800 . *www.watertowerinn.com. 180 rooms.* ✕ Spa ♿ P . This hotel has a dual personality: it provides modern services for the business traveller, yet functions as a resort through its Trailhead Program *(www.algomastrailhead.com)*, which connects visitors with the recreational possibilities of the surrounding wilderness. Rooms and suites are modern, with all the amenities; many come with a whirlpool tub. The on-site restaurant, **Casey's ($$)**, serves up steak, chicken, seafood and pizza.

$$ Errington's Wilderness Island Resort – *44 Great Northern Rd., Sault Ste. Marie.* ☎705-884-2215 *(May–Sept)*

or 705-946-2010. www.wildernessisland. com. 6 suites, 5 cabins. Closed late-Sept– early May. ✕ P

For something completely different, try this wilderness resort in the Chapleau Game Reserve, which is accessible only by the Algoma Central Railway or by float plane. Set on two islands on Lake Wabatonguishi, the resort caters to wildlife watchers (no hunting allowed) and fishing enthusiasts (northern pike and walleye).

Every two adults are provided a cedar boat with outboard motor and fish-finder; canoes and kayaks are also available. American plan and dinner-only plans are options. Hearty meals feature beef, chicken and generous desserts, as well as vegetarian fare.

$$ Laurentian Lodge – *Off Hwy. 639, north of Elliott Lake.* ☎705-848-0423. *www.laurentianlodge.com. 4 cottages, 1 bunkhouse sleeping 8. Open summer (May–Sept) and winter seasons.* ✕ P

This comfortable wilderness retreat on Flack Lake sits 20mi north of Elliott Lake near Mississagi Provincial Park and the Deer Trail, a scenic 109km/67 road loop with several accessible hiking trails. Area lakes and streams offer excellent fishing, and hunters appreciate abundant game. Tennis courts and a sauna can be found on premises, golf courses within 90min driving. Boat rentals are available.Meals are served in a new dining room with lake views.

WHERE TO EAT

$ Los Mexicanos – *678 Second Line E., Sault Ste. Marie.* ☎705-942-6394. *www. losmexicanos.ca. Open Thu–Sat lunch and dinner, Tue–Wed dinner only.* **Mexican.** A true surprise on the Canadian Shield, this restaurant was founded by the Garcia family hailing from Guadalajara, and they take Mexican cooking seriously. The traditional menu features shredded meats and vegetables wrapped in delicious variations of the tortilla. The El Mercado de Mexico plate provides a small sampling of popular dishes. Also on the menu are vegetarian dishes and an "American" plate of Tex-Mex specialties.

$$ Arturo Ristorante – *515 Queen St. E., Sault Ste. Marie.* ☎705-705-253-0002. *www.arturo.ca. Dinner only Mon–Thu; Fri–Sat breakfast, lunch & dinner.*

Italian. In a modern, subdued room somewhat overwhelmed by the owner's naïf artwork, simple fare is served as well as specialties including several veal preparations, notably a grilled veal chop in a port and mushroom sauce. Catch of the day often includes lake fish.

$$ Buttermilk Mountain Ski Village – 44 Robertson Lake Rd., Goulais River. ☎705-649-3124. www.buttermilkresort. com. Dinner only, Thu–Sun. **International.** North of the city, off Highway 17, this resort's restaurant brings the wide world to the ski hill. Staples at Buttermilk Restaurant include raspberry and soy-glazed Chilean sea bass or roast duck breast with berry sauce (this far north, berries are the only local fruit). But chef Sarah Birkenhauer doesn't hesitate to branch into garam masala spiced duck breast and other challenging fare. Desserts are delicious—try the mini lime pie with raspberries and blueberries. Extensive wine list. The resort's **bistro ($)**, open in ski season, serves up a varied menu for breakfast or a light meal of high standard.

$$ Franzisi Ristorante – 265 Bruce St., Sault Ste Marie. ☎705-253-1500. www.franzisiristorante.com. Dinner only, Mon–Sat. **Italian.** In the Italian tradition, owners Sal and Maria Franzisi pride themselves on home-made pasta and gnocchi, so delicious and artfully sauced they constitute a perfect meal by themselves. The spinach gnocchi in gorgonzola cheese is especially popular, but you can hardly go wrong. The marinated lamb, and the salmon steamed with herbs and vegetables are also delicious. The nicely garnished plates delight the eye. Typical of Italy, the dining room features simple wooden chairs and tables on a black-and-white tiled floor.

$$ Thymely Manner – 531 Albert St. E., Sault Ste Marie. ☎705-759-3262. www.thymelymanner.com. Dinner only, Tue–Sat. **Italian.** In this modern dining room, located within an old house, Italian cuisine, adapted to local tastes and produce, is served with flair. Main courses include rack of lamb and local duck, but the appetizers are the most inventive part of the menu.

world, was completed in 1895. Sault Ste.-Marie was launched as an industrial centre with the arrival of American **Francis Hector Clergue** (1856-1939) in the late 19C. In short order, Clergue set up a pulp mill, which has developed into St. Marys Paper, then founded the Algoma Steel Company, the Algoma Central Railway and a hydroelectric plant. A museum at the Ermatinger-Clergue Historic Site describes his extraordinary career.

The Algonquins called the lake Ke-che-gum-me, meaning "mighty lake," a word transformed by English-speakers into "Gitchee-gumee." Starting with the **Group of Seven** in the early 19C, artists have hiked into the wilderness (or made use of the Algoma Central Railway) to capture the aesthetically compelling contrast of lush forest, granite and water, washed by the thin northern light that shifts from clear blue to looming grey in minutes, sometimes followed by fierce storms.

Today the locks at Sault Ste. Marie are the world's busiest, handling traffic on the St. Lawrence Seaway. The old 1895 Canadian lock, refitted, accommodates recreational craft. The city has developed its riverfront, which lies close to the downtown core, into an attractive venue for sightseeing, boating, fishing and shopping. The city itself has many handsome buildings and residences.

Ermatinger House

Sault/Ontario Tourism

Sault Ste. Marie★★

POPULATION 74,948 – MAP P 241

Connected to Michigan's city of the same name by the International Bridge and railway bridges, Sault Ste. Marie [Soo Sainte Mar-EE] is an industrial centre renowned for the huge Algoma Steel Inc. works, the city's biggest employer, and the St. Marys Paper Corporation's mill. The Canadian "Soo," as it is commonly called, lies on the north side of St. Mary's River, the international boundary and waterway that connects Lakes Superior and Huron, forming an important link in the Great Lakes/St. Lawrence Seaway system. Freighters pass through two locks on the Michigan side, the world's busiest canal by tonnage, while pleasure craft and tour boats pass through the canal and lock on the Ontario side. Sault Ste. Marie has a sizeable Franco-Ontarian population, but visitors are often surprised at the large Italian community, drawn here by the steel mill, a fact reflected in the profusion of Italian restaurants. The attractive city centre is compact and easy to visit on foot; older residential areas around the core contain substantial early 20C houses, a reminder of the city's considerable wealth. Many of the most interesting sights lie along the riverfront walkway, which also gives access to restaurants and shops. Not far away lies the beautiful, uninhabited Algoma Region of the Canadian Shield—a favoured subject of the Group of Seven painters—with its stunning views and recreational opportunities. Since winter lasts so long here, snow activities are a major tourist draw. Nearby rise two alpine ski hills, and the renowned **Stokely Creek Lodge** in Goulais River, one of Canada's premier cross-country ski sites. Another popular winter pastime is climbing frozen waterfalls, of which there are many. The 10-day **Bon Soo Winter Carnival** (☎705-759-3000 or 866-899-1607; www.saultfestivals.com), held every February, provides plenty of activities, including a polar-bear swim.

- **Information:** Tourism office at the Civic Centre, 99 Foster Dr. ☎705-759-5442 or 800-461-6020. www.saulttourism.com.
- ▶ **Orient Yourself:** The city core lies along Bay St. and Wellington St. East, which run parallel to the riverfront park. Pim St. intersects Bay and Queen St. East at the south end of downtown, near the river, and heads north becoming the Great Northern Road, which is Hwy 17. Queen St. East continues to follow the river.
- **Don't Miss:** A train ride into the wilderness to the Agawa Canyon on the Algoma Central Railway.
- **Organizing Your Time:** The surrounding area is wilderness punctuated by parks, with some lovely drives and plenty of hiking, biking and skiing opportunities.
- **Especially for Kids:** Mockingbird Hill Farm and the playground at Hiawatha Highlands provide kid-style entertainment.
- **Also See:** NORTH BAY REGION

A Bit of History

The rapids in the river between the two identically named cities were a gathering place from earliest times when Ojibwa Indians came to catch whitefish here. Étienne Brûlé visited the rapids in 1622, as did many of the great explorers of New France: Nicolet, Radisson, de Groseilliers, Joliet, La Salle, the La Vérendrye family and others. In 1668 Jacques Marquette, a Jesuit missionary and explorer, established a mission here, calling it Sainte Marie du Sault (sault means "rapids" in French). The Ojibwa called the spot Bawating, meaning "water flowing over rocks," and congregated here annually to socialize and trade, as well as fish. The name is often found in local references. To bypass the rapids, the **North West Company** completed the first lock and canal in 1798; it was destroyed during the War of 1812.

Bellevue Park and its lighthouse

Howe/Ontario Tourism

Sault Ste. Marie is also the birthplace of **Roberta Bondar**, Canada's first woman astronaut, for whom several city properties are named; in 1992 she was a member of the crew on the space shuttle *Discovery*.

Sights

Sault Ste. Marie Canal National Historic Site★

Lock ⊙open early-Jun–Labour Day daily 9am–9pm, mid-May–early Jun & early Sept–mid-Oct daily 11:30am–7:30pm. zJul–Aug site tours 11am & 2pm. 🅿$1.90. ☎705-941-6262. www.pc.gc.ca. Visitor centre at 1 Canal Dr.

The boats plying the Great Lakes bypass the rapids through two parallel locks (the Poe and the MacArthur) on the American side of the river. The Poe lock is equipped to handle freighters up to 305m/1,000ft long; the MacArthur takes boats up to 262m/800ft long. These locks are the last of 16 lock complexes on the seaway and the busiest section of the entire system. The 1895 lock on the Canadian side, once the world's longest lock, was taken out of service in 1987, refitted and now handles recreational craft *(mid-May–mid-Oct)*; it measures 76m/250ft long. At the base of Huron Street, there is a reconstruction of the first lock (**A** *on map*). Made of stone, with a wood-locking structure, it is a "bateau" lock, designed to give passage to the flat-bottomed, barge-like boats used in canals at the time.

The vast lock system and the busy shipping and industrial activity of the Soo can be appreciated by taking a **boat trip** (⊙*departs from Roberta Bondar Park mid-May–Sept daily 12:30pm & 3pm, Jul–*

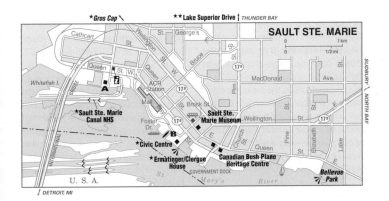

Aug additional 6pm departure; first 2 wks Oct 12:30pm only; Round-trip 2hrs; ⊙$27; Lock Tours Canada ✕☎705-253-9850 or 877-226-3665.www.locktours.com).

The tour leaves from the downtown waterfront and passes upriver through the Canadian side lock, then circles around to pass downriver through a lock on the American side, rising 7m/21ft. The lock is huge, but the cruise boat is big enough to permit a fine view of canal infrastructure. Passengers have the sense of rubbing shoulders with the big "lakers" that can reach 328m/1,000ft, and ocean-going vessels called "salties," whose size is limited by the dimentions of the Welland Canal. The enormous Algoma Steel complex is seen close up, and the boat permits views of the International Bridge, the railway bridge, the riverside park area and heritage buildings. Peppered with statistics, the commentary helps identify sights.

Riverfront★

Sault Ste. Marie has redeveloped its riverfront as a pleasant park, dominated by its attractive **Civic Centre** *(99 Foster Dr.)*, built of copper-coloured reflecting-glass. A boardwalk along the water between the civic centre and the Sault Ste. Marie Canal National Historic Site leads past the rapids that once were 1.6km/1mi long and roared so loudly that human voices were drowned out. Where the Ojibwa caught whitefish, today's fishermen try their luck, standing on platforms along the walk. Fanciful wooden carvings punctuate the space, and plaques en route describe city history. A notable landmark is the white tent-like pavilion in Roberta Bondar Park, just north of civic centre, named for Sault Ste. Marie's astronaut.

Nearby stands the permanently berthed **MS Norgoma (B** *on map)*, a passenger-carrying cargo ship that was the last overnight passenger ship used on the Great Lakes; the boat provided essential transport before good roads and bridges were constructed *(docked next to Roberta Bondar Park;* ⊙*may be boarded Jun–Aug daily 10am–8pm; Sept–Oct hours vary;* ⊙*$6;* ☎*705-256-7447; www.norgoma.org).*

Ermatinger/Clergue Historic Site★

831 Queen St. E. ⊙*Open June-Labour Day daily 9:30-4:30, mid-May-Jun and Sept-Dec Mon-Fri 9:30am-4:30pm.* ⊙*$7.* ☎*705-759-5443.*

Two 19C houses, among the oldest stone buildings northwest of Toronto, share this site, along with carefully maintained historic gardens. The attractive Georgian stone house was built in 1814 by Charles Oakes Ermatinger, a partner in the North West Company, and his Ojibwa wife, Charlotte. Known as the Blockhouse, the Clergue house was built in 1894 by Francis Hector Clergue and moved here in 1996; it served as both a home and trading post. Clergue, a lawyer from Maine, went on to found Algoma Steel, the Algoma Central Railway and the predecessor of St. Marys Paper. An incompetent manager, he unfortunately went bankrupt, but his companies survived. The city owns the buildings, which have been meticulously restored to their prime. Exhibits, interactive displays and artifacts bring the era of the fur trade to vivid life. In the Summer Kitchen Interpretive Centre, costumed interpreters demonstrate daily life in a frontier outpost.

Bellevue Park

Near corner of Lake St. and Queen St. E.

From this park situated along the river, east of the city centre, there are fine **views**★ of the ships using the locks and of the bridge to the US. The park has a lighthouse, botanical garden and greenhouses.

Canadian Bush Plane Heritage Centre

50 Pim St. ⊙*Open mid-May-mid-Oct daily 9am–6pm, rest of year daily 10am-4pm.* ⊙*$10.50.* ☎*705-945-6242 or 877-287-4752. www.bushplane.com.*

Just across the street from the Ermatinger-Clergue houses, a former hangar of the old Ontario Provincial Air Service contains a museum displaying 18 aircraft flown by intrepid bush pilots, including the iconic de Havilland Beaver, still in service around the world, and the Silver Dart (range: one mile), which made the first powered flight in Canada, on Feb.

23, 1909, at Bras d'Or, Nova Scotia. A film on bush pilots, *Wings over the North*, will have children asking for pilot lessons. An exhibit on Roberta Bondar includes photos, documents and artifacts.

Sault Ste. Marie Museum

690 Queen St. E. ◷Open Jun-Sept Mon-Sat 9:30am–5pm, rest of year Tue-Sat 9:30am-5pm. ☞$5. ☎705-759-7278. www.saultmuseum.com.
The amazing redbrick building that houses the museum was built in 1906 as a post office, and was surely the grandest building in town, topped by a baroque cupola with a clock face on each side. Inside, a glass floor allows light to stream down from upstairs windows; a massive oak stairway leads upward. The exhibits are static, with many glass cases, but useful in gaining insight into the area's ancient Indian inhabitants and local history. Marine buffs will appreciate a scale model of the *Edmond Fitzgerald*, the freighter wrecked in 1975.

Hiawatha Highlands Conservation Area

Northeast of downtown, between Fifth & Sixth Line roads, east of Great Northern Rd. (Hwy. 17N). ◷Open daily year-round. Sault Ste. Marie Conservation Agency. ♿P ☎705-946-8530. www.ssmrca.ca.
Within walking distance of downtown, this 1,214ha/3,000-acre recreation area provides hiking, biking, skiing and snowshoeing trails as well as a canoe route and children's playground. Visitors can observe the operation of a sawmill that processes trees harvested by park management. **Mockingbird Hill Farm** offers a glimpse of farm life, with a menagerie of domestic animals, a corn maze and wagon rides (*◷open mid-Apr-Oct daily dawn-dusk; in winter, sleigh rides and parties by appointment; ☞$6; ☎705-253-4712*).

Excursions

Gros Cap★

26km/16mi west by Hwy. 550.
From this headland there is a good **view**★ of Lake Superior and the beginning of the St. Mary's River. A hiking trail,

the Voyageur Trail, leads from Marshall Drive in Sault Ste. Marie to the bluffs; cyclists can follow Highway 550 or secondary roads from Highway 17.

St. Joseph Island

About 53km/33mi east of Sault Ste Marie via Hwy. 17 E. to Hwy. 548 and St. Joseph Island turnoff. St. Joseph Island Chamber of Commerce, Richards Landing. www.stjosephisland.net.
Accessible by bridge, this island, set in Lake Huron near the St. Mary's River, is both a historic site and a lovely scenic spot. Highway 548 *(72km/45mi)* circles the island, passing through Hilton Beach and Richards Landing. The ruined **Fort St. Joseph,** built in 1797 to protect fur routes from the Americans, was a strategic spot during the War of 1812; the site contains archaeological remains going back centuries (*◷open Jun-Labour Day daily 9:30am-5pm; ☞$4; ☎705-246-2664; www.pc.gc.ca*). The **view** of the St. Mary River from the fort is lovely. Hiking trails lead to picturesque spots, and fishing on the shore and in streams is popular. Birds frequenting the wetlands can be viewed from canoes. The St. Joseph Island Museum Village consists of six authentic pioneer buildings that trace life from the earliest settlement (*◷open late Jun-Labour Day Wed-Mon 9:30am-4:30pm; ☞$4; ☎705-246-2672*).

Train Trip to Agawa Canyon

183km/114mi. Departs from Bay St. depot in Sault Ste. Marie ◷late Jun–mid-Oct daily 8am, return 5:30pm. Also operates mid-Jun: call for schedule. Round-trip 9hrs. ☞$65 (summer), $85 (fall). Also late Jan–early Mar Sat 8am, return 5pm. ☞$65. Reservations required. Algoma Central Railway Inc. ✕♿☎705-946-7300 or 800-242-9287 (Canada/US). www.agawacanyontourtrain.com.
The train leaves the waterfront station and traverses miles of scenic Algoma wilderness north of Sault Ste. Marie, arriving at Agawa Canyon *(2hrs)*. The trip gives a superb perspective of the rugged southern edge of the Canadian Shield, passing through dense mixed-growth forest, providing views of lakes and muskeg bogs, and crossing cascading rivers over high trestles. The train

pauses on the floor of the Agawa Canyon, a rift 175m/575ft deep, formed by an earthquake 1.2 billion years ago. Travellers have a 90-minute stopover, during which time they can climb 300 stairs to a lookout 82m/250ft high for a fine **view**★ of the canyon and the Agawa River. The most popular period is late September to early October for the fall colours. The train ride is the only way, except for hiking trails, to access the Agawa Canyon, as there are no roads.

East Shore Lake Superior★★

MAP OF PRINCIPAL SIGHTS

The eastern shore of Lake Superior, a haunt of artists since the Group of Seven made it famous, offers superb views over the water from towering headlands and over vast stretches of forested wilderness punctuated with thousands of lakes and watercourses. Craggy outcroppings of pink granite, rock faces and canyons, all shaped by glaciers, volcanoes and earthquakes, characterize the Canadian Shield, among the oldest exposed rocks on the planet. Two forest types meet here, mixed forest and boreal; the maple, poplar, birch and spruce trees provide striking colours in the fall. Rivers descending from the higher interior plunge over cliffs, creating waterfalls and rapids, while ancient earthquakes have left sheered rock at Agawa Canyon, Agawa Rock and Old Woman's Bay.

Lake Superior's powerful waves have piled sand against the shore, creating miles of wide sandy beaches; the water is inviting, but quite nippy. Until the 1970s, the eastern shore of Lake Superior was wilderness, with the few visitors mostly arriving by boat. The land is so rugged that, notoriously, building the Canadian Pacific Railroad line in the 1880s nearly ruined the company. Completion of the Trans-Canada Highway 17 across this area opened it up and brought in the facilities needed to attract visitors. The Algonquins called Lake Superior Ke-che-gum-me, meaning "mighty lake," and it is not only the biggest freshwater lake in the world, it is also very treacherous. The coast is infamous for its sudden squalls and terrific storms, which make for great theatre when watched from a resort window, but which have sent many a boat to the lake bottom.

- **Information:** Tourism office. ☎705-759-5432 or 800-461-6020. www.northernontario.com.
- ▶ **Orient Yourself:** The route given here passes south to north, but it is equally stunning taken in the other direction.
- **Don't Miss:** Stop to enjoy the beautiful sand beaches; the pebble beach at Agawa is said to be one of the finest in the world.
- **Organizing Your Time:** Be sure the gas tank is full and bring along picnic supplies and water. With no stops and under ideal conditions, the trip to Wawa takes 3hrs.
- **Also See:** THUNDER BAY

The Drive

230km/143mi by Trans-Can Hwy. (Rte. 17) to Wawa.
The **route**★★ from Sault Ste. Marie northwest to Wawa is surely one of the most scenic in Canada, as Highway 17 hugs the twisting contours of the rugged coastline. Near the town of Goulais Bay, the road passes over a point 574m/1,883ft high, the highest on the itinerary, from which there is a splendid **view**★ of Batchewana Bay and the rocky shores beyond. **Batchewana Bay Provincial Park** (*◯open early May-Thanksgiving Day daily; ☜$11.85/vehicle;*

Ontario Tourism

Aerial view of Lake Superior

♿️🅿️☎705-882-2209; www.ontarioparks. com) is a favourite swimming spot for Sault Ste. Marie residents because of its very shallow, protected bay and sandy beach that is the warmest on the Superior coastline. There are also fishing, boating and camping facilities as well as a playground.

Farther on, 76km/47.5mi north of Sault Ste Marie, lies **Pancake Bay Provincial Park** (🕐*Same information as Batchewna Bay*). The bay was named by *voyageurs* who, camping here, made pancakes from the last of their flour, knowing the trading post was the next stop. From a viewing platform, visitors can see where the *Edmond Fitzgerald,* the freighter immortalized in the song by Canadian singer Gordon Lightfoot, sank when "the gales of November came early" in 1975. The deep, protected bay, with its 3.2km/2mi sandy beach, is relatively warm for swimming *(Jul–Aug)*. This park has campgrounds.

The highway follows the lakeshore for a lengthy stretch, with views of headlands, coves, islands, rocks and high granite bluffs pounded by the deepest of the Great Lakes. At **Alona Bay** (viewpoint after 108km/67mi) a turnout offers a fine **view** of sheer cliffs of granite and quartz. Near the mouth of the Montreal River, which flows along steep banks and cobble beaches formed by ancient glacial lakes, the road turns abruptly inland, ascending the mountains and offering superb **views**★★ of the river

and coastline. **Montreal River Provincial Park,** accessible only by boat, contains graphic geological evidence of a series of ancient beaches formed as lake waters rose and fell over the aeons.

The lookout at **Agawa Bay** (viewpoint after 151km/94mi) offers a **panorama** extending some 20km/12.5mi on a clear day. The pebble beach here is superb.

For 84km/52mi the road passes through **Lake Superior Provincial Park** *(swimming, hiking, boat rentals;* 🕐 *open early May–late Oct daily;* 🚗*$9/vehicle;* 🅿️♿️☎705-856-2284; www.ontario parks.com). A new **visitor centre** in the Agawa Bay Campground provides useful information on the park's natural and cultural history. The park is known for its Indian **pictographs**—rock paintings done in red ochre, largely dating from the 17C and 18C. About 8km/5mi past Agawa Bay, a road sign indicates Agawa Rock. A side road leads to a parking lot from which a rugged trail descends to the lake. A series of pictographs can be found on **Agawa Rock**, a sheer face of white crystalline granite rising 32m/98ft out of the water (🚸*accessible only when lake conditions are favourable; extreme caution advised*). The 35 drawings depict abstract forms, animals, a war party in canoes, and mythical figures. The **view**★ of the lake is excellent.

Farther on lies Old Woman's Bay, formed by an ancient earthquake, with cliffs rising to 120m/400ft, and offering yet more spectacular views.

TIMISKAMING REGION

From its headwaters in Quebec's Laurentian Highlands, the 1,271km/790mi-long Ottawa River flows westward to a point north of Temiskaming Shores, where it turns south and widens into 108km/68mi-long Lake Timiskaming. At its southern end, some 20km/13mi north of the town of Thorne, the lake narrows back into the Ottawa River, which continues southeast to the Canadian capital and empties into the St. Lawrence River. The river and lake form the boundary between Quebec and Ontario, which runs down the centre of the lake, and is the source of spelling inconsistencies for area toponyms. The federal and Ontario governments prefer Timiskaming, which they have given the lake and the district. But local residents opted for Temiskaming, which is closer to the French spelling of Témiscamingue. In Algonquin the name Timiskaming [Teh-MIS-kah-ming] means "at the place of the deep water." Extending west from the river halfway to Lake Superior, and roughly north of Temagami to just south of Timmins, and east to just north of Kirkland Lake, this vast region is the centre of year-round activities that appeal to outdoors enthusiasts. Among the many lakes and rivers, the best known are the Montreal River, Lady Evelyn Lake, Gowganda Lake and Lake Temagami.

At area resorts, which are numerous—and often quite rustic—the principal summer occupation is fishing. Northern pike, walleye pike, small-mouthed bass, pickerel and several species of trout are common. On Lake Temagami, which lies southwest of Lake Timiskaming, visitors can float around on houseboats. Those seeking wilderness adventures follow the extensive canoe routes first mapped by *voyageurs* in the 17C. Many hiking and portaging trails in Timiskaming connect with the ancient Nastawgan system around Lake Temagami, used by Algonquin, Ojibwa and Cree tribes for thousands of years. Boaters can travel between Arnprior, near Ottawa, and New Liskeard via the 457km/286mi Ottawa River Waterway; the system employs hydraulic trailers or vehicles to haul boats around portage sites and to circumvent hydroelectric dams. Hunting for moose, black bear, grouse and duck is popular in the region. Despite the influx of summer vacationers and year-round outdoor adventurers, the region remains fairly empty and untamed—an added enticement to those who want to escape from it all.

Fishing on Lake Temagami

Practical Information

AREA CODES

The area code for this region is 705. For local calls, dial all 10 digits (area code plus the number, but without the 1-prefix). For more information: ☎1-800-668-6878 or www.bell.ca.

GETTING THERE AND GETTING AROUND

BY AIR

The closest airports are those of North Bay: **Jack Garland Airport** and the **Greater Sudbury Airport** (& see *North Bay Region chapter's Practical Information*).

BY BUS

Greyhound provides service to this area. (☎800-661-8747. www.grey hound.ca).

Ontario Northland (555 Oak St. E., North Bay. ☎705-472-4500 or 800-363-7510. www.ontc.on.ca) operates daily bus service between Toronto and Hearst, along the Hwy. 11 corridor, serving Temiskaming Shores, Kirkland Lake and points north. One-way fare between Toronto and Kirkland Lake is $112.

BY TRAIN

The **Northlander** train, also operated by Ontario Northland (& see *By Bus*), serves North Bay, Temagami, Cobalt, New Liskeard and points north once daily except Sat. One-way fare between Toronto and New Liskeard is $91. ☎800-461-8558. www.ontarionorth land.ca or www.ontc.on.ca.

GENERAL INFORMATION

VISITOR INFORMATION

& *See also local tourism contacts in each section.*

Tri-Town Tourism Information Centre – 883356 Hwy. 65 E., New Liskeard, ☎705-647-5771 or 866-947-5753. www.tritownchamber.ca.

Temagami Tourist Information – www.temagamivacation.com.

ACCOMMODATIONS

For a selection of lodgings, & see the Address Book.

RECREATION

HIKING AND CANOEING

Hiking trails and canoe routes – www.ottertooth.com is a website maintained by Brian Back, a journalist who provides extensive information on trails and canoe routes in the Temagami region. **Nastawgan Trails Inc.** is a non-profit organization that provides information on trails in the Timiskaming and Temagami regions. www.nastawgan trails.org.

Ottawa River Waterway – (☎866-224-5244. www.ottawariver waterway.com).

SNOWMOBILING

Timiskaming and Abitibi Trail Assn., PO Box 1144, Kirkland Lake. ☎705-567-2088 or 888-828-2766. An association of snowmobiling clubs from Iroquois Falls to the Temagami, with trail maps and information.

RENTALS, OUTFITTERS AND CHARTERS

Xtreme Fishing Charters – 1 Whitewood Ave., New Liskeard. ☎705-647-0010. Set directly on the New Liskeard municipal marina (with a blue roof that can't be missed), this outfitter sells fishing and hunting equipment and supplies, and offers charters to select fishing spots on Lake Timiskaming in an 5.5m/18ft Lund aluminium boat that holds 3 passengers plus guide. A 3hr trip costs $250, a 5hr trip $350. Fish caught are walleye pike, northern pike and small mouthed bass.

Temagami Outfitting Co. – Mid-May–mid-Sept: 11 Lakeshore Dr., Temagami; ☎705-569-2595. Rest of the year PO Box 230, Nottingham PA 19363-0230; ☎484-467-1068. www.icanoe.ca. This company, located on the waterfront in Temagami, has been outfitting canoe expeditions for a century and offers a range of services, including bed and breakfast lodging, shuttle service for hauling canoes to the trailhead, and a water taxi. The company's outfitting store sells outdoor gear; rents canoe, kayak and equipment; and offers trip planning and the services of professional guides. Canoe rentals start at $28/day for a 5m/16ft Kevlar canoe.

Wolf Within Adventures – Box 31, Temagami. ◐Operates Jun–Sept. 10-day trip $1,450/person. ☎705-840-9002. www.wolfwithin.ca.

The base camp for this company is on Whitney Lake, north of Temagami. Custom-organized 3-day canoe trips include a day-long training and orientation session at base camp, which is a comfortable lodge.

Wanapitei Canoe and Northern Expeditions – 338 Caves Rd., RR#1, Warsaw. ☎705-652-9461 or 888-781-0411. www.wanapiteicanoe.com.

This company, established for 70 years, outfits both self-guided and guided trips in the Temagami area. Self-guided packages range from the basic (canoe and maps) to all equipment and food, plus float plane access to Lady Evelyn Lake. Guides are available for $180/day.

North Bay Charters – 631 Tackaberry Dr., North Bay. ☎705-497-8810. www.airnorthbay.com. Float-plane charters for the area around Lake Temagami (but not north of the lake) on a de Havilland Beaver: 4 passengers, $1200 one-way. Reservations required 2 weeks in advance.

FISHING AND HUNTING LICENCES

To fish in Ontario, you must have a fishing licence. ◔ For details, see Practical Information for the South Central Ontario chapter in this guide. The Ministry of Natural Resources contact is ☎800-667-1940. www.mnr.gov. on.ca. Holders of an **Ontario Outdoors Card** can obtain a small game hunting licence quickly (www.ontario.ca/outdoorscard). Otherwise, licences are issued specifically for the type of quarry hunted. Licences for non-residents are considerably more expensive than for residents. For example, a resident's moose-hunting licence costs $44, a non-resident's $373. Hunters must be 16 years old, although Ontario residents can obtain a licence at 15 years of age with parental permission. For details, ☎800-667-1940. www.mnr.gov.on.ca.

ENTERTAINMENT

Cobalt Classic Theatre – 30 Silver St.,(Hwy 11B), Cobalt. ☎705-679-8080.

www.classictheatre.net. Built in 1926 as the opera house that no silver boom town could be without, this 260-seat theatre was renovated in 1994 and today offers plays, concerts, pop/folk/rock bands, and variety shows as well as its own locally produced fare year-round, in a modernized burgundy-plush environment. On the mezzanine, local art is displayed for sale.

SHOPPING

Farmers' Market – *Riverside Place, Waterfront, New Liskeard.* ◐*Open Jun–Oct, Sat 8am-noon.* Fresh produce, flowers, meat, poultry, baked goods and crafts.

Belle Vallee Wools – *RR#1, Belle Vallée.* ☎*705-647-8686.www.bellevallee-wools.ca.* ◐*Open year-round Mon-Sat 8am–5pm. Pass through Belle Vallée, turn north on Brethour Rd., continue until the intersection with Wool Mill Rd. Turn E, go 2km.* Sheep from the local Wight Sheep Farm at Belle Vallée on Hwy. 11, about 15km/9mi north of New Liskeard, contribute to this boutique's wide variety of machine-washable woollen blankets and knitting yarn made on the premises on old machines, some dating from the early 20C. The blankets are available in several tartans, coloured and natural fibre tweeds, large checks as well as the classic northern trade blanket. Jackets and vests made from the blankets and knitted goods are also available.

The Highway Book Shop –*Hwy. 11B, Cobalt.* ◐*Open daily year-round 8am–10pm.* ☎*705-679-8375. www.highwaybooks.ca.* This virtually windowless white-frame building with "bookshop" written in large red letters across the front is a treasure trove of new and used material about the local area, including maps and guidebooks, much of it published by the shop. It's a bit crowded and musty, but if you've come this far, you probably need what's inside.

Boreal Cuisine Regional Food Kiosk – *883356 Hwy. 65 E., New Liskeard.* ◐*Open Sept–Apr Mon–Fri 9am–5pm; Sat 9am–4pm; Sun 11am–4pm. Phone for hrs rest of the year.* ☎*705-563-8100. www.borealcuisine.com.* This specialty shop sells products from northern Ontario, everything from pickled sausage to wool socks. Food items include wild rice, jams and jellies, chocolate, whole grain flour, herbal tea and much more. The many colourful soaps make excellent gift items, as do the creatively arranged gift baskets.

Thornloe Cheese Shop – *999697 Hwy 11, New Liskeard.* ⏱*Open mid–May–Oct Mon–Sat 8am–8pm, Sun 9am–6pm. Rest of the year Mon–Fri 8am–5pm, weekends 9am–5pm.* ☎*705-647-7441.*

All those cows ambling about the green pastures of the Little Clay Belt are, in fact, hard at work producing milk for this little white and maroon cheese shop set on the highway. Products are freshly made in the factory right behind the shop. The house special-ity is flavoured cheese: tomato/basil,

lemon/dill, salsa, Colby/garlic. Also try the ice-cream, sold by the cone with a few flavours available in containers.

The Quilting Barn – *883356 Hwy 65 E., New Liskeard.* ⏱*Open Jan–Nov Mon–Fri 9am–5:30pm (Fri 6pm), Sat 9am–4pm. Dec daily 10am–4pm.* ☎*705-647-0081.* This green and red barn, which once held horses, has been handsomely renovated with pines walls and a stone fireplace. The barn sells supplies for quilters and petit-point enthusiasts as well as, in the adjacent **Cosy Country Pine Shop**, gift items such as carved wood, candles and lavender sachets. Beautiful quilts are on display, and a few are for sale.

Address Book

⏱*For dollar sign categories, see the Legend on the cover flap. Lodgings below are grouped by geographic location as follows:* Lady Evelyn Lake, Gowanda Lake, Elk Lake, Temagami area, Lake Temagami (houseboats), and Moosonee and Moose Factory.

WHERE TO STAY

⏱*Accommodations in this area are gen-erally rustic, and oriented towards fishing and, often, hunting. Check carefully with resorts to know what guests must bring, such as towels or linen. Nearly all resorts and houseboats do not allow pets. Be sure to bring bug repellent.*

$ Cheminis Lodge – *1 Government Rd., Kearns.* ☎*705-634-2400. www.cheminis lodge.com. 6 rooms and 3 housekeeping units.* ✗. Located 40km/25mi east of Kirkland Lake, near Larder Lake Provin-cial Park, this bed and breakfast offers the wilderness experience in comfort. Cosy rooms have ensuite bathrooms, and guests enjoy a sunny living room with fireplace. For longer stays, there are packages offering three meals a day, transport to sites for ice fishing, canoeing, skiing, ice-fishing. Hunting on 36ha/90 acres of private land can be arranged. Boat, canoe, ice-shack rentals are available, fishing and hunt-ing licences sold, and passes for snow mobile trails obtainable. Nearby Mt. Cheminis (Mt. Chaudron on the Quebec

side) has a popular hiking trail to the summit.

$$ Cedar Ridge Lodge – *Off Hwy. 66, 30km/19mi west of Kirkland Lake.* ☎*705-624-6465. www.cedarridgelodge. ca. Suites in lodge and 6 housekeeping cabins.* Located on Burt Lake, west of Kirkland Lake, this lodge offers fishing, hunting, boating and swimming. American plan meal arrangements are available in lodge dining room, or guests can make their own meals in housekeeping cabins. The resort is affiliated with Wyndy River Expeditions (www.wyndyriver.com), which offers horseback riding excursions, including both day rides and pack expeditions lasting a week. The lodge also arranges excursions to the polar bear reha-bilitation centre in Cochrane (www. polarbearhabitat.ca). Special packages for families.

$$ Waterfront Inn – *2 Cedar Ave., New Liskeard.* ☎*705-647-8711 or 800-461-4644. www.waterfrontinn-ontario. com. 41 rooms.* ✗⏱. Located on Timiskaming Lake within New Liskeard, this modern motel provides direct access to the beach from ground-floor rooms. Some rooms have lakeside views; others (less expensive) face the parking lot. Rooms are spacious and have all modern amenities, including access (for a charge) to the local recrea-tion complex offering fitness facilities, a pool, sauna and squash courts. Open to the public, **Rooster's Bar and Grill ($$)** serves breakfast, lunch, and dinners of steaks, chicken and other Canadian standards.

The following **Resorts on Lady Evelyn Lake,** *located southwest of Temiskaming Shores, are accessible only by boat or float plane. Resorts provide water-taxi service from Mowat Landing, off Hwy 558 west of Haileybury.*

$$ Ellen Island Camp *– Cobalt.* ☎705-679-5145 or 888-679-5145. *www. ellenislandcamp.com. 5 cottages. Closed mid-Sept–early May.* This island resort on Lady Evelyn Lake offers excellent fishing as well as comfortable lodgings in new, clean housekeeping cottages. All units have private bathrooms, screened porches and decks with propane barbecues. Cottage rental includes one fully equipped boat per 2 adults, 15-20hp motor and gas, plus use of canoes and paddleboats. A children's playground and swim toys are on hand to entertain the young ones.

$$ Red Pine Wilderness Lodge *– Haileybury.* ☎705-679-5677 (summer), 905-689-3000 (winter) or 800-585-8069. *www.redpinelodge.com. 7 cabins. Closed Oct–mid-May.* ✂ Set on a 3ha/7.5acre island in Lady Evelyn Lake, this resort leaves guests plenty of time to fish or relax by offering complete meal service in the dining room . Guests can choose an American plan, or cook for themselves in two- or three-bedroom, completely equipped housekeeping cottages, each with a bathroom, pine-walled living room and dock. The resort provides one boat per 2 adults and 20hp motors, and canoes, as well as boats for use on six nearby lakes reached by boat and portage.

The following **Resorts on Gowanda Lake** *are accessible by a road off Hwy. 560, west of Temiskaming Shores.*

$ Auld Reekie Lodge *– Gowganda.* ☎705-624-3512 or 800-511-1191. *www. auldreekielodge.com. 6 suites in lodge, 6 housekeeping cottages with 2-4 bedrooms.* ✂. Package plans include a full American plan and a housekeeping plan. Amenities include canoes, kayaks, and pedal boats, a sand beach, hiking and ATV trails. In addition to Lake Gowganda, 7 other fishing lakes

are accessible. In winter snowmobiling (including overnight tours), cross-country skiing and ice-fishing are popular activities. Hunting for black bear, moose and grouse can be arranged with guide service. The spacious, pine-panelled cottages are fully equipped with kitchen, microwave and linens. All accommodations have TV, DVD and Internet access, and come with maid service, a boat, motor, gas and fish-finder. There's also a sauna. The restaurant serves hearty fare, with a Swiss influence, especially at breakfast time, and will cook up guests' fish catch.

$$ Gowganda Lake Camp *– Gowganda.* ☎705-624-3446.*www.gow gandalakecamp.com. 9 housekeeping cottages with 2 or 4 bedrooms.* Located on the north shore of Gowganda Lake, the cabins cover a range of comfort but all have wireless Internet, barbecues, and all equipment and linens as well as a boat and 15hp motor; deluxe cabins have satellite TV and microwave. There's a sandy, shallow protected beach suitable for children. The camp includes a laundromat, post office and general store that also provides fishing and hunting licences as well as bait and tackle. In winter snowmobiling, ice-fishing and skiing are popular.

$$ Lookout Point Camp *– Gowganda. Closed Oct-Apr.* ☎705-624-2035. *www. lookoutpointcamp.com. 4 pine cabins, 2-, 3- and 4-bedrooms.*✂. A full American plan is available. All cabins are fully equipped with microwave, TV, VCR, linens and barbecues and all have screened porches and fireplaces. Boat and motors are provided. There's a sandy swimming beach. Other activities include ATV riding and mountain biking on logging roads, moose and grouse hunting.

The following **Resorts in Elk Lake** *area can be reached off Hwys. 560 and 65, west of Hwy. 11, between Temiskaming Shores and Kirkland Lake.*

$ Long Point Lodge *– 19km/12mi west of the town of Elk Lake.*☎705-624-2419. *www.duenorth.net/longpoint lodge. 12 cottages, with 1, 2 or 3 bedrooms.* ✂ American plan is available. Located 22km/14mi east of Gowgonda, this resort provides fully equipped waterfront cottages (guests provide towels and TVs), with decks. Some are bunga-low-style, while others are A-frame; all have large windows. Boats and motors included in cottage packages; boat and motor rental available. Guide and fly-in service available for fishing. Bear, moose and small game hunting. In winter, snowmobile packages offered, including meals. Laundromat. Sauna. Camping facilities also provided.

$ Twin Bear Camp Resort – *RR#2 Kenabeek, 12mi east of Elk Lake off Hwy 65.* ☎705-563-8393. *www.ontariooutdoors.net/twinbear. 7 cottages with 2 or 3 bedrooms.* Located on the Montreal River, these fully equipped housekeeping cabins (guests provide towels and soap) come with a microwave and barbecue. Cottages are trim, white bungalows around an open, grassy area that helps keep mosquitoes at bay; interiors are finished in pine. Motor boat rentals, with canoe or paddle boat free with rental. Activities include fishing, hunting (moose, black bear, grouse, duck), swimming, hiking, ATV riding on trails.

$$ Golden Eagle Camp – *Hwy 65 W., Elk Lake.* ☎705-565-2566 or 877-565-2566. *www.goldeneaglecamp.com. 9 cottages, with 2-3 bedrooms.* ✖ Located on Sydney Creek, a tributary of the Montreal River, near Sydney Lake, this full-service camp can also provide access to several other lakes. An American meal plan is available. Some cottages are rustic log cabins; others are more modern with large windows and pine finishing. Guests supply own towels. The camp offers trailer sites, and campsites as well as boat rentals, fishing supplies, gas, groceries and a laundromat. A sauna, beach and playground are on-site. Activities include fishing, bear and moose hunting, hiking, ATV riding and snowmobiling.

The following **Resorts in Temagami** *area and on Lake Temagami can be reached by boat from a dock at the end of the access road (signposted on Hwy. 11) south of the village of Temagami.*

$ Mountain Home Lodge – *Marten River.* ☎705-892-2385. *www.mountain-homelodge.com. 9 cottages, with 1-4 bedrooms, and 3 bed-and-breakfast rooms. Campground.* ✖. Located on Red Cedar Lake, off Hwy. 64, south of Lake Temagami, this resort offers fully equipped rustic cabins, with electric refrigerators, appliances including microwave oven, bathrooms with showers and screened porches. Linens are provided, but guests bring towels. The main lodge has a comfortable lounge area with satellite TV movies; meals are taken family-style at long tables. Various packages, including full American plan, and fishing and hunting packages are available. Fishing boats, 14ft and 16ft, and motors for rent, canoes, kayaks, pedal boats and rowboats provided. Swimming beach.

$ Temagami Lodge – *Temagami Island.* ☎705-237-8935. *www.temagamilodge.com. 5 cottages, with 1-3 bedrooms. Closed Oct–early May. Weekly rentals.* This lodge on Temagami Island in Lake Temagami is accessible by water taxi from Temagami. The lodge has operated since 1905, although the massive Temagami Inn building is no more. The old billiard hall now serves as the main lodge. All cottages are modern, have kitchens equipped with refrigerators and appliances including microwave oven, bathrooms with showers, covered porches with barbecues. Linens are provided, but guests are asked to bring beach towels. Internet access and fax can be arranged on request. There's access to docks, and 16ft fishing boats with motors can be rented; canoes and kayaks are provided. On the island are extensive stands of old-growth white and red pines as well as hiking trails.

HOUSEBOAT RENTALS ON LAKE TEMAGAMI

$$ Ket-Chun-Eny Lodge – *Temagami.* ☎705-237-8952. *www.ketchuneny lodge.com. Available mid-May–Oct. Two houseboats, each with 2 double beds, 2 single beds.* These 11m/36ft identical houseboats were built on Lake Temagami. Each has a fully equipped galley, bathroom with shower and toilet, depth finder and CD player. Lights run off the boat battery. Guests bring bed linen, towels. Accommodation also at **Ket-Chun-Eny Lodge,** with three 2-bedroom suites, and 4 lakeside housekeeping cottages. Variety of packages including American plan. Boat, motor and canoe rentals; laundry facilities;

bait shop. Lodge is open mid-May-Oct and Jan-Mar for ice fishing.

$$ Leisure Island Houseboat Rentals – *115 Lakeshore Dr., Temagami. ☎705-569-3261 www.leisureisland houseboats.com. Weekly rentals only in summer, 2-day minimum spring and fall. Available mid- May–early Oct. 13 boats, each with 2 double beds, one bunk.* Cruise Lake Temagami on a pontoon houseboat. Each 8m/26ft houseboat cabin measures 10ft by 16ft , with a fore and aft deck, and has an indoor toilet (no shower), an equipped galley with propane stove and refrigerator, barbecue and heater. Guests supply sleeping bags, but towels are provided. The houseboat is powered by a 4-stroke 9.9hp motor. The company also rents small pontoon boats for fishing.

$$$ Three Buoys Houseboats – *Temagami. ☎705-569-3455. www. lakelandthreebuoys.com. Available mid-May-Sept. Variety of packages. 7 boats, each with 5 double beds.* Two-deck, 12m/40ft Sportcruiser houseboats offering considerable comfort, with a stateroom, sleeping deck, bathroom with shower and tub, fully equipped galley, furnace and a CD player. Electrical lights run off the boat battery. Guests provide bed linen and towels.

$$$ Canusa Vacations – *Temagami. ☎705-237-8965. www.canusavacations. ca. Available late May- Oct. Variety of packages. 4 houseboats each with 5 double beds.* Spacious 13m/44ft Suncruiser two-deck houseboats with fully equipped galley, living room, deck with barbecue, bathroom with tub and shower, stateroom, depth sounder, CD player, TV with DVD player. Appliances operate on propane, but electricity for lights is provided by the boat battery. Guests supply bed linen or sleeping bags and towels. Canusa also rents lakeside cottages.

The following lodgings in **Moosonee and Moose Factory** *on James Bay can be reached by train from Cochrane or by plane from Timmins (☉see Kirkland Lake Excursion below)*

$ Station Inn – *200B Railway St., Cochrane. ☎705-272-3500 or 800-265-2356. www.northlander.ca. 23 rooms.* Visitors taking the Polar Bear Express will find that this comfortable, modern hotel at the Northland train station is extremely convenient. There is also a **restaurant ($)** in the hotel that is open to the public.

$ Tamarack Suites and Lodging – *21 Waburn Rd., Moosonee. ☎705-336-2496. www.tamaracksuites.ca. 3 suites.* Located a short distance from downtown, the hotel sits on the Moose River. Its attractive suites feature one or two bedrooms, a kitchen and a living room with TV. Walls, ceilings and cabinets are done in red cedar, and rooms have generous windows. The hotel offers sunset cruises on the Moose River in a pontoon boat daily in good weather in summer *(7pm and 9pm, $20)*.

$$ Cree Village Ecolodge – *Moose Factory. ☎705-658-6400 or 888-273-3929. www.creevillage.com. 17 rooms, 1 suite.* This very comfortable hotel, constructed in 2000, provides facilities for conferences as well as tourists. The **Shaapuhtuwaan restaurant ($$)** serves delicious meals based on local game and fish such as bison and pickerel. The restaurant name refers to the Cree's communal lodge, and the spectacular architecture, a high, arched room with ribbed construction made of logs and cedar shingles, draws from this tradition. Bike and canoe rentals, boat tours arranged with local operators.

$$ Niska Inn – *141 Ferguson St., Moosonee. ☎705-336-2226. www. niskainn.com. 11 rooms, 1 suite.* Guests very far from home enjoy the comforts of a modern hotel near the shores of the Moose River. Wireless Internet and a dining room with continental breakfast are provided. Shuttle service to the airport or train station is available.

WHERE TO EAT

$ Elk Lake Eco Centre – *Ontario St., Elk Lake. ☎705-678-2433 or 877-678-2248. www.elklakeeco.ca. Closed Sat.* **Canadian.** In a beautiful modern conference centre constructed of glass and wood, lunch and dinner are open to the public weekdays and Sunday. Meals are served in the small, cozy lounge, which has a bar. Menus stress local produce, such as grilled salmon, Timiskaming steak, bison burgers and local vegetables, including delicious "ecological" mixed salads. The centre has six modern chalets on the property with 35 guestrooms **($)** available to the public .

$ Silverland Inn & Motel – *7 Prospect Ave., Cobalt. Open Mid-May-mid-Oct Mon-Sat 11am-11pm (Sun 6pm). Rest of year call ahead for hrs.* ☎*705-679-2115 or 866-544-3344. www.silverlandinn.ca.* **Canadian.** The distinguished-looking building was constructed by the Bank of Ottawa in 1913 as the most modern building in the north; most importantly, it was fireproof. Today, the outside is beautifully restored, while the interior is modernized, with hardwood floors. The **Silver Nugget,** much appreciated by visitors to the Classic Theatre nearby, serves pizza, salads and sandwiches, but what everyone talks about is the fudge (no less than 60 varieties of home-made fudge, including the Québec classic *sucre à la crème* and a cranberry- raspberry combo) and the ice-cream—12 kinds are offered. Upstairs are 3 guestrooms, sharing a lounge and bathroom facilities, and next door is a 10-unit **motel ($)**.

$ Voyageur Cafe – *Outside Temagami Outfitting Co., Temagami.* ☎*705-368-2023. www.icanoe.ca.* **Canadian.** Enjoy an espresso or a light meal while waiting for your canoe to arrive. This waterfront cafe, run by the outfitters, is a good place to study maps and gather information from the people at the next table. Or fire up your laptop: the entire complex is covered by wireless Internet.

$$ Green Tomato Bar & Grill – *998006 Hwy. 11 N., New Liskeard.* ☎*705-647-4003.* **Canadian/Fusion.** Unprepossessingly located in an Econo Lodge Motel, although with a separate entrance, this deliberately low-key spot is a local favourite due to Chef Hans Hopp's inventive cuisine, Every evening, along with the regular menu, he offers two specials, such as bison sirloin with red onion jam and balsamic blueberry sauce with garlic mashed potatoes or pecan-crusted arctic char with maple vinegar sauce. He also prepares a delicious rack of lamb with red wine and thyme. Desserts favourites include apple tart with maple custard sauce and crème brûlée.

Lake Timiskaming's width varies from a few hundred metres to 8km/5 mi, and most of the waters are quite deep, at 122m/372 ft because the lake follows an ancient fault line, the Timiskaming Rift Valley; earthquakes from 3 to 5 on the Richter Scale are not uncommon. Geologically, the region has formed along fault lines, including the Timiskaming Fault, which produced such dramatic features as Devil's Rock south of Haileybury, formed during an ancient earthquake. The rock rises some 100m/300ft above the lake, scarred by old silver-mining pits. The area also possesses kimberlites, extrusions in which diamonds are often found; exploration is continuing. In contrast to the boreal forests, muskeg and craggy rocks of the Canadian Shield, the area around New Liskeard lies on the Little Clay Belt, an area of rich soil formed on an ancient glacial lakebed. For a look at the effect of the Wisconsin Glacier, Esker Lakes Provincial Park just north of Kirkland Lake, is an essential visit. The region offers four definite seasons, with cold winters (January between –19.8°C/–4°F and –9.5°C/15°F) and hot summers (July between 14°C/57°F and 24.5°C/76°F). As elsewhere in the northern woods, bug repellents are a necessity from May to September.

Temiskaming Shores (the city has a different spelling from the lake and region), Cobalt and Kirkland Lake have had a rough-and-tumble history, as gold and silver mines near which the towns sprang up created vast wealth in the early 20C, then played out. Lumber and farming also supported settlement, which began in the late 19C. Tourists seeking wilderness adventure began arriving in the early 20C, with the coming of the train line. Lake Temagami was once the home of Grey Owl, an Englishman named Archibald Belaney (1888-1938) who, arriving here at age 17, passed himself off as an Ojibwa trapper and wrote popular books promoting conservation.

Temiskaming Shores

POPULATION 10,723 – MAP OF PRINCIPAL SIGHTS

Created in 2004 from two towns, New Liskeard and Haileybury, as well as the township of Dymond, this sprawling city lies on Wabi Bay at the northern end of elongated Lake Timiskaming. The new city adopted the spelling Temiskaming, but the district and the lake are officially spelled Timiskaming. Poised amid a lacework of lakes and rivers, the city is a hub for outdoor sports: fishing, hunting, boating, hiking, skiing and snowmobiling. The fall brings bear- and moose-hunters. Resorts, some more rustic and isolated than others, abound.

- 🅸 **Information:** Tri-Town Tourism Information Centre, 883356 Hwy. 65 E., New Liskeard. ☎705-647-5771 or 866-947-5753. www.tritownchamber.ca.
- ▶ **Orient Yourself:** Haileybury lies 8km/5mi south of New Liskeard, on Hwy. 11B, Lakeshore Road, which also threads through Cobalt south of Haileybury.
- 😊 **Don't Miss:** RockWalk Park in Haileybury.
- 🄺🄸🄳 **Especially for Kids:** Local beaches, particularly in Haileybury.
- 🕐 **Organizing Your Time:** Best to stay several days at a lakeside resort.

A Bit of History

Settled in the late 19C as by lumbermen and farmers, the towns that form Temiskaming Shores boomed when railroad workers discovered silver in 1903 at the site of what became Cobalt, igniting a frantic scramble that launched Canada's hard-rock mining industry. Today, this heritage is perpetuated at the Haileybury School of Mines, founded in 1912, and now one of four campuses of Northern College. Farming proved more durable than mining. The flat, fertile fields of the Little Clay Belt, a 56km/35mi swath at the north end of Lake Timiskaming, make a striking contrast to the muskeg and granite outcroppings of the surrounding Canadian Shield. The growing season of 90 days is short, but the area supports dairy and beef farms, sheep raising and feed-grain production. The Little Clay Belt is actually the bottom of an ancient glacial lake, where sediment accumulated and forest detritus created fertile soil. Unfortunately, the area is periodically swept by great forest fires.

Haileybury Beach

City of Temiskaming Shores

Haileybury's Hardy Boys

The author of the first 11 Hardy Boys children's detective books, Leslie McFarlane (1902-1977), who wrote the books under the pen name Franklin W. Dixon, grew up in Haileybury as the son of the public school principal. He left in 1920 to pursue a career as a newspaper reporter, but returned to his hometown to write the books while living at 580 Brewster Lane from 1932-1936. Thus, the prototypical American teenagers, Frank and Joe Hardy of Bayport, a waterside town in New York, are based on impressions of a lakeside youth in northern Ontario. Haileybury residents recognize the location of *The House on the Cliff* as Devil's Rock, which plunges 91m/300ft into Lake Timiskaming. McFarlane enjoyed a successful writing career, including a period in Hollywood, where a documentary he wrote was nominated for an Academy Award.

Sights

Town Waterfronts

Erected at Haileybury's lakeshore pavilion, a **monument** depicts Haileybury residents escaping the Great Fire of 1922 by plunging into the lake. The fire spared the mansions of mining tycoons along Haileybury's **Lakeshore Road,** generally called Millionaires Row, as well as along adjoining Brewster and Latchford streets, worth strolling down. **Haileybury Beach** is enclosed and the water is cleaned with a chlorine filter system. The beach is supervised *(Jul-Aug)*, and includes a children's wading pool and water slide (*open Mon–Fri 11am–7pm, weekends 1pm–5pm).

Along New Liskeard's waterfront stretches 1.6km/1mi Algonquin Memorial Beach Park with a boardwalk, public recreational facilities and a picnic area. In the nearby town of Latchford, located south of Cobalt on Hwy. 11, **Latchford Beach** provides a stretch of sand on Bay Lake, where swimming as well as camping are popular.

Haileybury RockWalk Park★

Next to parking lot for Haileybury School of Mines, off Hwy. 11B. *Open year-round.* *705-672-3376. www.rock walkpark.com.*

Dotted with boulder-size rocks and minerals from around the country, this 2ha/5acre landscaped park offers a lesson in Canada's ancient geologic past. Lined with explanatory panels, a trail wends around displays divided by rock types, such as metallic ore, gold and silver ore. The gold ore samples demonstrate how difficult it is to recognize ore-bearing rock with the naked eye. The Timiskaming district itself sits on a fault zone where earthquakes occur occasionally, a factor that may account for the silver and gold deposits. The origin of rocks is explored with samples showing strata, as well as a model volcano illustrating how magma is extruded to form new rock. The **Inca Trail** shows how people have used rock over the ages to express cultural ideas: examples include megalithic monuments found in Europe and the inukshuk of the Inuit.

Little Claybelt
Homesteaders Museum

883356 Hwy. 11, New Liskeard (near the information centre). *Open mid-Jun–Labour Day daily 9am–5pm.* *705-647-9575. www.museumsnorth.org.*

Housed in a red barnlike building with a cupola on the roof, this modern museum celebrates the homesteaders who began arriving in the area in the late 19C. A giant fibre-glass Holstein cow named "Ms. Claybelt" stands outside at the front. Created and staffed by volunteers, the well-planned museum presents an authentic look at settler life through some 5,000 objects displayed on a changing basis. Equipment, tools and other artifacts gleaned from local sources include primitive washing machines, a "high-tech" indoor hand pump, and food-preserving implements. Interestingly, even pioneers believed they needed telephones, and an exhibit explains that in the early years, lines were strung along fence posts and treetops to effect this means of communication.

Cobalt ★

Named after a metal found in silver ore, the little town of Cobalt, with just over 1,000 residents, has been designated a National Historic Site because of its importance as the cradle of Canada's hard-rock mining industry. Although similar boom towns were abandoned, Cobalt has survived due to tenacious local efforts. At the **welcome centre,** an excellent video *(20min)*, *Cradle of Canadian Mining*, describes the history of the Cobalt and its mining industry. Another film *(12min)* produced in 1919 by the Ontario government shows scenes that are astounding by today's safety standards: a miner lights a series of dynamite fuses, then runs for his life; another worker wearing no eye protection opens a door to peer into a furnace. The town's 1928 opera house, now the **Classic Theatre** *(✆ see Practical Information)*, has been renovated and offers some 70 performances a year, while small businesses and restaurants, some in heritage buildings, cater to the many tourists who are drawn here.

- 🅸 **Information:** Welcome centre at the train station, 1 Station St. ☎705-679-5191. www.cobalt.ca
- ▶ **Orient Yourself:** Cobalt lies about 2km/1.5mi south of Temiskaming Shores, via Hwy 11B.
- ⌖ **Don't Miss:** The Northern Ontario Mining Museum, and a stroll around this former silver-rush boom town.
- 🕐 **Organizing Your Time:** Allow at least one day.
- 👣 **Also See:** NORTH BAY

A Bit of History

For a few short years, peaking in 1911, Cobalt was the world's fourth-biggest producer of silver. Lumps of silver were discovered in 1903 by two tie-cutters on the Northern Ontario Railroad. Within a few short years, more than 50 mines were in operation, eventually extracting some $80 million of silver. The town of Cobalt sprang up overnight, and the population soon hit 10,000. The community supported a streetcar line, an opera house, a stock exchange and

Right-of-Way Mine on the Heritage Silver Trail

Cobalt Mining Museum

perhaps most importantly, a National Hockey Assoc. hockey team, the Cobalt Silver Kings. Mining continued sporadically until the 1970s, leaving the town surrounded by craggy piles of tailings and collapsed tunnels from the frenetic digging. Miners from Cobalt dispersed elsewhere in northern Ontario and across Canada, applying their hard-won skills to develop the country's mining industry.

Sight

Northern Ontario Mining Museum★★

1 Station St. ⏱Open Jun–Sept daily 9am–5pm. Rest of the year Mon–Fri 9am–4pm. ✎$3.25. ☎705-679-8301. www.museums north.org.

This charming old-fashioned museum, located across from the welcome centre at the train station, provides an explanation of the geology of the area. Exhibits in seven rooms include extensive mineral samples, and displays about the short period of local prosperity. The collection of **silver ore samples** from the Cobalt area is particularly fine. Most displays are enclosed by glass cases, but a few interactive exhibits will be introduced during a 2009 renovation. The Colonial Adit (an adit is a mine-tunnel entrance) can be toured upon request. The self-guided, 6km/4mi **Heritage Silver Trail,** which loops around Cobalt Lake, with several spurs into the hills, takes visitor to abandoned mining sites: the McKinley-Darragh Mill Site was named for the two sharp-eyed railroad workers, and the Ragged Chutes Compressed Air Plant forced air into the tunnels through a network of pipes. Also on the tour, the Larose Blacksmith Shop was named for another railroad worker, a blacksmith named Fred Larose. Fred threw his hammer at a fox and chipped off silver fragments that led to the first registered mining claim in the area.

Lake Temagami★

MAP OF PRINCIPAL SIGHTS

Ringed with small towns and back roads, this sprawling, many-armed lake encompasses 3,000km/1,875mi of shoreline and 1,200 islands. It has drawn tourists since the first trains arrived in the early 20C. Fishing resorts on this and the many surrounding lakes are numerous; vacationers routinely catch good-size trout, small mouthed bass and walleyed pike. Lake Temagami is known for its houseboats, which can be rented from several suppliers (♣see Address Book). The name Temagami [Tee-mah-GAW-mee] comes from the Ojibwa Te-mawg-a-mee, meaning "deep water by the shore"—in some places the lake drops to a depth of 16m/50ft near the shore. Today, the Temagami First Nation lives on Bear Island in the lake. The Temagami area covers some 12,000sq km/4,630sq mi of wilderness, most of it government (Crown) land. A network of canoe routes and hiking trails following ancient Indian portages is collectively called the Nastawgan, linking the many lakes and rivers. Among the seven provincial parks in the area, the two best-known are Finlayson Point and Lady Evelyn-Smoothwater.

🛈 **Information:** Information Centre, Lakeshore Dr. (behind the gas station), Temagami. ☎705-569-3421 or 800-661-7609. www.temagamiinformation.com.

▸ **Orient Yourself:** The lake lies west of Hwy. 11, about 55km/35mi southwest of Temiskaming Shores and 100km/63mi northwest of North Bay. Principal access is at Finlayson Point Provincial Park, just off Hwy. 11, on the northeast arm of the lake, just 1km/.5mi south of the town of Temagami.

👁 **Don't Miss:** Views from Caribou Mountain in Finlayson Point Provincial Park; they are best from the fire tower.

🕐 **Organizing Your Time:** Allow at least two to three days to enjoy this scenic area.

Sights

Finlayson Point Provincial Park

1km/.5mi south of the town of Temagami. ⏱*Open late May–late Sept.* ⊜*$12/vehicle.* ☎*705-569-3205.* www.ontarioparks.com. Maps of the trail system and other trails in the region are available at the Temagami Information Centre in town. Finlayson Point Park serves as the gateway to Lake Temagami and the region. The park offers extensive facilities for canoeing, swimming, fishing, camping and hiking. The celebrated 30m/100ft **fire tower** can be reached from a park road that leads to the summit of Caribou Mountain. At the summit there is an interpretive centre *(next to the parking lot)* and a wooden lookout cupola for those who do not wish to climb the tower; the view from the lookout over the town of Temagami is expansive. From the fire tower (⊜*$2 to climb the tower)*, the **view**★★ on a clear day is spectacular, reaching 40km/25mi and taking in Lake Temagami, abandoned mining and logging sites, White Bear Forest and the Trans-Canada pipeline. There is also a sanctuary at the summit for peregrine falcons, once abundant in the area. Near the main boat launch, a **plaque** memorializes the English conservationist known as Grey Owl (⬦*see sidebar).*

Adjacent to the park, White Bear Forest is threaded by a network of hiking paths. One of several entrances to the **White Bear Forest Hiking Trail** is located at the foot of Caribou Mountain, near the road's initial ascent to the summit. The forest, with stands of old-growth white pines, was named after White Bear (Wabimaka), a chief of the Ojibwa tribe, whose family once hunted these lands. The 28km/18mi network of trails through the 1,242ha/3,070-acre forest, now a conservation area, is part of an ancient portage system, portions of which are more than 3,000 years old. Some of the trees in the forest, most of which has never been logged, are 350 years old.

Lady Evelyn-Smoothwater Provincial Park

Accessible only by boat or float plane: from the town of Elk Lake, then by canoe or hiking; from Temiskaming Shores via Hwy. 558 west to Mowat Landing on the Montreal River, then across Lady Evelyn Lake; by water from Lake Temagami in Finlayson Point Park or by float plane. ⏱*Open late May–late Sept.* ☎*705-569-3205.* www.ontarioparks.com.

Inaccessible by road, this park is popular for wilderness canoeing and hiking excursions. It is the site of **Ishpatina Ridge,** a bulge in the Canadian Shield that rises to a peak at 693m/2,274ft above sea level—the highest point in Ontario, although only about 300m/915ft above the plateau. It is the highest point between here and the North Pole. The name means "high hill" in Ojibwa. Maple Mountain, 32km/20mi to the east, rises only 642m/2,106ft above sea level, but its vertical rise is actually 37m/113ft higher than that of Ishpatina Peak. Located on Scarecrow Lake, Ishpatina can be reached by determined canoers, who then climb a 3.4km/2mi trail. Maple Mountain can

Grey Owl

"Grey Owl," who posed as an Indian, dressing in buckskins and wearing his long hair in braids, travelled throughout North America and Europe with a conservation message, even lecturing to the British monarch George VI in 1937. Trying to reestablish beaver colonies, he worked for Canada's national park service, living first in Riding Mountain National Park with his pet beavers Rawhide and Jelly Roll. At his death in 1938, he was exposed as an Englishman, **Archie Belaney,** who had taken the Indian name Wa-sha-Quon-Asin ("the Grey Owl") about 1920. Though an impostor, Grey Owl remains one of Canada's finest nature writers and among the first to promote preservation of the wilderness. His most famous books are *Tales of an Empty Cabin, Pilgrims of the Wild* and *Sajo and Her Beaver People.* A 1999 film, Grey Owl, directed by Richard Attenborough and starring Pierce Brosnan, is a respectful tribute to his accomplishments.

be reached more easily, via Lady Evelyn Lake, and then via a 3.2km/2mi hike from Tupper Lake. Another highlight is **Helen Falls,** on the Lady Evelyn River, which plunges 25m/76ft. Lady Evelyn was the elder daughter of John Graves Simcoe, first lieutenant-governor of Upper Canada. The younger daughter had nearby Lady Sydney Lake named after her, and Lord Simcoe himself got the large lake south of Muskoka, now known as Lake Simcoe.

Kirkland Lake

POPULATION 8,248 – MAP OF PRINCIPAL SIGHTS

Kirkland Lake is the El Dorado of Ontario, the place where gold fever in the early 20C created vast fortunes. The town once again produces gold, but has reinvented itself as a destination for tourists drawn to its beautiful hinterland. Activities that beckon include hiking, notably at Esker Lakes Provincial Park, canoeing several established routes, fishing for unusual varieties such as Aurora trout and splake (a cross between brook and lake trout), downhill and cross-country skiing, snowmobiling and golf at the local club. Kirkland Lake has also gained fame as the home of a remarkable number of early National Hockey League players and the site of the Hockey Heritage North museum. As for the lake, named after Winnifred Kirkland, a secretary in the Ontario Department of Mines, it disappeared years ago, buried by mine tailings.

Discovery of silver in nearby Cobalt in 1903 flooded the area with prospectors, and eventually two of them, out rabbit hunting in 1911, came upon an extremely rich vein of quartz containing gold. The discovery, coming just as the Yukon gold rush was flagging, brought in prospectors from all over the world and launched the Toronto Stock Exchange. Many people became very rich, including Sir Harry Oakes, whose chateau now holds the Museum of Northern History, and such unlikely characters as Roza Brown, a Hungarian boarding house operator so unwashed and fierce that she frightened everyone but Harry Oakes, and Charlie Chow, a Chinese restaurant owner prescient enough to buy some of Oakes' shares.

- **Information:** Kirkland Lake. ☎800-249-8933. www.town.kirklandlake.on.ca.
- **Orient Yourself:** The downtown area lies along, and south of, Government Road (Hwy. 66), which Main Street transects north to south.
- **Don't Miss:** The Museum of Northern History, both for the mining information and for a look at the interior of an attractive, highly individual house.
- **Organizing Your Time:** Kirkland Lake is a pleasant town whose principal attractions lie in outdoor activities; take a couple of days to explore the surrounding wilderness.

Sights

Museum of Northern History★

2 Chateau Dr. ◷ *Open year-round Mon–Sat 10am–4pm, Sun noon–4pm.* ☎*$5.75.* ☎*705-568-8800. www.museumsnorth.org.*
This museum is particularly noteworthy for the structure in which it is housed, the **Sir Harry Oakes Chateau.** The dwelling was built twice, in 1919 as a large log cabin and in 1929 as a three-storey, 19-room chateau, by magnate Harry Oakes (1874-1943), founder of the Lake Shore Mine and victim of a notorious, unsolved murder.
At the entrance to the museum stands a remarkable **monument** to the tenacious miners who brought glory to the town. Carved out of black granite by Sally Lawrence and Rob Muir, it shows the figures of five miners labouring underground

Museum of Northern History

Ontario Tourism

as well as a mine head frame that can be compared to the Old Toburn Mine head frame preserved on the town's east side. Along with photos of colourful local characters, exhibits of preserved wolves and small animals, works by local craftspeople, mementoes of hockey heroes are souvenirs of Sir Harry's fabulous career. The original building was largely destroyed in a 1928 fire, so Sir Harry—a highly educated individual who graduated from Bowdoin College in Brunswick, Maine—rebuilt it according to his own plan, using a bar and joist system familiar to him from mining; he borrowed from several architectural styles, including Frank Lloyd Wright's Prairie House designs. The result is gracious and well suited to the hilly site, which overlooks the gold mine. Visitors particularly appreciate the nursery of the eldest daughter, Nancy, with its plaster frieze of childhood motifs.

Hockey Heritage North

400 Government Rd. W. ○*Open Sept–Jun Mon–Fri 10am–5pm, weekends 10am–4pm. Rest of the year, call for hrs.* ○*Closed Jan 1 & Dec 25.* ⊗*$12.* ☎*705-568-4420 or 866-568-4420. www.hockeyheritagenorth.ca.*

For hockey buffs, this new (2006) 1,665sq m/18,000sq ft museum and archives is a must-see. Exhibits include hockey

Sir Harry Oakes

A native of Sangerville, Maine and a dropout from Syracuse University School of Medicine, Harry Oakes led an adventurous youth, following rough and dangerous trades to Alaska, New Zealand and the Belgian Congo, among other landfalls, but he was always drawn to mining. In 1912, with $2.65 in his pocket, he arrived in Kirkland Lake, where he staked a claim to a goldmine that was to make him the richest man in Canada. The Midas touch stayed with him, and he made a fortune in land speculation in Florida, where he built another mansion in North Palm Beach. Yet another home, Oak Hall in Niagara Falls, where Sir Harry was remarkably generous during the Depression, now shelters the Niagara Parks Commission. In 1935 Sir Harry took up residence in the Bahamas to avoid Canadian taxes; he became a British citizen and received a baronetcy for his philanthropy. On July 8, 1943, Sir Harry's body was found with its skull battered in his Nassau bedroom; suspicion immediately focused on his son-in-law, playboy spouse of Oakes' eldest daughter, Nancy, whose testimony largely led to her husband's acquittal; other suspects were house guest Harold Christie and mob boss Meyer Lansky. The island's governor, the Duke of Windsor, pursued the investigation with remarkable ineptitude, provoking more rumours. Sir Harry's murder has, in turn, proven a gold mine for crime literature, where it lurks in many plot outlines.

memorabilia, dioramas of beloved north Ontario arenas, interactive displays on today's hockey heroes, an area where visitors can play hockey-based games, a theatre and a souvenir shop. According to the museum's record, some 330 NHL players have hailed from northeastern Ontario, and some of the most heart-felt exhibits are those celebrating local teams, members of the Northern Ontario Hockey Association. For example, there was the glorious moment when the local Lake Shore Blue Devils defeated the Calgary Stampeders in three straight games to win the 1940 Allan Cup.

Esker Lakes Provincial Park

37km/23mi northeast of Kirkland Lake via Hwys. 66 & 672. ⏱*Open mid-May–Sept* ⮞*$9.* ☎*705-568-7677. www.ontario parks.com.*

Set on the 250km/156mi Munroe Esker, the park provides a rare opportunity to view the work of glaciers that occurred some 10,000 years ago. An esker is a long ridge of sand and gravel formed when melting water within a glacier flows down a tunnel, leaving debris. The park holds smaller eskers as well as sand dunes and 29 kettle lakes. Within the park's forests are easy to difficult hiking trails with helpful interpretive stops that explore the landscape. Camping, swimming, boating, fishing and biking are offered. The park lies on the divide separating rivers flowing into the Arctic from those flowing into the Atlantic.

Excursion

Polar Bear Express★★

Departs from Cochrane, 176km/110mi north of Kirkland Lake, late Jun–Aug Sun–Fri. Rest of year Mon–Fri. ⮞*Return fare $90. 2week advance reservations recommended. Ontario Northland, 555 Oak St. E., North Bay.* ☎*705-472-4500 or 800-363-7510. www.ontc.on.ca. Passengers can book a 1day return trip, with a brief stay in Moosonee, or stay on for a day or longer (*⮞*for suggested lodgings, see Address Book). Moosonee is accessible by air from Timmins (flights year-round twice daily weekdays, one flight per day weekends; call ahead for fees & schedules;* ☎*819-825-8375 or 800-567-6567; www. aircreebec.ca).*

This fascinating, all-day train excursion operates year-round between Cochrane and **Moosonee** *(Moosonee Town Hall, 5 First St.;* ☎*705-336-2993; www. moosonee.ca)*, an outpost on James Bay, which is an inlet of vast Hudson Bay some 560km/350mi to the north. The route takes passengers across terrains of giant boreal forests, bushland and muskeg through the Arctic watershed to Moosonee. Arriving mid-day, visitors have ample time to take in the island of **Moose Factory** *(by boat taxi from dock, $10 one-way; in winter, by helicopter from airport, $35 one way)*, some 3km/2mi offshore, where a Hudson's Bay Company post was established in 1673, making it the earliest English-speaking settlement in Ontario; the island is still an important fur-trading centre, now operated by the North West Company. The two-storey white frame **Hudson's Bay Staff House,** dating from 1850, has been acquired by Ontario Heritage Trust, along with smaller factors' houses that have been moved nearby (⏱*open Jul–Aug; for hours: Town of Moosonee:* ☎*705-336-2993; www.moosonee.ca).*

The fur-trading posts drew Cree Indians to the area. Today the Moose Cree First Nation reserve on Moose Factory operates tourist programs *(*☎*705-658-4619. www.moosecree.com).* The Cree Village EcoLodge (⮞*see Address Book)* serves as a tourist centre for the island.

Tidewater Provincial Park (⏱*open Jul–Aug;* ☎*705-262-2746; www.moosonee. ca/tidewater)*, run by the municipality, lies on Charles Island and three other islands in the Moose River, between Moosonee and Moose Factory. Charles Island sits about 1.5km/1mi from each shore and is accessible by water taxi or canoe. The islands are forested, and offer glimpses of small wildlife, the occasional seal or beluga whale offshore, as well as sub-Arctic plants like the Labrador tea plant, bog laurel and calypso orchid. Park recreational activities include camping, hiking the easy 2km/1.5mi Riverside Trail, fishing for brook trout, and stopping by the visitor centre. ⚠*Tides and currents make the area too dangerous for swimming.*

THUNDER BAY
AND LAKE SUPERIOR

The largest city on Lake Superior, Thunder Bay is situated almost in the centre of Canada. It lies on a deeply indented curve of shoreline at the western edge of the bay of the same name. At the city's south end, the Kaministiquia River, which was part of the trade route to the northwest, empties into Thunder Bay; to the east the bay is protected by the Sleeping Giant Peninsula, and Pie Island to the south. As a major inland port and the Canadian western terminus of the Great Lakes/St. Lawrence Seaway system, the city receives over 400 ships annually and is a hub for both water and land transport. Its rail lines and roads carry a wide range of commodities. Prairie grain, coal, potash, petroleum products, and other goods arriving by railway or truck are transshipped to lakers for ports to the east. The Canadian Pacific and Canadian National railways both serve the city, although there has been no rail passenger service since 1990. The city is well-connected by road, since Trans-Canada Highways 11 and 17 meet here, and Highway 61 continues south through the Pigeon River border crossing, only 52km/33mi away, to merge with US Interstate 35 southwest of Duluth, Minnesota.

Near Thunder Bay, the Canada/US border runs through Lake Superior just north of elongated Isle Royale on the US side. This northernmost and westernmost of the five Great Lakes lies well and truly on the Canadian Shield—extremely ancient rock ripped by long-ago earthquakes, as at Ouimet Canyon, and scoured by the Wisconsin Glacier, which retreated some 10,000 years ago. Traces of aboriginal presence here go back 10,000 years as well, to shortly after the glacier's retreat. Needless to say, the north shore of Lake Superior is spectacularly scenic; dramatic views of the lake, vast stretches of boreal forest and the Shield's rugged landscape accompany a drive along Highway 17 from Thunder Bay to Schreiber.

Kakabeka Falls

Thomson/Ontario Tourism

Practical Information

AREA CODES

The area code for this region, which includes Kenora and western Ontario, is 807. This code covers two time zones, Eastern and Central. For more information: ☎1-800-668-6878 or www.bell.ca.

GETTING THERE AND GETTING AROUND

BY AIR

Thunder Bay International Airport (YQT) (340-100 Princess St. ☎807-473-2600. www.tbairport.on .ca.), about a 10min drive southwest of the city centre, is served by **Air Canada Jazz** (direct flights to Toronto, Ottawa and Winnipeg) **Bearskin Airlines** (direct flights to Sault Ste-Marie, Sudbury, Fort Frances, Dryden and Sioux Lookout) and **WestJet** (direct flights to Winnipeg and Toronto). Car Rentals: Avis (☎807-473-8572 or 800-879-2847. www.avis.com), Budget (☎807-473-5040 or 800-268-8900. www. budget.com), Enterprise (☎807-473-5222 or 800-261-7331. www.enterprise. com) and National (☎807-577-1234 or 800-227-7368. www.nationalcar.com) have counters at the airport.

BY RAIL

Via Rail Canada passes through the town of Armstrong, located on Hwy. 527, some 242km/152mi north of Thunder Bay. The train shelter is located on King Street and ⏱48 hrs notice must be given for the train to stop. For information ☎888-842-7245. www.viarail.ca. The train is useful for accessing certain remote resorts; otherwise, there is no passenger train service to Thunder Bay.

BY BUS

Greyhound Bus (815 Ft. William Rd. ☎807-345-2194 or 800-661-8747. www. greyhound.ca) provides scheduled bus service to Thunder Bay.

GENERAL INFORMATION

VISITOR INFORMATION

Thunder Bay Visitor Information –500 Donald St. E. ☎807-625-2149 or 800-667-8386. www.visitthunderbay.ca.

Northwest Ontario Tourist Outfitters Assn. – 386 Algonquin Ave., North Bay. ☎705-472-5552 . www.noto.net.

Northwest Ontario Sunset Country Travel Assn. – Kenora. ☎807-468-5853 or 800-665-7567. www.ontariosunset country.ca.

North of Superior Tourism Assn. – Kenora. ☎807-346-1130 or 800-265-3951 .www.nosta.on.ca.

ACCOMMODATIONS

👍For a selection of area lodgings, see the Address Book.

RECREATION

OUTFITTERS

Archie's Charters – Thunder Bay Marina. ☎807-473-8437 or cellphone 807-624-7096 .www.archiescharters.com. Fishing excursions on Lake Superior on a sleek 9m/30ft Bay Liner boat with guide Archie Hoogsteen.
Fish for Chinook salmon, lake trout and rainbow trout. $500 for 2 anglers, $50 for each additional angler. Winter ice-fishing ($65/day) on Lac des Mille Lacs in huts equipped with heating, electric light and a propane stove for cooking the catch.

Canadian Quetico Outfitters – 1184 Mountain Rd. ☎807-929-2177 (summer) or 807-475-3786. www.cqo2000. com. Outfitting for Quetico Provincial Park. Full range of outfitting, from complete package including transportation to just helping out.

Wilderness North – Strathcona RPO. ☎807-583-2047 or 888-465-3474. www.wildernessnorth.com. Fly-in fishing trips, from plane base in Thunder Bay or on Waweig Lake, Armstrong, 242km/150mi north of Thunder Bay via Hwy. 527. Fly in to 9 outpost cabins or 5 lodges set on northern lakes. Lodges offer either full American or housekeeping plans. Prices for 3-day packages, based on 4 people, range from $1000/person to $2000/person. Wilderness North provides list of supplies to bring (guests provide own lifejackets.) but weight restrictions apply. Guides available at Strikers Point Lodge, $175/day.

Wild Waters Nature Tours & Expeditions Ltd. – *856 N. Vickers St.* ☎*807-622-7200. www.wabakimi. com.* Outfitting for canoe trips in the Wabakimi Provincial Park. Wild Waters will supply everything from complete outfitting (all equipment and food) to providing just what is needed, and full guided tours including transportation. Specialized tours for beginners, family groups, experienced canoers, women-only and some routes for serious outdoor adventurers. Also an aboriginal sites tour, and sea-kayak trips on Lake Nipigon. Price per person for 7-day excursions $1700-$2000. Also fishing cabins reached by train or float plane, and customized eco-tours.

LEISURE

Thunder Bay Community Auditorium – *1 Paul Shaffer Dr.* ☎*807-684-4444 or 800-463-8817. www. tbca.com.* This 1,500-seat theatre, with exceptionally fine acoustics, hosts productions including performances by the Thunder Bay Symphony Orchestra.
Magnus Theatre – *10 S. Algoma St.* ☎*807-345-5552. www.magnus.on.ca.* The site of this 35-year-old professional theatre company is exceptional: the former Port Arthur Central School, a red brick structure with an impressive bell tower, at the eastern end of Waverly Park. A lovely flower garden, laid out on the former baseball diamond, is lit at night. Six productions a season and a summer show.

Kangas Sauna – *379 Oliver Rd.* ☎*807-344-3761. www.kangassauna. com. Sauna open year-round Mon–Fri 7:30am–11pm.* As Finns believe, a trip to the sauna relieves illness, relaxes the joints and calms the spirit. On-site are 18 private saunas, large, medium and small, that can be rented for 90min to 4hrs, each with shower and changing room. If, like Finnish cabinet ministers, you hold meetings in the sauna, Kangas can accommodate you with 2 conference rooms. The interior is done in neatly finished wood in the Finnish style. A small room rents for $11 for one person, $28 for 4 people. Hot tub, tanning salon. A pleasant **restaurant ($)** with Finnish decor serves pancakes, salt fish on rye bread and borscht, among more Canadian items.

SHOPPING

Thunder Bay Country Market – *CLE, Dove Building, just off Memorial Ave. Saturdays, 8am–1pm.* ☎*807-622-1406. www.thunderbaycountrymarket.com.* Produce, baked goods, crafts, and more.
Thunder Bay Farmers Market – *Victoriaville Shopping Centre. Open daily 9am–4pm.* ☎*807-473-9597.* Seasonal produce.
Amethyst Gift Centre – *400 E. Victoria Ave.* ☎*807-622-6908. www.amethyst mine.com.* Amethyts in many shapes and forms, from the Amethyst Mine Panorama. Workshop tours available.

Address Book

WHERE TO STAY

$ Birch Point Resort – *Kashabowie, 100km/63mi west of Thunder Bay via Hwy. 11.* ☎*807-926-2412 (May–Sept), 807-939-1320 (winter). www.duenorth. net/birchpoint resort. 8 cabins, 15 campsites. 2-night minimum.* This resort offers an easily accessible wilderness fishing on Lake Kashabowie, 27km/17mi long. Simple but comfortable cabins have bathrooms with showers and fully equipped kitchens with propane stoves and electric refrigerators. Linens are provided; guests provide towels. A convenience stores sells fishing tackle

and basic supplies. Rental of 14ft and 16ft boats and 15hp motors. Swimming beach. Guests clean and freeze their catch (walleye, northern pike, bass, lake trout) in fish house. Kashabowie Provincial Park, accessible only via the lake, is notable for remains of the Wisconsin Glacier 10,000 years ago including an esker and deposits left by retreating ice.
$ Chippewa Park Cabins – *Chippewa Park, south of the Kaministiquia River. Turn east on Chippewa Rd. off Hwy. 61, go 10km/6mi to park; Chippewa Rd. becomes City Rd. at Bannon's Gas Bar.* ☎*807-625-2447 or 888-771-5094. www.*

thunderbay.ca/chippewapark. Closed mid-Sept–mid-May. 21 Cabins. ✗ ♿ The city's 110ha/270acre Chippewa Park, on the shore of Lake Superior, offers a splendid view of Sleeping Giant. Seven modern cabins have two queensize beds, electric heating, refrigerators and microwave ovens, and wide decks. The 14 historic cabins have wood stoves; five cabins have two double beds and a cot; nine have two double beds. Extra cots provided. Although bedding is supplied, there is neither cutlery nor dishes. Washrooms and showers are situated in a nearby well-maintained, modern communal building. A communal kitchen has 2 stoves, 2 microwave ovens, sinks with hot/cold water and picnic tables. There is a small grocery shop, as well as a food concession in the park.

$ Thunder Bay International Hostel *– Longhouse Village, 1594 Lakeshore Dr., 18km/11mi east of Thunder Bay, just off Hwy. 11/17 at MacKenzie Station Rd.* ☎*807-983- 2042. www.thunderbayhostel.com. 11 rooms, with various combinations of beds.* This hostel offers rooms as well as camping facilities. There are family facilities, a communal kitchen, bicycles for use and Internet access. Swimming in the MacKenzie River. Greyhound buses will pick up and deposit guests if alerted beforehand.

$$ Mink Mountain Resort *– 240 Mink Mountain Dr., Neebing.* ☎*807-622-5009 or 888-616-6465. www.superiornorth. com. 10 cabins, 3 units in main lodge. Cabin have 1, 2 or 4 bedrooms.* ✗ ♿ 𝗣 These comfortable cabins on Mink Bay on Lake Superior are more like houses, each one individual and set on generous .5ha/1-acre lots. All have satellite TV, expansive kitchens, balconies, fireplaces and barbecues. Most have hot-tubs or Jacuzzis. The 4-bedroom has a recreation room with pool table. Lodge units have bar refrigerators and microwave ovens; two have fireplaces. A small convenience store is on-site, and the **Eagle's Nest Bar and Grill ($$)** offers dinner Fri and lunch and dinner weekends and holidays. Canoe and mountain bike rentals available. Close by are downhill skiing (Candy Hill and Loch Lomand), four golf courses and hiking trails. In winter, snow-shoeing and cross-country skiing are popular.

$$ Prince Arthur Waterfront Hotel *– 17 N. Cumberland St., Thunder Bay.* ☎*807-345-5411 or 800-267-2675. www.princearthur.on.ca. 120 rooms.* ✗ 𝗣 ♿ . In the tradition of Canada's great railroad hotels, this venerable 1911 landmark has taken the best location in the city, directly on the waterfront, with views of the Sleeping Giant. Although the elegant lobby area speaks of times gone by, the renovated rooms may be short on charm, but offer modern comfort and amenities. The **Portside Restaurant ($$)** serves prime rib and Yorkshire pudding on Fri and Sat evening and is open from 7am–9pm daily.

$$ Rose Valley Lodge and Restaurant *– 56 Rose Valley Rd., South Gillies.* ☎*807-473-5448 summer. www.rosevalleylodge. com. 2 one-room cabins.* ✗ 𝗣 . Located just off Hwy. 608, a short drive southwest from Thunder Bay, this lodge, owned by a Swiss native, is known for its excellent **restaurant ($$)**, which serves a three-course meal Mon–Wed, or 5-course meal Thu–Sun evenings. The menu varies but may include veal Zurich style, in a mushroom sauce with rösti potatoes; pickerel cooked with Pernod; or pork stuffed with prunes in a juniper sauce. Unlike many resorts, this lodge does not have minimum stay requirements. The one-room log cabins are new and simply furnished with a queen-size bed and futon sofa that folds into a double bed, a wood stove and table, as well as a bathroom. Child-care services available. The surrounding 178ha/440acres are suited to hiking, skiing and snow-shoeing.

$$ White Fox Inn *– 1345 Mountain Rd., Thunder Bay.* ☎*807-577-3699 or 800-603-3699. www.whitefoxinn.com.* ✗ ♿ 𝗣 9 rooms. A country retreat within city limits, this comfortable modern inn on 15 acres of woodland offers rooms from small to large, with fireplaces, Jacuzzi tubs and TV/DVD. The **dining room ($$)** has a formal decor and a relaxed dress code, and a menu stressing grilled meats accompanied by inventive vegetable dishes. The signature rack of lamb is accompanied by grilled courgette with marsala and pepper ragout and garlic potatoes; duck is served with dill spaetzle, fennel slaw and blueberry relish. Desserts includes warm chocolate soufflé or pineapple baked in a mille-feuille crust, with blueberry sauce; or the optional cheese tray.

$$$ Dog Lake Resort – *Dog Lake Rd., Thunder Bay. ☎807-933-4407 summer, 807-767-1809 winter or 800-466-1908. www.doglakeresort.com. 9 cabins, 2 houseboats, 100 RV sites. Minimum 3-night stay.* ✕

This resort lies a short drive away from Thunder Bay and offers both cabins and houseboats. Although the resort is 60 years old, the log cabins, all with lake views, are modern and furnished with attractive furniture and recent appliances, including microwave ovens, satellite TV and wireless Internet. The 40ft and 36ft houseboats are also fully equipped, with bathrooms, linens, kitchens; interiors resemble a house trailer. Rentals of boats and motors, canoes and paddle boats. Full American plan or housekeeping plans available, both including boat rental. Dog Lake has some 800km/500mi of shoreline and many islands, with fishing for wall-eye, northern pike, bass, pickerel and perch. Moose and bear hunt outfitting also offered.

WHERE TO EAT

$ Fox and Hedgehog Irish Pub – *450 Memorial Ave., Thunder Bay. ☎807-345-3430. www.foxandhedgehog.ca.* **Pub Fare.** The beer is of course a prime consideration, but the food here is also good. Items include the inevitable chicken wings, fish and chips and shepherds pie, but check out the jambalaya, with chicken, shrimp and chorizo sausage combined with peppers, or the *perogies* and cabbage rolls. Sunday evening is amateur entertainment night.

$ Hoito Restaurant – *314 Bay St., Thunder Bay. ☎807-345-6323. www. hoito.ca.* **Finnish.** Located on the ground floor of the Finnish Labour Temple, this 90-year-old restaurant is a local institution, serving three meals daily. It is a popular stop for breakfast. Hoito means "care" in Finnish: the dining room was opened as a co-operative in 1918 to provide nourishing meals for poor Finnish workers. Here you will find rib-sticking traditional dishes such as beef stew *(mojakka)*, Karelian pasties

(karjalanpiirakka) and *pulla,* the most delicious cardamom-flavoured bread ever invented, as well as the ever-popular pancakes. Baked goods are ferried in from the Kivela Bakery. Nordic egalitarianism reigns: seat yourself and pay at the cash register.

$ Metropolitan Moose Beanery & Café – *Kakabeka Falls. ☎807-473-5453.* **Canadian.** This cafe in the centre of town is a place to recharge your body's batteries with a healthy snack or light meal after clambering around the falls. Highly recommended baked goods, sandwich wraps, gluten-free products, and a range of coffee brews greet patrons here. Open at 7am weekdays and 9am weekends, the restaurant sits in a building that is a log cabin, on a wooded lot.

$$$ Bistro One – *55 Dunlop St. off Memorial Ave., Thunder Bay. ☎807-622-2478. www.bistroone.ca. Dinner only, Tue–Sat.* **Contemporary.** Chef Jean Robillard provides a daily changing menu, with a marked Italian tilt. Favourite dishes are rosemary-flavoured rack of lamb with gorgonzola butter, or roasted Atlantic salmon with seafood risotto and lobster sauce. The dessert chef, Maria Costanzo, is justly appreciated for her warm chocolate gâteau with raspberry coulis, or lemon-flavoured mille-feuille with pistachio meringue and lemon cream. Bistro One is located near the waterfront.

$$$ Caribou Restaurant and Wine Bar – *727 Hewitson St., between Balmoral St. & Memorial Ave., Thunder Bay. ☎807-628-8588. www.caribou restaurant.com. Lunch Wed–Thu.* **Italian.** Situated near the waterfront, this low-key but very pleasant watering hole boasts a bar with comfortable seats, and softly-lit tables in the dining space. Guests are treated to an extensive menu that includes wild boar baked in tomato sauce and served with pappardelle egg noodles, or roast duck served with caramelized onion-mushroom risotto. The lighter fare is also tasty: wood-oven pizzas and inventive appetizers such as fried calamari coated in chick-pea flour and served with tamarind sauce.

The first French outpost here was Fort Caministigoyan, founded by Daniel Greysolon in 1679. After the American Revolution, the North West Company's Grand Portage fort, some 52km/33miles southwest, found itself on the US side of the border and subject to American duties. In 1803 the directors moved to the old French site, naming it in 1807 Fort William after William McGillivray, the company superintendent. Thunder Bay was created in 1970 when two storied and rival towns at the mouth of the Kaministiquia River, Fort William and nearby Port Arthur, amalgamated.

The new city's name was taken from the Ojibwa, who called the bay Animikii, or "thunder," while the French called it *"la baie du tonnerre"*. Within the region, people often refer to Thunder Bay as Lakehead. The area has a well-earned reputation for cold winters, due to icy blasts off the lake. Summer temperatures range between 15°-30°C/59°-86°F, averaging just under 25°C/75°F, with generally cooler nights. Winter temperatures can hit −35°C/−31°F or even lower, to which must be added the wind chill. But the mean temperature in January is −15°C or 5°F.

Thunder Bay★★

POPULATION 122,907 – MAP P270

Sitting on the northwestern shore of Lake Superior, the city of Thunder Bay is an important port. On its waterfront the 32ha/79-acre Keefer Terminal shifts cargoes among ships, trains and trucks. Prairie grain arriving by rail, accounting for about 70 percent of port activity, is cleaned and stored in the port's nine grain terminals for transfer to the huge ships of the Great Lakes fleet. Port facilities also include two terminals for coal, potash and other dry-bulk commodities—just under 30 percent of the port's tonnage—and facilities for petroleum products and bagging specialty grains, a malting plant and a general cargo area noted for its ship/rail heavy lift transfers. In 2007 more than 400 vessels used the port's installations. In addition to rail, road and water transport, Thunder Bay's airport is the third busiest in Ontario, with 75 departures daily. As the largest Canadian city on the lake, Thunder Bay has assumed the role of a metropolis, despite its relatively small population; it boasts a symphony orchestra that performs in a 1,500-seat community auditorium; an art gallery *(www.theag.ca)* noted for its collection of contemporary aboriginal art; and a lively theatre scene. Within the city, great tracts are reserved for parks and recreation areas, including the second oldest municipal park in Ontario. Thunder Bay lies on the edge of a vast region of lakes, rivers and boundless forests that draw fishing and hunting enthusiasts, as well as canoers, hikers, snowmobilers and skiers. Three alpine ski hills and tens of cross-country ski venues are easily accessible.

- **Information:** Tourism Thunder Bay, 500 Donald St. E. ☎807-625-2149 or 800-667-8386. www.visitthunderbay.com. An information centre, in service since 1909, operates June–Labour Day weekdays at the pagoda *(corner of Walter St. and Red River Rd.)*. Another kiosk stands at the Terry Fox momument (↻*see below*).
- ▶ **Orient Yourself:** The main shopping areas are located near the waterfront. An area bounded by Water and Algoma Streets, on either side of Red River Road encompasses the historic shopping district, with many restaurants. Except for Fort William, attractions lie mostly along the lake to the east of the city.
- ☺ **Don't Miss:** The harbour as seen from Marina Park.
- ◔ **Organizing Your Time:** Allow 2 days minimum to enjoy this area.
- Kids **Especially for Kids:** Fort William offers a look the life of northern fur traders and explorers. Rides and amusements at Chippewa and Centennial parks.
- ◔ **Also See:** SAULT STE. MARIE

©Fort William Historical Park

Aerial view of Fort William Historical Park

A Bit of History

In 1803 the North West Company chose the site of an old French trading post to replace its fort at Grand Portage on the Pigeon River which, following the American Revolution, found itself in the US (present-day Minnesota). Originally named Fort Kaministiquia, for the river on which it sat, the fort was renamed in 1807 in honour of William McGillivray, chief superintendent of the company. Until 1821 the fort hosted the summer **Great Rendezvous** of Scottish traders, French-Canadian *voyageurs,* and the aboriginals whose fur trapping supported the industry. When the Hudson's Bay Company took over the North West Company in 1821, Fort William lost its importance, carrying on as an outpost until 1883.

Port Arthur first appeared as a silver-mining camp in the 1850s. Then in 1870, it was chosen as a transshipment point for materials going to the Red River Colony in Manitoba, and docks were constructed. Its name came from the Duke of Connaught, a son of Queen Victoria then doing military service in Montreal. The arrival of railroads reinforced the town's importance as a grain transport site, still a major activity today. Port Arthur merged with Fort William in 1970 to create Thunder Bay. The Waverly Park Heritage Conservation District encompasses old houses and buildings at the old city centre.

The major commercial employer in Thunder Bay is Abitibi-Bowater Inc., which operates the largest pulp and paper mill in Canada. Bombardier Transportation, another big employer, manufactures mass transit equipment. The city also serves as a regional health care centre. The largest single employer is the municipal government, followed by health care and education. Two institutions of higher education, Lakehead University, located in the former Port Arthur, and Confederation College make their home in Thunder Bay.

The city has an interesting mix of ethnic groups. As the many Italian restaurants attest, a major group is Italian, but there are also residents of Finnish, Polish and Ukrainian extraction, whose ancestors arrived mostly in a wave of immigration from 1900 to 1913. As well, the Ojibwa First Nation, with a reserve adjacent to the city, is a significant part of the population.

Sights

The Waterfront★

To appreciate the impressive port, and the sheer size of the grain terminals and ships, view them from **Marina Park** *(end of Red River Rd. ◷Open daily year-round).* The largest of these ships measures 222m/728ft by 23m/75ft, capable of carrying up to a million bushels of grain—the yield of 20,650ha/51,000 acres of land. The breakwater protecting the harbour from the storms of Lake Superior can also be seen. Waves can reach 12m/40ft in height in autumn. In summer the lake is calmer, and sailboat races are held weekly within and outside of the breakwater. The park itself is the site for summer festivals and events, and lies near the shops of the CN railroad station. On summer Wednesday evenings, public concerts feature local talent.

Viewpoints★

Thunder Bay is surrounded by the hills of the Canadian Shield, called the Nor'wester Mountains. The city is hemmed in across the bay by a long peninsula that forms a cape called **Sleeping Giant** because it resembles the prone figure of a man. Its sheer cliffs can be seen along the horizon.

Mount McKay Scenic Lookout★

At end of Mission Rd., on Fort William First Nation Reserve. ◷*Open mid-May–early Oct 9am–10pm.* ☎*807-622-3093. www.fwfn.com.*

This prominent flat-topped peak is the highest (488m/1,600ft) of the Nor'western chain. From a ledge 180m/600ft high, there is a fine **view** on clear days of the city, port and Sleeping Giant guarding the entrance to the harbour. The park includes a snack bar and an easy hiking trail to the top of the mountain.

Hillcrest Park★

High St. between John St. Rd. and Red River Rd.

Located on a cliff above former Port Arthur, this park provides a good **view** of the port installations and in the distance, Sleeping Giant and the islands that close the harbour mouth. The park includes a formal flower garden and a small children's playground.

Thunder Bay Historical Museum

425 Donald St. ◷*Open mid-Jun–Labour Day daily 11am–5pm. Rest of year Tue–Sun 1pm–5pm.* ✸*$3.* ✕&☎*807-623-0801. www.thunderbaymuseum.com.*

This small museum is housed in an imposing 1910 former police station and courthouse near City Hall. Exhibits tracing aboriginal occupation of the region include copper tools made 5,000 years ago. Collections about local history, including railroad lore, are quite touching because many items are personal belongings of immigrants, workers and leading citizens. The museum has a remarkable assemblage of decorative beadwork by Swampy Cree Indians living near York Factory on Hudson Bay, amassed by Anglican missionary Richard Faries, as well as a smaller collection of Ojibwa beadwork gathered from around Thunder Bay. A reconstructed 1928 theatre projects old films, including some made in the area.

City Parks

☎*807-625-2313. www.thunderba.ca/parks.*

Within city limits are many parks with acres of green space and residents take full advantage of their recreational facilities. The 74ha/183-acre park around **Boulevard Lake,** created in 1901 by damming the Little Current River, has a trout stream running through it and offers swimming, sailing, windsurfing, hiking, fishing and walking the 5km/3mi path. The 60ha/148-acre 🧒 **Centennial Park and Logging Camp** (*enter at Arundel St.*), a favourite with children, offers a replica 1910 logging camp, rides on a narrow-gauge railway, the *Muskeg Express,* a playground and hiking trails; in the winter, skiers and sleighs fly down the trails. From the Bluffs Scenic Lookout, there is a view of the city and Sleeping Giant. (◷*park open year-round; logging camp open mid-Jun–Sept daily 8am–8pm; Muskeg Train rides Jun weekends only 11am–4pm, Jul–first Mon in Sept Wed–Sun 11am–4pm;* ☎*807-683-5723).* Centennial Park is linked to the 142ha/350-acre **Cascades Conservation Area,** where trails, including a .7km/.4mi paved & trail for wheelchairs, lead through a birch and poplar forest. Across a bridge from Centennial Park stretches 600ha/1,500-acre **Trowbridge Falls Park,** which offers forest hiking trails, wading spots on the Little Current River, and camping. **Waverly Park,** 2ha/5acres, in former Port Arthur (*between Algoma, Red River Rd. and Waverly St.*), dates from 1871 and is

Ontario's second-oldest municipal park. Residents appreciate its enormous old cottonwood trees, the 1790 Hogarth Fountain, transported from England in 1964, the cenotaph and the modern bandstand. The park lies at the centre of the Port Arthur conservation district. **Kids Chippewa Park** (🕙 *open late-May– first Mon of Sept;* ☎*807-625-2447; www. chippewapark.ca*), located directly on Lake Superior, incorporates within its 109ha/270acres a children's amusement park dating to 1920s (🕙*open Jul–Aug daily 1pm–8pm, Jun weekends 1pm–8pm; small rides* ☞*$1.50, large rides $2.70*) as well as a petting zoo, rental cabins, campgrounds and a sandy, protected swimming beach.

Additional Sight

Fort William Historical Park★★
1350 King Rd., 16km/10mi south by Broad- way Ave. 🕙*Open late-May–mid-Oct daily 9am–5pm (mid-Jun–Labour Day 6pm). Early Jan–late May Mon–Fri by guided tour only, 11am &1pm.* ☞*$14 summer, $7 win- ter.* ✕ ♿ ☎*807-473-2344. www.fwhp.ca.* ☛*Guided tours (1hr 30min) offered every half hour during summer season.* **Kids** Located at Pointe de Meuron on the Kaministikwia River, this recreated fort is a superb reconstruction of the head- quarters of the North West Company, site of the Great Rendezvous—the annual

meeting of voyageurs, Scottish traders and aboriginal fur trappers. A project of the Ontario Ministry of Tourism, which operates the site, the replica represents the fort as it would have appeared in 1815, at the height of its activity. Some 42 structures on the 10ha/25 acre site represent all aspects of early-19C fur- trade society. The reconstructed fort sits about 14km/9mi upriver from the actual fort, whose one surviving building was demolished in 1902 for construction of a Canadian Pacific rail yard.

From the visitor centre, visitors can walk through the woods to the palisaded fort. Inside the palisade there is a large square of dovetailed log buildings, two raised above the ground on stilts (the river still floods, inundating the fort as recently as 2003 and 2006). Costumed guides help recreate fort life. The North West Company partners can be seen discuss- ing business in the council house; the warehouses are full of furs and trading goods; and birchbark canoes, tinware and barrels are being crafted by hand. Other highlights include a farm, apoth- ecary and a jail.

🕙Special events, such as re-enactments of the Great Rendezvous or of old bat- tles, are staged throughout the year. The Anishnawbe Keeshigun Native Festival is a major August attraction (*informa- tion can be found on the Fort William website*).

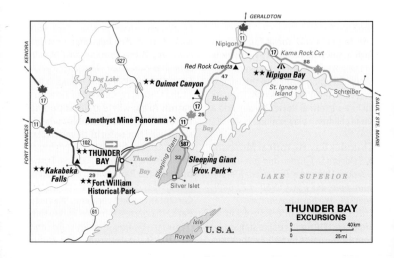

THUNDER BAY
EXCURSIONS

Excursion

Kakabeka Falls★★

29km/18mi west by Trans-Canada Hwy. 17. Provincial park ⏱ open year-round. Park ⏱ open to vehicles mid-May–early Oct daily. ⛽$10/vehicle. Hiking, camping, fishing, canoeing. ☎807-473-9231. www. ontarioparks.com.

The Kaministiquia River plunges 39m/128ft over a cliff around a pinnacle of rock into a narrow gorge. Formed by surging glacial meltwater that cut through the hard Precambrian rock some 10,000 years ago, the escarpments hold 1.5 billion-year-old fossils. These falls were the first harrowing obstacle negotiated by the fur traders of the North West Company between 1803 and 1820 when they left Fort William on the return trip to the northwest. A hydroelectric complex has harnessed the falls since 1904.

Visitors tracing the portage route should imagine themselves carrying 80kg/175-pound packs several times around each of the portages between here and Lac la Croix; a common cause of death among *voyageurs* was a strangulated hernia. The falls themselves can be reached from a parking lot near the park entrance. A bridge crosses the river to enable visitors to view the falls from both sides. Platforms accessible from footpaths around the gorge give dramatic views.

North Shore Lake Superior★★

MAP P 270

This route departs from Thunder Bay and continues 211km/131mi to Shreiber along Trans-Canada Highway 11/17. Along the way are dramatic natural sites, as well as lovely views of the lake.

- ℹ **Information:** Tourism Thunder Bay, 500 Donald St. E. ☎807-625-2149 or 800-667-8386. www.visitthunderbay.com.
- ▶ **Orient Yourself:** Lake Nipigon, to the north of this route, marks the traditional frontier of Ontario's vast northern wilderness.
- ⊘ **Don't Miss:** The great fault at Ouimet Canyon astonishes visitors.
- ⏱ **Organizing Your Time:** Calculate 2-4 hours to see Sleeping Giant Park. Allow 2 days to take the driving tour.
- Kids **Especially for Kids:** Marie Louise Lake in Sleeping Giant Park has a sand beach for swimming.

Driving Tour

211km/131mi from Thunder Bay to Schreiber by Trans-Can Hwy. 17.

Terry Fox Monument and Scenic Lookout

1km/.6mi east of Hodder Ave., Thunder Bay.

The 3m/9ft high bronze statue, set on a granite base, commemorates the heroic efforts of **Terry Fox** (1958-1981) to raise money to fight cancer. Deprived of his right leg by the disease at age 18, he undertook a 5,342km/3,339mi cross-Canada run in 1980, starting in Newfoundland. Two months later, he was forced to abandon his run close to this spot because of recurring cancer from which he died on June 28, 1981. From the monument, a splendid view of Lake Superior is afforded.

An **information centre** for the city of Thunder Bay lies close by (⏱ *open Jun–Labour Day daily 8:30am–8:30pm; rest of the year daily 9am–5pm; ☎807-983-2041 or 800-667-8386).*

▶ *After 51km/32mi, take Rte. 587.*

Sleeping Giant Provincial Park★

Park headquarters and campground ⏱ open daily late-May–mid-Oct and

Jan–Mar. Trails accessible year-round. 🚗*$10/car.* 🚹☎*807-977-2526 or 888-668-7275. www.ontarioparks.com.*

Seen from the opposite side of the bay, this dramatic landform, 8.3km/5.2mi long, with cliffs 240m/787ft high, resembles a sleeping giant; the Ojibwa called it Nanabijou. Occupying most of the peninsula that has the Sleeping Giant at its end, this pleasant 2,443 ha/6,037-acre park features 80km/50mi of trails, high cliffs, **views**★ of Lake Superior and the remains of the village of Silver Islet.

On Marie Louise Lake are a sandy swimming beach, a campground and a visitor centre. In the summer, the park offers interpretive programs and guided walks. A 11km/7mi **Top of the Giant trail,** not for the faint-hearted, leads up to spectacular views from towering cliffs. The Thunder Bay Lookout, which can be reached by car, offers a distant view of the city; the viewing platform extends out over the edge of the cliff.

Some 190 species of bird pass over the park, which lies on a north-south migration route. The **Thunder Cape Bird Observatory** at the peninsula's tip logs the traffic. In addition, the park encompasses an unusual mix of boreal and southern plant life; some 24 types of orchids can be found.

At the very tip of the peninsula lies Silver Islet, founded in 1868 and for a brief decade the richest silver mine in the world, yielding $300 million worth of ore. Its shaft, on a tiny islet offshore, extended over 381m/1,250ft below the lake.

▶ *After 56km/35mi, take E. Loon Rd. for 8km/5mi.*

Amethyst Mine Panorama

🕐*Open Jul–Aug daily 10am–6pm. Mid-May–Jun & Sept–mid-Oct daily 10am–5pm.* 🚶*Guided tours daily.* 🚗*$3.* 🚹☎*807-622-6908. www.amethystmine.com.*

This open-pit mine is a rock hound's delight as pieces of amethyst can be collected *(charge per pound)* and polished stones purchased. The tour offers interesting background information on mine history and on the geology of amethysts. The mine, which has operated since 1960, was discovered during roadwork in the area. While part of the

mine is a serious commercial operation, an area is reserved for visitors, who often find specimens. A gift shop sells jewellery, carvings and gift items.

▶ *After 76km/47mi, take road for 12km/8mi.*

Ouimet Canyon★★

🕐*Open mid-May–mid-Oct daily dawn–dusk.* 🚗*$2.* 🚹☎*807-977-2526. www.ontarioparks.com.*

This great gash in the landscape was caused by a fault line in the Canadian Shield, which was then scoured by glaciers during the last Ice Age. The canyon measures 100m/330ft deep, 150m/500ft across and more than 1.6km/1mi long. The walls are sheer drops.

Two viewing platforms along a wheelchair-accessible trail allow visitors to peer into the depths, where rare Arctic plants, remains of the last ice age, thrive because the temperature is considerably colder than on the surface. A chill breeze often wafts from the canyon floor.

Just after the Red Rock turnoff on the Trans-Canada Highway stands a cliff of layered limestone coloured red by hematite, the **Red Rock Cuesta,** nearly 210m/690ft high and about 3km/2mi long. A cuesta is slope that ends abruptly in a cliff, caused by unequal erosion.

▶ *Continue northeast to Nipigon. From Nipigon continue 88km/55mi on Hwy. 17 to Schreiber.*

Nipigon Bay★★

After crossing the Nipigon River, which descends from Nipigon Lake to the north, the Trans-Canada Highway runs along the shore of this bay, offering **views**★★ of rocky islands covered with conifers and rocks worn smooth by Lake Superior.

The **view**★★ of Kama Bay through the Kama Rock Cut *(27km/17mi from Nipigon)* is particularly fine. Rock such as this posed problems during the construction of this highway in 1960, and in the building of the Canadian Pacific Railway. In the winter, ice-climbers can sometimes be seen scaling the sheer cliffs.

For the best little places, follow the leader.

Looking for the latest news on today's best hotels and restaurants? Pick up the Michelin Guide and look for the Bib Gourmand and Bib Hotel symbols. With 45,000 addresses in Europe, in every category and price range, the perfect place to dine or stay is never far away.

MICHELIN
A better way forward

INDEX

INDEX

S

INDEX

WHERE TO STAY

INDEX

WHERE TO EAT

INDEX

MAPS AND PLANS

LIST OF MAPS

COMPANION PUBLICATIONS

MAP 583 NORTHEASTERN USA AND EASTERN CANADA

MAP 585 WESTERN USA AND WESTERN CANADA

- ✦ Large-format maps providing detailed road systems; includes driving distances, interstate rest stops, border crossings and interchanges.
- ✦ Comprehensive city and town index
- ✦ Scale 1:2,400,000 (1 inch = approx. 38 miles)

NORTH AMERICA ROAD ATLAS

- ✦ A geographically organized atlas with extensive detailed coverage of the USA, Canada and Mexico. Includes 246 city maps, distance chart, state and provincial driving requirements and a climate chart
- ✦ Comprehensive city and town index
- ✦ Easy to follow "Go-to" pointers

Historic Urban Plans

Canada (1719)

LEGEND

★★★ **Highly recommended**
★★ **Recommended**
★ **Interesting**

Sight symbols

Recommended itineraries with departure point

Church, chapel – Synagogue	Building described
Town described	Other building
AZ B Map co-ordinates locating sights	Small building, statue
Other points of interest	Fountain – Ruins
Mine – Cave	Visitor information
Windmill – Lighthouse	Ship – Shipwreck
Fort – Mission	Panorama – View

Other symbols

Interstate highway (USA)	US highway	Other route
Trans-Canada highway	Canadian highway	Mexican federal highway

Highway, bridge
Major city thoroughfare
Toll highway, interchange
City street with median
Divided highway
One-way street
Major, minor route
Pedestrian Street
15 (21) Distance in miles (kilometers)
Tunnel
2149/655 Pass, elevation *(feet/meters)*
Steps – Gate
△6288(1917) Mtn. peak, elevation *(feet/meters)*
Drawbridge - Water tower
Airport – Airfield
Parking – Main post office
Ferry: Cars and passengers
University – Hospital
Ferry: Passengers only
Train station – Bus station
Waterfall – Lock – Dam
Subway station
International boundary
Digressions – Observatory
State boundary, provincial boundary
Cemetery – Swamp
Winery
Long lines

Recreation

Gondola, chairlift	Stadium – Golf course
Tourist or steam railway	Park, garden
Harbor, lake cruise – Marina	Wildlife reserve
Surfing – Windsurfing	Wildlife/Safari park, zoo
Diving – Kayaking	Walking path, trail
Ski area – Cross-country skiing	Hiking trail

Sight of special interest for children

Abbreviations and special symbols

MP Marine Park	NP National Park	NF National Forest
NHS National Historic Site		PP Provincial Park

Visitor centre : Local - 🛈   Provincial - 🛈

⑯ Yellowhead Highway   Ⓜ Subway station (Montreal)

All maps are oriented north, unless otherwise indicated by a directional arrow

Michelin Apa Publications Ltd

A joint venture between Michelin and Langenscheidt

Suite 6, Tulip House, 70 Borough High Street, London SE1 1XF, United Kingdom

No part of this publication may be reproduced in any form
without the prior permission of the publisher.

© 2009 Michelin Apa Publications Ltd
ISBN 978-1-906261-56-6
Printed: August 2008
Printed and bound: Himmer, Germany

Although the information in this guide was believed by the authors and publisher to be accurate
and current at the time of publication, they cannot accept responsibility for any inconvenience,
loss, or injury sustained by any person relying on information or advice contained in this guide.
Things change over time and travellers should take steps to verify and confirm information,
especially time-sensitive information related to prices, hours of operation, and availability.